Transforming Scholarly Publishing With Blockchain Technologies and AI

Darrell Wayne Gunter
Gunter Media Group, USA

A volume in the Advances in Data
Mining and Database Management
(ADMDM) Book Series

Published in the United States of America by
    IGI Global
    Information Science Reference (an imprint of IGI Global)
    701 E. Chocolate Avenue
    Hershey PA, USA 17033
    Tel: 717-533-8845
    Fax: 717-533-8661
    E-mail: cust@igi-global.com
    Web site: http://www.igi-global.com

Library of Congress Cataloging-in-Publication Data

Names: Gunter, Darrell Wayne, 1959- editor.
Title: Transforming scholarly publishing with blockchain technologies and
  AI / Darrell Wayne Gunter, editor.
Description: Hershey, PA : Information Science Reference, [2021] | Includes
  bibliographical references and index. | Summary: "This book explores the
  application of artificial intelligence and blockchain technologies in
  scholarly publishing"-- Provided by publisher.
Identifiers: LCCN 2020009641 (print) | LCCN 2020009642 (ebook) | ISBN
  9781799855897 (hardcover) | ISBN 9781799855903 (paperback) | ISBN
  9781799855910 (ebook)
Subjects: LCSH: Scholarly publishing--Technological innovations. |
  Blockchains (Databases) | Artificial intelligence.
Classification: LCC Z286.S37 T73 2021 (print) | LCC Z286.S37 (ebook) |
  DDC 070.5--dc23
LC record available at https://lccn.loc.gov/2020009641
LC ebook record available at https://lccn.loc.gov/2020009642

This book is published in the IGI Global book series Advances in Data Mining and Database Management (ADMDM) (ISSN: 2327-1981; eISSN: 2327-199X)

British Cataloguing in Publication Data
A Cataloguing in Publication record for this book is available from the British Library.

For electronic access to this publication, please contact: eresources@igi-global.com.

Advances in Data Mining and Database Management (ADMDM) Book Series

ISSN:2327-1981
EISSN:2327-199X

Editor-in-Chief: David Taniar, Monash University, Australia

MISSION

With the large amounts of information available to organizations in today's digital world, there is a need for continual research surrounding emerging methods and tools for collecting, analyzing, and storing data.

The **Advances in Data Mining & Database Management (ADMDM)** series aims to bring together research in information retrieval, data analysis, data warehousing, and related areas in order to become an ideal resource for those working and studying in these fields. IT professionals, software engineers, academicians and upper-level students will find titles within the ADMDM book series particularly useful for staying up-to-date on emerging research, theories, and applications in the fields of data mining and database management.

COVERAGE

- Data Analysis
- Text Mining
- Predictive Analysis
- Data Mining
- Cluster Analysis
- Enterprise Systems
- Decision Support Systems
- Profiling Practices
- Association Rule Learning
- Heterogeneous and Distributed Databases

IGI Global is currently accepting manuscripts for publication within this series. To submit a proposal for a volume in this series, please contact our Acquisition Editors at Acquisitions@igi-global.com or visit: http://www.igi-global.com/publish/.

Titles in this Series

For a list of additional titles in this series, please visit: http://www.igi-global.com/book-series

701 East Chocolate Avenue, Hershey, PA 17033, USA
Tel: 717-533-8845 x100 • Fax: 717-533-8661
E-Mail: cust@igi-global.com • www.igi-global.com

Table of Contents

Detailed Table of Contents

Chapter 1
Value Creation With Information-Based Products and Services 1
> *Roland Dietz, Focused Growth Partners, Inc, USA*
> *Neil Posner, Digital Publishing Partners, LLC, USA*
> *Darrell W. Gunter, Seton Hall University, USA*

This chapter provides an overview of how scholarly publishing and information-based services have evolved over the last 20 years, and how these activities are fundamental to enabling scientific research and education to improve on the key performance indicators of speed, quality, contextualization, discoverability, enablement of creativity and innovation, and developing the talent pipeline. The authors delve into the exciting prospects for value creation using new business models and patterns of cooperation and co-innovation between stakeholders.

Chapter 2
Business Model Developments: The History, Current Situation, and Future
Outlook of Business Models in Academic Publishing 32
> *Joost Kollöffel, J & J Marketing Solutions, The Netherlands*

Academic publishing is a 'need to have' process that is very important in the academic world. This chapter focuses on the business models that were/are/might be used to finance the processes and the innovation in scholarly communication. What sparked the serials crisis? Is Open Access publishing feasible? Why are there predatory publishers? Can scientometrics and altmetrics be made into saleable products? These types of questions are answered in this chapter, where the focus lies on the financial feasibility of the main processes that occur in academic publishing.

Chapter 3

The legal developments in scholarly publishing began back at the time of the Guttenberg press. The scholarly journal publishing industry evolved over the centuries. The 1960s through the launch of the internet saw the industry explode with growth. With the advent and development of the digital journal, open access, and other clandestine illegal databases, it is essential that the industry work to protect its interests. This chapter will provide a history, overview, and developments that will be required to ensure the ongoing concerns of the industry.

Chapter 4

Publication is an essential step in research and is the responsibility of all scientists. Scholarly publications should provide a comprehensive and detailed record of scientific discoveries. They affect not only the research community, but society at large. Scientists have a responsibility to ensure that their publications are complete, detailed, clear, honest, balanced, and avoid misleading, selective, or ambiguous statements. Journal editors are also responsible for ensuring the integrity of the research literature. Publishers are adapting their roles in response both to changing needs and to these new competing services that can include researchers, research institutes, universities. Aside from their traditional roles in supporting quality assurance and peer review, publishers participate in many initiatives and develop services, often in partnership with universities and other organisations, to support communication and develops standards. This chapter shows the importance of standards and presents some concrete examples of standards organizations and perpetual evolution.

Chapter 5

This chapter reviews the history of blockchain from its ideation in the early 1990s to the widespread development efforts of private enterprise and governments two decades into the 21st century. The chapter covers the early developments in securing the digital record; the origins of the immutable, decentralized ledger; and trustless digital transactions. The key people in blockchain's development are addressed including the pseudonymous Satoshi Nakamoto, developer of the first cryptocurrency, Bitcoin, which became for a while synonymous with blockchain. The successes and failures of blockchain are covered in this history as well as its status and the problems that need to be solved for blockchain to have a global economic and cultural impact.

AI was first coined by John McCarthy in 1956. Vannevar Bush penned an article, "As We Make Think," that was first published in The Atlantic, and five years later, Alan Turning wrote a paper on the notion of machines being able to simulate human beings. AI had a number of significant contributors, which this chapter chronicles along with the definitions and their achievements. This chapter will provide an introduction, history, and overview of AI. It will also provide examples of the four waves of AI and the current applications and future applications of AI.

Organizational changes are made for business decisions that aim to improve performance and achieve short- and long-term strategic goals. The decisions to change are usually based on analysis of the organization, and success is evaluated by improving bottom-line performance. And many changes are unplanned. Despite all the preplanning, external factors can change or even divert the progress of the organization. Change is inevitable, and a good change management process can help ensure the potential for success.

In this chapter, the authors explore the potential for actors across the scholarly publishing industry to increase revenues while decreasing costs by using AI and blockchain to capture and leverage many of the intangible assets continually being generated across the industry. Where these assets bring more value than cost, they are referred to as intellectual capital. Areopa's 4-Leaf Model is used to examine how organisations serving the scholarly publishing industry can gain increased future economic benefit from identifying their intellectual capital and then capturing, storing, and making it re-usable.

The COVID-19 pandemic created significant problems for everyone and every business, but a few enterprises thrived, and Amazon was at the top of the list. Through their AWS (Amazon Web Services), Amazon controls many companies' information flow and data of all sizes. But what the general public does not know is that Amazon has been working on several blockchain and AI initiatives for over a decade. This chapter will provide a detailed narrative about Amazon's activity, patents, databases, and services that will leverage blockchain technology. The many patents filed by Amazon will greatly benefit Amazon both now and in the future.

Digital transitions have had strong headwinds in scholarly publishing for the past decade. It started with digitising content and is resting somewhere between tying up diverse content and catering to diverse end users. The goal is still to keep up with the changing landscape, and a demonstrable way of doing so is to actively participate by quickly adapting to standards. Artificial intelligence (AI) has a proven track record of helping with this and is an integral part of the solution frameworks. The chapter content includes a brief insight into some practices and workflows within scholarly publishing that stand to benefit from direct intervention of AI. These include editorial decision systems, metadata enrichments, metadata standardization, and search augmentations. The authors bring to light various developments in scholarly publishing and the status of some of the best implementations of AI techniques in aiding and upkeep of the 'digital transformations'.

The internet of things (IoT) is proving to be a seminal development amongst this century's most productive and pervasive high-tech revolutions. Increased reliance on the internet of things (IoT) is one of the foremost trends, and the financial services industry is a major contributor to that trend. IoT's influence on our daily lives is noteworthy, and it has become imperative for financial services organizations to evolve to adapt to these changes. Digital devices have started to interconnect with each other and possibly with other peripheral entities. Owing to the explosion of these devices and digitization in the banking and financial services industry, businesses are discovering the possibility of IoT in finance to control data and to minimize the risk. This chapter focuses on the impact of internet of things on financial services. It discusses the various applications, trends, challenges, and risks associated with adoption of IoT by financial services institutions. This chapter also discusses Indian and global cases of application of internet of things by financial services institutions.

Chapter 12

Anthony L. Paganelli, Western Kentucky University, USA
Andrea L. Paganelli, Western Kentucky University, USA

This chapter will examine the theoretical uses of blockchain technologies in research libraries. Technology has enhanced the services and operations of research libraries since the early implementation of computerized cataloging systems. Blockchain technology provides research libraries with the opportunity to decentralize services, while also maintaining and strengthening digital rights management. Research libraries will be able locate services that can be decentralized to provide patrons with a more effective and efficient service. The blockchain technology has the potential to expand library collections through distributed verifiable sovereign identity, which would allow patrons to securely access information from multiple libraries while maintaining their privacy. Libraries will be able to evaluate services and programs to determine best uses for blockchain technology.

Chapter 13

Leslie McIntosh, Ripeta, USA

While technology advances, the applications of those technologies within the scientific publishing ecosystem have lagged. There has never been a greater time to increase the speed and accuracy of scientific reporting. Researchers are under immense pressure to conduct rigorous science, and the publishing industry continues to act as a facilitator. Yet, inefficiencies stall the speed and prohibit the consistency of communicating research. This chapter proposes automating quality checks as a means to scale science. The author also explores the publishing process and potential places to use machine learning and natural language processing to enhance the quality—and thus rigor—of reporting scientific research.

Chapter 14

Shantanu Kumar Rahut, Saarland University, Saarland, Germany
Razwan Ahmed Tanvir, East West University, Bangladesh
Sharfi Rahman, East West University, Bangladesh
Shamim Akhter, International University of Business Agriculture and
Technology (IUBAT), Bangladesh

The paper reviewing process evaluates the potentiality, quality, novelty, and reliability of an article prior to any scholarly publication. However, a number of recent publications are pointing towards the occurrence of the biasness and mistreatments during the progression of the reviewing process. Therefore, the scientific community is involved to standardize the reviewing protocols by introducing blind and electronic submission, selecting eligible reviewers, and supporting an appropriate checklist to the reviewers. The amplification of reviewing with decentralization and automation can solve the mentioned problems by limiting the possibility of human interaction. This chapter proposes and implements a decentralized and anonymous paper reviewing system (DJournal) using blockchain technology. DJournal eliminates all the trust issues related to the reviewing process but improves reliability, transparency, and streamlining capabilities with up-gradation of the machine learning-based reviewer selection approach.

Chapter 15

Darrell W. Gunter, Gunter Media Group, Inc., USA

This chapter will explore how blockchain and AI technology will address the current problems in the current publishing workflow including the author manuscript submission systems, peer review process, editing, production process, and dissemination process. Further, after the article has published, blockchain and AI technologies will allow all of the stakeholders in the value chain to benefit from a more efficient and effective upstream and downstream publishing process. This chapter will explore rights and royalties, anti-piracy and ebooks, and how blockchain and AI will create new research and business opportunities.

Chapter 16

Edward Reiner, New York University, USA
Darrell W. Gunter, Seton Hall University, USA

Blockchain has broad application in academic publishing and addresses necessary benefits in cost containment, improved workflow, and business management. In particular, blockchain facilitates greater control over copyrighted content and royalty administration, citations, and billing and collection. Blockchain is a user-friendly technology that can improve profitability and cash flow while reducing administrative errors. Blockchain technology has become ubiquitous within various market segments but slow to be adopted within academic publishing environments, but with the pressure on revenue growth and cost containment, blockchain represents a new tool in the arsenal of workflow products to create more accurate reporting. In particular, royalty accounting has been an area of varying reliability and uncertainly, relying on many data sources and data aggregation generally confusing to authors, researchers, and writers. Blockchain takes the guesswork out of this process by documenting digital content access and usage through artificial intelligence engines and machine learning tools.

Foreword

Data is the life blood of a digital transformation. And data production is now on steroids. I remember not too long ago when 50 gigabytes of data storage seemed like an enormous amount, which could last a lifetime. We're no longer talking of gigabytes; we're speaking of terabytes, petabytes, exabytes, and zettabytes. To provide some perspective on this, a zettabyte is equal to a trillion gigabytes. In 2020 it is estimated that there were 59 zettabytes of information in the world, and that is likely to triple by 2024. While it is true that most of this data is neither scientific or scholarly, much is, and the fundamental growth trends for research data follow similar levels of exponential growth. Researchers, it is often said, are drowning in data, while starved for knowledge.

Transforming Scholarly Publishing With Blockchain Technologies and AI looks at the important question of how the scholarly publishing industry can continue to meet the needs of researchers in a world of metastasized data growth. There are four basic tenets in scholarly communication: verify authorship, vet the content, distribute the findings, and store the work. There was a time, to be sure, in the history of scholarly communications, when publishing houses could identify, verify, control the distribution, deliver, and store content for researchers in a timely and consumable manner on their own. Those times now seem long ago and as quaint as a fax machine.

What *Transforming Scholarly Publishing With Blockchain Technologies and AI* takes head on is how scholarly publishing must 1) innovate; 2) authentic and vet content as it moves through a variety of alternative forms and distribution channels; and 3) transform its delivery and search systems to allow researchers access to the information they need within their workflow and in a reasonable time at the point of demand.

The prospect of how scholarly communications is changing and must continue to change in the face of this data explosion is mind boggling. This work is important for anyone interested in how this transformation is occurring and how it can develop in the near future. It describes in fine detail through its 16 chapters how scholarly publishing needs to change through radical innovation; the value that the community will realize through the increased use of artificial intelligence (AI) in empowering search services; and how blockchain technologies can genuinely improve the very basic need to establish authorship and the source of scholarly content as well as maintain the integrity of scholarly content as it moves through a variety of distribution cycles.

In short, *Transforming Scholarly Publishing With Blockchain Technologies and AI* simply is a view of a scholarly communication in likely near future, written by experts and visionaries who should be hear and engaged by all interested in scholarly research and scientific communications.

John J. Regazzi
Independent Researcher, USA

Preface

The year was 2014, and I attended a NY Times symposium on Finance and Technology at the Time Center in Manhattan. The day-long conference featured several speakers on various topics, and during the Wall Street discussion, a woman from the audience posed a question to the panel that stumped the panel. The look on each of the panelists' faces was quite astonishing. I have attended many conferences throughout my career, and never have I ever experienced an expert panel being dumbfounded. The question from the woman was about Blockchain. The moderator was equally stunned, and then he asked the woman to explain what is Blockchain. The entire audience turned their heads to the woman, who then discussed how Blockchain technology is being applied in the financial markets.

After the session ended, the audience immediately turned their attention to the woman who posed the question to introduce themselves and exchange business cards. Usually, the audience would rush up to the podium to the panel, but not this time.

This meeting was my first encounter with Blockchain, and I did not take my interest any further as I was very focused on AI and Semantic Technology. Outside of a few industry colleagues and friends who would speak about how Bitcoin was built on Blockchain technology, my knowledge of Blockchain was limited. As It happened, a good friend of mine, Carlos Fernandez, called me one Saturday morning in June of 2018. My wife, daughter, and I had just moved to Ambler, PA, and I had moving boxes on my mind, not Blockchain. Carlos shared with me his idea of how Blockchain would have many applications. His excitement lit a fire in me, and over the next few weeks, I was reading anything and everything about Blockchain. I arranged a call with another friend, ironically with the same name Carlos, who was quite successful with Bitcoin. Then in the middle of July, I got a call from another friend John Larrier who works with Andrew Frazier on his Power Breakfast Conferences. John stated that their Blockchain speaker for their August 9 conference had to cancel his speaking appearance, and they needed another speaker and would I be interested. I jumped at the invitation and said yes. My wife, Deb, said to what do you know about Blockchain? I replied, "by August 9, I will know enough". So over the next few weeks, I continued my cram course on Blockchain.

I watched many videos and read articles on Medium. In conducting my research on Blockchain, I found the MIT 7 week course on Blockchain and its Applications that would begin in September.

On the day of the Power Breakfast, I was pretty nervous but prepared. I explained to the audience that I was not a Blockchain expert but an "enthusiast." I was also signed up for the MIT Blockchain course that would begin in the first week of September 2018.

Taking the MIT Blockchain course was one of the most enriching experiences that I have experienced. It truly propelled my interest in understanding how this technology could transcend everyday applications. The course required me to write a case study weekly on an area that Blockchain was applied.

In December 2010, an industry friend asked me to submit a chapter for her IGI book on Semantic Technology. Since that time, I had given thought to be becoming an editor of a book. In 2019, I drafted an outline of a book on Blockchain and AI. That outline then resulted in a proposal that IGI accepted. In recruiting authors for my book, I encountered many skeptical people who said "no." The book's objective became even more clear that I wanted it to be a thought leader book. A book that would not provide precise answers but would provoke the reader to read on. A book that would make some bets and would take a few years for them to be proven.

This thought leader book is 15 chapters and focuses on three sections. The first five chapters set the stage for the introduction to the industry, the academic colleges and Universities, business models, legislative developments, standards, and best practices for incorporating change.

The second block of five chapters begins with a history of Blockchain, Intellectual Capital and Blockchain, Amazon and Blockchain, AI-led content publishing, and IoT. The third block details Blockchain and Research Libraries, automating quality checks in the publishing process, Blockchain and peer review, new efficiencies, and applications.

CHAPTER OVERVIEW

Chapter 1: Value Creation With Information-Based Products and Services

This chapter provides an overview of how scholarly publishing and information-based services have evolved over the last 20 years, and how these activities are fundamental to enabling scientific research and education to improve on the key performance indicators of: - speed - Quality - contextualization - Discoverability - Enablement of creativity and Innovation, and - Developing the talent pipeline We delve into the exciting prospects for value creation using new business models and patterns of cooperation and co-innovation between stakeholders.

Chapter 2: Business Model Developments – The History, Current Situation, and Future Outlook of Business Models in Academic Publishing

Academic publishing is a 'need to have' process that is very important in the academic world. From its birth in 1665, to the current situation and beyond, this chapter focuses on the business models that were/are/might be used to finance the processes and the innovation in scholarly communication. What sparked the serials crisis, is Open Access publishing feasible, why are there predatory publishers? Can scientometrics and altmetrics be made into saleable products? These types of questions are answered in this section, where the focus lies on the financial feasibility of the main processes that occur in academic publishing.

Chapter 3: Legislative Developments in Scholarly Publishing

The legal developments in the scholarly publishing began back at the time of the Guttenberg press. As the scholarly journal publishing industry evolved over the centuries, the growth in the 60's through the launch of the internet saw the industry explode with growth. The advent and development of the digital journal, open access and other clandestine illegal databases, it is essential that the industry work together to protect its interest. This chapter will provide a history, overview and developments that will be required to ensure the ongoing concern of the industry.

Chapter 4: Standards Developments in Scholarly Publishing

The publication is an essential step in research and is the responsibility of all scientists. Scholarly publications should provide a comprehensive and detailed record of scientific discoveries. They affect not only the research community but society at large. Scientists have a responsibility to ensure that their publications are complete, detailed, clear, honest, balanced, and avoid misleading, selective, or ambiguous statements. Journal editors are also responsible for ensuring the integrity of the research literature. Publishers are adapting their roles in response to changing needs and to these new competing services that can include researchers, research institutes, universities. Besides their traditional roles in supporting quality assurance and peer review, publishers participate in many initiatives and develop services, often in partnership with universities and other organizations, to support communication and develop standards. This chapter shows the importance of standards and presents some concrete examples of standards organizations and perpetual evolution.

Chapter 5: A Brief History of Blockchain

This chapter reviews the history blockchain from its ideation in the early 1990's to the widespread development efforts of private enterprise and governments two decades into the 21st century. The chapter covers the early developments in securing the digital record, the origins of the immutable, decentralized ledger and trustless digital transactions. The key people in blockchain's development are addressed including the pseudonymous Satoshi Nakamoto developer of the first cryptocurrency Bitcoin which became for a while synonymous with blockchain. The successes and failures of blockchain are covered in this history as well as its status and the problems that need to be solved for blockchain to have a global economic and cultural impact.

Chapter 6: Is AI in Your Future? A.I. Considerations for Scholarly Publishers

AI was first coined by John McCarthy in 1956. AI, Vannevar Bush penned an article, "As we make think" that was first published in The Atlantic and five years later Alan Turning wrote a paper on the notion of machines being able to simulate human beings. AI had a number of significant contributors which this chapter chronicles along with the definitions and their achievements. This chapter will provide an introduction, history, and overview of AI. It will also provide examples of the four waves of AI and the current applications and future applications of AI.

Chapter 7: Best Business Practices for Incorporating Change

Organizational changes are made for business decisions that aim to improve performance and achieve short- and long-term strategic goals. The decisions to change are usually based on analysis of the organization and success is evaluated by improving bottom-line performance. And many changes are unplanned. Despite all the preplanning, external factors can change or even divert the progress of the organization. Change is inevitable, and a good change management process can help ensure the potential for success.

Chapter 8: Scholarly Publishing's IC in the Age of AI and Blockchain

In this chapter, the authors explore the potential for actors across the scholarly publishing industry to increase revenues while decreasing costs by using AI and Block Chain to capture and leverage many of the intangible assets continually being generated across the industry. Where these assets bring more value than cost, they are referred to as Intellectual Capital. Areopa's 4-Leaf Model is used to examine how organizations serving the scholarly publishing industry can gain increased future economic benefit from identifying their Intellectual Capital and then capturing, storing and making it re-usable.

Chapter 9: Amazon Blockchain-Enabling Commercial and Governmental Applications – Amazon Leveraging Blockchain for the Advancement of New Technologies

The COVID-19 pandemic created significant problems for everyone and every business, but a few enterprises thrived, and Amazon was at the top of the list. Through their AWS (Amazon Web Services), Amazon controls many companies' information flow and data of all sizes. But what the general public does not know is that Amazon has been working on several blockchain and AI initiatives for over a decade. This chapter will provide a detailed narrative about Amazon's activity, patents, databases, and services that will leverage blockchain technology. The many patents filed by Amazon will greatly benefit Amazon both now and in the future.

Chapter 10: Artificial Intelligence-Led Content Publishing, Metadata Creation, and Knowledge Discovery – In Quest of Sustainable and Profitable Business Models

Digital transitions have had strong headwinds in Scholarly Publishing for the past decade. It started with digitizing content and is resting somewhere between tying up diverse contents and catering to diverse end users. Goal is still to keep up with the changing landscape and a demonstrable way of doing so is to actively participate by quickly adapting to standards. Artificial Intelligence (AI) has a proven track record of helping with this and is an integral part of the solution frameworks. Chapter content includes a brief insight into some practices and workflows within scholarly publishing that stand to benefit from direct intervention of AI. To name a few; Editorial decision systems, Metadata enrichments, Metadata standardization and Search augmentations. With the authors bring to light various developments in scholarly publishing and the status of some of the best implementations of AI techniques in aiding and upkeep of the 'digital transformations'.

Chapter 11: Internet of Things and Its Impact on Financial Services

The Internet of Things (IoT) is proving to be a seminal development amongst this century's most productive and pervasive high-tech revolutions. Increased reliance on the internet of things (IoT) is one of the foremost trends, and financial services industry is a major contributor to that trend. IoT's influence on our daily lives is noteworthy and it has become imperative for financial services organizations to evolve to adapt to these changes. Digital devices have started to interconnect with each other and possibly with other peripheral entities. Owing to the explosion of these devices & digitization in the banking and financial services industry, businesses are discovering the possibility of IoT in finance to control data and to minimize the risk. This paper focuses on the impact of internet of things on financial services. It discusses the various applications, trends, challenges & risks associated with adoption of IOT by financial services institutions. This paper also discusses Indian and global cases of application of internet of things by financial services institutions.

Chapter 12: Blockchain and the Research Libraries

This chapter will examine the theoretical uses of Blockchain technologies in research libraries. Technology has enhanced the services and operations of research libraries since the early implementation of computerized cataloging systems. Blockchain technology provides research libraries with the opportunity to decentralize services, while also maintaining and strengthening digital rights management. Research libraries will be able locate services that can be decentralized to provide patrons with a more effective and efficient service. The Blockchain technology has the potential to expand library collections through Distributed Verifiable Sovereign Identity, which would allow patrons to securely access information from multiple libraries, while maintaining their privacy. Libraries will be able to evaluate services and programs to determine best uses for Blockchain technology.

Chapter 13: Automating Quality Checks in the Publishing Process

While technology advances, the applications of those technologies within the scientific publishing ecosystem have lagged. There has never been a greater time to increase the speed and accuracy of scientific reporting. Researchers are under immense pressure to conduct rigorous science and the publishing industry continues to act as a facilitator. Yet, inefficiencies stall the speed and prohibit the consistency of communicating research. This chapter proposes automating quality checks as a means to scale science. The author also explores the publishing process and potential places to use machine learning and natural language processing to enhance the quality - and thus rigor - of reporting scientific research.

Chapter 14: DJournal – A Blockchain-Based Scientific Paper Reviewing System With Self-Adaptive Reviewer Selection Sub-System

The paper reviewing process evaluates potentiality, quality, novelty, and reliability of an article prior to any scholarly publication. However, a number of recent publications are pointing towards the occurrence of the biasness and mistreatments during the progression of the reviewing process. Therefore, the scientific community is involved to standardize the reviewing protocols by introducing blind and electronic submission, selecting eligible reviewers, and supporting an appropriate checklist to the reviewers, and etc. The amplification of reviewing with decentralization and automation can solve the mentioned problems by limiting the possibility of human interaction. This article proposes and implements a decentralized and anonymous paper reviewing system (DJournal) using blockchain technology. DJournal eliminates all the trust issues related to the reviewing process but improves reliability, transparency, and streamlining capabilities with up-gradation of the machine learning-based reviewer selection approach.

Chapter 15: Blockchain and the Scholarly Publishing Industry – Current Use Cases: New Efficiencies in Scholarly Publishing

This chapter will explore how Blockchain and AI technology will address the current problems in the current publishing workflow including the author manuscript submission systems, peer review process, editing, and production process to the dissemination process. Further, after the article has published, Blockchain and AI technologies will allow all of the stakeholders in the value chain to benefit from a more efficient and effective upstream and downstream publishing process. This chapter will explore rights and royalties, anti-piracy and ebooks, and how Blockchain and AI will create new research and business opportunities.

Chapter 16: Blockchain and Scholarly Publishing Industry (Potential Uses Cases) – Applications of Blockchain in Academic Publishing

Blockchain has broad application in Academic Publishing, and addresses necessary benefits in cost containment, improved workflow and business management. In particular, Blockchain facilitates greater control over copyrighted content and royalty administration, citations and billing and collection. Blockchain is a user friendly technology that can improve profitability and cash flow while reducing administrative errors. Blockchain technology has become ubiquitous within various market segments but slow to be adopted within academic publishing environments, but with the pressure on revenue growth and cost containment, Blockchain represents a new tool in the arsenal of workflow products to create more accurate reporting. In particular, royalty accounting has been an area of varying reliability and uncertainly, relying on many data sources and data aggregation generally confusing to authors, researchers and writers. Blockchain takes the guesswork out of this process by documenting digital content access and usage through artificial intelligence engines and machine learning tools.

The scholarly publishing industry is primed for positive disruptions. These positive disruptions will provide the scholarly publishing industry with a host of new opportunities to improve the speed and accuracy of research. Considering the rapid rise of infectious diseases, academic research will greatly benefit from these potential new applications that Blockchain and AI can provide.

This book is not only for academe but for administrators, venture capital, entrepreneurs and anyone who participates in the scholarly research process.

We hope that this book, *Transforming Scholarly Publishing With Blockchain Technologies and AI*, will answer many of your questions and prompt you to challenge the many hypotheses presented in the book. More importantly, encourage you to challenge the status quo and select one application that Blockchain and AI could apply. It is vital for scholarly publishing to have a host of new technology champions to usher in a new era of applications to advance scholarly research.

This past year we experienced the phenomenon of a vaccine being researched, developed, clinically trialed, and launched within a year. The dissemination of scholarly research is essential to humanity, and any increases in efficiency would save lives. We look forward to hearing from you, and your thoughts about what we have written, pro or con, as this book is not about being right or wrong but provoking your thought.

As a Seton Hall Alum, I must close out this preface with "Hazard Yet Forward," whatever the peril, ever forward.

God bless,

Darrell W. Gunter
Gunter Media Group, USA

Acknowledgment

This edited volume came about after a good friend of mine, Carlos Fernandez, called me up in June of 2018 to share his excitement about Blockchain and the potential for many applications. I want to thank Carlos for that phone call that lit the spark for me to understand the technology and the potential for many applications.

I want to thank all of the authors who believed in the book and the technology and contributed their expertise and chapter to all of my industry colleagues who cheered me on and provided me with positive encouragement.

Thank you to my publishers IGI for their support and belief in the project.

As I conducted my research on Blockchain and AI, a few conferences provided me the opportunity to present to their audience. The Charleston Conference, SAMA, and the Power Breakfast were excellent venues to present my thoughts about how Blockchain and AI can improve scholarly Publishing.

Most of all, I want to thank my wife Deb, who always provides me with her knowledge, insight, encouragement, advice, counsel, and constructive advice to challenge my thoughts to make this book better.

Introduction

This edited volume Transforming Scholarly Publishing with Blockchain Technologies and AI was developed to educate the key stakeholders about the technology and how it can be of service to the scholarly publishing industry.

New technology can be fascinating with the promise of delivering further productivity gains. However, the acceptance of new technology can sometimes be very challenging. History has shown us how some companies got it right, and some called it wrong. We have seen many great technologies utilized in other countries, but I must ask the following questions.

- Why doesn't the US have a modern high-speed train system? (Quora, 2017)
- Why hasn't the US solved the water levy issue in Houston and New Orleans? (Rogers and Hasselmann, n.d.)
- Why can't the US have a national water system to transport clean water to all 50 states? (Water Resources of the United States, n.d.)
- Why is it that the US doesn't have a national electronic grid to leverage solar and wind power? (Simon, 2021)

Have you heard of the semantic web? (*The Semantic Web*, n.d.) What is the semantic web? Why is the semantic web important? How does the semantic web fit into the Internet of Things?

I want to share with you my thoughts about what a Blockchain/AI future might contain, a future that demonstrates the full force of Tim Berner Lee's paper about the semantic web. A lot has been said about Blockchain/AI, some good and some bad, but I stand here today to tell you that the Blockchain train is about to leave the station and make sure you get your ticket and get on board.

I always like to start with the PPP for our session today. The Purpose, The Process, and most importantly, the Payoff for the time you are investing today.

This book aims to provide you with a solid fundamental understanding of Blockchain/AI, its function, application, and future possibilities.

The 16 chapters of this book will provide a comprehensive overview of Blockchain /AI and representative applications.

TECHNOLOGY HISTORY: WINNERS AND LOSERS

If history has taught us anything, is it that we are not perfect in our assessment of new technology and that even the most brilliant minds can miss an opportunity?

Can someone share an example of how a company missed out on a technology opportunity?

How many of you have heard of Bloomberg? Everybody right!

How many of you have heard of Telerate? Not too many people. Before Bloomberg, there was Telerate. The Telerate system was the dominant terminal for Fixed Income Securities in the world. Founded in 1969, they were a leader in their space. Dow Jones & Company, Inc. initially purchased a 32% stake in 1985 for $285 million in 1985. Eventually, DJ would buy the remaining shares and bringing their total investment to $2 billion.

Bloomberg was founded in 1981; their terminals started to show up first in Merrill Lynch offices in 1985. Merrill Lynch was an investor in the new company. The Bloomberg terminals were installed exclusively in the Merrill Lynch office, with 1 terminal per office. The feature-rich terminal was priced hundreds of dollars more than the Telerate terminal. Once they started to sell their service to other financial houses, these financial houses had several Telerate terminals they could only afford 1 or 2 Bloomberg terminals.

By 1998 Bloomberg had displaced Telerate, and Dow Jones had to sell Telerate to Bridge Information Systems for $510 million, a loss of $1.4 billion!

What happened? How did Telerate lose their luster, their dominance, and market share to Bloomberg? Data analytics, back-office systems, and customer service were the culprits.

Blockbuster was founded in 1995 and became the dominant player in the consumer movie rental business, only to be upended by Netflix founded in 1997. Netflix created a new business model with their mailing DVDs versus Blockbuster with their brick-and-mortar stores. The Netflix business model provided selection, convenience, low price, and satisfaction. Blockbuster has moved into the closed business museum along with the Skytel pager.

But NetFlix did not stop there. Instead of just shipping DVD's Netflix created a streaming service that would compete with the premium channels like HBO.

Back in 2011, HBO's CEO stated that NetFlix was not a competitor. Only for him to see NetFlix overtake them. HBO, a part of Time Warner, was recently sold to AT&T and back in March 2019. The HBO Executive, Mr. Greenblatt, was quoted saying, "NetFlix doesn't have a brand. It's just a place you go to get anything — it's like Encyclopedia Britannica. That's a great business model when you're trying to reach as many people on the planet as you can."

Last but not least is Sears, who had the Christmas wish book catalog, craftsman tools, the Kenmore brand only to be squashed by Amazon.

In each of these case studies, we have seen how newcomers utilizing new technology and business models overtake the industry leaders.

If we achieve our objective by the time you finish the book, you will have a strong foundation of knowledge about Blockchain and AI and how each of these technologies can utilize in your industry and your company.

REFERENCES

Quora. (2017, March 11). Why Doesn't The United States Have High-Speed Bullet Trains Like Europe And Asia? *Forbes*. https://www.forbes.com/sites/quora/2017/03/11/why-doesnt-the-united-states-have-high-speed-bullet-trains-like-europe-and-asia/?sh=2f1fa6dc0804

Rogers & Hasselmann. (n.d.). *Historic Background of the New Orleans Levee System*. University of Missouri-Rolla. Retrieved from: https://web.mst.edu/~rogersda/levees/Historic%20background%20on%20the%20New%20Orleans%20Levee%20system%20-Chapter%204.pdf

Semantic Web. (n.d.). *Scientific American*. https://www-sop.inria.fr/acacia/fabien/lecture/licence_travaux_etude2002/TheSemanticWeb/

Simon, M. (2021, February 26). The Texas fiasco makes the case for creating a national power grid. *Mother Jones*. https://www.motherjones.com/environment/2021/02/the-texas-fiasco-is-a-case-for-creating-a-national-power-grid/

Water Resources of the United States-National Water Information System (NWIS) Mapper. (n.d.). https://maps.waterdata.usgs.gov/mapper/index.html

Chapter 1
Value Creation With Information–Based Products and Services

Roland Dietz
Focused Growth Partners, Inc, USA

Neil Posner
Digital Publishing Partners, LLC, USA

Darrell W. Gunter
Seton Hall University, USA

ABSTRACT

This chapter provides an overview of how scholarly publishing and information-based services have evolved over the last 20 years, and how these activities are fundamental to enabling scientific research and education to improve on the key performance indicators of speed, quality, contextualization, discoverability, enablement of creativity and innovation, and developing the talent pipeline. The authors delve into the exciting prospects for value creation using new business models and patterns of cooperation and co-innovation between stakeholders.

INTRODUCTION

This first chapter serves to describe how technology has enabled and triggered transformation in the science eco-system, what role scholarly publishing has played, and how both of these things are likely to change in the next decade. Digital Technologies have not just provided new functionality in products and services, but

DOI: 10.4018/978-1-7998-5589-7.ch001

also enabled completely new uses, and empowered the consumers of the information to have a more direct impact along the whole lifecycle of knowledge creation, and associated educational practices and pathways. The next period will be more driven by business model innovation and re-imagining the roles of knowledge lifecycle participants.

Publishers exist to help participants in a community of practice with their information needs, and through their products and services, contribute to the performance of the communities' activities, outcomes, and impacts.

For science, technology and medicine (STM) communities in particular, we are looking at key performance dimensions:

- Speed of Knowledge creation
- Quality (and integrity) of Knowledge
- Contextualization of Knowledge
- Discoverability, Accessibility, and Usability
- Enablement of creativity (supporting idea generation for hypotheses etc)
- Developing the talent pipeline
- The development and monetization of Intellectual Capital

We believe that:

- there is a huge need for a more significant impact of science on society,
- there is a huge need for much more effective and efficient talent development through education, and finally,
- what we currently call scholarly publishing will undergo rapid change to serve the needs of the various communities and stakeholders involved.

SCHOLARLY PUBLISHING DEFINED

Scholarly (STM=Science-Technology-Medicine) publishing has been around for a very long time. Like all publishing activities, it focuses on serving a specific set of audiences and communities with their specific information needs. These needs vary significantly based on audience:

- the core: Researchers, Students and their institutional infrastructure (Universities, Institutes, Corporations)
- the periphery: funding organizations, policy makers, consultants, professionals, and their institutions
- the general public

2

The mission of scholarly publishing is to serve the needs of these various audiences by:

- disseminating,
- enhancing the trio: accessibility – usability - findability,
- contextualizing,
- presenting - visualizing, and
- facilitating dialogue to help further the development of science.

Of course, the core of all these activities is the scientific information itself (generated and provided by authors and verified by peers), but with increasing technological advancements considerable added value is provided by scholarly publishers. More on this evolution later in this chapter when we discuss the time periods: print (pre-digital), transition (to digital), and acceleration.

Initially scientific results were predominantly communicated and debated inside the discipline of relevance, and the added value of the publisher was mostly in editing, formatting, distributing and promotion of awareness. With other audiences looking to consume and act upon scholarly information, the need for optimized value chains for each use-case became necessary, leading to specific products and services for these audiences. These use-cases present significant value creation opportunities for scholarly publishers.

Examples are:

- Information to the **general public** through **carriers** like PubMed, Scientific American, the New Scientist, Nature and Science
- **Review journals** to allow for quick review of progress in a discipline
- **Textbooks** to support educational needs in and between disciplines
- **Clinical Databases** about application of methodology or medicine in practical settings and related databases
- **Engineering toolkits**, enabled by digital technology, to simulate, predict and design structures and solutions to real world problems
- **Scientific conferences and meetings**, formal and informal to exchange ideas, status updates, preliminary findings etc. frequently using poster sessions and other highly interactive formats.

Publishing for any community tends to mirror the organization of the community it services, so it would be good to elaborate a bit more on the specifics of the "Science Information Ecosystem".

Scientific Research itself can be further segmented into:

- Basic Research (What are the right questions to ask? How do we understand foundational phenomena.)
- Applied Research (What are answers we have discovered? How do we apply the knowledge to address as specific problem(set), that help frame hypotheses or even solutions?
- Clinical Research. (How do solutions fit together into a context that delivers solutions for society? What have we learned about implementation aspects that are transferable to other implementations? Impact studies.) With the availability of huge data sets from numerous sensors and observations, this area is undergoing explosive growth.

Scientific Research is a highly specialized activity, and given that practices and needs vary substantially by field of study, new results are primarily communicated to peers in the (sub) discipline. As Science is constantly evolving and our understanding of phenomena grows along the way, this is a never-ending endeavor, with sometimes fundamental resets on models and hypotheses that may have been in place for a long time. Scholarly publishing provides not just service to the specialists in a field, but also to the interdisciplinary researchers, students and general public to enable the application of scientific information to education and problems or opportunities in our society.

Examining the **Science Eco-system**, we can see 6 major areas of impact:

- Research findings – Phenomena – Knowledge
- Education
- Source knowledge to power Innovation
- Policy input
- Funding and Research priority setting
- Citizen outreach and debate to understand Science, its' potential and its' limits

COVID-19 and PrePrints

The recent developments around Covid-19 and Climate change as examples, have highlighted that proper engagement of the general public is hugely important to enable consistent progress and secure appropriate funding. Political structures and belief systems have shown that they can easily override rational debate and dominate immediate implementation. Understanding the knowledge fact base, the limits of our knowledge and the scenarios that could result from certain interventions is crucial to enable sound policy decisions and public opinion development.

PrePrints have been with us since 1961 as the NIH launched a program called Information Exchange Groups, designed for the circulation of biological preprints, but shut down in 1967. While PrePrint exchanges in various subject areas have grown over the years, the affect of COVID-19 on the global environment in all aspects created an opportunity for the science community to cooperate and share information on an unprecedented basis. For example in March of 2020 there were about 500 preprints about COVID-19, by mid August this number exploded to more than 13,000 preprints. While these preprints are essentially grey literature and have not yet been verified through the peer review process, they do provide for a faster awareness of preliminary results and ideas. With this clarity on definition, it is a very valuable tool for communication and collaboration between scientists.

Unfortunately it has taken a global crisis for scholarly parties around the world to figure out the importance of cooperation and consideration to achieve an overarching goal.

Figure 1.

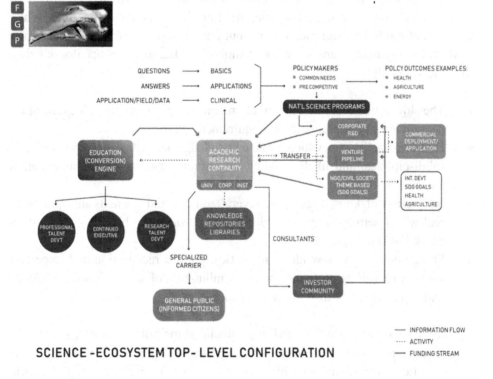

SCIENCE -ECOSYSTEM TOP- LEVEL CONFIGURATION

THE SCIENCE ECO-SYSTEM AND ITS EVOLUTION

Universities and Research institutions are centrally placed in the science eco system, but in most cases have to rely on partnerships with a variety of stakeholders to generate outcomes and impact in the larger socio-economic context and our day-to-day lives.

In the remainder of this chapter we will focus on the Research (and Development) and Education impact areas.

During the period from the 1600's until approximately the late 1990's, while print media proliferated in terms of format, focus and context, these publications had severe limitations in accessibility, searchability, usability, derivative research enablement, facilitation of more advanced educational approaches and the like.

Technology, specifically the move toward digital libraries, typically accompanied by vast expansion in access to literature, enabled significant progress in many of these areas, and has generated whole new formats, even companies and organizations dedicated to significantly improving the understanding of Science, Technology and Medicine and the application in our day-to-day lives.

At the same time, as a society, we are confronted with many big challenges for which Science may provide (partial) answers, and we are confronted with the need to understand how we can use this scientific knowledge as best as possible. While Science definitely has significant contributions to offer to problem solving and product development, there are inherent limitations because Science doesn't have all the answers all the time:

- The slow speed of knowledge creation, due to rigor in methodology, need for peer review and reproducibility requirements, a.o.
- Hyper specialization, which leads to knowledge being distributed over several subdisciplines, and likely residing in different channels of communication (Journals)
- Integration of knowledge from several sources and contexts into practical, real-world settings requires skillful navigation and ability to "fill-in-the-blanks" where necessary
- Sometimes use of new ideas, heuristics, pattern recognition and imperfect knowledge will be necessary, in the combination of solid scientific evidence and expert opinion, insights and hunches.

Recently the general public and in particular some policy makers, spurred by comments from Government leaders have grown impatient with, and suspicious of, scientific research findings. In some cases even outright rejecting scientific evidence. Sometimes scientific progress can be confusing due to insights having changed between various study results (inherently a sign of strength of the scientific methodology). The complexity of real-world problems can make it harder to see consequences of change in a particular scientific result, and how it impacts the solution in its' entirety. In addition, the trend toward the rejection of experts, those who are best positioned to translate scientific findings into actionable plans, is yet another factor that adds complexity and challenges to those in the scientific community.

There seems to be a significant opportunity for scholarly publishing in this area as many of the current media do not sufficiently cover the real-world application of science and its' potential benefits and risks.

In the longer run, we believe these doubts may prove to be transient, and a responsible education of general public and policy makers should be a top priority of the stakeholders in field of scientific knowledge discovery. It is essential that those issues that don't lend themselves to a simple "yes/no" or "black/white" answers (e.g. most of Science) can be discussed and understood along with the inherent nuances contained in these subjects.

While the main subject of this book is the impact of technology on scholarly publishing, we believe the most important impacts are not just the direct ability to provide new functionality or context, but to enable new business and funding models in order to unleash the value that is inherent in the information and insights that are produced by scientific research.

ROLE OF SCIENCE IN SOCIETY TODAY

Science is more needed than ever at the moment to help humanity address serious problems we are confronted with. A recent example is Covid-19 and health care, but clearly there is also climate change, food supply chains, safety and stability etc.

- Many tough problems exist that need holistic thinking (systems approach) due to their complex nature with many moving parts. Science is only able to provide component answers. Somebody needs to integrate science with heuristics and new ideas to develop solutions in the short term.
- Scientific progress, by its nature, is both slow, and regularly updating itself as new concepts replace old ones, and we understand phenomena better. We need to develop credible, long-lasting solutions in the shortest time possible.
- Problem owners and stakeholders in society find it difficult to navigate the maze of ever finer specialism, and integration of various views is hard.
- Frequently the big problems society is confronted with are referenced back to a state called VUCA (Volatility, Uncertainty, Complexity and Ambiguity), a term borrowed from the military and indicating that many interacting phenomena, with uncertain aspects, lead to very unpredictable system

behavior. On top of that we require an ability to accurately perceive all critical data and "warning signs". (Ambiguity) challenges traditional decision making, problem solving and governance structures. The combination of these pose further challenges to the appropriate application of scientific knowledge in these efforts.

- Complex problems increasingly are politicized by people simplifying problems, seeking the lowest hanging fruits and solutions, selectively referencing component results. And both policy makers as well as the general public and the media do not spend enough time to argue at high quality, comprehend and mobilize.
- Universities are often very internally focused and not good at technology or knowledge transfer.
- Institutions of higher education tend to educate for science, rather than for application, which is understandable, but this results in a disconnect with the majority of students that are seeking to have a career outside academia.
- In many competency areas there is a huge shortage in sound education and practice. The connection between a degree and a career is haphazard in most cases.

A clear example of course is the COVID-19 crisis. It has shown that medical and healthcare structures designed for a steady state situation do not necessarily respond with speed and agility once the going gets tough. It has also shown a lack of resilience in many areas of first responder infrastructure. At the same time we have mobilized tremendous resources for the creation of vaccine candidates, and the subsequent necessary steps in trials and assessments. From all of this it should be abundantly clear that we need better and faster science contributions to address and manage the various aspects of community crisis. Quick development of a Covid-19 vaccine has been demonstrated to be possible given a single-minded focus accompanied by substantial and focused investment. Surely other problems can be addressed in similar ways.

Another example is the long-term orientation of the Chinese government, where critical investments and incentives in Scientific research going back 20 years now, have generated significant centers of excellence and knowledge in areas like Artificial Intelligence, visualization and other computer science areas. With the enormous advantage of scale, scientific man/woman power, work ethic and discipline, due to its population and demographics, it has been able to innovate faster and is arguably ahead of other countries in the world in tactical AI applications.

The general public and policy makers need solid information about what those contributions can be, what the limits of our knowledge are, and how risks and incomplete information can be managed. Universities and research institutions play a key role, and so can a variety of publishers and 3rd party solution providers.

While these 'external to the science eco-system' factors are increasing the emphasis on applied and clinical research, and these trends have been in place for decades already, we also need to realize that applied and clinical research efforts can only thrive if there is enough pure basic research taking place to replenish the pipeline of ideas and concepts. Universities and independent research institutes fulfill essential roles and need to be funded adequately. A shining example that speaks to all of us today is that the internet would not have existed without early-stage funding by the US government, and there are plenty other examples of this.

This leads us to the critical subject of funding, funding mechanisms, resource allocation, and objectives of the various stakeholders.

FUNDING OF UNIVERSITIES AND RESEARCH

Before digging deeper into past, present and future of scholarly publishing and information service provision, it is useful to examine how science is being funded today and what trends are emerging. While we will not go through an exhaustive review of this sizable and complex subject here, we will point out a few fundamental shifts that will affect our perspective on the future of publishing for science.

Scientific knowledge is mostly created in universities, government institutions, independent not-for-profit institutions, and corporate R&D departments. Within this context, the university environment is functioning as the prime wellspring of both basic scientific knowledge, as well as crucial talent development to provide the human brain power for the advancement of science, whether in academic or corporate settings.

Commercial opportunities are increasingly dependent on the application of science into products and services, examples are pharmaceuticals, medical devices, alternative energy, self driving cars, food supply chains, and many other areas. Because of this there is a very substantial corporate R+D investment and an increased emphasis on public-private partnerships.

On a global scale Universities have diversified their funding sources considerably between tuition, public government support, grants, endowments, contract research, and IP monetization. But Universities, particularly in the USA, primarily rely on Tuition revenue and State & Local government support, and this government funding has been rapidly decreasing, and is expected to continue to decline. Because of this very large dependency on tuition it is useful to go a bit deeper on the analysis of trends in that area.

Figure 2. (College Board, pg. 22)

Percentage of Institutional Revenues from Various Sources

	Net Tuition Revenue	State and Local Appropriations	Federal Appropriations and Federal, State, and Local Grants and Contracts
Public Doctoral			
2007-08	32%	37%	32%
2012-13	41%	27%	32%
2017-18	43%	27%	30%
Public Master's			
2007-08	40%	46%	13%
2012-13	52%	36%	13%
2017-18	48%	39%	13%
Public Bachelor's			
2007-08	36%	49%	15%
2012-13	44%	41%	15%
2017-18	42%	44%	15%
Public Associate			
2007-08	26%	59%	15%
2012-13	35%	51%	14%
2017-18	30%	55%	15%

CollegeBoard   Source: The College Board, Trends in College Pricing and Student Aid 2020, Page 22.

As the chart below demonstrates, the published (e.g. list) prices for Tuition and Fees by both public and private institutions has grown tremendously over the past 30 years. Interestingly, the published prices for public institutions have increased at a greater rate than for private institutions. Perhaps this is merely a reflection of the extent and degree of how public institutions have needed to obtain greater amounts of funding from tuition to survive given decreases in governmental support.

However, it is equally fascinating to see that these institutions (both public and private) have started acting more and more like businesses by finding ways to offset these higher list prices with selective discounts to those students they most want to attract and keep. See the following two charts – the first for Public institutions and the second for Private institutions.

The level of (average) net Tuition and Fees achieved between 2006 and 2020 is remarkably stable (see the line at the bottom of each chart) as compared to published list price changes during the same time period. But within this dynamic and for those not receiving these discounts, there is increasingly an unequal impact. This in a nutshell is the reason for the need for the increasing levels of student loans needed by those not receiving sufficient cross-subsidies.

Figure 3. (College Board, Figure CP-3)

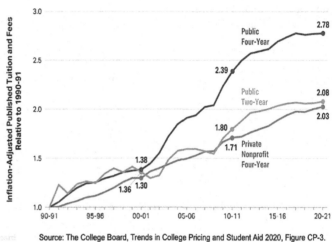

Inflation-Adjusted Published Tuition and Fees Relative to 1990-91, 1990-91 to 2020-21 (1990-91 = 1.0)

Source: The College Board, Trends in College Pricing and Student Aid 2020, Figure CP-3.

We know that foreign students are typically not receiving discounts and therefore represent one group of students that subsidize those that do receive discounts. While mathematically we know this group doesn't represent the entire amount of the cross subsidy, and there are many other dynamics at play, the recent limits imposed on the number of permitted foreign students in the U.S. make it more difficult for these institutions to balance their budgets. In addition, the lower perceived value of an online experience a la Covid-19 puts yet additional pressure on these institutions.

Interestingly, although we focus in this chapter primarily on U.S. institutions, those in Canada and Australia would appear to have even greater challenges as shown in the chart below.

In addition to all the pressures mentioned above, as reported extensively by McKinsey, institutions have been adjusted their spend away from the core-business of research, education and seeding innovation to aspects like student services to ensure their tuition funding remains intact by attracting greater numbers of students.

On the one hand it might indeed represent a rational step for these institutions to spend more on things like gyms and stadiums in order to attract and compete for students, on the other hand this behavior effectively serves to limit the amount of funds available to address deeper academic needs and experiences for these students as well as societal and especially scientific needs.

Figure 4. (College Board, CP-9)

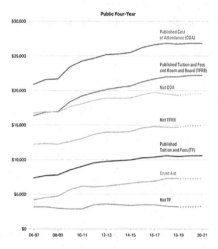

Average Published and Net Prices in 2020 Dollars, First-Time Full-Time In-State Undergraduate Students at Public Four-Year Institutions, 2006-07 to 2020-21

Source: The College Board, Trends in College Pricing and Student Aid 2020, Figure CP-9.

Figure 5. (College Board, CP-10)

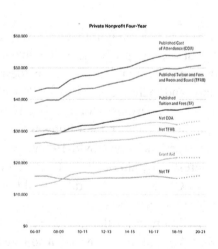

Average Published and Net Prices in 2020 Dollars, First-Time Full-Time Undergraduate Students at Private Nonprofit Four-Year Institutions, 2006-07 to 2020-21

Source: The College Board, Trends in College Pricing and Student Aid 2020, Figure CP-10.

Figure 6. (Dua et al., 2020)

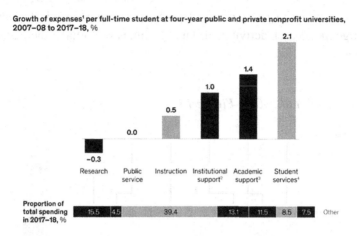

Growth of expenses[1] per full-time student at four-year public and private nonprofit universities, 2007–08 to 2017–18, %

The model of a university with substantial undergraduate population and associated business model aspects, combined with world class research in basic, applied and clinical stages, may need a real rethink. The drivers for success in the undergraduate area are substantially different from the graduate and prost-graduate levels.

As it isn't reasonable to expect the situation to change overnight, it becomes imperative for institutions to seek new funding sources, for example in the form of partnership with corporations who can provide funding for specific objectives. As reported extensively by the Wall Street Journal (Stoll, 2020) and other publications, more and more institutions have been moving in this direction (Mitchell, 2020).

Bringing educational institution practices and resource allocation decisions more in line with the needs of society and business community objectives may not be a bad development if it would also include a commitment by those funders to set aside a portion of the funding for basic research as well. This may serve to force institutions to utilize a different set of lenses to determine what is indeed of value to them in the future. It may also create greater incentives for publishers and other market stakeholders to invest in higher level tools and technological advance to enable innovation.

On a global-scale, investments in research and development are increasing steadily, both in Universities as well as commercial and government organizations. This reinforces the notion that, with the right innovation orientation, there is a very substantial business opportunity in scholarly publishing and scholarly information service provision. The daily practices in the scientific endeavor are still relatively poorly supported by collaboration and workflow/workbench digital tools. Companies like Mendeley and others have started to deliver some functionality, but real in-depth productivity tools for scientists are still absent.

Science is a quintessential global activity, and therefor the STM publishing industry has always had a global perspective. The leaders in the industry have moved with the surge in research activities in Japan, China and India in the past, and now more and more in Africa too.

Figure 7. (Robbins et al., 2020, Figure 13)

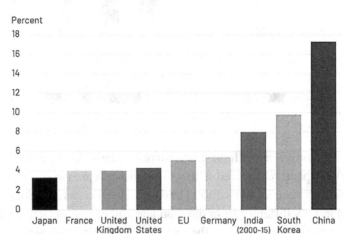

NOTE: The EU includes France, Germany, and the United Kingdom.
SOURCES: NCSES, National Patterns of R&D Resources; OECD, MSTI 2019/1; UNESCO, UIS R&D.
Indicators 2020: R&D

One key finding is that China and India, and before that Japan, have been strategically prioritizing research and development. They have followed a consistent strategy to accumulate capability in strategic areas like Robotics, Artificial Intelligence, Material science etc. In terms of global expertise we have seen a tremendous growth of high quality research from these countries because of the investments and focus.

Companies, both large corporations as well as entrepreneurial units, are more and more invested in research and development as the frontier for value creation in commercial settings is moving into areas like application of computer science for social media and information services for consumers, applications in areas like Health, Energy, Agriculture and food-supply chains etc. With this momentum comes the notion of proprietary research and the interaction between public and civils society funded research and corporate research. A real risk is now apparent in the aspect of securing the free flow of ideas and the ability to cooperate for the advancement of science, while providing incentives for innovators as well.

Figure 8. (Robbins et al., 2020, Figure 11)

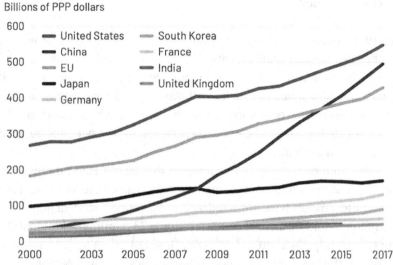

NOTES: PPP is purchasing power parity. Data are for the top eight R&D-performing countries and the EU. Data are not available for all countries for all years. The EU includes France, Germany, and the United Kingdom. See p. 22.

SOURCES: NCSES, National Patterns of R&D Resources; OECD, MSTI 2019/1; UNESCO, UIS R&D.

Indicators 2020: R&D

COVID-19 DISRUPTION

While the financing and internal practices of public and private Universities and research institutions may not have been of direct relevance in the context of scholarly publishing in the past, the future may require these and other stakeholders to reassess their practices. Certain trends are very substantial, and have further accelerated due to the occurrence of Covid-19.

Examples of trends in the U.S. that were in place before the crisis:

- Published tuition prices far outpacing inflation
- Total cost for students escalating even faster
- Student Debt driving domestic student reluctance
- Grants and other "discounts" increasingly given unevenly to a select subset of students to offset what they otherwise would need to pay
- Rapid inflow of foreign students at full price to help finance the universities
- Recent America First Policies that have created problems to sustain foreign student acquisition for universities

- Increasing on-line education to reach more students without increasing on-campus population

Covid-19 of course has created a "forced transition" to on-line learning and has educated the students and their parents about the nature of the value proposition in relation to on-campus teaching. It is already having a big impact on enrollment and it is uncertain how much this factor will stay in place once we return to normal operations, whatever that new normal may be. Online education at this level is simply not comparable to an on-campus experience for the personal development of higher education students.

The United Nations recently issued a report that nearly 1.56 billion learners in more than 190 countries and all continents, have experienced a severe impact from the pandemic. These closures have impacted 94% of the world's student population and up to 99% of lower-middle income countries. Some 23.8 million additional children and youth (from pre-primary to tertiary) may drop out or not have access to school next year due to the pandemic's economic impact alone(United Nations, 2020).

Due to access to online classes, there may even be a systemic change in education across the globe, especially if good students can compete for online training/degrees in pretty much any University they want. It may radically change the education system and its foundation. On the flip side universities may also adopt newer revenue models both for engaging the "best" educators from anywhere in the world, and vie for the "best" students (pre-qualified or not) who are willing to pay for the experience. There is a real opportunity for institutions of education to re-imagine the best, most effective way to reach a certain educational challenge, independent of the research objectives of the university.

VALUE IN SCIENTIFIC INFORMATION

Information products (books, journal articles, datasets etc.), in the print world, were generally being priced by publishers in sort of an industry standard approach, typically developing yearly price adjustments off of a historic base for a title, and reflecting aspects like volume of content and circulation. Setting prices for STM information in a print only paradigm, by definition limited the publishers' ability to meet the needs of different types and sizes of institutions in terms of how products are packaged and priced. While the move to digital delivery of information allowed for far more flexibility by publishers, there remains the basic challenge that it is very hard to know a priori which products deliver the most value (in terms of immediate benefit to the user). There have been several studies on hits for movies and music production and it is notoriously difficult in these genres to pick winners versus losers.

Scientific Information products are even more difficult, since many of them cover a very specialized area, and may represent different stages of scientific knowledge creation. What is relevant today in computer science may be outdated or superseded in a year. What is relevant in Chemistry today will most likely still be relevant two centuries from now. New research sometimes needs long periods of debate and integration into other knowledge to show its true impact.

Carl Grant stipulates in his article (Grant, 2018) that information products are of limited value inside the container they were originally published in, and would have substantial potential value if the information was allowed outside the container to be used in different context.

This is an important avenue to pursue, because context in which information is presented is quite important to address applicability, usability, and utility. Creating the new context is a non-trivial activity (possibly a derivative work, or a remix if you will). There will be a wide variety of possible contexts/frames for STM information, as it is optimized for certain purposes. This leads to questions about how much value is being created by what party, and how this reflects on fair distribution of this value across parties involved.

The knowledge (and value) locked up in a piece of information is brought to the user, generally by a combination of author-editor-publisher activities focused on a specific goal (representing a specific value chain for a specific audience-purpose combination). That same information may be instrumental in a different context to prove a theory, induce creative thinking, formulate a new testable hypothesis etc. It is understandable that readers and their buyer (e.g. the institution that funds the bulk of the price of the original building blocks) want to be able to allow this recontextualization of content to get this value in their process, but exactly how this would work and how value is shared remains a key discussion item. Libraries and technology tools can provide additional opportunities to "reframe" atoms of insight into a new context. This is very exciting and certainly something that needs full support by all stakeholders.

Publishers today, remain relatively restrictive in what they allow with the information in "their" containers and in their "artifacts", this of course is partly because of the legal regimes governing copyright, first sale doctrine, licensing parameters etc. And, partly it is just sheer inability to predict what "derivative" uses could lead to what value and how that value would be reasonably divided between publisher, author, and user.

Many times the value of a piece of information is only expressed effectively when a reader applies it and gets some sort of new result. Since a journal is a collection of articles where some are very high value and others not so high, and we do not know upfront which articles represent the value now and in the future…. Pricing is really hard.

If we want to promote innovation in STM publishing value chains we will have to find ways for publishers and communities of practice to work together and experiment on new "containers" and "distribution mechanisms" to discover how best to maximize value delivered, AND how to distribute it in a reasonable way. Investment in innovation will only occur if the stakeholders see a path toward receiving a financial return and/or another tangible benefit from the activity. Technology will enable us to do more, but the real challenge is business models, legal structures etc.

We advocate the creation of strategic partnerships between stakeholders and sandbox environments where new formats and contexts can be explored before commercialization is being considered.

THE PRINT ERA: THE 1600'S TO THE LATE 1990'S

Print formats like journals (primary, secondary, Tertiary, Review, Textbooks, Workbooks, Academic ability testing) and complementary services have been very successful in communicating scientific results, enabling high education, etc.

At the same time the economic models applied by publishers, as described before had severe limitations. Budget constraints at universities and libraries did not account for the exponential growth of number or researchers and research output. These two factors combined led to antagonism between publishers and librarians, and more importantly to a severe reduction in availability and accessibility for the community of scientists in the universities, corporations and research institutes. The SERIALS CRISIS was born. In the print era, on an annual basis it was typical for Institutions to put in place "cancellation committees" to evaluate which journal subscriptions can go unrenewed – not necessarily for lack of need by the community, but rather due to lack of financial resources.

Libraries in a print world were in a difficult spot. Budgets were under pressure as the function of archival information was typically less valued by researchers as compared to current awareness and other new functions. These new functions were only partly serviced by libraries – for example scientific conferences and peer exchanges.

Educational publishing models for publication:

The adoption cycle and the need for publishers to ensure the industry stayed sustainable, also led to an ever-increasing price for textbooks. Editions only showed marginal improvements year on year, while just enough to ensure students had to buy the new version.

The print version of published media lacked the flexibility of context, the ability to embed and re-embed in working documents, the wide scale accessibility at the point of work or study, the ability to simultaneous access and so on. The print media relied heavily on the complementarity of physical and digital infrastructure at universities, corporations and research institutions. (Libraries, Catalogues, Databases)

THE TRANSITION TO DIGITAL MEDIA: LATE 1990'S - PRESENT

Publishers and service providers to research, education and professional audiences moved from an almost exclusive print paradigm to an electronic one, over a 20 year period. During that time, improvements in value delivered were realized in what is to be characterized as mostly an effort to stabilize the industry and improve the economics for all concerned.

Stakeholders were both eager as well anxious about the unbundling of traditional aspects of the journals (archive, news, awareness) functionality in digital media, and hopeful that substantial increases in functions and benefits for users could be accomplished. Publisher and Librarians were in a tug-of-war around the financial parameters and the sustainability of the infrastructure.

Publishers were now able to increase significantly the functionality locked inside the information itself:

- Extensive meta-data for each atom / article of information to enable search, browse and interconnection between articles
- Granular SGML encoding to enable reference links to all source materials and to re-embed information into workflow and workbench solutions being built either on institutional or discipline level or both.

Elsevier, as the largest STM publisher and the one with the most impact on library budgets and operations developed an economic model, the "Big Deal" that was designed to stabilize the funding situation and allow for stakeholders to work together on innovations that they believed would in the end substantially improve the situation.

Fundamental to this pricing mechanism was the intention to rebalance the value equation between publisher and library and enable maximum access, use and usage in the institutions.

The chart below provides a visual example of this dynamic at the journal title level, and can be roughly compared to how academic institutions have been steadily increased Tuition list prices, but overall have offset these increases with selective discounts. The chart only goes through 2010, but the trend shown has clearly continued. This trend shows a combination of higher serial LIST prices but with a simultaneous large increase in "serials taken" and lower resulting costs per serial.

Figure 9.

Typical STM Industry Pricing Model Structure

- Spending level agreement is typical (includes subscribed print journal value) governed by multi-year contract
- One list price per journal (per billing currency). Annual list price changes are consistent for most journals.
- Small effective discount on subscribed titles
- Non-subscribed title access (via Unique Title List fee; Subject Bundle fee; Flat price for small institutions, etc). Typical discount 90-99%.
- Focus on overall customer cost per use

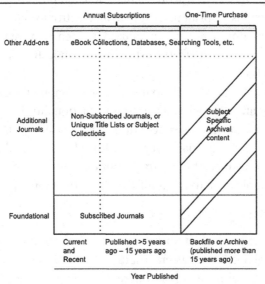

Earlier Project TULIP had proven that library-publisher cooperation was very promising. Under the big deal umbrella Elsevier started strategic partnerships with leading institutions like Los Alamos National Laboratory, University of Michigan, Naval Research Lab, University of Toronto, National Library of the Netherlands, Tsukuba University in Japan, CSIRO Australia and many others.

While these projects have led to some improvements here and there, the main problem was and is still today, the lack of incentive for key stakeholders to address the need for innovation, the organizational aspect of siloed specialists with way too little cross collaboration, and the general lack of budget or a budget sitting with the wrong party in University contexts. This structure represents substantial constraints to potential financial payback for those willing to make an investment in innovation. University Libraries, as the custodians of information and knowledge, were often stuck in old paradigms, not focused enough on value creation, but more on cost reduction, and with only a few exceptions most did not show institutional leadership, and therefore proved to generally be less of a player to help develop more innovative solutions.

Figure 10. (Anderson, 2013)

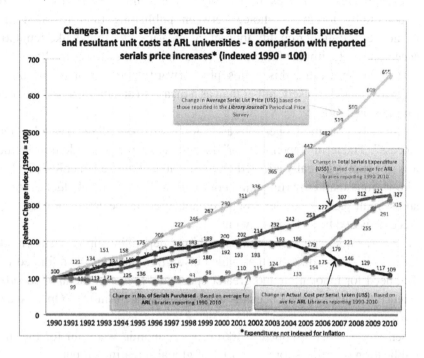

Technology holds immense opportunity to provide better utility to users of STM information, but traditional roles, budget and decision making authority can stand in the way of actually transforming this potential utility in real value creation for all concerned.

Additionally, there has been a decades long and continuing push from many stakeholders for "Open Access" to scientific publications and/or to an entirely "Open Access" publishing model and/or an "Open Access" philosophy. While Open Access and open science efforts have had some positive effects, it seems a very minor part of the solution needed by the community. Maintaining a primary focus on the individual article or individual journal seems akin to looking at each tree when an entire forest needs to be the focus. But nevertheless, Open Access has been a primary focus for many stakeholders and to date it has resulted in a disjointed situation.

At this point only a few things about the Open Access effort seem clear:

- This activity does not fundamentally alter the value proposition of scientific publishing for the various stakeholders
- It represents mostly a change in who pays, from which budget the payment comes, and when the payment is made

- It complicates or makes impossible a publishing choice for an author – potentially forcing a choice between publishing their research in an acknowledged higher quality journal (as measured by things like reputation, acceptance rate, impact factor, etc.) versus a journal of lower quality
- The focus on driving this philosophy forward appears to have become an objective in and of itself, rather than as a means to achieving a particular goal for the stakeholders
- As time goes on, more questions arise about what actually is meant by "Open Access". The term "Open Access" does not have a standard definition, much less one that is globally adopted or enforceable (Janicke Hinchliffe, 2020).
- The various market participants, both within a given stakeholder group and across multiple stakeholder groups, do not agree on the details of what "Open Access" is and how it will play out.
- "Open Access" can mean different things depending upon a stakeholders location in the world as well as which institution they may be affiliated with
- The need for innovation and greater speed and focus on the applied side of science to solve societal needs is absent as a concept in the "Open Access" movement
- Open Access focuses on re-working the economic waterfall for the initial publication of articles for a minority of global scientific output

The recent formalization of a neutral third party company called the Open Access Switchboard illustrates that all the different formulations of "Open Access" and the resulting complexities of implementing these derivative formulations now require a centralized authority to manage and operationalize them on behalf of the stakeholders – for yet another fee. But with what benefit to Science at large?

While the Open Access effort continues to focus mainly on adherence to "principles" and the pressuring of for-profit publishers, is there a larger and more significant opportunity and need being ignored and/or foregone?

- To truly innovate, it seems the various stakeholders need to move toward a view that encompasses far more than either the article, the journal or the textbook, but rather focus on the delivery of this information to those that need it.
- Greater levels of focus and investment should be given to meeting researcher (e.g. user) needs
- Publishers are slowly moving to compete at this higher level, but as long as the focus from a significant portion of the community remains on the value carrier of the past (e.g. the journal) it is likely the transition will be longer rather than shorter.

Partnering between academic institutions and those companies investing in, and attempting to solve societal problems with Science would seem a good model to use. In and of itself, undertaking these partnerships would put added pressure on publishers to innovate. There are of course many types of barriers to this happening, including existing systematic funding mechanisms as well as individuals with the incentive to preserve their existing budgets and funding levels and therefore their institutional power and sphere of influence. It is not an easy situation to address, and will likely require external forces to act as a change agent.

There is also a need to reconsider the language and metrics utilized by the community to assess things like value and performance. As pushed by the library community, publishers have taken to measuring overall cost per download annually across all titles for each institution. While a vast improvement as compared to metrics that existed in a print only world, the cost per download metric doesn't get at the true value and/or benefit of the information. While the cost per download has generally been decreasing over time, and this is a good thing, it would seem that alternative metrics and approaches need to be developed and agreed by the community which would serve to better evaluate "value". By definition, **if cost per download is the only metric used, it could serve to effectively limit investment in, and spending on, valuable contextual tools needed by the community**. This is yet another reason for quickly pursuing academic, corporate, and government partnerships to help stimulate progress and innovation.

Users of the published material are still going through learning curves to fully understand the "art-of-the possible" to be able to use already embedded functionality (for instance the power of meta-data), and also to conduct meaningful interaction with publishers about what would help them further.

Publishers have slowly adapted to the new "toolbox" provided to them, in regard to the potential to create utility for users with new products and services. Many assumptions of user behavior now and in the future are grounded in older paradigms, and may not fully utilize the potential of specific technology. New product development in publishing companies has largely been incremental as big shifts would have required substantial new purchasing power on the institutional level or wholesale changes to how institutions are organized and funded.

At the same time, in the area of education there has been very substantial innovation both by selected key professors in Universities (still a minority amongst academic teachers) and EdTech companies. Efforts have been substantial in experimenting with media, flipped classroom operations[1], and assessment-and-adaptation technologies. Many universities have moved a substantial part of their activities in Education on line through the use of external OPM providers. Interestingly, prices for these on-line courses are largely at the same level as for in person learning, while the external providers get 60%,[2] to sometimes even 75%, of that tuition charge as revenues for their help! Colleges had no problem deciding to go along with this business model at a time when most of the on-line education was incremental to their normal on-campus activity. It effectively represented an incremental revenue source, without increasing the cost base at the college or university. With the COVID-19 crisis forcing Universities and Colleges to bring their core activity on-line, this picture changes dramatically. Paying 60%-75% of their core tuition revenues is unlikely to be supportable in the near future, and calls into question the current OPM outsourcing model. This is particularly true given the pricing pressure on the college tuition due to COVID-19 crisis and the widespread realization that on-line teaching does not represent the same value as on-campus.

The confluence of all these factors creates a huge strategic issue for Universities and Colleges to consider. A range of questions present themselves, such as:

1. What is the role of education within our institution?
2. How much of the education experience should be on-line and how much on-campus?
3. What value is delivered in our education approach and how will we capture that?
4. Do we want to build our on-line education infrastructure ourselves, or do we want to buy it as a service from organizations like the OPM's, or do we band together with other institutions and develop a shared infrastructure?
5. How do we ensure the economics of the chosen approach are sound and sustainable?

We do not believe we are in a position to project what the future outcome of these strategic reviews at Universities and Colleges are likely to be. But we do know that it will require a thorough review of strategic intent and mission of the institutions, and will also impact the diverse set of stakeholders in the eco-system as well.

Here we see essentially the same issue as with the research enterprise aspect of the university: Too little funding / buying power is available to take full advantage of the very substantial innovation capacity that is available, potentially, to create utility for the learner/student and teacher. Examples are AR/VR teaching tools and enhancements, AI driven teaching pathway optimizations etc.

Concluding: The transition period from purely print to digital media has been characterized by stakeholders trying to preserve their positions and funding, while gradually introducing new capabilities in an effort to show the industry what technology enabled innovation would be capable of. An incremental, careful approach to avoid discontinuity risks. There have been some casualties in the process, like subscription agents that lost their ability to add value. At the same time, innovation was not inhibited by lack of opportunity to add utility for users, but more importantly by lack of budget and buying mechanisms at the scientific institution level. This will need to change to unleash significant improvements possible. And COVID-19 vaccine development has shown that it is possible. But it will require a new answer to the question: "what business are we in", and re-imagined process and organization at the institutional level. It will undoubtedly create new opportunities for stakeholders and question past activities and their viability,

Figure 11. (The Anatomy of an OPM, 2020)

ACCELERATION: THE DEVELOPMENT TOWARDS INTELLIGENT MEDIA AND FUNCTIONALITY

We are now entering into a period where students, researchers, professionals and consultants have become aware of the "art of the possible" not just as a technology push, but more importantly because we all have seen substantial new functionality and context presented to us in the form of consumer products, social media, advance business applications using data etc. And the STM audiences expect those functionalities and containers to be available for their line of activity as well.

Technology has enabled many direct and indirect contributions, some examples:

- Embedded intelligence into the content itself (for instance Meta Data)
- Functionality of the delivery systems (usability and utility at the point of use)
- Integration, search, browse, mining utility functionality
- Facilitation of interactivity and community collaboration tools
- Optimization of presentation of content and usability based on specific needs of the user/consumer
- Business models that allow larger access and usability, shifting costs between stakeholders to more efficient operators

Earlier we talked about the various impact pathways for research and the implications this has for publishing and technology support. Specifically we identified the following key pathways:

- (Basic) Research to Scientific Knowledge
- Innovation based on research, partnering with commercial actors
- Talent Development for Scientific work
- Education pipelines for high level professionals as well as continued and executive education
- Research to Policy development
- Involvement of the general public to ensure realistic understanding of the advancement and potential impact of science, possibly the involvement of citizen science projects and schools as well

Technology enables new products and services, but also enables new, more collaborative business models. It allows stakeholders to fundamentally rethink their collaboration and value added patterns, which in turn should help the eco-system to perform better on the earlier mentioned dimensions of Speed, Quality, Integrity, Agility and applicability as well as the all important aspect of integration of scientific knowledge with empirical and situational information to enable better decision making and execution of critical processes.

We focus ourselves here on the innovation and education pathways only for practical reasons of scope. But for the other pathways there will prove to be huge opportunities for improvement and innovation as well.

Driving forces in the larger context of scholarly publishing impact areas:

- Data and Analytics availability
- Education can be optimized for individual students, using proven pathways and individual assessments and learning patterns
- Unrelenting demand for talent that can drive faster value creation in companies and organizations they will work in after college or university

- Bigger community involvement and information flow to the general public and help communities get appropriately educated about the potential impact of science and how it operates.
- Better transfer of science knowledge to the corporate sector to allow faster and more high volume innovation in critical fields to support society: EdTech, FinTech, AgTech etc

Figure 12.

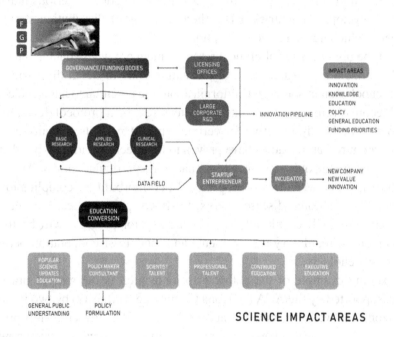

SCIENCE IMPACT AREAS

We believe that stakeholders in the science eco-system need to work together and define sandbox situations to experiment with new business models and deploy new technology aggressively to drive the faster and more efficient adoption of knowledge.

Examples of cases that show progress are in evidence based medicine and recent similar areas in environmental science and agriculture.

A very good example of a project in agriculture is plantwise, where proven scientific information is used to help farmers with critical problems of pest and disease management and control of invasive species (www.plantwise.org). In these settings proven, evidence-based interventions, are being recommended and huge amounts of data with regard to clinical settings, efficacy and safety are continuously generated in the field. These data in turn lead to significant input into the scientific process of finding even better intervention and management methods. The project was a brilliant example of how Science/Research was embedded in a practical in the field application environment supported by governments, donors and researchers, while managed and delivered through the leadership of the CABI team (www.cabi.org)

An example of where handoffs between science and innovative entrepreneurs is essential and currently being missed is the development of fortified seed varieties by Harvest+, and initiative of CGIAR, the worlds' largest source of R+D in agriculture outside universities with a budget of well over $1B, controlled by the world bank and sourced from a variety of not-for-profit funding organizations. Harvest+ has discovered and proven very powerful seed varieties to address serious nutritional deficits in developing countries. BUT, there is a lack of distribution strategy for these seeds, which has led to poor adoption.

One of the big promises of clinical research in an era where data is much more available, reliable and usable: One of our authors had in depth discussions with medical school dean in southern California about the potential to harvest electronic medical records from cancer patients and detect treatment protocol deviations that may prove to be highly effective for certain types of patients. Usually treatment protocols set in research studies have proven to be effective and safe, but that does not mean they are the only options with impact for a particular patient. As we learn more about links between treatment protocols, co-morbidities, complications and interactions with chronic disease factors, treatment protocols can be optimized. Technology tools will enable all this, but the key for progress will be funding, business models, regulatory arrangements and models of cooperation between a variety of stakeholders.

An exciting example of the pathway to innovation is the current practice in Arizona, supported by the ACA (Arizona Commerce Authority) by two initiatives, The Arizona Innovation Challenge and he Venture Ready mentorship program. These two processes have enable entrepreneurs to take critical science knowledge and turn them into completely new business in healthcare, marketing technology, educational technology, financial technology and many other areas. Similar programs exist or are being developed in other geographic areas. Linking the universities to the innovation pipelines can still be significantly improved and would generate many benefits for parties concerned.

These cases show the need for public-private partnerships, where each provider works from their strong capabilities and develops a way to deliver a societal outcome of importance.

Funding by the Bill and Melinda Gates foundation and similar groups is essential to get structures and priorities in place that are not addressed by governments due to the rapid changes in political landscape and short-term orientation that flows from it.

Figure 13.

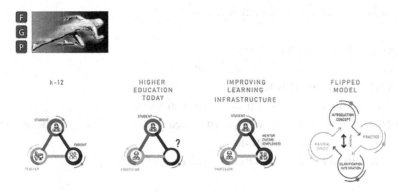

CRITICAL STRUCTURES FOR LEARNING

In the field of education there are huge opportunities to improve the student experience, deliver a better connection between university and the future employers, and optimize the process for continued education. Technology will allow educators to optimize the learning pathways for specific students by using AI engines, assessment tests and proven remediation and acceleration techniques.

Textbook / Materials are likely to follow more of a Netflix subscription model, where students have access to all their materials for a monthly flatrate. Professors and Tutors will be less bound to a specific set of materials, but rather will have to be flexible about how the students get their foundational input. Cengage, a major textbook publisher has introduced their subscription model for textbooks called Cengage Unlimited that provides a student access to their corpus of books at a fraction of the reqular print book price (*Save on Course Materials – Cengage Unlimited.*

The role of for profit investors like VC and PE funds, as well as private charities and not-for-profit funders will increase significantly as government steps back.

We are very optimistic about what can be achieved with Science and Science integration into pragmatic solutions. Technology will allow us many new opportunities, but the key will be cooperation, funding and incentives for parties to work together.

This book is intended to facilitate further discussion and most importantly, implementation of new ideas in the STM publishing and technology provision industry to help the science community achieve their goals and increase performance significantly. Here we circle back to the all important performance dimensions for the Science Eco-system we defined at the very start of this chapter. And implore all stakeholders to carefully think how to improve on these dimensions significantly in the next decade.

For science, technology and medicine (STM) communities in particular, we are looking at key performance dimensions:

- Speed of Knowledge creation
- Quality (and integrity) of Knowledge
- Contextualization of Knowledge
- Discoverability, Accessibility, and Usability
- Enablement of creativity (supporting idea generation for hypotheses etc)
- Developing the talent pipeline
- The development and monetization of Intellectual Capital

ACKNOWLEDGMENT

The authors of this Chapter are thankful for the review and contribution of the following key people: Dr. Prem Warrior, Drs. Edwin Scholte, Prof. Penny Carnaby, Drs. Chris Kluiters, Carl Grant, Dr. Andy Robinson, Don Muccino, Nick Turner, Tim Hoctor.

REFERENCES

Anderson, K. (2013, January 8). *Have Journal Prices Really Increased Much in the Digital Age?* The Scholarly Kitchen. Retrieved from: https://scholarlykitchen.sspnet. org/2013/01/08/have-journal-prices-really-increased-in-the-digital-age/

CollegeBoard. (2020a, October). *Trends In Higher Education Series Trends in College Pricing and Student Aid 2020*. Retrieved from: https://research.collegeboard.org/ pdf/trends-college-pricing-student-aid-2020.pdf

CollegeBoard. (2020b, October). *Trends In Higher Education Series Trends in College Pricing and Student Aid 2020*. Retrieved from: https://research.collegeboard.org/ pdf/trends-college-pricing-student-aid-2020.pdf

CollegeBoard. (2020c, October). *Trends In Higher Education Series Trends in College Pricing and Student Aid 2020*. Retrieved from: https://research.collegeboard.org/ pdf/trends-college-pricing-student-aid-2020.pdf

CollegeBoard. (2020d, October). *Trends In Higher Education Series Trends in College Pricing and Student Aid 2020*. Retrieved from: https://research.collegeboard.org/ pdf/trends-college-pricing-student-aid-2020.pdf

Dua, A., Law, J., Rounsaville, T., & Viswanath, N. (2020, December 4). *Reimagining higher education in the United States.* McKinsey & Company. Retrieved from: https://mck.co/3u0vM2S

Grant, C. (2018). We are the change we want to see. *Information Services & Use, 38*(1-2), 45–59. doi:10.3233/isu-180011

Janicke Hinchliffe, L. (2020, April 8). *Seeking Sustainability: Publishing Models for an Open Access Age.* The Scholarly Kitchen. Retrieved from: https://scholarlykitchen.sspnet.org/2020/04/07/seeking-sustainability-publishing-models-for-an-open-access-age/

Mitchell, J. (2020, October 19). How Apprenticeship, Reimagined, Vaults Graduates Into Middle Class. *Wall Street Journal.*

Robbins, C., Khan, B., & Okrent, A. (2020, January 15). *Science & Engineering Indicators.* National Science Foundation. Retrieved from: https://ncses.nsf.gov/pubs/nsb20201/global-r-d

Save on Course Materials – Cengage Unlimited. (n.d.). Cengage. https://www.cengage.com/unlimited/

Stoll, J. D. (2020, November 9). This College Degree Is Brough to You by Amazon. *Wall Street Journal.*

The Anatomy of an OPM and a $7.7B Market in 2025. (2020, August 18). HolonIQ. Retrieved from: https://www.holoniq.com/news/anatomy-of-an-opm/

United Nations. (2020, August). *Policy Brief: Education during COVID-19 and Beyond.* United Nations. Retrieved from: https://www.un.org/development/desa/dspd/wp-content/uploads/sites/22/2020/08/sg_policy_brief_covid-19_and_education_august_2020.pdf

ENDNOTES

[1]   Flipped classroom operations refers to the practice pioneered by the Kahn Academy, where the efforts of the teacher are much more directed by immediate needs of the students after they have attempted to internalize the study material on their own., and related formats.

[2]   The business model arrangements in place for OPM have been the subject of some scrutiny in the recent Huffington Post Highline article: "the Corporations Devouring American Colleges."

Chapter 2
Business Model Developments:
The History, Current Situation, and Future Outlook of Business Models in Academic Publishing

Joost Kollöffel
J & J Marketing Solutions, The Netherlands

ABSTRACT

Academic publishing is a 'need to have' process that is very important in the academic world. This chapter focuses on the business models that were/are/might be used to finance the processes and the innovation in scholarly communication. What sparked the serials crisis? Is Open Access publishing feasible? Why are there predatory publishers? Can scientometrics and altmetrics be made into saleable products? These types of questions are answered in this chapter, where the focus lies on the financial feasibility of the main processes that occur in academic publishing.

BUSINESS MODEL DEVELOPMENTS

The History of Academic Publishing Business Models

Early Days

Academic publishing as we currently know it was established in 1665, notably by the publication on March 6 of that year of the United Kingdom's *Philosophical Transactions of the Royal Society*. An earlier publication had already come out in January of that year, so two months before, with the French publication of *Journal*

DOI: 10.4018/978-1-7998-5589-7.ch002

des sçavans by Mr. Denis de Sallo, making this the very first academic publication. The *Journal des sçavans* however ceased to exist in 1752, and the *Philosophical Transactions of the Royal Society* is still being published, although the journal has split into two separate publications: one serving physical sciences and one serving the life sciences. Academic publishing as we know it has existed for 355 years! The 'philosophical' from the title should be read as 'natural philosophical', which we currently name: 'science'.

Figure 1. Front page of Philosophical Transactions.
Attribution: CC BY 4.0 via Wikimedia Commons

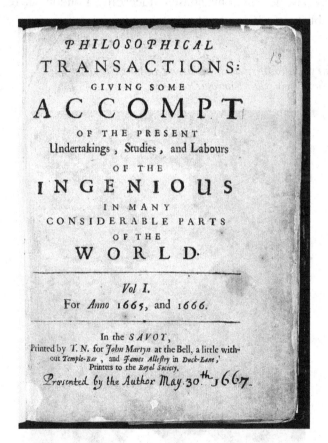

With the topic of this section in mind, it is interesting to know that the first publisher of the *Philosophical Transactions of the Royal Society* was the German-born Henry Oldenburg, who was the Society's First Secretary. Four and a half years after the Society was formed, he decided to publish the journal. In the Society's council minutes can be found: "the Philosophical Transactions, to be composed by Mr. Oldenburg, be printed the first Monday of every month, if he has sufficient matter for it, and that that tract be licensed by the Council of this Society, being first revised by some Members of the same". This last part means something very important; it means that peers were to be used for reviewing. Peer review in these days was not always mandatory, as it became in the 20th century. He financed the journal himself, and was allowed to keep the profits from selling it to the Society's members. This means that in its origin, academic publishing was conceived with a commercial 'reader pays' business model.

For Mr. Oldenburg, this did not bring much success: with the profit generated, he could barely pay the rent of his house in Piccadilly, London. He passed away in 1677, after publishing 136 issues of his 'Transactions'.

Figure 2. Henry Oldenburger by painter Jan van Cleve.
Attribution: Public domain, via Wikimedia Commons

In the 18th century, approximately 1000 different journals emerged, most of them were published over short time spans. This means that it was not an easy business to maintain over a longer period. It was expensive to print a scientific journal: the demands on printing quality were high and especially the illustrations were the largest expense. Illustrations had been a natural and essential aspect of the scientific periodical since the later seventeenth century. Engravings (cut into metal plates) were used for detailed illustrations, particularly where realism was required; while wood-cuts (and, from the early nineteenth century, wood-engravings) were used for diagrams, as they could be easily combined with letterpress (Kronick, 1976).

In addition to being able to share human knowledge and push its boundaries, another important goal of academic publishing is solving the issue of 'first inventor'/ scientific priority. Mr. Robert K. Merton, a sociologist, found that 92% of cases of simultaneous discovery in the 17th century ended in dispute. The number of disputes dropped to 72% in the 18th century, 59% by the latter half of the 19th century, and to 33% by the first half of the 20th century (Merton, 1963). The decline in contested claims for priority in research discoveries can be credited to the increasing acceptance of the publication of papers in modern academic journals, with estimates suggesting that around 50 million journal articles have been published since the first appearance of the Philosophical Transactions. The Royal Society was steadfast in its not-yet-popular belief of that time that science could only move forward through a transparent and open exchange of ideas backed by experimental evidence (Jinha, 2010).

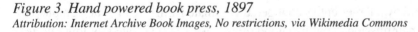

Figure 3. Hand powered book press, 1897
Attribution: Internet Archive Book Images, No restrictions, via Wikimedia Commons

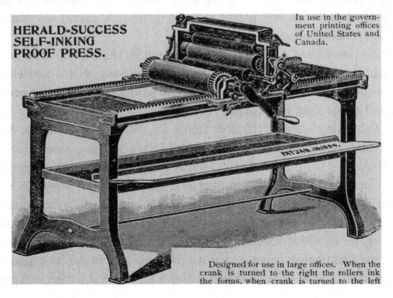

Academic journals were mostly published by societies, and were financed by the members fee's, and by selling the journals as subscriptions to non-members. Until recent years, this was the common business model.

Market Consolidation

After the Second World War however, a shift started to take place in academic publishing: enterprises started to take over the publishing of the academic journals from the societies. To produce an academic journal, you need to master the functions of organizing the peer review process, editorial services, desk top publishing, production of the paper journals, distribution, sales and marketing. Certain companies gathered this required specific expertise and could offer it with a higher efficiency than the society-run operations, whose directors were in the first place scientists, not publishers... Data from the mid-1990s by Tenopir and King suggests an increase of commercial publishers' share of the article output; by then, commercial publishers accounted for 40% of the journal output, while scientific/professional societies accounted for 25% and university presses and educational publishers for 16% (Tenopir & King, 1997). Slowey but surely academic publishing became an industry.

While many academic publishing companies had the expertise to run their operations, there often was a lack of capital. From the 1960s on, there were companies who understood that a way to gain capital is by merger and acquisitions. In his memoir *The Business of Books: How International Conglomerates Took Over Publishing and Changed the Way We Read*, André Schiffrin describes how the acquisition of a smaller firm by a larger entity changed the climate from one in which employees believed in their mission to publish good titles, which compensated for low salaries, to one in which each title is expected to make money and executives demand the salaries and perks of industry moguls.

The 1961 purchase of Alfred A. Knopf by Random House created an unusually large establishment for the time, but the 1965 purchase of Random House by entertainment firm RCA was more of a departure. The merger mania that characterized national and global economies in the 1970s and 1980s spread to publishing: in 1980, Advance Publishing acquired Random House for $80 million; Simon & Schuster bought Prentice Hall in 1984 for $718 million; I.R. Maxwell purchased Macmillian; Rupert Murdock's firm, News Corp., bought Harper & Row and merged it with Collins. Viacom, with Sumner Redstone as chairman, bought Simon & Schuster (Schiffrin, 2001). André Schiffrin's memoir is not specifically focusing on academic publishing, but similar events occurred in the academic publishing sector. The example is Elsevier, which started operating as a scientific publisher in 1947 with the launch of the first English language journal *Biochimica et Biophysica Acta*. It then grew organically, and in 1970 acquired the North Holland Publishing company and in 1971 Excerpta Medica. In 1978 it acquired Dutch newspaper publisher NDU. In 1993 it merges with Reed International. In 2001 it acquires the publishers Mosby's, W.B. Saunders, and Academic Press.

Serials Crisis

(Academic) Publishing was not always looked upon as a high-profit sector. In the USA, since the 1920s average profits reported by publishers have hovered around 4%, after taxes. Among major independent French publishers, Gallimard had an annual profit of a bit over 3%, and Le Seuil just over 1% (Schiffrin, 1996). This however started changing in the seventies and eighties: the pressure for a scientist to climb the academic ladder by publishing his/her work was gaining momentum; 'publish or perish' became the mantra if your ambition was to climb the academic ranks. The scientific community realized that through publishing articles, and by how many times these were referenced by peers, it was possible to quantify scientific output. Publishers understood this very well. Instruments to measure quality and quantity of academic output were developed. An example such as the Impact Factor was devised by Eugene Garfield, the founder of the Institute for Scientific Information (ISI). Impact factors are calculated yearly starting from 1975 for journals listed in the Journal Citation Reports (JCR), which currently is a list of over 8,000 academic journals. The index measures for a given journal title the number of citations in a year, divided by the number of articles published in the two previous years. The higher this number, the more citations the articles in the journal have, the higher its reputation. So, a researcher not just wants to publish his/her article, but wants to publish it in the best journal possible. This drives up the importance of the publishing process for the academic world. Similar to publishing in the legal segment, academic publishing is not a 'nice to have', but a 'need to have'.

In the nineties and the new millennium, the subscription prices started to increase faster than national inflation rates. Every year the Library Journal publishes a summary of periodical pricing and inflation. "The rate of price increase is analyzed for more than 18,000 e-journal packages handled by EBSCO Information Services... For 2019, the average rate of increase over two years was 5.5%, up slightly from 5% in 2018 (Bosch, 2019)."

First the publishers started raising the prices of their top-rated journals. Since there are no substitutes for this unique journal, if an institute wanted to have access to its articles, they just had to swallow the price increase. In economic terms this is called price inelasticity. Another possible set of factors in this situation includes the increasing domination of scholarly communication by a small number of commercial publishers, whose journals are far more costly than those of most academic societies (Mayer, 2006).

Figure 4. Title: Eugene Garfield.
Attribution: Science History Institute, CC BY-SA 3.0 via Wikimedia Commons

Over the years, there was also significant growth in academic publishing taking place: every year there were more articles per journal published, more issues per year, and more journal titles in scientific specialty areas that appeared, and this trend could justify a part of the price increases, but not all librarians were convinced. This growth in scientific output was not taking place at the same rate as the growth of the library budgets, who also needed to invest in the computer infrastructure of their traditionally paper-based worlds. While the budgets of the institutes often were increasing, the library's budget was not, making their slice of the pizza relatively smaller, as the whole pizza was growing. What started happening, is that budgets earmarked for other purposes, such as acquiring monographs, were siphoned off to keep pace with the yearly increasing journal subscription fees. For example, the Association of Research Libraries (ARL) described in a report in 2002 that in "1986, libraries spent 44% of their budgets on books compared with 56% on journals; twelve years later, the ratio had skewed to 28% and 72%."

In the new Millennium, librarians got increasingly frustrated about the publisher's price increases, and started to cancel journal subscriptions. This had an effect on the publishers, who had to make up for the loss of revenue by increasing the subscriptions for the remaining clients, who then decided to cancel their subscription too, and there you have a negative spiral; the serials crisis was born.

The librarians wanted to break out of this mechanism and developed more efficient ways of accessing the articles: services such as 'interlibrary loan' and buying separate articles from aggregators instead of having subscriptions were increasingly being used. Libraries started to organize themselves into consortia, where they could negotiate better terms and conditions with the commercial publishers as a buying combination, compared to when they operate as a separate library. The consortia are often organized on a national or state level.

The Electronic Library

While the Serials Crises unfolded, the internet, hypertext and the browser were being introduced to the world, and soon the benefits of these technology developments were discovered by academia and by publishers alike. This meant a major shift in how libraries operated and how they could offer their services to their users. A librarian now can for example get the insight in which journals and books are being used, by whom, for how much time, when, etc. The usage data was giving meaningful indications into a library's collection: is it relevant? Is it efficient? What is the price per downloaded article in the last year? To this day and in the foreseeable future, usage analysis is important in the buying decisions of a librarian. Previously, librarians had to use indicators such as the 'dust test': if a journal or book had collected a lot of dust in the shelves since the last round, maybe it should move to the archive...

In the late 1990s, as online editions of journals became widely available, business models changed drastically. With online editions, there are no printing or mailing costs, and the marginal cost to the publisher of permitting another user is essentially zero. Moreover, the internet enabled commercial publishers to develop new pricing methods that allowed them to exercise their market power much more effectively than in the print-only environment (Bergstrom, 2012).

An effect of the internet was that publishers could put all their content in online searchable databases. Not only from the current publications; they started digitizing their archives, going back to Volume 1, Issue 1. In the example of the famous medical journal *The Lancet*, that means you can search for and read articles that were published going back to 1823. (Which on another note, is curious from a social historic standpoint, because in a Lancet article of 1877 it was discussed that it might not be a good idea if women should be allowed to follow medical training. The doctor who had this opinion, is now probably spinning in his grave of frustration...) (Ferry, 2015). This development of opening up of archives and putting all content online meant that there currently is no scarcity in scientific information. With your smart electronic device, you can access millions of articles with a few swipes and clicks from your couch. The ubiquity of scientific content (not only from a production standpoint, but also from an access standpoint), means that the value perception of it comes down, and so does the price, comparable as to what happens in other content sectors that moved online, such as the music and movie industry: information is becoming a commodity.

In the 2000s and beyond, more librarians started to complain about the price increases and the gross profit margin of the commercial publishers of academic content. In their annual financial reports, you could see that the profits were regularly above 30%. Pressure groups, websites, meetings, conferences, journalists and newspapers were discussing this topic. Their story line was: most articles are written by researchers who are employed by universities or not-for-profit institutes. They are being paid by tax payers' money. Authors send their articles to commercial parties to get published, and do this free of charge. The publisher does not pay for this work, or for the peer review process that mainly takes place between academics. Publishers even charge for author services, such as proof reading, lay-out and illustrations. Then the publishers sell the journals and books to the libraries, who too are financed by the governments, and the tax payer pays again. It is clear that publishers add value in the publishing process, but it was felt that annual profit margins of above 30% were too much.

Figure 5. Modern library, where the computer is more used than the books.
Attribution: Informationwave at English Wikipedia, CC BY 3.0

Big Deal Offerings

The trend described earlier of the consolidation of the publishers kept progressing. Reed-Elsevier, Wiley-Blackwell, Springer, and Taylor & Francis increased their share of the published output, especially since the advent of the digital era (mid-1990s), mainly by growing through mergers and acquisitions. Combined, the top five most prolific publishers account for more than 50% of all papers published in 2013 (Larivière, 2015).

To counter the negative sentiment, the publishers thought of solutions to lower prices and/or increase value. One solution that was quickly adopted, was to bundle their content and offer it with substantial discounts to librarians. Libraries normally would select the titles from a publisher's catalog ('pick and choose'), however in the digital age the publishers would offer access to all of their journals and all of their books with steeply discounted prices. The price on a per title basis came down.

While in the traditional paper world everybody paid the same subscription price, for the 'big deals' every institute would get an a la carte price. Publishers added non-disclosure agreements to their contracts, so the offerings could be not be compared. To estimate how much a library would pay for a big deal, a publisher would not need to know the buyer's valuation for any single journal, but could simply estimate the library's willingness to pay for the entire package of previously unsubscribed journals. The initial price for a big deal contract would be a library's then-current total expenditure on the publisher's offerings, plus an additional 5–15%. These contracts had a duration of 3–5 y with built-in annual price increases of about 6%. A subscribing institute would continue to pay the full cost of all of the journals that it previously purchased, and for a relatively small additional fee it could also electronically access the journals that it had previously chosen not to purchase. Publishers could be assured of increased revenue from any library that accepted the big deal and would lose no revenue from those that did not. The initial big deals were based on the assumption that institutions would be willing to pay at least an added 10–15% of their current expenditure in return for access to the unsubscribed journals. Although there were built-in price increases, the increments were gradual, so that libraries could adjust their budgets to these increased costs (Bergstrom, 2014).

'Pay by the Drink' vs. 'All You Can Eat'

Before the electronic library emerged, it already was possible to request a single article or book chapter from another library, or from a commercial provider. Publishers allow academic libraries under strict conditions to make a copy of an article of a subscribed journal and send that to another library. This is called interlibrary loan (ILL), and it used to take a long time with the mail. In the eighties, the speed increased because copies could be sent by fax, but still a lot of manual processing were required. In the days of internet, search software, email and PDF, the ILL process can be quite fast. It allows for libraries to have a shared catalogue; however, the publishers try to make this hard. It is for example not allowed to send a PDF file by email to another library as a machine-readable file, only as a flat image. However, the electronic library has made this process logistically easier and faster. In the context of the big deal cancellations by several library systems, data analysis tools like Unpaywall Journals are being used by libraries to assist in calculating whether alternative access methods like ILL and Open Access end up being more effective and less expensive, than a potential subscription (Wolfe, 2020). Open Access is discussed in the next paragraph.

Especially in corporate libraries of R&D intense industries you see this a lot: corporate Information Professionals (in the corporate world they do not embrace the function title of 'Librarian') do not have the same goal as their academic counter parts, whose ultimate goal is to make as much content available to their users in the easiest way ('All you can eat'). Industries with a strong R&D focus are for example the pharmaceutical, automotive, agricultural, and air & space industries. The corporate Information Professionals are more focused on efficiency: if a journal is being used a lot, or important for a certain innovative project, they might consider taking a subscription. The main provider of the scientific content comes from document delivery providers, who do a type of corporate ILL. They have a large catalogue that can be searched, and articles are being sent as PDF files within a few minutes. On average, these cost $60 per article, and in most cases, they may not be stored on a shared network drive ('Pay by the drink'). Here the so called 'Tokens' come into play: upfront a company can for example acquire 100 tokens, that allow for 100 downloads. They can negotiate a better price with the upfront payment. Often the tokens have a validity period; after 24 or 36 months there are not valid anymore.

If corporate libraries would like to store the PDFs, and make them available for reuse for colleagues, then a copyright license is required, such as the one offered by the Copyright Clearance Center, which you can almost see as some kind of a subscription license for PDF documents that first had to be acquired.

When a (corporate) researcher is looking for information, and finds an article from an unsubscribed journal, he can see the meta data of the article: who is the author, what is the title, where was it published, what are the key words, etc. Based on the meta data information, the next step is to decide to buy the article. It might happen that the $60 article unfortunately is not relevant, and the PDF is seen as useless. There are companies who have a solution for this issue: article rental. You can access an article for 24 hours, but cannot print or share it. DeepDyve delivers this service and their business model is that you pay $500 annually and can search and read in the 18 million articles in their database.

Open Access and Reform of Academic Publishing

Although the move to electronic files, internet and new business models such as the Big Deal meant that libraries could obtain cheaper, faster and easier access to more academic information, the librarians / academic world did not agree with the large profits of the publishers, their market power, and in many instances also objected principally to the process of academic publishing. The biggest change in this sector, not only from a business model standpoint, must be the Open Access movement, where not the reader pays through a subscription, but where the author pays to get his/her article or book (chapter) published, or where sponsors, such as an institute, national research fund, NGO, philanthropy, etc. pick up the costs of publishing. In the case of publishing journal articles, these costs are referred to as Article Processing Charges (APCs). Access to this content becomes free of cost or free of other access barriers, not locked behind a pay-wall for the reader. There are many different versions of Open Access, identified by a color (Gold, Green, Bronze, Hybrid, Diamond, Black) where the main differences lie in what type of copyright exists, and with whom, in (self) archiving and in which party pays the APCs.

Figure 6. The Open Access logo.
Attribution: Rafabollas, CC BY-SA 4.0, via Wikimedia Commons

CURRENT SITUATION: A VARIETY OF OPTIONS

What has changed in the last few years and is still valid today, is that when you are an academic author wanting to publish, or when you are a student or researcher and are looking for specific information, there are numerous options to choose from. It can be head spinning. Let us look from a business model perspective at the current situation in academic publishing.

Open Access Is Here to Stay

An author wanting to publish an article can choose to do it the traditional way where you select a journal with the best reputation, based on its scientific subject, the journal's ISI Impact Factor, who is in the editorial board, frequency, etc. This journal is paid for by the readers, so by subscription income, institutional license, consortium agreement and by pay-per-view income. This is still how approximately 50% of articles are published, however the number of OA published articles grows fast (Piwowar, 2018). Academic publishing is tipping towards OA published articles, but when we look at the speed of change in this sector in the past, the traditional model will be around for some time to come. A recent effect is that publishers need to follow the market trend, so cannot request annual price increases above the consumer price index / inflation correction.

If the author prefers to publish under an Open Access license, then it requires understanding of what all the different OA flavors entail, not just about the price of the APCs, but also from where the budget comes from to pay the APCs, to regarding the copyright position (ownership, re-use and archival rights). There are OA or hybrid journals that have an ISI Impact Factor, but most do not have this; they have been launched in the last 10 years, so do not have built up a strong academic reputation yet. In the second to next paragraph is explained what hybrid journals are.

Academic Institutes Stop Renewing Licenses

Since 2010, an increasing number of universities and library consortia have not renewed their 'big deal' licenses with the large publishers, or did after bitter negotiations. According to SPARC, these big deal cancellations happened 65 times since 2009, and the main publishers involved were Elsevier, Springer Nature, Taylor & Francis and Wiley. High profile examples are the cancellation of all members of the University of California System that in 2019 did not renewed the license with Elsevier (who own 26% of all academic journals globally). No renewals either for Elsevier in 2020 for the Massachusetts Institute of Technology (MIT), State University of New York System (SUNY) and the national Finnish library consortium FinELib (SPARC, 2020).

Open Access Mandate

Certain research funding agencies object to the commercial academic publishing process in such a degree, that they mandate the authors that they fund, to publish only under Open Access licenses, to avoid that their work which is funded by the public, is being 'locked away' behind the pay walls of the commercial academic publishers. The list of research or funding institutes who mandate this publishing policy is growing, and some well-known high-quality institutes follow this policy. Among the universities that have adopted open-access mandates for faculty are in the United States of America: Harvard University and the Massachusetts Institute of Technology, in the United Kingdom: University College London, in Belgium: University of Liege and in Switzerland: ETH Zürich. Among the funding organizations that have adopted open-access mandates for grant recipients are in the USA: National Institutes of Health, in the UK: Research Councils UK and the Wellcome Trust, in Belgium: National Fund for Scientific Research, and the European Union's European Research Council.

As of December 2020, there are 834 research organizations (e.g. university or research institution), 82 sub-units of research organizations (e.g. departments, faculties or schools), 11 multiple research organizations, 86 funders and 57 funder and research organizations who have adopted a form of an OA publishing mandate. For a full index of institutional and funder open-access mandates adopted to date, see the Registry of Open Access Mandatory Archiving Policies (ROARMAP). A current OA mandatory initiative that is being discussed is: 'Plan S', which was launched in 2018 by "cOAlition S", a consortium of national research agencies and funders from twelve European countries (Economist, 2018). Some parties signed up, and others stepped out. From a business model perspective, it is remarkable to see that the national R&D funding agencies (basically the federal governments) try to steer this industry in the direction of Open Access.

Hybrid Journals

From a business model perspective, a hybrid journal is interesting: it has a mix of traditionally financed articles, and of OA articles. The advantage of a hybrid journal is that an author can publish OA in an already existing title, that has an established reputation. A hybrid journal's income stream is more complex. Critics of this set-up also call this: 'double dipping', because the publisher requires readers to pay for the traditionally published articles, and at the same time collects APCs for the OA published articles. Publishers say that they can lower the subscription license fee for the hybrid journal, but the critics say that the hybrid journals lack transparency, and the publisher may just turn the knobs in such a way that the revenue stream of a hybrid journal is generating the highest yield (Mittermaier, 2015).

Predatory OA Publishers

Since the market of OA published journals was growing, combined with the pressure to publish of the author/researcher, plus the up-front payment of the APCs which on average are $3000, meant that new publishing companies emerged who wanted to skim off the APCs, and were not really interested in developing a respected academic journal. These 'fake' publishers were coined 'predatory' in 2010 by librarian Jeffrey Beall, who at the time worked at University of Colorado Denver.

He started 'Beall's list' listing OA publishers who did not comply with 26 quality features that Jeffrey Beall had stated for a properly run OA publisher (Beall, 2016). In 2017 he stopped his efforts. Irony is that the company Cabell's took over the management of the predatory publisher's list, and put it behind a paywall... More than half of all articles published in predatory journals do not get cited. Today's early career researchers get warnings and education from the institutes that employ them how to avoid publishing with a predatory publisher.

Scientometrics and Altmetrics

The academic publishing's move to electronic journals and the internet not only had an impact on the insights that librarians, authors and publishers got on how academic content was actually being used; it is also a development that is interesting from a business model / business opportunity side. Usage analysis can be aggregated not only to an institute level, but also regional, national, continental and even global levels. Usage analysis can be combined with other data sources, such as article output, citation analysis and R&D budget level. These insights are not on the level of an individual article, but are on aggregated levels above and next to it.

To make this more concrete, think of a national research foundation, like the Deutsche Forschungsgemeinschaft (DFG) in Germany, the National Science Foundation (NSF) in the United States of America or the National Research Foundation (NRF) in South-Africa. Every budget cycle, they need to decide which universities, faculties and research groups get funding, and how much. In the case of the NSF, that budget is $8,3 billion in 2020. They need to understand what the successful and strong areas of research are in their country, and what the status is of the competition (on global, national, state, institute and research group levels). Countries decide on a R&D policy: which areas are important to grow in or maintain their position? There is a segment of policymakers, scientists and businesses that focus on solving these questions. What is the position of the universities in a country? What are the best performing research teams? How do you measure that? What is the effect on shifting budget to a certain research topic? ISI's Impact Factors are the first step into this direction, and now the large publishers have moved into this field, which is named 'Scientometrics', which has the aim to measure the quality, quantity, performance, efficiency and effectiveness of the academic process (Mingers, 2015). 'Altmetrics' basically has the same goal, but uses non-traditional indicators, such as usage/downloads of the content or 'likes'/retweets on social media platforms, so are looking at using alternative research assessment methods.

As described before, the relative value of academic content is being perceived lower, there is pressure from OA and non-profit publishing initiatives, resulting in publishers that find it more challenging to maintain their profit levels. The scientometrics field requires large databases with complex datasets, such as author details, publications, citations, journal data, topic areas, funding, etc. Products and services in this field are difficult to develop and hard to replicate, so publishers can still get a good margin. Examples of products in this space are Elsevier's Pure, Clarivate's Conversis and Digital Science's Dimensions. A revenue stream is not being generated by publishing itself, but on the analysis and insights thereof, in combination with other indicators.

Transformative Agreements: Read and Publish Licenses

Most academic publishers allow for traditionally published articles and OA published articles, sometimes as separate journals, but often mixed in the same title ('Hybrid' journal, see above). Since 2019, publishers started offering a business model that fits well with this 'hybrid' set-up. It is referred to as a 'transformative agreement' or more precisely the 'Read & Publish' license. From an academic institute's perspective, to be able to get access to the traditionally published journals, they firstly need a subscription license. To publish in OA journals, they secondly need to pay the APCs. The Read & Publish license combines these two payments: a package deal is made, based upon the wishes for the license and by estimating how many articles by that institute (or consortium of institutes) will be published as OA. The publisher can give a discount on the APCs, which per article average $3000. In certain negotiations, the APCs are waved completely. For a university, this can be a very interesting offer (Hinchliffe, 2019). The advantage for a publisher is that in many cases the budget for publishing under OA can be on a different location than the content budget, so these two budgets can both be tapped in to. Another advantage of a Read & Publish agreement is that a publisher can secure a stream of OA articles and increase this body of academic content. For publishers who do not have such a license in place, it can mean that the number of submissions for OA articles decline, and over time this might even erode the publisher's position.

The transformative part is that it is seen as a stronger shift towards OA publishing, because the traditional model is combined with OA in one license. Many see this type of license as a temporary solution, an in-between thing, with the end situation being a complete conversion to OA, where the Read & Publish licenses will not be needed anymore.

WHAT WILL THE FUTURE BRING?

Will Open Access Live Up to Its Promises?

The move to OA financed publishing will continue, as more librarians and research funders mandate this business model. Whether it in the long term is feasible remains to be seen; publishers have developed numerous innovative products and services, and the funding for this came from the revenues generated by the readers, who had annual licenses and subscriptions. For a given published peer reviewed article, there is a continues income stream, and this could be used for the development of new innovative products and services. Under OA however, there is a one-time payment of the article, and until eternity this document needs to be hosted in an online database, indexed and being in a format that people can read (currently mainly XML, HTML and PDF, but this might change in the future). Because the academic article output is growing (more published articles in a growing number of journals), and the relative share of OA is also growing, there is more revenue coming in, but in the long run, it might be a challenge if the financing of the publishing process is still feasible. Another risk of OA are the predatory publishers and even the independence of a publisher: imagine a publisher that is almost bankrupt, and he receives an article to publish, that does not meet the quality standards, will he bend the rules a bit and publish it anyway if it can save his company? What will the effect be for researchers who would like to publish, but their institute is located in a low-income country and the $4000 requested for the APC is a challenge? Perhaps the flow of budget for OA publishing will increase in the direction of national and local research grant agencies and philanthropy, with a threshold built in on how much profit margin may be made by a commercial party.

Increased Scattering

Already discussed above is the increase in parties involved in the academic publishing process, and the increase in products and services offered in this industry. The growing ease of using computer power and software development, combined with a decrease of costs involved of these, mean that more institutes, agencies and companies will start publishing initiatives, such as publishing organizations, archives, indexing and search platforms, etc. There will be winners and losers in this segment, however the future of the landscape of academic publishing will be even more scattered. To make the right choice in where and how to publish, for an author, and to choose what products and services to offer to the library users, for a librarian will become less obvious. The winners and losers will also (dis)appear in a higher frequency. Think of the example of the social media platform MySpace: in its days the leading social media platform, which only a few years later has become obsolete.

Open Science / Open Data

This paragraph is comparable to the 'Scientometrics and Altmetrics' above, in the sense that is about data regarding publication, but not in the direction of accumulation to higher levels, but the opposite way: into granularity. In many fields of science, large datasets are being used and/or generated. Think for example in bio-informatics or physics. The author of an article extracts, combines or summarizes his/her findings of these specific datasets, and publishes the article. It is currently possible to let readers access the raw datasets that led to a publication. There is discussion going on currently under the title 'Open Science' and 'Open Data', where the proponents would like to see a development comparable to Open Access licensed information. The publishers might see an opportunity to establish the infrastructure to make this possible. One of the more discussed topics regarding Open Data is indeed on how to put data sets and software of various types, formats and sizes available online in an efficient way, and how to do that in a feasible way. It is yet to be seen which business models will be used in the new Open Data / Open Science movement.

The Power of the Crowd

There are projects looking at using the 'power of the crowd' in academic publishing processes, with many focusing on the peer review process. Peer review may take a few months, and the people who carry this out are often very busy. The thought here is not to have a selected group of peer reviewers who do this 'Blind' (not knowing who wrote the manuscript that needs to be reviewed), but to do this in an open and transparent way, that should improve the speed and efficiency of this process, by using the 'crowd'. At the 2016 SpotOn conference in London, the main subject was the future of peer reviews (Academy, 2020). Those who regularly participate in the publishing process (e.g., publishers, stakeholders) were asked for their input on peer review by 2030. The discussions centered around the fact that the process is slow and inefficient and, as stated above, often subject to bias. Some of the suggestions for change were as follows:

- Expand the role of technology, such as artificial intelligence to match reviewers with the subject matter.
- Increase reviewer diversity in, for example, age and geographic area.
- Increase transparency.

- Use new artificial intelligence to detect inconsistencies in a manuscript, such as throughout figures.
- Use newly created programs to better detect plagiarism.
- Increase reviewer recognition to increase their incentives.

Publishers are starting to offering this service too, for example Thieme Chemistry offers since 2018 their 'Select Crowd Review' service.

Needs

In such as diversified playing field, with many newcomers entering the academic publishing segment, for stakeholders it will be important that they can quickly establish trust between each other or between the providers and that the processes used demonstrate integrity and transparency. Many think that blockchain technology can play a strong role here. It is still too early days to see a clear business model of how Blockchain technology can/will be used, and it is exciting to see how that will develop.

The traditional business model will lose territory, and new ways how to finance academic publishing will develop. The high profit margins will disappear; however, a publisher might develop a specific golden goose. Looking at the music industry, you can see that the profit margins per song or record are in decline, and that a new platform like Spotify opens up a lot of music to listeners for a fixed price, still making it a feasible business model for the stakeholders involved.

REFERENCES

Beall, J. (2016). *List of Publishers*. Scholarly Open Access.

Bergstrom, T. C., Courant, P. N., McAfee, R. P., & Williams, M. A. (2014). Evaluating big deal journal bundles. *Proceedings of the National Academy of Sciences of the United States of America*, *111*(26), 9425–9430. doi:10.1073/pnas.1403006111 PMID:24979785

Bergstrom, T. C., Courant, P. N., McAfee, R. P., & Williams, M. A. (2014). Evaluating big deal journal bundles. *Proceedings of the National Academy of Sciences of the United States of America*, *111*(26), 9425–9430. doi:10.1073/pnas.1403006111 PMID:24979785

Enago Adacemy. (2020). *Will Crowd-based Peer Review Replace Traditional Peer Review?* Enago Adacemy.

Ferry, G. (2015). Medical periodicals: Mining the past. *Lancet, 385*(9987), 2569–2570. doi:10.1016/S0140-6736(15)61151-5 PMID:26122152

Janicke Hinchliffe, L. (2019). *Transformative Agreements: A Primer*. The Scholarly Kitchen.

Jinha, A. E. (2010). *Article 50 million: An estimate of the number of scholarly articles in existence*. Academic Press.

Kronick, D. A. (1976). *History of Scientific and Technical Periodicals* (2nd ed.). Scarecrow.

Larivière, V., Haustein, S., & Mongeon, P. (2015). The Oligopoly of Academic Publishers in the Digital Era. *PLoS One, 10*(6), e0127502. doi:10.1371/journal.pone.0127502 PMID:26061978

Library Journal. (2019). *Deal or No Deal: Periodicals Price Survey 2019*. Author.

Mayer, K. (2006). *Journal subscription costs continue to climb*. UW News.

Merton, R. K. (1963). Resistance to the Systematic Study of Multiple Discoveries in Science, *European Journal of Sociology, 4*(2), 237–282. doi:10.1017/S0003975600000801

Mingers, J., & Leydesdorff, L. (2015). A Review of Theory and Practice in Scientometrics. *European Journal of Operational Research, 246*(1), 1–19. doi:10.1016/j.ejor.2015.04.002

Mittermaier, B. (2015). Double Dipping in Hybrid Open Access – Chimera or Reality? Forschungszentrum Jülich.

Modern Language Association. (2002). *Report from the Ad Hoc Committee on the Future of Scholarly Publishing*. Author.

Piwowar, H., Priem, J., Larivière, V., Alperin, J. P., Matthias, L., Norlander, B., Farley, A., West, J., & Haustein, S. (2018). The state of OA: A large-scale analysis of the prevalence and impact of Open Access articles. *PeerJ, 6*, e4375. doi:10.7717/peerj.4375 PMID:29456894

Schiffrin, A. (1996). The Corporatization of Publishing. *Nation (New York, N.Y.)*, 29–32.

Schiffrin, A. (2001). *The Business of Books: How International Conglomerates Took Over Publishing and Changed the Way We Read*. Academic Press.

SPARC. (2020). *Big Deal Cancellation Tracking*. SPARC.

Tenopir, C., & King, D. W. (1997). Trends in Scientific Scholarly Journal Publishing in the U.S. *Journal of Scholarly Publishing, 28*(3), 135–170. doi:10.3138/JSP-028-03-135

The Economist. (2018). European countries demand that publicly funded research should be free to all. *The Economist.*

The Royal Society. (2015). *Philosophical Transactions: 350 years of publishing at the Royal Society (1665–2015).* Author.

The Royal Society-Publishing. (2010). *Philosophical Transactions of the Royal Society of London – History.* Author.

Wolfe, D. (2020). *SUNY Negotiates New, Modified Agreement with Elsevier.* Libraries News Center University at Buffalo Libraries.

Chapter 3
Legislative Developments in Scholarly Publishing

Carlo Scollo Lavizzari
Lenz Caemmerer, Switzerland

ABSTRACT

The legal developments in scholarly publishing began back at the time of the Guttenberg press. The scholarly journal publishing industry evolved over the centuries. The 1960s through the launch of the internet saw the industry explode with growth. With the advent and development of the digital journal, open access, and other clandestine illegal databases, it is essential that the industry work to protect its interests. This chapter will provide a history, overview, and developments that will be required to ensure the ongoing concerns of the industry.

LEGAL DEVELOPMENTS: THE PRISM OF THE FIVE FLOWS

Content industries are said to thrive in relative stability, if they are able to align a "three-legged stool" comprising the legs of business model, legal rules and technology in such a way to create value for all participants. This Subsection will focus on the leg of "legal rules" of that stool, with a special emphasis of legal rules on the horizon or emerging for scholarly publishing in the context of Blockchain and AI.

Yet, legal rules are not art for art's sake. It is for any legal rules important to keep in mind what they try to regulate: In order to engage successfully in any Content or Tech industry, the writer has embraced, for analysis purposes, the concept of five inter-connected flows along which legal rules can be defined:

DOI: 10.4018/978-1-7998-5589-7.ch003

1. **Content flow:** Content understood here as the output of Scholarly publishing, including increasingly datasets, databases, metadata and raw data:

Legislative Developments concerning Content include the implementation of the Digital Single Market Copyright Directive (DSM): These rules will be implemented in the EU by 7 June 2021 and include new rules on platform responsibility, affecting article sharing on social scientific networks, as well as rules on text and data mining. EU and national consultations on AI and IP augur legislative reform in 2021: chiefly about the value to be appropriated from owners of databases or the return of a portion of the value created through AI to them; further rules will include the Digital Services Act with rules on harmful and illegal content as well as rules on the responsibility of digital market places, also expected for 2021, and also set rules on due diligence about customer identity online (know your customer rules);

2. **Rights flow**: publishing relies on intellectual property, chiefly copyrights and database rights[1] that subsist in the Content (as defined above): the review of the EU legislation on Collective Management Organisations and crossborder licensing by way of Independent Management Entities will continue into 2021; Standards on safety and reliability of AI devices, eg medical diagnostic devices may stipulate access to training data rules to ensure "explainability" and guard against biased decision making.

3. **Money flow**: to be sustainable, compensation both monetary and non-monetized but otherwise valuable reputation or intangible benefits frequently flow in opposite direction to the flow of Content: Part of legislative developments under this title are rules on the re-use of public sector information to be included in the Data Governance Act of the EU, as well as internationally the UNESCO draft Recommendation on Open Science, the coming into force of Horizon Europe with new Open Access and Open Science rules, as well as the policy agreed by some science funders known as "plan S" and various policies. Money flow elements also concern commitments by owners of technology, trade secrets or patents that negotiate reasonable licensing fees, so called FRAND licensing of Standard Essential Patents.

4. **Data flow**: "Data" for purposes of "Data flow" is to be understood as distinct from "Data" that is part of Content, ie the object of scientific output. Data here denotes "data about data", ie metadata about Content and any stakeholder or event relevant in the flow, as well as data about any of the other four flows, ie money, culture/social, rights. Also as distinct from the other flows, the "Data flow" is at least bi-directional, if not multi-directional (Aschermann, 2018)[2]: GDPR, Privacy Shield, WTO rules on free flow of non-personal data and local data retentions rules chiefly form Russia, China, India, as well as ePrivacy

Directive and Regulations in the EU, as well as expected new rules on In Vitro Diagnostic Devices, and IoT data. ;

5. **Culture/Social flow:** The human-centred element. In Scholarly Publishing this element is addressed through identification of parties, including researchers as well as show-casing author's research in social scientific networks. This development is further complemented by rules on data ownership and control and reward of data altruism fall into this category, as well as information rights under the GDPR where decisions are made by fully automated AI processes, eg in human resources. Other elements include preservation and access to orphan works and out of commerce works, the cultural patrimony of Europe.

Blockchain and AI may however in the longer term even shake our understanding of what constitute "legal" rules. Traditionally these are laws applicable in certain countries or regions, especially but not only, about intellectual property (IP) and laws governing competition (antitrust), personal data, human rights, and contractual rules such as licensing of IP and datasets.

A greater and greater source of rules relevant here are standards developed by so-called SSOs or Standard Setting Organisations. As it may turn out. Blockchain itself can be interpreted as a set of **standards, as a code,** akin to software, or even akin to legal rules, set by virtue of technology, rather than applicable territorially in a jurisdiction (almost like a "planet Blockchain", where different laws apply and may be **self-enforced through code**, without needing to resort to a judicial process).

This Sub-section discusses below in a discursive manner the above five flows as they relate to the topic of Scholarly Publishing, Blockchain and Artificial Intelligence. As these concepts are delineated differently by different commentators, the investigation is prefaced by a brief description of the these three elements for purposes of discussing legal developments.

The legal developments summarized above will then be contextualized with developments of the Scholarly Publishing market:

*   Evolution and transformation of publishing towards Open Access and Open Science
*   Sharing of scholarly communication through social scientific networks
*   Access to research data and finding reward model for making scientific data discoverable, curating data, verifying and assuring provenance, ethical collection of data
*   Rules on text and data mining that will underpin collaboration between publishers and technology companies in areas such as human language processing and machine learning.

- Developments around the GDPR, including SCCs and US-EU Data Shield and Brexit, data ePrivacy, free flow of data.

In keeping with Yogi Berra's adage that predictions are perilous, especially about the future, this sub-section will only sketch out legal rules that either have changed in 2020, or are expected to change in 2021 or shortly beyond that horizon.

Geographically, this sub-section will center mainly around developments in Europe, as the writer has most to say about rules in Europe, not because other developments elsewhere are unimportant or perhaps would need to be considered with even greater curiosity and attention. That said, legal developments taking place in other geographic regions will be touched upon occasionally as well.

What Is Scholarly Publishing and How Is It Concerned With Blockchain or Artificial Intelligence?

Scholarly Publishing: A Broad Concept

Surprisingly, "Scholarly Publishing" is neither only about "Academic" or "STM" (as in Scientific Technical and Medical), nor solely about "Research Publishing" (as in publishing a stand-alone book or journal article that can be placed on a shelf or displayed on a website). Instead, Scholarly Publishing includes any form of academic, scholarly and professional publishing and communication. This is well beyond the publication of individual titles of authors, and comprises a host of services around publications, including, and ever increasingly, the underlying data, abstracts, referencing and cross-referencing with permanent, yet dynamic links, creating effectively a web of interconnected resources. Increasingly Scholarly Publishing also offers decision tools, text and data mining applications, software, discovery and search algorithms and rankings, video tutorials explaining research experiments or outcomes to interested audiences, or workflow tools and applications.

Moreover, "Scholarly" includes the Arts, History and Social Sciences (sometimes referred to as AHSS), a field that with the advent of Industry 4.0 is believed to be of increasing importance to understand the "soft skills" needed for an increasingly fragile planet. Some also start to include law, accounting and tax and indeed any professional publication in the broader concept of "Scholarly Publishing", some draw the line at humanitarian law and transparent and ethical accounting and taxation rules.

Rather than a specific discipline of science, or a method of communication, what sets Scholarly publishing apart from its close cousin, the broader concept of tertiary educational publishing is that Scholarly publishing is concerned, predominantly, with primary publications (and more recently digital product solutions and services) as opposed to secondary publications. Primary publications are those that publish new scientific discoveries, scientific claims or present new evidence corroborating or falsifying state of the art scientific hypotheses and link such claims with the underlying datasets, databases and sometimes all the way down to the raw data. In other words, Scholarly publishing is not so much concerned with synthesizing, summarizing and in some form re-publishing acquired state of the art knowledge about a subject, but is concerned with new findings, never before published.

Blockchain and Artificial Intelligence

Blockchain is a ledger architecture that comes in many different shapes and kinds. At heart, it is a concept for the creation of trust between parties that do not really know each other and that enable the fixation or recording of certain events or terms and conditions with a great degree of confidence. Blockchain allows the association of in a secure way of metadata "about" a product or service with a product or service and is very versatile. As such the concept even though it has a multitude of applications is well understood by now. A Blockchain application may be administered entirely by humans or the application of a service could be run by a set of algorithms described as artificially intelligent as an assisting technology or entirely run by an artificial intelligence entity.

Regulation of Blockchain is foremost discussed in the context of FinTech and Cryptocurrencies. More generally, the area of law that could or should take a closer look at Blockchain is the law of antitrust (in the US) and competition law (in the EU). Blockchain applications to be effective will need to be standardized and this may also be an effective way to address antitrust and competition law concerns within Standard Setting Organisations (SSOs), like ISO or NISO etc. One of the chief aims will be to make Blockchain technology inter-operable more widely and also to develop a good governance of Blockchain inside SSOs. This will often be coupled with IP policies that involve undertakings by patent and other IP holders to license their Standard Essential Patents (SEPs) and other technologies on Fair, Reasonable and Non-Discriminatory, "FRAND", terms and conditions. What constitutes FRAND has so been worked out so far case by case in a number of courts all over the world ranging from Australia to China, to Canada, to France, Germany, UK and US, mainly in the context of mobile smart phones and related applications. In many cases Alternative Dispute Resolution (ADR) may be a promising answer to arrive at multi-jurisdictional understandings rather than to litigate country per country. 2021, it is expected, will see these discussions which have been especially prevalent in the mobile telecoms market around cellular networks, to other connected devices (IoT) and AI entities (eg self-driving vehicles, if not generally already in 2021, then at least in designated spaces such as factories, harbours, mines or in agricultural settings).

Artificial Intelligence (AI), on the other hand is defined in many different ways and for many different purposes. The writer stresses that it comprises a man-made capacity to comprehend information along certain dimensions only and is thus neither "artificial", as it is made by humans, nor "intelligent" understood as comprising a degree of consciousness or imagination rivalling the human (Rebouillat et al, 2020).[3] Consequently, AI is here simply understood as any human-machine co-production in which the machine performs tasks it has learnt through any type of data analysis. Whilst itself a fast evolving subject, all practical AI to date rests on the availability of "clean data" – data that is fit for use in reinforced, supervised or unsupervised machine learning, either immediately or after pre-processing. Some, notably Vas Narasimhan, CEO of Novartis, have for this reason also stated that the success of AI depends foremost on "data first" (Shaywitz, 2019).

To date, AI as a useful combination of "clean data", algorithms and unparalleled computing power utilizing human language processing and machine learning, has seen Scholarly publishers participate as partners contributing to machine learning or language projects, and also as developers and customers of AI technologies to accelerate the use of high-value high-quality publisher-owned Content for the benefit of the wider scientific community. At the Frankfurt STM Conference, Springer Nature presented a book on the subject of a kind of battery that has been entirely written by an AI entity (Vincent, 2019)[4]. The book has no human author as such, but the electrical engineering title has an ISBN and is, as far as the writer knows, for sale as the first fully AI-generated book of the Scholarly Publishing world.

AI emerged in earnest as one of the hot topics in 2019, as also predicted by the Future Lab of STM's STEC back in 2017/2018. "Clean data" comprises both completely unstructured data (like plain text and video) and highly structured data (like metadata, tables and well-formatted records), and any combination thereof or anything between that falls into one of the layers (in reality a continuum) of the "Data Pyramid", a term coined by Eefke Smit, Director, Standards and Technology of the STM Association.

For at least the next three years, it must be anticipated that individual Scholarly publishers will rightly seek to realize the tremendous opportunities in front of them, but also be faced with great risks associated with AI. Publishers' valuable services and skills in generating, curating and validating data need to be seen by all relevant stakeholders for what they are: an indispensable piece of the puzzle to humanize and make AI useful and ethical. Datasets and databases represent commercially value created or used and 2021 especially during the 2nd half will see in Europe and in the UK a policy debate over exceptions or encouragement to licensing data and datasets: how much of the value should be sent back to database owners? This is the question that remains all up for play!

As a sector, Scholarly Publishing, including through a cross-cutting working group within the STM Association, will focus immediately on the creation of an enabling framework for responsible human machine co-production, including establishing standards and regulations as well as processes for testing and validation of data, taking into account:

- The fast evolving nature of AI.
- The need for data markets for training, testing and validation data.
- The risks and efficiencies associated with intensive and wide data usage.
- The need to balance negative incentives for data harvesting, generation and marketing with positive incentives.
- The need to take public security, safety and the legitimate interests of third parties into account.
- The need to enable diverse and parallel usability of data as input, output, by-product and training data.
- The need to take into account network effects and benefits and risks of data pooling.

Traditionally, Scholarly Publishing is Built on Licensing of Copyright: This Remains So Even as the Industry Transitions to Open Access and Open Science Based Business Models

Whilst this chapter discusses legislative developments and illustrates areas in Scholarly Publishing that relate to Blockchain technology and also to AI, the bigger picture must not be let to go amiss: after all, the main thing, is to do the main thing; and in the field of scholarly publishing the main thing is still the hunt for the best manuscript in my view for the publisher, and the hunt for the most prestigious communication channel from the researcher/author's perspective: the medium is the message and the message is also the medium. In spite of the exciting opportunities Blockchain and AI herald to advance science and to accelerate knowledge for the greater public interest, the nuts and bolts of publishing, the life blood of the endeavor is still the vision of publishing, the spine to publish what is worth publishing and to resist publishing what is unsound or unfit to be published, unapologetically. The life blood of this endeavor remains intellectual property, copyright, in particular, and licensing.

Open Access Snapshot and Trend for Books and Journals

Open Access started in earnest as a business model from 2002 (Poynder, 2020). From about 2010, a 2nd phase of OA has started seeing a broader expansion of open access, which has seen most traditional scholarly publishers adopting (to a greater or lesser extent) open access publishing practices, and new open access journals becoming well-established within their disciplines. This expansion is reflected in the growing number of OA journals and articles.

As of end September 2019, the number of open access journals was approximately 13,700 (of which ¾ were published in English) as per DOAJ. 70% of journals in the DOAJ do not charge author-side fees and their sustainability may thus not be assured. Among the accepted Open Access sustainable funding models is Gold Open Access as well as the hybrid model. Both essentially rely on Article Publication Charges (APCs). Whilst Open Access articles as a proportion of all articles (as of 2018) across all disciplines range between 20% and 30% (but when Green OA, which still essentially relies on the subscription model continuing is excluded, falls to about 15-18%). Be that as it may, it is anticipated that journal articles available open access as a proportion will continue to grow as a share of all articles for the foreseeable future (DOAJ, n.d.). In 2019 and 2020 a further effort is under way meant to accelerate the transition to Open Access: plan S with a controversial so-called "Rights Retention Strategy" (which in truth entails a mandatory imposition of CCBY end-user licenses on plan S-funded authors for accepted manuscripts) seeks unilaterally to impose its vision of Open Access. More encouraging, by contrast are additional funding models such as "Diamond" Open Access and crowdfunding efforts that might also be a mechanism to address other areas where the transition to Open Access underserves the market: publishing opportunities for authors of the so-called Global South, ie opening Open Access also to authors from Small and Middle Income Countries.

By contrast, despite strong year-on-year growth, the OA book market is still less than 1% of all scholarly and professional e-book publishing: according to some estimates there were only around 10,000 titles in 2016, with humanities and social sciences (HSS) accounting for almost three quarters of all OA books published. Among the more successful OA book publishers are The University of California Press and the University College London Press (UCL Press). Among commercial publishers, Ubiquity Press has an important role in supporting university and society-based publishing and driving growth in the sector. Ubiquity also works outside English-speaking countries where growth in open access publishing among not-for-profits is slower.

For commercial book publishers the dominant OA business model became charging Book Publishing Charges (BPC). A typical BPC is currently around £10,000. Palgrave, which is the humanities and social sciences imprint of Springer Nature, have a similar arrangement: their BPC ranges from £11,000 to £17,000. Springer, Taylor & Francis/ Routledge also have OA book options. These charges and the current lack of funding at this level for book authors is hampering the spread of open access in the academic book market. An alternative solution, pooling library resources, was by Knowledge Unlatched. French platform OpenEdition operates on a "freemium" model, offering a catalogue of over 6,000 e-books in the humanities and social sciences. Books are made freely available online but libraries can choose to pay for premium services such as downloadable file formats.[5]

Offsetting Deals

While publishers have globally discounted the subscription rates of journals which also benefit from APC revenues for a number of years, uneven take up of hybrid to date has seen some countries and institutions experience increased costs. Meanwhile the corresponding savings on global subscriptions are widely distributed and may be obscured by price changes arising from inflationary pressures, increasing article volumes and a range of other factors. Thus, in response, several publishers have entered into local offset agreements designed to reduce the overall cost faced by research organisations or consortia. Under an offset agreement, open access publication costs are offset by lower subscription costs. There are different approaches to achieving this (OpenAccess, 2019).[6] Some offset agreements reduce the cost of APCs and some reduce the amount an institution pays for a subscription in proportion to the amount it pays for APCs. Some publishers offer credits against future APCs when subscriptions are taken out; others offer credits against future subscription payments when APCs are paid; a third approach bundles subscriptions with future APCs for modest additional payments.

Offsetting deal or transformational agreements and transformative journals, read and publish or publish and read deals, all will have to dove-tail or at least run side by side with the aforementioned "plan S". For now the expectation is that in 2021 this will be worked out, sometimes more smoothly than at other times.

A further development in Open Science will be the emergence of EU and international regulation on Open Science and I list below a few initiatives and programmes that should be considered going forward:

- **UNESCO draft Recommendation on Open Science**: a first draft is available and will be iterated throughout 2021. The recommendation will try to galvanise at time conflicting expectations about the nature of Open Science and Open Access and also its import and effect. Particularly a difference according to trading blocs is noticeable, as well as the division into Global North and South with different path-dependent effects of Gold Open Access and also different expectations about sovereignty over Data. 2021 will make apparent if the divisions can be bridged or at least reconciled to enable a global understanding of the evolution of Open Science.

- **Draft Data Governance Regulation:** In November, the European Commission published a draft <u>Data Governance Regulation</u>. This is intended to facilitate data sharing across the EU and between sectors, and to "offer an alternative model to the data-handling practices of the big tech platforms". The Regulation provides for neutral and transparent data-sharing intermediaries who will not be able to deal with the data on their own account. It includes:
  - ○ measures to increase trust in data sharing
  - ○ EU rules on neutrality to allow data intermediaries to function as trustworthy organisers of data sharing
  - ○ measures to facilitate re-use of public-sector data, for example health data, and re-use of even certain protected data held by public sector bodies. Those are both personal and non-personal data and cover sensitive data that is potentially the subject of third party rights including IPRs and trade secrets.
  - ○ measures to give Europeans more control over the use of their data, in a chapter dubbed "*data altruism*" (other chapters refer to existing safeguards in GDPR and by virtue of fundamental rights).

The Regulation is the first legislative initiative to come out of the European Data Strategy, published in February 2020 (see above). More dedicated proposals on common EU data spaces are expected in 2021, including a much awaited implementing act on so-called "high value datasets" that will give flesh to Article 14 of the Public Sector Information Directive, together with a Data Act to foster data sharing among businesses and between businesses and governments.

Changing Nature of Scholarly Communications – Social Scientific Networks

One of the most significant developments in the STM landscape is the rapid rise of Social Scientific or "Collaborative" Networks ("SCNs") in the academic environment, most notably Mendeley, SSRN, ResearchGate, Scholix, Figshare and Academia.edu, but many more offer their platform services for new forms of science communication, collaboration and for integrating science, data clinical evidence and experiences into an exciting new mix of scientific discourse and engagement.

Typically, SCNs are platforms aimed at connecting researchers with common interests. Users create profiles and are encouraged to list their publications and other scholarly activities, upload copies of manuscripts they have authored, and build connections with scholars they work or co-author with. However, as of the date of writing, much of this content is posted without permission and contrary to the STM Principles (STM 2016). Academia is probably still used more by social sciences and researchers in the humanities but there is pressure to pay for a premium service that is off-putting to many researchers. Some academics have thus created ScholarlyHub, a non-profit open access repository that gives access to academic papers, research projects and researchers. The platform aims to become a member-run and owned SCN that aggregates research, teaching and other professional resources. Another network, Colwiz (collective wizdom), launched in 2011 and provided interactive digital collaboration and free reference management services for researchers in academia, industry and government globally. Colwiz also developed the ACS Chemwork platform for the American Chemical Society. In 2013, Taylor & Francis incorporated Colwiz's interactive PDF reader into their journals platform and in 2017 its parent, Informa, acquired the whole company. In 2016, the company also developed the wizdom.ai research intelligence product (see section 4.7 Tools, apps and new services for funders and institutions). At the time of writing, Colwiz functionality was being merged into wizdom.ai to develop an intelligent research assistant under the wizdom.ai brand.

Bibliography management software (such as Endnote (Thomson Reuters), Flow (Proquest), Pages (Springer), Zotero, etc.) also allows users to share their research libraries with other users but typically the sharing is inherently one-to-one or one-to-few, or restrictions on the numbers of users with whom content may be shared are explicitly enforced

The popularity of SCNs is perhaps an indication of the way in which authors prefer to share their articles. However, uncertainty over the copyright status of academic papers hosted on social networking sites raises concerns over the persistence of such content. To counter this, STM has developed the <u>STM Voluntary Principles for Article Sharing</u> – the Principles have been developed between 2014 and 2015, widely consulted and provide a very useful base-line for any SCN or platform offering SCN services. The website https://www.howcanishareit.com/ provides more information and also a tool to check the status of published works and links to the sharing policies of individual publishers.

The Main legislative impact on SCNs and publishers supporting the sharing of scholarly articles on SCNs, is the Digital Single Market Copyright Directive, the DSM, and more particularly Article 17 DSM which transforms the concept of ISP liability limitation ("safe harbor") to a new concept of Platform responsibility (closing the "Value Gap"): Online Content Sharing Service Providers ("Platforms") are responsible for pre-identifying works and or expeditiously removing non-compliant content with a system of "notice and stay-down". The details of the mechanisms are currently implemented into national law and implementation is expected to be in place mostly by mid-2021 for EU member countries. The UK, with Brexit, will not implement the DSM and domestic UK law will have to be used to hold Platforms accountable there, although UK platforms doing business in the EU will remain subject to EU law in any case.

Access to Research Data and Finding Reward Model for Making Scientific Data Discoverable, Curating Data, Verifying and Assuring Provenance, Ethical Collection of Data

One of the over-arching trends in research publishing is linked to the global trends of big data and increased computing power, which also underlies the developments in text and data mining and artificial intelligence discussed below.

In order to understand the role of data, STM's Eefke Smit, Director for Innovations and Standards has coined the "Data Pyramid" as a way to structure the discussion: at the top of the pyramid sits "data" that forms part of research publications, the layer below includes processed data and data representations (which form the basis for data in publications); that pyramid layer is in turn supported by data collections and structured data, which in turn relies and is sources from both "raw data" and data sets.

One of the key elements that STM collaborated on is to make the different layers of the pyramid more interconnected. STM worked on this with DataCite, the main organization driving the discoverability and citability of data. DataCite in turn is working with Crossref, the industry body that applies Digital Object Identifiers (DOI) to publications and now also data.

There are various competing initiatives that try to define, or imagine, the "article of the future", a collection or node rather than a fixed document. In this way, it is possible to envisage the future "article" really to be a "knowledge stack".

For the Scholarly Publishing sector, a key initiative is the Research Data year of 2020 declared by STM as well as the collaboration of publishers in setting useful standards that maintain inter-operability. This will be key for the wider use and penetration of Blockchain technology, that may be a useful component of ensuring association of Content and data with provenance assured metadata.

Standardisation and codes of ethic on data disclosure and availability statements, standards on reproduceability and explainability of AI to the standardization of test to detect or guard against image manipulation will be important components. This latter element is key as frequently data needs to be visualized to be interpreted. What is needed is the definition of standards, guidelines or best practices on issues like a) permissible "manipulation", b) range of reactions to impermissible manipulation during peer review, c) determine how to posture post-publication. As technology evolves very fast in this area and as conclusions and interpretations of what and how machines learn will keep changing, standards and technology will play an even greater role than the adoption of hard to change, difficult to adapt legal rules.

From a policy and legal development perspective the above industry-internal work will be complemented by initiatives such as the European Open Science Cloud.

The European Open Science Cloud (EOSC) is an environment for hosting and processing research data to support EU science.

The process to create the EOSC was initiated by the Commission in 2015. It aimed to develop a trusted, virtual, federated environment that cuts across borders and scientific disciplines to store, share, process and re-use research digital objects (like publications, data, and software) following FAIR principles.

The EOSC brings together institutional, national and European stakeholders, initiatives and data infrastructures to develop an inclusive open science ecosystem in Europe.

This can lead new insights and innovations, higher research productivity and improved reproducibility in science.

The European Data Strategy recognises the EOSC as the nucleus for a science, research and innovation data space which will become articulated with the 9 sectoral data spaces foreseen by the strategy.

The EOSC timeline indicated in the European Data Strategy foresees the following stages

- by 2025: deploy EOSC operations to serve EU researchers
- from 2024: open up, connect and articulate EOSC beyond the research communities, with the wider public sector and the private sector
- post-2020: establish a renewed, stakeholder-driven EOSC governance structure possibly in connection with the launch of a corresponding EOSC European Partnership in the first quarter of 2020

Text and Data Mining

Text and data mining Text and data mining (TDM) has the potential to transform the way scientists use. The Publishing Research Consortium report Text Mining and Scholarly Publishing (Clark 2013) gives a good introduction to TDM.

TDM draws on natural language processing and information extraction to identify patterns and find new knowledge from collections of textual content. Semantic enrichment and tagging of content are likely to enhance TDM capabilities. At present TDM is most common in life sciences research, in particular within pharmaceutical companies, but relatively little used elsewhere.

The main challenges for more widespread adoption were for a while legal uncertainties as to what is permitted, and the lack of an efficient licensing regime; technical issues such as standard content formats including basic common ontologies; the need for content aggregation to permit mining cross-publisher corpuses; the costs and technical skills requirements for mining; limited incentives for researchers to use the technique and a lack of understanding on the part of publishers.

These challenges associated with TDM have been addressed via a number of initiatives:

- STM and PDR, the leading pharmaceutical sector research infrastructure group, issued an updated joint sample licence in 2012 that includes a TDM clause. TDM is one of the developments that has been prevalent in the corporate R&D world for some time and only later did the academic sector also approach STM and look to governments to address licensing issues.
- STM publishers issued a statement in November 2013 committing its signatories to implementing the STM sample licence clause, or otherwise to permit noncommercial TDM of subscribed-to content at no additional cost; to develop the mineability of content; and to develop platforms to allow integration of holdings across institutions for TDM purposes. The statement has been subsequently updated, with most recent version dating from 2017.
- CrossRef's text and data mining tools (originally Prospect): this offers a metadata API and services that can provide automated linking for TDM tools to the publisher full text, plus a mechanism for storing licence information in the metadata, and optionally, a rate-limiting mechanism to prevent TDM tools overwhelming publisher websites.
- Copyright Clearance Center (CCC) offers a service targeted at life science companies. RightFind XML for Mining provides access to approximately 10 million articles in XML content from more than 60 STM publishers with normalised metadata, and consistent licensing terms for mining the content for internal research. The system reduces the necessity for one-off licensing negotiations, along with the associated administration costs, while providing additional royalties to rightsholders when their content is used for textmining.

The last legislative element in the development is Art. 3 and 4 of the Digital Single Market Copyright Directive (DSM). Art. 4 is the over-arching clause which permits TDM for Content or data openly and legitimately available online freely, while Art. 3 is a *lex specialis* for Content and Data lawfully accessible to research institutions and universities. These latter entities benefit from a non-commercial use research exception, while the more general open internet TDM exception is always subject to publishers not reserving their TDM rights with machine-readable disclaimers.

Scholarly publishers continue to develop the field and also to accompany the implementation of the EU's Digital Single Market (DSM) Directive that provides an exception for reproductions necessary as part of TDM with certain safeguards and for "Research Organisations" as defined, if they have lawful access to the content in question (eg a subscription). The DSM Directive also makes it clear that commercial uses generally and non-commercial uses falling outside scientific research or of non-subscribed content remains subject to licensing.

For a US perspective of TDM and its clear connection to AI, see the US PTO report on AI and IP, especially also page 23 et seq. and footnote 121: *"STM further explained that the deployment of AI tools and mining tools is becoming more commonplace and that STM publishers "increasingly publish copyright works and associated datasets with AI ingestion technologies in mind. In other words, copyright content of 'look-up' type information will increasingly be published in ways that facilitate machine reading, learning, etc. It follows that licensing...should in most instances be the method of choice for enabling access to copyright works."*

GDPR: Data Privacy, Free Flow of Data, Data Shield

CJEU decision in Schrems II: the CJEU ruled in July that the EU-US Privacy Shield adequacy decision was invalid because it failed to protect EU personal data from unnecessary and disproportionate access by US intelligence agencies. While it upheld the adequacy decision on Standard Contractual Clauses (SCCs, *see further below heading also on the new draft SCCs out now*) as a data export mechanism, the same issues regarding access by intelligence authorities in the US apply to transfers made from the EEA to the US under them.

Going forward, the CJEU placed the onus on data exporters and importers to decide whether the data transferred to third countries under SCCs is adequately protected and to use enhanced protections if needed. If they do not, transfers may be open to challenge and to action by supervisory authorities (SAs) which can prohibit the transfers on a case by case basis. This may potentially impact data transfers from the EEA to the UK after Brexit if the UK does not get adequacy, which at the time of writing is very much in doubt. While SCCs can be used in theory, exporters will need to assess whether data transferred to the UK will be adequately protected, introduce supplementary measures if not, and cease transfers if they deem those measures to be insufficient.

The US Department of Commerce issued updated FAQs on the continuing use of the Privacy Shield following its invalidation by the CJEU. While acknowledging that reliance on the Privacy Shield will no longer legitimise data transfers from the EEA, the FAQs suggest that signing up to the Privacy Shield remains a good way to demonstrate a high standard of data protection and security. The US then issued a White Paper, arguing that the CJEU had failed to take account of the full range of US protections available to EU data. The European Data Protection Board (EDPB) adopted recommendations on measures to supplement transfer tools to ensure personal data transferred to third countries is adequately protected. It also adopted recommendations on the European Essential Guarantees for surveillance measures. Discussions have begun between the US and the EU, yet the effect of the CJEU's Schrems II decision goes far beyond the issue of EEA to US data transfers. Consequently, this will remain an issue to watch throughout 2021.

New Draft Standard Contractual Clauses

The European Commission published the long-awaited draft implementing decision on Standard Contractual Clauses (SCCs) for the transfer of personal data to third countries together with draft new SCCs covering four different categories of transfer. The Commission says the new SCCs are intended to be modular so different processing scenarios can be woven into a single document tailored to the individual situation. As a result, more than two parties will be able to sign up to a single set of SCCs. The SCCs are expected to be adopted in 2021. Organisations will then have a year in which to replace their existing SCCs with the new versions.

ePrivacy Regulation

The year 2020 has come and gone without a draft ePrivacy Regulation, a fate it shares with previous years as various EU Council Presidencies have failed to progress this work. In March 2020 the Croatian Presidency published a revised text of the Regulation. It introduced changes to Article 6 (permitted processing of communications metadata) and Article 8 (protection of end-users' terminal equipment information including cookies rules) and related recitals. It aimed to simplify the text and further align with the GDPR, principally by introducing the possibility of processing based on legitimate interest in both cases, subject to conditions and safeguards. This would have represented a major change, and meant that cookies would not necessarily require user consent. However, the German Presidency is believed to have removed this element, instead permitting general processing of metadata on the basis of legitimate interests. The latest draft also suggests processing of metadata in online communications to monitor epidemics and help in natural or manmade disasters will be allowed and clarifies that nothing in the Regulation will prevent Member States carrying out lawful interception of electronic communications and requiring providers to help them.

Proposals to Amend the ePrivacy Directive

Absent an ePrivacy Regulation, the European Commission has proposed a new Regulation which would introduce a limited exemption to the obligations in Articles 5(1) and (6) of the ePrivacy Directive. The intention is to exempt providers of number-independent interpersonal communications services (eg VoIP, IM) from obligations to respect the confidentiality of communications and traffic data where those conflict with their voluntary activities to detect child sexual abuse online. These types of providers will come within the scope of the ePrivacy Directive once the European Electronic communications Code is implemented which must be by 21 December 2020. The proposed Regulation would apply until December 2025, or until relevant longer-term legislation is adopted if earlier.

EC 2021 Work Programme and Data

The European Commission has published its 2021 work programme. Initiatives of interest in the context of rules on data include:

- following the principles of right to privacy and connectivity, freedom of speech, free flow of data and cybersecurity
- legislation covering safety, liability, fundamental rights and data aspects of AI
- a Data Act to set conditions for better control of data and data sharing for citizens and businesses
- a new EU digital identity to make it easier to do tasks and access online services across Europe

SUMMARY AND CONCLUSION

Licensing of electronic content is the life blood of Scholarly Publishing. At this juncture of Open Access and Open Science, and an impeding Big Data Tsunami, the role of the publisher as organizer and curator of data will be even more crucial. To fulfill this role, publishers have to continue doing what they are doing and seek high-value content and help authors to present their findings. At the same time, publishers have to collaborate and adapt to harness new technologies such as Blockchain and ready themselves to stay relevant in a world of Artificial Intelligence. The year 2021 will see many new rules that will clarify the extent to which publishers can take part and claim a return on investment for providing and curating high-value Content of assured provenance and that is trustworthy and guards against manipulation and bias.

NOTE

https://resource-cms.springernature.com/springer-cms/rest/v1/content/16216770/data/v1

ACKNOWLEGMENT

Carlo Scollo Lavizzari would like to thank Mathilde Renou, Founder, Legal Consultant, RC Rendel Consulting, Brussels, Belgium for assisting with the sourcing of some of the legislative developments referred to in this chapter, that remain in progress.

REFERENCES

Aschermann, T. (2018, August 30). *Was weiss das Auto über mich?* [What does my car have on me/know about me?"]. CHIP. Retrieved from https://praxistipps.chip.de/was-weiss-mein-auto-ueber-mich-diese-daten-speichert-ihr-kfz-ueber-sie_100613

DOAJ. (n.d.). *Transparency & best practice*. Retrieved from https://doaj.org/apply/transparency/

Marques, M. (2016, October 24). *Offsetting models: Update on the Springer Compact deal*. JISC. Retrieved from https://scholarlycommunications.jiscinvolve.org/wp/2016/10/24/offsetting-models-update-on-the-springer-compact-deal/

OpenAccess. (2019, January 15). *"Publish and Read" contract with Wiley concluded* [Notes]. Retrieved from https://openaccess.mpg.de/2336450/deal-contract-with-wiley-signed

Poynder, R. (2020, December 2). *Open access: Information wants to be free*. Retrieved from https://richardpoynder.co.uk/Information_Wants_to_be_Free.pdf

Rebouillat, S., Steffenino, B., Lapray, M., & Rebouillat, A. (2020). New AI-IP-EI trilogy opens innovation to new dimensions: Another chip in the innovation wall, what about emotional intelligence (EI)? *Intelligent Information Management, 12*(04), 131–182. doi:10.4236/iim.2020.124010

Shaywitz, D. (2019, January 16). Novartis CEO who wanted to bring tech into pharma now explains why it's so hard. *Forbes*. Retrieved from https://www.forbes.com/sites/davidshaywitz/2019/01/16/novartis-ceo-who-wanted-to-bring-tech-into-pharma-now-explains-why-its-so-hard/?sh=370f17cd7fc4

Vincent, J. (2019, April 10). *The first AI-generated textbook shows what robot writers are actually good at*. The Verge. Retrieved from https://www.theverge.com/2019/4/10/18304558/ai-writing-academic-research-book-springer-nature-artificial-intelligence

ENDNOTES

[1] And it will be the database directive that will undergo a review in the 2nd half of 2021 as part of the EU's copyright infrastructure initiative and the IP action plan. One of the reasons will be to guard against AI entities themselves becoming owners of automatically generated datasets/databases, which a German judgment (German Federal Supreme Court - ZR47/08, judgment of 25 March 2010) relating to data collected on the German *Autobahn* for purposes of identifying payees of a highway levy (*"Autobahnmaut"*) might suggest.

[2] Some articles about data collection "about" German car drivers, suggests the car knows them better than the drivers know themselves! Der Spiegel, titled already on 5 August 2016, an article *"Was weiss das Auto über mich?"*- Figuratively: "What does my car have on me/know about me?"

[3] For a discussion of Ai-IP and the element of Emotional Intelligence: Serge Rebouillat, Benoit Steffenino, Miroslawa Lapray, Antoine Rebouillat: New AI-IP-EI Trilogy Opens Innovation to new Dimensions; Another Chip in the Innovation Wall, What about Emotional Intelligence (EI)?, Intelligent Information Managemetn,2020, 12, 131-182, published by Scientific Research Publishing, DOI:10.4236/iim.2020.124010, July 30, 2020.

[4] The book, titled Lithium-Ion Batteries: A Machine-Generated Summary of Current Research, https://www.theverge.com/2019/4/10/18304558/ai-writing-academic-research-book-springer-nature-artificial-intelligence; *"Writing in the introduction, Springer Nature's Henning Schoenenberger (a human) says books like this have the potential to start "a new era in scientific publishing" by automating drudgery. Schoenenberger points out that, in the last three years alone, more than 53,000 research papers on lithium-ion batteries have been published. This represents a huge challenge for scientists who are trying to keep abreast of the field. But by using AI to automatically scan and summarize this output, scientists could save time and get on with important research."* https://futurism.com/the-byte/springer-machine-learning-textbook.

[5] https://resource-cms.springernature.com/springer-cms/rest/v1/content/16216770/data/v1, page10.

[6] See for instance SpringerNature: https://scholarlycommunications.jiscinvolve.org/wp/2016/10/24/offsetting-models-update-on-the-springer-compact-deal/; or Wiley: https://openaccess.mpg.de/2336450/deal-contract-with-wiley-signed.

Chapter 4
Standards Developments in Scholarly Publishing

Virginie Simon
MyScienceWork, France

ABSTRACT

Publication is an essential step in research and is the responsibility of all scientists. Scholarly publications should provide a comprehensive and detailed record of scientific discoveries. They affect not only the research community, but society at large. Scientists have a responsibility to ensure that their publications are complete, detailed, clear, honest, balanced, and avoid misleading, selective, or ambiguous statements. Journal editors are also responsible for ensuring the integrity of the research literature. Publishers are adapting their roles in response both to changing needs and to these new competing services that can include researchers, research institutes, universities. Aside from their traditional roles in supporting quality assurance and peer review, publishers participate in many initiatives and develop services, often in partnership with universities and other organisations, to support communication and develops standards. This chapter shows the importance of standards and presents some concrete examples of standards organizations and perpetual evolution.

1. HISTORY, KEY NUMBERS AND DEFINITION OF STANDARDS

1.1 History

Eugene Garfield originally designed the Journal Impact Factor (JIF) to help librarians choose journals that deserved a subscription. The JIF aggregates number of citations

DOI: 10.4018/978-1-7998-5589-7.ch004

to articles published in each journal, and then divides that sum by the number of published and citable articles. Since that time, the JIF has become the hallmark of the quality of the journal and has been widely used for the evaluation of research and researchers, even at the institutional level. It therefore has a major role in the field of research (Quader, 2021).

Deep changes have affected scholarly publishing, but the process itself has remained remarkably stable during centuries. It includes four key functions that have accompanied scientific publishing since the 17th century:

1. Registration with attribution system
2. Certification with peer review system
3. Dissemination with distribution and access system
4. Preservation with permanent archiving system

The main objective of this practice is therefore to improve the relevance and accuracy of scientific discussions by bringing knowledge, perspective and experience. Although experts often criticize peer review for a number of reasons, the process is still often considered the "gold standard" of science.

Academic publications have been used for years to disseminate academic research and scholarships. Articles from academic journals, books, thesis etc. are published and the quality of these results are guaranteed by the peer review quality system. Peer review quality and selectivity standards vary greatly from journal to journal, publisher to publisher, and field to field.

To publish a research article in the United States, the time between submission and publication of an academic article can vary a lot. In average, it takes about 4 to 8 months for publishers and reviewers to get a return after submitting the article.

Most researchers are still evaluated to date by their number of scientific publications and by their number of citations. The part of academic written output that is not formally published but merely printed up or posted on the web is called *grey* literature (Systematic review, n.d.). Most scientific and scholarly journals, and many academic and scholarly books, though not all, are based on some form of peer review or editorial refereeing to qualify texts for publication. In this context standards are essential to guarantee the quality of the productions of the research results.

1.2 Some Key Numbers

- 1945: Scientific scholarly publishing has deeply changed since the second world war. With few exceptions, organizations and association-based publishing have declined in importance, while commercial publishing has become dominant. Then, in the 1970s, the JIF is become the standard of blibliographic tool based on citations. This metric has contributed to re-organizing the competition among scholarly journals, and has led to a mode of research evaluation based on which journal researchers manage to publish. Standards have become increasingly important.

- 50 million: 50 million scientific articles published since 1665 were reached in 2009 according to a study from the University of Ottawa (Jinha, 2010).
- 2.6 million: New scientific papers published each year(White, n.d)
- 2.55 million: Total number of journal articles in 2018
- 23,764: ISO has developed over 23,764 International Standards(ICS, n.d.).

1.3 Definition of Standard

A standard is something established by authority, custom, or general consent as a model or example. A standard is something considered by an authority as a basis of comparison; an approved model. The ISO organization is comprised of 161 standards bodies globally with 776 technical committees and subcommittees (What is iso 9001, n.d.).

In scholarly publishing industry, publishers adapted their roles in response to changing needs and to these new competing services which may involve researchers, universities and research institutions, as well as funders. Aside from their traditional roles in supporting quality assurance and peer review, publishers participate in numerous initiatives and develop services, often in partnership with universities and other organisations in support of scholarly communication, such as:

- Open standards or metadata standards such as Crossref and ORCID
- Indicators or services that seek to evaluate research such as ImpactStory, Plum Analytics, Altmetric or Scimago

The standards in the scholarly publishing industry concern virtually all levels of scientific writing. Far from being exhaustive, standards could also concern tag, abstract, scientific and technical reports, number format and creation, bibliographic references, standard address number (SAN) (ANSI/NISO Z39.43-1993, n.d.), bibliographic items, metadata element set etc.

2. BENEFITS AND PROCESS OF STANDARDS IN THE SCHOLARLY PUBLISHING INDUSTRY

2.1 What Are the Standards Key Benefits?

Standards are used by all research organizations such as universities, funders and professional societies. Standards are promoted by editors and publishers. Their goal are to aid in research integrity training.

The global mission of scholarly publishing industry is to help to:

- Curate, maintain and develop a source of reliable information
- Verify that entries on the list comply with reasonable standards
- Increase the visibility, dissemination, discoverability and attraction of scientific journals

Enable scholars, libraries, universities, research funders and other stakeholders to benefit from the information and services provided

- Facilitate the integration of scientific journals into library and aggregator services
- Assist publishers and their journals to meet reasonable digital publishing standards

Support the transition of the system of scholarly communication and publishing into a model that serves science, higher education, industry, innovation, societies and the people.

To summarize standards has been developed in order to bring scientific those key benefits:

1. Soundness and reliability
2. Honesty
3. Balance
4. Originality
5. Transparency
6. Appropriate authorship and acknowledgement
7. Accountability and responsibility
8. Adherence to peer review and publication conventions
9. Responsible reporting of research involving humans or animals

2.2 When and How Could a Scientist Suggest a New Standard?

Any scientists and anytime people can suggest a new standard. Scientists can suggest a new standard directly online in the website of editors and publishers. Then active committees with specific working group will work on this new suggestion and act or not on the creation of a new standard. Standards may be revised or withdrawn at any time.

For example, new standards submitted to the National Information Standards Organization (NISO) are developed by working groups within the NISO organization under the supervision of a topic committee. The development process is a strenuous one that includes a rigorous peer review of proposed standards open to each NISO voting member and any other interested party. Final approval of the standard involves verification by the American National Standards Institute (ANSI) that its requirements for due process, consensus, and other approval criteria have been met by NISO. Once verified and approved, NISO Standards also become American National Standards (ANS).

3. CONCRETE EXAMPLES OF STANDARDS ORGANIZATIONS AND STANDARDS IN SCHOLARLY PUBLISHING INDUSTRY

3.1 Crossref

Crossref makes research outputs easy to find, cite, link, assess, and reuse. Crossref is a not-for-profit membership organization that exists to make scholarly communications better.

Crossref is one of the most successful examples of co-operation across the publishing community. It is run by the Publishers International Linking Association Inc. (PILA) and was launched in early 2000 as a cooperative effort among publishers to enable persistent cross-publisher citation linking in online academic journals.

Crossref interlinks millions of content such as journals, books, conference proceedings, technical reports, data sets and working papers. Linked content includes materials from Social Sciences and Humanities (SSH) and Scientific, Technical and Medical (STM) disciplines. When members register their content with Crossref it collects both bibliographic and non-bibliographic metadata, which is processed so that connections can be made between publications, people, organizations, and other associated outputs. The metadata is preserved for the scholarly record. It is also made available across a range of interfaces and formats so that the community can use it and build tools with it, with the expense paid for by Crossref member publishers.

Most services provided by Crossref, or into which Crossref has a major input, are based on Digital Object Identifiers (DOIs). The DOI is not managed by Crossref but by a separate body, the International DOI Foundation (IDF).

3.2 DOI

DOI is the web site of the International DOI Foundation (IDF), a not-for-profit membership organization that is the governance and management body for the federation of Registration Agencies providing Digital Object Identifier (DOI) services and registration, and is the registration authority for the ISO standard (ISO 26324) for the DOI system. The DOI system provides a technical and social infrastructure for the registration and use of persistent interoperable identifiers, called DOIs, for use on digital networks.

Status: Operational System

- Foundation launched to develop system in 1998. First applications launched 2000
- Currently used by well over 5,000 assigners, e.g., publishers, science data centres, movie studios, etc.
- Approximately 190 million DOI names assigned to date
- Over 260,000 DOI name prefixes within the DOI System
- Over 5 billion DOI resolutions per year
- DOI names are assigned by multiple RAs worldwide (DOI Registration Agencies, n.d.).
- Over 28 million shortDOI (Shortdoi Service, n.d.) links to DOI names are in use
- Initial applications are simple redirection — a persistent identifier
- More sophisticated functionality available, e.g., multiple resolution, data typing
- International Standard: ISO 26324, Digital Object Identifier System, 1 May 2012 (available from the ISO Store (ISO Store, 2020).

Scope

- *Digital Identifier* of an *Object* (not "Identifier of a Digital Object")
- Object = any entity (thing: physical, digital, or abstract)
  - Resources, parties, licenses, etc.
- Digital Identifier = network actionable identifier ("click on it and do something")

- Generic framework
- Initial focus on entities was documents/media e.g., articles, data sets
  - Now also moving into parties and licenses
  - Extending to other sectors
- Extensible by design to any sector: not intended as a publishing-only solution (digital convergence)
- International coverage

The DOI achieves the following:

- Provides an *actionable, interoperable, persistent* link
- *Actionable* – through use of identifier syntax and network resolution mechanism (Handle System®)
- *Persistent* – through combination of supporting improved handle infrastructure (registry database, proxy support, etc) and social infrastructure (obligations by Registration Agencies)
- *Interoperable* – through use of a data model providing semantic interoperability and grouping mechanisms

3.3 ResearcherID (Researcher ID, n.d.)

The ResearcherID system has been developed by Thomson Reuters and is connected to the Web of Science database. ResearcherIDs can be obtained by registering online and provide citation statistics including the h-index.

After Thomson Reuters was sold to Onex Corp OCX.TO and Baring Private Equity Asia for $3.55 billion, the new owners named the new company Clarivate Analytics. The newly minted CEO of Web of Science, Annette Thomas acquired Publons and integrated ResearcheID into Publons.

Web of Science ResearcherID is a unique identifier for researchers on Publons. Register on Publons and import your publications from the *Web of Science* to become eligible for a Web of Science ResearcherID.

Each night, Publons assigns a Web of Science ResearcherID to any profiles with one or more *Web of Science*-indexed publications that do not yet have a ResearcherID.

Any publications you add to your Publons profile will then be linked to your Web of Science ResearcherID when anyone searches for you on *Web of Science*. Please allow up to two weeks for changes you make on Publons to be reflected on Web of Science.

If you do not have any *Web of Science* indexed publications but require a *Web of Science* ResearcherID please follow this link (Pub Ions, n.d.)t o generate one for your account.

Note that during 12th - 14th of April, all public ResearcherIDs will be moved to Publons. From 15 April 2019, Publons will be the new environment where researchers can benefit from an improved Web of Science ResearcherID.

ResearcherID identifiers, claimed publication history and other ResearcherID account information will be moved to Publons. All existing links to ResearcherIDs will redirect to the new Web of Science ResearcherID, hosted on Publons, including from any ResearcherID badges created.

3.4 Scopus Author ID

Scopus Author ID: unlike DOI and ResearchID, the Scopus author ID does not need to be created manually. Every author with articles indexed in the Scopus database will be automatically assigned a Scopus Author ID, which includes citation information and the h-index similarly to ResearcherIDs.

3.5 National Information Standards Organization (NISO)

NISO is a US standards organisation with an international role which extends well beyond standards as usually defined. Its Recommended Practices play a major role in journal publishing. It is recognized as a secure place to hold and develop codes of practice which have been initiated elsewhere.

The concrete example of NISO's latest NISO standard with his Standards Tag Suite (STS): The Standards Tag Suite (STS) provides a common XML format that developers, publishers, and distributors of standards, including national standards bodies, regional and international standards bodies, and standards development organizations, can use to publish and exchange full-text content and metadata of standards. Structures are provided to encode both the normative and non-normative content of: standards, adoptions of standards, and standards-like documents that are produced by standards organizations

3.6 International Standard Serial Number (ISSN)

The International Standard Serial Number (ISSN) is an 8 digit serial number used to uniquely identify a serial publication. The ISSN is especially helpful in distinguishing between serials with the same title. ISSN are used in ordering, cataloguing, interlibrary loans, and other practices in connection with serial literature. Other systems are based on ISSNs and it is crucial for publishers to obtain one. The ISSN identifies the publication as such, in reference to its title and its medium.

4. ONIX FOR BOOKS

ONIX for Books is the international standard for representing and communicating book industry product information in electronic form. ONIX for Books was developed and is maintained by EDItEUR, jointly with Book Industry Communication (UK) and the Book Industry Study Group (U.S.), and has user groups in Australia, Belgium, Canada, Finland, France, Germany, Italy, the Netherlands, Norway, Russia, Spain, Sweden and the Republic of Korea.

In April 2009, EDItEUR announced the release of a major new version of the ONIX for Books standard: ONIX 3.0. This release of ONIX is the first since 2001 that is not backwards-compatible with its predecessors and, more importantly, provides a means for improved handling of digital products. A revised version (3.0.1) was subsequently released in January 2012.

5. ISO STANDARD FOR BLOCKCHAIN

Currently there are 15 ISO standards for Blockchain (Standards by ISO/TC 307, n.d.). They are as follows:

- ISO/DTR 3242 - Blockchain and distributed ledger technologies
- ISO/WD TR 6039 - Blockchain and distributed ledger technologies - Identifiers of subjects and objects for the design of blockchain systems
- ISO/WD TR 6277 - Blockchain and distributed ledger technologies – Data flow model for blockchain and DLT use cases
- ISO 22739:2020 - Blockchain and distributed ledger technologies
- ISO/WD 22739 - Blockchain and distributed ledger technologies
- ISO/TR 23244:2020 - Blockchain and distributed ledger technologies — Privacy and personally identifiable information protection considerations
  - 35.030
  - 35.240.40
  - 35.240.99
- ISO/DTR 23249 - Blockchain and distributed ledger technologies – Overview of existing DLT systems for identity management
- ISO/DIS 23257 - Blockchain and distributed ledger technologies — Reference architecture
- ISO/DTS 23258 - Blockchain and distributed ledger technologies — Taxonomy and Ontology
- ISO/WD TS 23259 - Blockchain and distributed ledger technologies — Legally binding smart contracts

- ISO/TR 23455:2019 - Blockchain and distributed ledger technologies — Overview of and interactions between smart contracts in blockchain and distributed ledger technology systems
- ISO/TR 23576:2020 - Blockchain and distributed ledger technologies — Security management of digital asset custodians
- ISO/DTS 23635.2 - Blockchain and distributed ledger technologies — Guidelines for governance
- ISO/AWI TR 23642 - Blockchain and distributed ledger technologies - Overview of smart contract security good practice and issues
- ISO/WD TR 23644 - Blockchain and distributed ledger technologies - Overview of trust anchors for DLT-based identity management (TADIM)

6. ISO STANDARDS FOR AI

Standards for artificial intelligence are essential as artificial intelligence has become very prevalent in our past, current and future environments. We cannot escape artificial intelligence as it helps us to check the weather, play music, conduct searches for information, provide discoveries for new drugs, etc. In a July 2020 article by Ms. Elizabeth Gasiorowski-Denis, she discusses the necessity of trust of artificial intelligence and the algorithms that support it. The question of trustworthiness is key, explains Wael William Diab, Chair of SC 42, *Artificial intelligence*, a subcommittee operating under joint technical committee ISO/IEC JTC 1, *Information technology*: "Every customer – whether it's a financial services company, whether it's a retailer, whether it's a manufacturer – is going to ask: 'Who do I trust?' Many aspects including societal concerns, such as data quality, privacy, potentially unfair bias and safety must be addressed. This recently published technical report is the first of many works that will help achieve this." (Gasiorowski-Denis, 2020).

7. EVOLUTION AND DEVELOPMENTS OF STANDARDS

Today, the scientific communication system has a number of weak points that publishers and publishers must work on. Open Access knows so great success but will not reach the 100% of the publications and even when it is open, it is generally limited because of its access to the content which is not clear or which is lacking. On the technical side, the traditional article, often in PDF format, still predominates and the interoperability of platforms remains limited by the constraints of commercial publishing. Researchers are still prisoners of prestige because the evaluation systems of research have remained the same to judge their work based on the number of citations and the impact factor. The process of submitting scientific articles is always too long and sometimes opaque. The peer review, although essential to scientific communication, is criticized for its parties and remains a journal frozen in time, non-dynamic and at times unfair. Commercial enterprises also tend to treat new technologies as competitive elements, favoring fragmentation and tactics such as foreclosure. Finally, the journal market, which in itself is not fully aligned with the forum for searching theories, concepts and facts, also lacks transparency when considering the perspectives of production costs.

A concrete example where publishers have had to evolve and set new standards is the practice of publishing in pre-print. A pre-print is usually a version of a research paper that is shared on an online platform before or during a formal peer review process. Preprint platforms have become popular in many disciplines due to the growing trend towards open access publishing and can be led by publishers or communities. A range of discipline-specific or interdomain platforms now exist. Standards have helped to ensure the quality of this new type of scientific material and must continue to do so.

It is why, participating in industry initiatives such as developing standards and protocols, linking repositories, publications, and best practices can help ensure more consistent and reliable access. It is therefore essential to encourage and support the development of standard interoperability tools for citation and other purposes, such as "persistent identifiers".

The specific values of scholarly communication draw much attention to the issues of equity, diversity and inclusion, as well as the need to strengthen the community. They also raise a deep concern for the quality and integrity of scholarly contributions. Finally, science communication should be designed to promote flexibility and innovation while remaining focused on profitability. The economic model of publishers and publishers is also changing and turning to new technologies such as artificial intelligence, machine learning etc.

The next challenge of publishing industry will be to put in place the new standards of blockchain and AI.

8. CONCLUSION

The standards on which the publication process is based, from creation to preservation through distribution, are an indispensable part of the scientific publishing industry system. The network of organizations developing standards in our community as well as standards is broad, flexible and responsive to new technologies. The challenge for the coming years will be to define new standards to adapt scientific publishing to new technologies such as Blockchain and AI.

REFERENCES

ANSI/NISO Z39. 43-1993 (R2017) standard address Number (SAN) for the publishing industry. (n.d.). Retrieved May 07, 2021, from http://www.niso.org/publications/z3943-1993-r2017#:~:text=The%20Standard%20Address%20Number%20(SAN,%2C%20publishers%2C%20etc.)

Gasiorowski-Denis, E. (2020, July 7). Towards a trustworthy AI. Retrieved May 07, 2021, from https://www.iso.org/news/ref2530.html

ICS. (2019, May 23). Retrieved May 07, 2021, from https://www.iso.org/standards-catalogue/browse-by-ics.html

Jinha, A. (2010, July 1). *Article 50 million: An estimate of the number of scholarly articles in existence.* Retrieved May 07, 2021, from https://onlinelibrary.wiley.com/doi/abs/10.1087/20100308

Publons. (n.d.). Retrieved May 07, 2021, from https://publons.com/account/login/?next=%2Fdashboard%2Ftools%2Fcreate-rid%2F

Quaderi, N. (2021, April 22). *The JCR reload and a look ahead to the introduction of early access content in 2021.* Retrieved May 07, 2021, from https://clarivate.com/webofsciencegroup/article/the-jcr-reload-and-a-look-ahead-to-the-introduction-of-early-access-content-in-2021/

Registration Agencies, D. O. I. (n.d.). Retrieved May 07, 2021, from https://www.doi.org/registration_agencies.html

Researcher, I. D. (n.d.). Retrieved May 07, 2021, from https://www.researcherid.com/#rid-for-researchers

Shortdoi Service. (n.d.). Retrieved May 07, 2021, from http://www.shortdoi.org/

Standards by ISO/TC 307. (2021, May 5). Retrieved May 07, 2021, from https://www.iso.org/committee/6266604/x/catalogue/

Store, I. S. O. (2020, April 17). Retrieved May 07, 2021, from https://www.iso.org/store.html

Systematic reviews: The process: Grey literature. (n.d.). Retrieved May 07, 2021, from https://guides.mclibrary.duke.edu/sysreview/greylit

What is iso 9001:2015 and why is it important? (2019, February 1). Retrieved May 07, 2021, from https://www.qualitymag.com/articles/95235-what-is-iso-90012015-and-why-is-it-important#:~:text=ISO%20consists%20of%20161%20standards,776%20technical%20committees%20and%20subcommittees

White, K. (n.d.). *Science & engineering indicators*. Retrieved May 07, 2021, from https://ncses.nsf.gov/pubs/nsb20206/#:~:text=This%20report%20utilizes%20 data%20from,million%20to%202.6%20million%20articles

You are Crossref. (n.d.). Retrieved May 07, 2021, from https://www.crossref.org/ ANSI/NISO

ADDITIONAL READING

Tennant, J., Crane, H., Crick, T., & Quintero, D. (2019). Ten Hot Topics around Scholarly Publishing. *Publications.*, *7*(2), 34. doi:10.3390/publications7020034

Tennant, J. P. T. (2018). The state of the art in peer review. *FEMS Microbiology Letters*, *365*(19), 1–10. doi:10.1093/femsle/fny204 PMID:30137294

Chapter 5
A Brief History of Blockchain

John H. Larrier
Big Voice Productions, USA

ABSTRACT

This chapter reviews the history of blockchain from its ideation in the early 1990s to the widespread development efforts of private enterprise and governments two decades into the 21st century. The chapter covers the early developments in securing the digital record; the origins of the immutable, decentralized ledger; and trustless digital transactions. The key people in blockchain's development are addressed including the pseudonymous Satoshi Nakamoto, developer of the first cryptocurrency, Bitcoin, which became for a while synonymous with blockchain. The successes and failures of blockchain are covered in this history as well as its status and the problems that need to be solved for blockchain to have a global economic and cultural impact.

A BRIEF HISTORY OF BLOCKCHAIN

The Origins of Blockchain

During the 1980's more and more of the worlds data was being digitized. The age of computing in all facets of business and daily living was being fully launched. The question of how to ensure that the integrity and authenticity of that data was maintained in perpetuity was a concern of a young research scientist and doctoral student at Stanford University named W. Scott Stornetta. While finishing his doctorate in the late 80's, Scott worked at Xerox Parc (**P**alo **A**lto **R**esearch Center) where his adviser had a joint appointment. This placed him at one of the business centers at the forefront of adopting digital record keeping. Scott became obsessed with the idea of securing the digital record from manipulation to maintain its integrity for

DOI: 10.4018/978-1-7998-5589-7.ch005

future generations. He wanted to know if there was a way to create an immutable record that didn't rely upon a human, trusted third party, especially as it related to business financial transactions. (Stornetta W. S., 2018)

After receiving his Ph.D. in Physics from Stanford, Scott started working at Bellcore (Bell Communications Research) in 1989 shortly after the breakup of communications giant AT&T. The corporate culture at Bellcore encouraged new hires to determine what they thought were going to be important problems and to work on solving those problems. Scott's "big problem" and continued interest and focus was on how to create an immutable record with evidence that it had not been changed, but also without the need for a trusted third party institution or individuals in the process. Scott approached a colleague named Stuart Haber in the Cryptography group at Bellcore. He had met Stuart during his Bellcore interview process. Scott explained the concerns he had about creating an immutable record of digitized data and Stuart agreed to work with him on finding a solution. The two began to collaborate on how to create a system where digital data could be preserved during or after the digitization process. (Stornetta W. S., 2018)

The two colleagues worked closely for several weeks looking at various scenarios. None of the scenarios led to the conclusion they desired for an immutable record, where information could not be changed, unless everyone involved became aware of the change. There was always an opportunity for collusion between one or more parties without others being informed that a change had been made to a specific record. Stuart, two years senior to Scott eventually told Scott that he did not think it could be accomplished. Regrettably, all the various iterations of the process and systems they could think of led to the need for a trusted third party. Stuart, not wanting to abandon all the work they had put into the project and wanting to get something published from their research, suggested to Scott that they should instead prove that an immutable record *could not* be created. (Stornetta W. S., 2018)

They worked on creating a proof that a trusted third party had to be part of an immutable record system. In looking at the problem from this standpoint they ultimately had a breakthrough. (Stornetta W. S., 2018) According to Scott's wife, his eureka moment came while he was at a Friendly's restaurant in Morristown, NJ. (Stornetta M. F., 2019) They came to the realization that instead of looking to an individual person or entity for trust, if data or documents could be identified as having been created at a specific time and date with an identifying cryptographic "time stamp" that time stamps could be used to insure that the record could never be changed. Further to the "fingerprint" as it was described by Haber, distributing the fingerprint to as many parties as possible would be the method to remove the need for one individual or entity to be the trusted third party, as that single entity could be the single point of failure for the system. (Stornetta W. S., 2018) (Talks, 2019)

During the summer of 1990 Haber and Stornetta published their research in a paper titled *"How to Time Stamp a Digital Document"* at the Crypto 1990 conference in Santa Barbara, CA, the premier technical conference in the field of cryptography. (Talks, 2019) Stornetta and Haber decided to commercialize their idea in 1993. With three patents licensed from Bellcore, they launched a business in 1994 during the early dot-com years named Surety. (Stornetta M. F., 2019)

Haber and Stornetta realized that the time stamp "fingerprint" did not completely solve the problem. The fingerprint identified a document for instance but did not tell you anything about the document. With further research, during 1995 they decided to link document fingerprint ID's to the previous fingerprint ID to insure the immutability of each original document or transaction. These strings of digital ID's would be grouped into blocks with each block given a fingerprint of its own. These strings of "blocks" were the forerunner to what we now call blockchain technology. At Surety, they created the first blockchain, which they dubbed a "digital notary service". (Talks, 2019)

The launch of the software did not make a big splash in the booming dot-com world of the mid to late 1990's as Haber and Stornetta had hoped. Despite inquiries from some of the world's leading financial institutions they were not able to capitalize on their patents. Stornetta stepped down as CEO and Haber remained for a few years as Chief Scientist. Surety focused on its software instead of its technology. Ironically, this lack of focus led to the lapsing of the Bellcore licensed patents in 2004, opening the door for the global expansion and awareness of blockchain technology shortly thereafter. (Stornetta M. F., 2019)

In 2008 **Satoshi Nakamoto**, the name used by the unknown person or people who developed Bitcoin, authored a white paper entitled *Bitcoin: A Peer-to-Peer Electronic Cash System.* Three of the paper's eight references cited articles by Stornetta and Haber. (Stornetta W. S., 2018) In 2007 Satoshi used the lapsed patents to start coding and creating the Bitcoin blockchain and deployed Bitcoin's original reference implementation. (Stornetta M. F., 2019) As part of the implementation, they also devised the first blockchain database. In the process they were the first to solve the double-spending problem for digital currency using a peer-to-peer network. They were active in the development of Bitcoin up until December 2010. (About Bitcoin.org, n.d.)

Currently, a **blockchain**, ("Blockchain" n.d., para 1) originally **block chain**, is a growing list of records, called *blocks*, which are linked using cryptography. Blockchains which are readable by the public are widely used by cryptocurrencies. Cryptocurrencies such as Bitcoin, are the most familiar use of blockchain understood by the average person. Each block contains a cryptographic hash of the previous block, a timestamp, and transaction data (generally represented as a merkle tree root hash).

Figure 1.
https://commons.wikimedia.org/wiki/File:Hash_Tree.svg#/media/File:Hash_Tree.svg

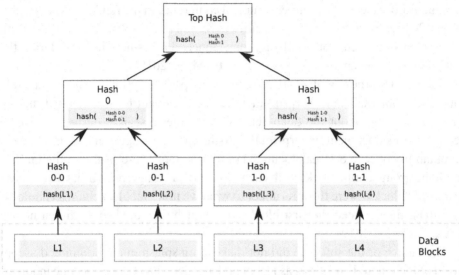

By design, a blockchain is resistant to modification of the data. It is "an open, distributed ledger whose users can record transactions between two parties efficiently and in a verifiable and permanent way". For use as a distributed ledger, a blockchain is typically managed by a peer-to-peer network collectively adhering to a protocol for inter-node (each person in the network is a node) communication and validating new blocks. Once recorded, the data in any given block cannot be altered retroactively without alteration of all subsequent blocks, which requires consensus of the network majority. (contributors, Distributed Ledger, 2020) (contributors, Peer-to-peer, 2020)

Private blockchains have been proposed and are in use for conducting business. In 2018, Stuart Haber announced that he is working on "cryptographic verifiability for audit & financial reporting of all sorts". A solution he called Auditchain.

Though blockchain records are not unalterable, blockchains may be considered secure by design and exemplify a distributed computing system with high Byzantine fault tolerance. Decentralized consensus has therefore been claimed with a blockchain. (contributors, Secure by Design, 2020)_(contributors, Decentralization, 2020) (contributors, Byzantine Fault, 2020)

BLOCKCHAIN IN THE 21ST CENTURY

Blockchain 1.0: Bitcoin

As mentioned above, Bitcoin came into being in 2008 as the first application of Blockchain technology. Satoshi Nakamoto in his whitepaper detailed it as an electronic peer-to-peer system. Nakamoto formed the genesis block, from which other blocks were mined, then interconnected, resulting in one of the largest chains of blocks carrying different pieces of information and transactions.

Bitcoin.org was registered in 2008. Bitcoin.org was originally registered and owned by Bitcoin's first two developers, Satoshi Nakamoto and Martti Malmi. When Nakamoto left the project, ownership of the domain was transferred to additional people, separate from the Bitcoin developers, to spread responsibility and prevent any one person or group from easily gaining control over the Bitcoin project.

From 2011 to 2013, the site was primarily used for releasing new versions of the software now called Bitcoin Core. In 2013, the site was redesigned, adding numerous pages, listing additional Bitcoin software, and creating the translation system. Updates, fixes, suggestions, and improvements from members of the community are welcome.

Today the site is an independent open source project with contributors from around the world. It is not the official site for the cryptocurrency. Final publication authority is held by the co-owners, but all regular activity is organized through the public pull request process and managed by the site co-maintainers. (About Bitcoin.org, n.d.)

Bitcoin the cryptocurrency has undergone a few highs and lows in its relatively brief history. One of the most notable was the Mt. Gox scandal. Mt. Gox was a cryptocurrency exchange. It was a website originally created by Jed McCaleb for players of the card game "Magic: The Gathering" so they could trade cards online. Mt. Gox was an abbreviation of Magic: The Gathering Online Exchange. McCaleb transferred ownership of the site to Mark Karpeles in 2011 and he became the CEO of Mt. Gox. The exchange went on to become the most influential bitcoin exchange in its time. At its most influential it was responsible for over 70% of all bitcoin transactions.

However, there were operational and security problems that caused thousands of coins to be "lost" in 2011 due to attacks by hackers. This was followed by increased concern from customers due to bugs in the software. In early 2014 the company suspended withdrawals after they discovered what they termed "suspicious activity" in their digital wallets. The suspension of withdrawals combined with the known software problems caused the value of bitcoin to plunge 20%. The company then announced that it has lost over 850,000 bitcoins.

The loss of so many bitcoins had a profound effect on the bitcoin market. Although, 200,000 of the lost bitcoins were recovered, the remaining lost bitcoins, valued at over $450 million US dollars, pushed Mt. Gox into insolvency. Mt. Gox filed for bankruptcy in Tokyo District Court and was ordered to liquidate in April 2014.

Multiple lawsuits were filed, and many are still ongoing in the early months of 2020. Karpeles was arrested and charged with embezzlement and fraud but was later cleared of those charges. In 2019 he was found guilty of falsifying data in Mt. Gox's bookkeeping. (Frankenfield J., Investopedia-Cryptocurrency-Cryptocurrency Strategy & Education, 2020) (Coindesk, 2020)

Bitcoin recovered from the Mt. Gox scandal to hit a peak price of $19,783 USD during November 2017. Just before this high value a new bitcoin was created. Unlike previous new coins, this new cryptocurrency clone created by existing bitcoin owners, and called Bitcoin Cash, also cloned the bitcoin blockchain. Normally when new alternative cryptocurrencies are created, developers just clone the code and not the blockchain. But Bitcoin Cash copied Bitcoin's blockchain as well, which created a situation in which everyone that had one bitcoin suddenly also had one Bitcoin Cash. Bitcoin owners were forced to ascribe value to a new coin created from nothing. The Bitcoin Cash creators all had to be in agreement for the new coin to be created, but it did cause discord within the Bitcoin and blockchain community because of how quickly it happened and the risk it posed if the community didn't generally agree that the new coin, in principle had value to it. (Mow, 2017)

As of January 2020, Bitcoin's original blockchain had grown to over 615,000 blocks and continues to grow. (Reiff, 2020)

Between 2018 and 2019 Bitcoin's bubble burst with the price declining as low as $3,983 in 2019. However, primarily due to the global coronavirus pandemic in 2020 and investors looking for safety the price stood at over $11,100 US dollars as of July 30, 2020.

Blockchain 2.0: Ethereum

In a world where innovation is the order of the day, Vitalik Buterin was among a growing list of developers who felt Bitcoin had much more potential beyond creating a ledger of document transactions. Buterin was an early contributor to the coding of Bitcoin. Concerned by Bitcoin's limitations, Buterin started working on what he felt would be a malleable blockchain that could perform various functions in addition to being a peer-to-peer network. Ethereum was born as a new public blockchain in 2013 with added functionalities compared to Bitcoin, a development that has turned out to be a pivotal moment in Blockchain history. (Goyal, 2018)

Buterin differentiated Ethereum from Bitcoin Blockchain by enabling a function that allows people to record other assets such as slogans as well as contracts. The new feature expanded Ethereum functionalities from being a cryptocurrency to being a platform for developing decentralized applications as well.

Launched in 2015, Ethereum blockchain has been developed to become one of the biggest applications of blockchain technology given its ability to support smart contracts used to perform various functions. Nick Szabo, an American cryptographer, and computer scientist proposed the idea of smart contracts in 1994. He defined smart contracts as computerized transaction protocols that execute the terms of a contract. (Frankenfield J., 2019) Smart contracts regulate the exchange of resources, services, products, and assets between the participants who have agreed to the contract. (Bartoletti, 2020) Given the decentralized nature of these contract agreements, since they don't require a bank or financial institution to be involved, blockchain and smart contract technologies function well in instances where legal contracts are required to maintain ownership rights and data privacy laws. These customizable, self-executing smart contracts on the blockchain can be easily managed by all parties. (Goyal, 2018)

Some concerns arose however with smart contracts since they cannot be changed. If any of the parties who have entered into the contractual agreement which is now coded and on the blockchain, changes their mind the contract cannot be changed quickly or easily. Smart contracts typically operate on an if/then contention. Ethereum's Solidity software calls it *assert/require.* (Bartoletti, 2020) *If* something occurs, *then* another action, previously agreed to by the parties will automatically occur. (CryptoNinjas-Home-What Are Smart Contracts, 2020) The actions can be positive or negative, either advancing the fulfillment of the contract or negating terms of the contract because one or more parties have not completed some agreed condition of the contract. These conditions usually have a time frame during which they must be completed, for the contract to remain valid.

Ethereum blockchain platform has also succeeded in gathering an active developer community that has seen it establish a true ecosystem.

Ethereum blockchain processes the greatest number of daily transactions thanks to its ability to support smart contracts and decentralized applications. Its market cap has also increased significantly in the cryptocurrency space. (Goyal, 2018)

Many other players have entered the arena of blockchain based smart contracts. These new players bring with them software and smart contract process innovations. Some of the challenges being tackled were how to tie digital assets to real world assets. (e.g. - real estate assets coded in a smart contract to the physical property whose ownership is being transferred via a smart contract). Increasing transaction security was also a key concern for smart contract users and cryptocurrency investors (Anwar, 2018) Ethereum based applications have been hacked several times. The most famous was The DAO hack of 2016.

A DAO or *"distributed autonomous organization"* is a digital platform upon which autonomous organizations can operate. A DAO is another computer code through which a set of smart contracts are connected and function as a governance mechanism. "The DAO" eponymously named, was launched as a virtual, decentralized venture capital fund on the Ethereum blockchain and went live on April 30, 2016. The only investment requirement was to invest Ether in The DAO. for which 100 DAO tokens were provided for each Ether. The fund had a 28 day funding period. Within two weeks $100M US dollars had been raised and a total fund investment of $150 million was attained by the end of the funding period. It went downhill from there.

Concerns were expressed that vulnerabilities were evident in The DAO coding. One was related to what was described as a "recursive calling bug". Before programmers could fix this bug, the fund was hacked on either June 16th or 17th, 2016 for approximately 3.6M Ether, about $50M US dollars. The hack was accomplished using a process meant to protect investors who were in the minority when funding proposals were approved by a majority of the investors. They could create a split DAO (child DAO) and retrieve their funds into the split DAO. The split procedure could be started by any token holder at any time regarding the retrieval of their own Ether. An investor had to wait 1 calendar week after creating the split DAO, before they could initiate the retrieval of funds into the split DAO. The weakness in the procedure was that the code allowed for the retrieval of the Ether without an immediate check of the The DAO's balance sheet. The DAO's coding allowed for a specified amount of time to pass after funds were retrieved before the balance sheet was automatically checked by the code. During that time, after the initial withdrawal, the attacker exploited the weakness and used The DAO's code to make repeated withdrawals from the fund. The attacker(s) continued retrieving Ether until the "recursive call exploit" was discovered. The price of Ether plunged from $20 to $13 once the hack was discovered. The attacker subsequently sent an open letter to The DAO community defending their actions, stating that the code allowed them to make the withdrawals. Since the coding also included a 48 day series of procedures before funds could be moved from a split DAO to an account fully under the control of the retrieving investor, the Ethereum community eventually made the difficult decision to create a "hard fork" of the Ethereum blockchain in order to nullify the attacker's child DAO. This was completed on July 20, 2016 and the funds returned to the investors. The new blockchain continued with the name Ethereum and the older original version was kept going under the name Ethereum Classic. (Güçlütürk, 2018) (Siegel, 2015)

By December 2016, The DAO was delisted on cryptocurrency exchanges and ceased operations. This attack further highlighted that there were weaknesses in smart contract blockchains and would be one of several drivers in blockchain development as it entered its second decade.

Blockchain 3.0: Beyond Cryptocurrency

Blockchain history and evolution does not stop with Ethereum and Bitcoin. However, it is still a relatively young technology that requires significant investment to resolve the challenges being faced in its second decade of existence. The 'killer app" has not yet appeared that will allow blockchain to be widely adopted and become a global commercial success. However, there is growing interest in its use and application on several fronts, most notably in finance, healthcare, entertainment, and government. (Goyal, 2018) (Ghosh, 2019)

Blockchain 3.0 is defined as the attempts to fix the current problems in the blockchain industry – specifically, issues regarding *scalability*, *interoperability*, and many would argue, *privacy*. Blockchain 3.0 should be the final push it needs to gain mainstream adoption. (Elev8, 2019)

Scalability

As blockchain entered its second decade, the issue of scalability to meet the growing demands of various enterprises is a growing concern. The popularity of Bitcoin for instance has caused its blockchain to have a 7 transactions per second (tps) processing rate as compared to Visa's 2000 tps. The computing power needed for Bitcoin to scale up their operation is tremendous and of course needs the investment of the nodes to bring this technology to bear on Bitcoin's processing power.

The idea of a second layer is becoming more prominent in the blockchain world. Basically, the second layer is what it describes; a group of projects, applications, and infrastructure software solutions that sit on top of a blockchain's base layer.

These extra layers are a second lane for traffic on the blockchain highway, add functionality to individual chains, but also improve their user experiences and impart benefits specific to unique decentralized concepts (like payments, storage, bandwidth sharing). (Vilner, 2019)

Some early examples are:

- **Lightning Network (LN)**: Bitcoin's second layer - The LN will lighten the load by hosting private 'payment channels' between two users, which is a mini balance sheet on which they can transact in BTC instantly, with the main Bitcoin blockchain used only to index and authenticate them.
- **Raiden:** Ethereum's Raiden Network is an off-chain solution that implements a similar payment channels model, the Raiden platform acts as a second layer payment channel for Ethereum. The ETH network is the second most used public blockchain in the world. The current slowness of it when processing

payments make it a bad contender for businesses as a point of sale (POS) service for groceries and other necessities.

- **EOS:** This blockchain was developed to respond to the growing need for a solution to address the need for scale and reduce the congestion on many original blockchain platforms. It is somewhat similar to Ethereum in its intention to host decentralized applications, but while featuring a more centralized Delegated Proof of Stake (DPoS) system, EOS developers still find themselves starved of the memory they need to easily create massively scalable open-source blockchain software (dApps). (Vilner, 2019)

Interoperability

As interest in blockchain grows there are numerous enterprises, governments and other organizations developing blockchains around the world. Like previous technological inventions there is a great desire for multiple proprietary systems to be able to communicate and interact with one another. The industry realizes the need for an interoperability standard to be developed so that the fullest potential of blockchain can be accessed and scaled for use in the global economy.

Blockchain interoperability means the ability to share, see, and access information across different networks without the need for intermediaries. Currently, blockchain networks operate independently from one another. The Bitcoin blockchain, for instance, operates entirely separately from the Ethereum network. (Perryman, 2020)

Interoperability is not only needed for blockchain-to-blockchain communication, but also for connecting the blockchain to traditional business and government infrastructure. Companies like Santander, Barclays and other are creating their own interoperability standards as well. (Elev8, 2019)

Examples of interoperable projects are:

- **Cosmos:** The Interchain Foundation (ICF) through a conservatively managed "fundraising" effort raised $17 million during its initial offering in April 2017. The funds were used to develop the Cosmos network. (Cuen, 2019)

Cosmos is an ecosystem of blockchains that can scale and interoperate with each other. The vision of Cosmos is to make it easy for developers to build blockchains and break the barriers between blockchains by allowing them to transact with each other. The end goal is to create an **Internet of Blockchains,** a network of blockchains able to communicate with each other in a decentralized way. (What is Cosmos?, 2020)

- **Polkadot:** Polkadot was founded and conceptualized by Gavin Wood, a cofounder of the Ethereum blockchain. A variety of assets will be enabled for cross-chain transfer to any of the blockchains within its expansive network. Many interoperability projects are focused on enabling assets to be swapped cross-chain, Polkadot goes further. It also enables data to be swapped in the same manner and supports cross-chain computation.

While at Ethereum, Wood founded along with other colleagues, the EthCore blockchain company. EthCore was formed to address some of the problems faced by Ethereum, in particular the issues concerning interoperability and privacy. Wood departed Ethereum on January 11, 2016. EthCore subsequently became known as Parity Technologies (Parity). Parity has developed several significant blockchain technologies available on the Ethereum blockchain.

Like the Ethereum DAO experience, Parity was attacked not once, but twice in 2017. The first time occurred on July 19th with a net loss of approximately $30 million in funds. Parity quickly explained the code weakness that was exploited. Since $164 million had been recovered, the incident and its handling did not become a death blow to the organization.

During the same summer, Wood and Peter Czaban of Parity, formed the Web3Foundation. One of its primary goals was to manage the funds raised in the Polkadot token sale which took place on October 25-27, 2017. The token sale was a huge success and raised $145 million. Just 10 days later another vulnerability coming from a fix of the previous hack allowed an attacker to freeze funds in many Parity wallets. The code was then, according to the attacker "accidentally" destroyed. The frozen funds included those of the Web3Foundation as well as those raised during the Polkadot ICO. At this writing in 2020, those funds have still not been recovered.

Unlike many other blockchain organizations whose companies floundered after hacks or other founding problems, Wood, and his colleagues behind Polkadot persevered despite the loss of funds and some professional credibility after the 2017 hacks. Two and a half years later, the initial interoperable, scalable functionalities of Polkadot were launched on May 26, 2020 during the global Covid-19 pandemic. Only time will tell if Wood's labors and patience will bring to blockchain the functionality desired to make blockchain the next blockbuster technology in the global economy. (Posnak, 2019) (Sedgwick, 2020) (Parity.io, 2017) (Polkadot, 2020)

- **Privacy and Security:** The more things change in some ways the more they stay the same. Human nature being what it is (as evidenced by the numerous attacks on crypto networks) has caused many individuals and companies to seek privacy solutions for blockchain users. Blockchain was developed as a trustless system, open transaction system. However, that very design that makes data publicly available can be used by those who are "untrustworthy" to trace data on the blockchain back to specific individuals and organizations.

Governments and many corporations are working on implementing blockchain for a variety of applications. Yet, because of the privacy and security concerns, their blockchains will be privately not public controlled. While these blockchains will likely have some element of decentralization, they will surely have a centralized party responsible for oversight to insure organizational control of the blockchain and all its user and customer data as well as any proprietary information. It is highly unlikely that this would be left to the general good will of the users of the blockchain whether internal or external.

There are now numerous blockchain initiatives and collaborations to bring blockchain to use in daily organization and personal life.

It has been used by the US Federal Government for public procurement, at the Department of Health and Human Services. HHS Accelerate, launched in early 2020 is the first blockchain platform approved for use by the US Federal Government and is expected to save $30 millions over the next five years. (Kirkland, 2020)

Walmart, and other global companies in the food supply chain, including Kraft and Unilever, partnered with IBM as early as 2016 to develop blockchain technology to improve food safety. IBM's Food Trust solution built on IBM's Blockchain Platform, uses Hyperledger Fabric one of the Hyperledger projects of the Linux Foundation to ensure food safety through enhanced supply chain tracking. A Walmart case study showed that it reduced identifying the source of mangoes sold to its stores in the US from 7 days to 2.2 seconds. This time savings is a crucial enhancement in prepared and fresh produce recalls. Hyperledger is a prominent open source platform for modular, interoperable blockchain use, which notably says it preserves privacy. (Hyperledger.org, 2020) (Miller, 2018)

Blockchain nears the end of its third decade from initial conception and is in its second decade since practical commercial implementation. The global coronavirus pandemic (Covid-19) in 2020 will surely spur blockchain development, use and interest in some enterprises and governments. However, the impact of the pandemic on economies will likely have a limiting effect on the amount of financial and intellectual resources that will be available to further blockchain research and development. As noted above, only time will tell how successful blockchain technology is in changing the global economic and cultural landscape.

As the technology evolves, Gartner Trend Insights expects at least one business built on blockchain to come into being valued at more than $10 billion by 2022. The research firm expects business value because of the digital ledger technology to grow to over $176 billion by 2025 and exceed $3.1 trillion by 2030. (Goyal, 2018)

REFERENCES

About Bitcoin.org. (n.d.). Retrieved from Bitcoin.org: https://bitcoin.org/en/

Anwar, H. (2018, July 19). *101 Blockchains - Home»Guides»Smart Contracts: The Ultimate Guide for the Beginners.* Retrieved from 101Blockchains.com: https://101blockchains.com/smart-contracts/#15

Bartoletti, M. (2020). *Smart Contracts Contracts. Frontiers in Blockchain, 5.*

Brenig, C., Accorsi, R., & Muller, G. (2015). Economic Analysis of Cryptocurrency Backed Money Laundering. In C. Brenig, R. Accorsi, & G. Muller (Eds.), *ECIS 2015 Completed Research Papers* (p. 19). Association for Information Systems.

Brito, J., & Castillo, A. (2013). *Bitcoin: A Primer for Policymakers.* Mercatus Center: George Mason University.

Coindesk. (2020). *Coindesk-Mt. Gox-Tokyo.* Retrieved from Coindesk: https://www.coindesk.com/company/mt-gox

Contributors, W. (2020a, August 2). *Byzantine Fault.* Retrieved from Wikipedia, The Free Encyclopedia: https://en.wikipedia.org/w/index.php?title=Byzantine_fault&oldid=970825345

Contributors, W. (2020b, August 2). *Decentralization.* Retrieved from Wikipedia, The Free Encyclopedia: https://en.wikipedia.org/w/index.php?title=Decentralization&oldid=970789219

Contributors, W. (2020c, July 5). *Distributed Ledger.* Retrieved from Wikipedia, The Free Enclyopedia: https://en.wikipedia.org/w/index.php?title=Distributed_ledger&oldid=966156176

Contributors, W. (2020d, july 5). *Distributed Ledger.* Retrieved from Wikipedia, The Free Encyclopedia: https://en.wikipedia.org/w/index.php?title=Distributed_ledger&oldid=966156176

Contributors, W. (2020e, July 27). *Peer-to-peer.* Retrieved from Wikipedia, The Free Encyclopedia: https://en.wikipedia.org/w/index.php?title=Peer-to-peer&oldid=969866372

Contributors, W. (2020f, May 11). *Secure by Design.* Retrieved from Wikipedia, The Free Encyclopedia: https://en.wikipedia.org/w/index.php?title=Secure_by_design&oldid=956142127

CryptoNinjas-Home-What Are Smart Contracts. (2020). Retrieved from CryptoNinjas.com: https://www.cryptoninjas.net/what-are-smart-contracts/

Cuen, L. (2019, November 11). *Coindesk - Business.* Retrieved from Coindesk. com: https://www.coindesk.com/how-to-turn-a-17-million-ico-into-104-million-the-cosmos-story

Elev8. (2019, August 23). *Elev8 Blog.* Retrieved from Elev8.com: https://www. elev8con.com/what-is-blockchain-3-0-a-guide-to-the-next-phase-of-dlt/

Frankenfield, J. (2019a, November 8). *Block Time.* Retrieved from Investopedia: https://www.investopedia.com/terms/b/block-time-cryptocurrency.asp

Frankenfield, J. (2019b, October 8). *Investopedia-Cryptocurrency-Blockchain.* Retrieved from Investopedia.com: https://www.investopedia.com/terms/s/ smart-contracts.asp#:~:text=Smart%20contracts%20were%20first%20 proposed,bitcoin%2C%20which%20he%20has%20denied

Frankenfield, J. (2020, February 2). *Investopedia-Cryptocurrency-Cryptocurrency Strategy & Education.* Retrieved from Investopedia: https://www.investopedia.com/ terms/m/mt-gox.asp

Ghosh, P. (. (2019, October 31). *Dataversity - Data Topics - Data Education>Smart Data News, Articles, & Education>The Future of Blockchain.* Retrieved from Dataversity.net: https://www.dataversity.net/the-future-of-blockchain/

Goyal, S. (2018, November 3). *101blockchains.com-Reviews.* Retrieved from 101 Blockchains: https://101blockchains.com/history-of-blockchain-timeline/

Greenberg, A. (2017, January 25). *Wired.com - Security.* Retrieved from Wired.com: https://www.wired.com/2017/01/monero-drug-dealers-cryptocurrency-choice-fire/

Güçlütürk, O. G. (2018, August 1). *Medium.com - Cryptocurrency.* Retrieved from Medium.com: https://medium.com/@ogucluturk/the-dao-hack-explained-unfortunate-take-off-of-smart-contracts-2bd8c8db3562

Hileman, D. G., & Rauchs, M. (2017). *Global Cryptocurrency Benchmarking Study.* Centre for Alternative Finance - University of Cambridge.

Hyperledger.org. (2020). *Hyperledger - How Walmart.* Retrieved from Hyperledger. org/Learn: https://www.hyperledger.org/learn/publications/walmart-case-study

Kirkland, R. (2020, March 31). *Execs to Watch - Execs to Know.* Retrieved from WashingtonExec.com: https://washingtonexec.com/2020/03/how-jose-arrieta-became-a-blockchain-champion/#.XynYeihJF3g

Kopfstein, J. (2013, December 12). *New Yorker.com-Tech.* Retrieved from New Yorker: https://www.newyorker.com/tech/elements/the-mission-to-decentralize-the-internet

Levine, B. (2018, June 11). *Martech: Marketing.* Retrieved from Martech Today: https://martechtoday.com/a-new-report-bursts-the-blockchain-bubble-216959

Marsh, A., & Brush, S. (2019, March 3). *Bloomberg Technology.* Retrieved from Bloomberg.com: https://www.bloomberg.com/news/articles/2019-03-03/why-crypto-companies-still-can-t-open-checking-accounts

Marvin, R. (2017, August 30). *PCMag Australia - Features.* Retrieved from Au PCMag: https://au.pcmag.com/features/46389/blockchain-the-invisible-technology-thats-changing-the-world

Miller, R. (2018, September 24). *Walmart is betting on the blockchain to improve food safety.* Retrieved from TechCrunch.com: https://techcrunch.com/2018/09/24/walmart-is-betting-on-the-blockchain-to-improve-food-safety/

Mow, S. (2017, August 7). *Fortune-Commentary-Bitcoin.* Retrieved from Fortune.com: https://fortune.com/2017/08/07/bitcoin-cash-bch-hard-fork-blockchain-usd-coinbase/

Orcutt, M. (2017, September 11). *MIT Technology Review/Blockchain/Cryptocurrency.* Retrieved from MIT Technology Review: https://www.technologyreview.com/s/608763/criminals-thought-bitcoin-was-the-perfect-hiding-place-they-thought-wrong/

Parity.io. (2017, November 15). *Parity.io - Security- A Postmortem on the Parity Multi-Sig Library Self-Destruct.* Retrieved from Parity.io: https://www.parity.io/a-postmortem-on-the-parity-`multi-sig-library-self-destruct/

Perryman, E. (2020, January 26). *Yahoo! Finance.* Retrieved from Finance.yahoo.com: https://finance.yahoo.com/news/blockchain-interoperability-key-successful-projects-140034557.html

Polkadot. (2020, May 25). *W3F Initiates Launch: Polkadot is Live.* Retrieved from Polkadot.network: https://polkadot.network/web3-foundation-initiates-launch-polkadot-is-live/#:~:text=26%20May%202020%2C%20Zug%2C%20 Switzerland,together%2C%20seamlessly%20and%20at%20scale.

Posnak, E. (2019, May 27). *Medium.com - On the Origin of Polkadot.* Retrieved from Medium.com: https://medium.com/on-the-origin-of-smart-contract-platforms/on-the-origin-of-polkadot-c7750e2fc5ff#:~:text=History,figure%20in%20 Ethereum's%20early%20history.&text=While%20still%20at%20Ethereum%2C%20 Wood,hereafter%20referred%20to%20as%20Parity)

Raymaekers, W. (2015). Cryptocurrency Bitcoin: Disruption, challenges, and opportunities. *Journal of Payments Strategy & Systems*, 30-46.

Raymond, E. S. (1996). *The New Hacker's Dictionary, 3e*. MIT Press.

Reiff, N. (2020, February 1). *Investopedia - Blockchain Explained*. Retrieved from Investopedia: https://www.investopedia.com/terms/b/blockchain.asp

Sedgwick, K. (2020, Jan 22). *News - Blockchain - Polkadot Will Finally Launch*. Retrieved from News.Bitcoin.com

Siegel, D. (2015, June 25). *Coindesk.com - Markets*. Retrieved from Coindesk.com: https://www.coindesk.com/understanding-dao-hack-journalists

Stornetta, M. F. (2019). Retrieved from Google Docs: docs.google.com/document/d/1xYmwJQK-pi9fr6yOq5RzQBaRzoQuEpSUQyvjOzkAjQc/edit?usp=sharing

Stornetta, W. S. (2018, September 6). *The Missing Link between Satoshi & Bitcoin: Cypherpunk Scott Stornetta* (N. Brockwell, Interviewer). Academic Press.

Talks, T. (2019, February 20). *Blockchain: Decentralization is Central*. TEDxBeaconStreet.

Tapscott, D., & Tapscott, A. (2016). *The Blockchain Revolution: How the Technology Behind Bitcoin is Changing Money, Business and the World*. Penguin Group.

The Economist. (2015, October 31). *The Great Chain of Being Sure About Things*. Author.

Vilner, Y. (2019, April 25). *Forbes - Crypto & Blockchain*. Retrieved from Forbes.com: https://www.forbes.com/sites/yoavvilner/2019/04/25/down-the-next-rabbit-hole-exploring-biockchains-second-layer/#2f57c4af278f

What is Cosmos? (2020). Retrieved from Cosmos.Network: https://cosmos.network/intro

Chapter 6

Is AI in Your Future?
AI Considerations for
Scholarly Publishers

Darrell Wayne Gunter
https://orcid.org/0000-0001-5717-8342
Gunter Media Group, Inc., USA

ABSTRACT

AI was first coined by John McCarthy in 1956. Vannevar Bush penned an article, "As We Make Think," that was first published in The Atlantic, and five years later, Alan Turning wrote a paper on the notion of machines being able to simulate human beings. AI had a number of significant contributors, which this chapter chronicles along with the definitions and their achievements. This chapter will provide an introduction, history, and overview of AI. It will also provide examples of the four waves of AI and the current applications and future applications of AI.

INTRODUCTION

I thought about the title for my talk about A.I. quite a bit and felt asking the question, "Is A.I. in your future?" would help position this talk on a more strategic basis. I say strategic because implementing A.I. requires vision, leadership and significant investment.

In this chapter, we will discuss the following topics:

- Opening Hypothesis
- History of A.I. & Definitions

DOI: 10.4018/978-1-7998-5589-7.ch006

- The Art of the Possible
- A Few A.I. Examples
- The Path to Success
- The Art of the How
- Summary and Conclusions

My hypothesis is that A.I. should be in your plans to create new products and services to improve the scholarly research eco-system. It will provide many opportunities to improve the efficiencies of scholarly publishing and data analytic tools. Let's look at the various areas where A.I. can be of service to Scholarly Publishers.

- Peer Review
  - Analyzing submitted manuscripts
  - Selecting relevant peer reviewers
- Search and Discovery Platforms
  - Semantic Search
- Hypothesis Generation – Determining where research is going
- Selecting employees for specific positions

HISTORY OF A.I.

The term artificial intelligence was first coined by John McCarthy in 1956 when he held the first academic conference on the subject (Peart, 2020). But the journey to understand if machines can honestly think began much before that. In Vannevar Bush's seminal work "As We May Think" he proposed a system that amplifies people's own knowledge and understanding (Bush, 1945).

"As We May Think" is a 1945 essay by Vannevar Bush described as visionary and influential, anticipating many aspects of the information society. It was first published in *The Atlantic* in July 1945 and republished in an abridged version in September 1945—before and after the atomic bombings of Hiroshima and Nagasaki. Bush expresses his concern for the direction of scientific efforts toward destruction, rather than understanding, and illustrates a desire for a sort of collective memory machine with his concept of the memex that would make knowledge more accessible, believing that it would help fix these problems. Through this machine, Bush hoped to transform an information explosion into a knowledge explosion.

Five years later, Alan Turing wrote a paper on the notion of machines being able to simulate human beings and the ability to do intelligent things, such as play Chess (Stezano, 2018).

John McCarthy

John McCarthy (September 4, 1927 – October 24, 2011) was an American computer scientist and cognitive scientist. McCarthy was one of the founders of the discipline of artificial intelligence. He coined the term "artificial intelligence" (A.I.), developed the Lisp programming language family, significantly influenced the design of the ALGOL programming language, popularized timesharing, and was very influential in the early development of A.I.

McCarthy spent most of his career at Stanford University. He received many accolades and honors, such as the 1971 Turing Award for his contributions to the topic of A.I., The United States National Medal of Science, and the Kyoto Prize.

Artificial intelligence (A.I.), sometimes called machine intelligence, is intelligence demonstrated by machines, in contrast to the natural intelligence displayed by humans and other animals. In computer science, A.I. research is defined as the study of "intelligent agents": any device that perceives its environment and takes actions that maximize its chance of successfully achieving its goals. Colloquially, the term "artificial intelligence" is applied when a machine mimics "cognitive" functions that humans associate with other human minds, such as "learning" and "problem-solving" (IBM, 2020).

The scope of A.I. is disputed: as machines become increasingly capable, tasks considered as requiring "intelligence" are often removed from the definition, a phenomenon is known as the A.I. effect, leading to the quip, "A.I. is whatever hasn't been done yet." For instance, optical character recognition is frequently excluded from "artificial intelligence", having become a standard technology. Modern machine capabilities generally classified as A.I. include successfully understanding human speech, competing at the highest level in strategic game systems (such as chess and Go), autonomously operating cars, and intelligent routing in content delivery networks and military simulations (Skinner, 2021).

Artificial intelligence was founded as an academic discipline in 1956, and in the years since has experienced several waves of optimism, followed by disappointment and the loss of funding (known as an "A.I. winter"), followed by new approaches, success, and renewed funding. For most of its history, A.I. research has been divided into subfields that often fail to communicate with each other. These sub-fields are based on technical considerations, such as particular goals (e.g., "robotics" or "machine learning"), the use of particular tools ("logic" or artificial neural networks), or deep philosophical differences. Subfields have also been based on social factors (particular institutions or the work of particular researchers).

The traditional problems (or goals) of A.I. research include reasoning, knowledge representation, planning, learning, natural language processing, perception and the ability to move and manipulate objects. General intelligence is among the field's long-term goals. Approaches include statistical methods, computational intelligence, and traditional symbolic A.I. Many tools are used in A.I., including versions of search and mathematical optimization, artificial neural networks, and methods based on statistics, probability, and economics. The A.I. field draws upon computer science, information engineering, mathematics, psychology, linguistics, philosophy, and many others (Findlay, 2020).

The field was founded on the claim that human intelligence "can be so precisely described that a machine can be made to simulate it". This raises philosophical arguments about the nature of the mind and the ethics of creating artificial beings endowed with human-like intelligence, which have been explored by myth, fiction, and philosophy since antiquity. Some people also consider A.I. to be a danger to humanity if it progresses unabated. Others believe that A.I., unlike previous technological revolutions, will create a risk of mass unemployment.

In the twenty-first century, A.I. techniques have experienced a resurgence following concurrent advances in computer power, large amounts of data, and theoretical understanding; and A.I. techniques have become an essential part of the technology industry, helping to solve many challenging problems in computer science, software engineering, and operations research.

"As We May Think" is a 1945 essay by Vannevar Bush described as visionary and influential, anticipating many aspects of information society. It was first published in *The Atlantic* in July 1945 and republished in an abridged version in September 1945—before and after the atomic bombings of Hiroshima and Nagasaki. Bush expresses his concern for the direction of scientific efforts toward destruction, rather than understanding, and explicates a desire for a sort of collective memory machine with his concept of the memex that would make knowledge more accessible, believing that it would help fix these problems. Through this machine, Bush hoped to transform an information explosion into a knowledge explosion.

Vannevar Bush

Vannevar Bush (/væ'niːvɑːr/ *van-NEE-var* March 11, 1890 – June 28, 1974) was an American engineer, inventor and science administrator, who during World War II headed the U.S. Office of Scientific Research and Development (OSRD), through which almost all wartime military R&D was carried out, including important developments in radar and the initiation and early administration of the Manhattan Project. He emphasized the importance of scientific research to national security and economic well-being, and was chiefly responsible for the movement that led to the creation of the National Science Foundation.

Alan Turing

Alan Mathison Turing OBE FRS (/ˈtjʊərɪŋ/; 23 June 1912 – 7 June 1954) was an English mathematician, computer scientist, logician, cryptanalyst, philosopher, and theoretical biologist. Turing was highly influential in the development of theoretical computer science, providing a formalisation of the concepts of algorithm and computation with the Turing machine, which can be considered a model of a general-purpose computer. Turing is widely considered to be the father of theoretical computer science and artificial intelligence.

THE FOUR WAVES OF ARTIFICIAL INTELLIGENCE

- The first wave is "Internet A.I."
- The second wave is "Business A.I."
- The third wave of A.I. -call it "Perception A.I."
- The fourth way is the most monumental but also the most difficult: "Autonomous A.I."

Artificial Intelligence is omnipresent—what we once thought of as a futuristic technology will soon permeate all life spheres. So how will it impact business and the world in general? In his book, *A.I. Superpowers*, Kai-Fu Lee, a prominent Chinese I.T. investor with an executive background in Google, Apple, and Microsoft, dwells on four waves of A.I., their present and future use cases (Diamadis, 2018; Wikipedia, 2021).

In Lee's opinion, the four waves are Internet A.I., Business A.I., Perception A.I., and Autonomous A.I.

Internet A.I.

Internet A.I. is already familiar to most of us. There are recommendation engines out there, collecting your browser data and offering you exactly the information you're interested in based on your browsing behavior. Facebook seems to know exactly what you've been thinking—so does YouTube and Amazon. That's Internet A.I. at work. On the Internet, A.I. is fueled by user-submitted data—our clicks or non-clicks, likes, comments, shares and time spent on a webpage.

But the future will take Internet A.I. even farther. What started now as complex data analytics, sketching a detailed portrait of your personality based on your web-surfing behavior, will soon bring us to fully personalized Web, tailored to your desires and needs with even headlines rewritten to appeal to your individual taste.

Chinese content aggregator Toutiao already uses natural language processing (NLP), computer vision along with data analytic tools to bring users fully personalized news feeds, based on detailed analysis of preferences and behavior. The platform now has 120 million users daily and looks like it's setting the standard for Web 3.0.

Business A.I.

Business A.I., on the other hand, will work with data previously recorded and submitted during our interactions with financial, healthcare, legal and business institutions. Using complex data analytics, which, unlike the human brain, are trained to detect and process weakly correlated data, business A.I. can predict your future health and wellness, financial status and social behavior. For example, it can predict your likelihood of becoming a regular offender, if you already have a record of criminal suits and even the probability of getting into a car accident.

Currently, Chinese mobile app Smart Finance, intended for mobile payments and microloans, can determine your capacity to repay loans based on seemingly unrelated data stored in your phone. In the future, the same approach applied by insurance, health, travel and legal institutions will change our habits and lifestyles forever.

Perception A.I.

Perception A.I. may sound like we are entering the science fiction realm but is, in fact, our nearest future. Smart homes and IoT devices, A.R. and V.R. combined with artificial eyes, ears, and other sensors will erase the line between digital and physical environments, and online-merged-offline (OMO) world will enrich physical reality with the variety and endless opportunities of the Web.

Imagine, what it would be like entering a grocery store and being reminded by a personalized virtual assistant (aware of your nutrition needs and family status) to pick up veggies and milk — and paying with your face instead of credit card since there are facial recognition systems everywhere.

Autonomous A.I.

But the final frontier of Artificial Intelligence, according to Kai-Fu Lee, will be autonomous A.I. Powered with all the sensory and intellectual abilities, the machines will finally be capable of operating on their own as separate entities. This, in fact, is happening now, as Elon Musk promises to go on a first road trip in a self-driving car by end of 2018. According to Musk, autonomous vehicles will become common during the upcoming decade. Driving your own car could soon become a recreational hobby, just like horse riding. This, of course, will imply building smart roads equipped with sensors and allowing the cars, roads, and vehicles to interact with each other. Moreover, all manual labor in production and agriculture will be done by machines (Ossawa, 2018).

The term "artificial intelligence" was coined in 1956, at a historic conference at Dartmouth, but it has been only in the past 10 years, for the most part, that we've seen the first truly substantive glimpses of its power and application. A.I., as it's now universally called, is the pursuit of performing tasks usually reserved for human cognition: recognizing patterns, predicting outcomes clouded by uncertainty, and making complex decisions. A.I. algorithms can perceive and interpret the world around us—and some even say they'll soon be capable of emotion, compassion, and creativity—though the original dream of matching overall "human intelligence" is still very far away.

What changed everything a decade or so ago was an approach called "deep learning"—an architecture inspired by the human brain, with neurons and connections. As the name suggests, deep-learning networks can be thousands of layers deep and have up to billions of parameters. Unlike the human brain, however, such networks are "trained" on huge amounts of labeled data; then they use what they've "learned" to mathematically pick out and recognize incredibly subtle patterns within other mountains of data. A data input to the network can be anything digital—say, an image, or a sound segment, or a credit card purchase. The output, meanwhile, is a decision or prediction related to whatever question might be asked: *Whose face is in the image? What words were spoken in the sound segment? Is the purchase fraudulent?*

This technological breakthrough was paralleled with an explosion in data—the vast majority of it coming from the Internet—which captured human activities, intentions, and inclinations. While a human brain tends to focus on the most obvious correlations between the input data and the outcomes, a deep-learning algorithm trained on an ocean of information will discover connections between obscure features of the data that are so subtle or complex we humans cannot even describe them logically. When you combine hundreds or thousands of them together, they naturally outstrip the performance of even the most experienced humans. A.I. algorithms now beat humans in speech recognition, face recognition, the games of chess and Go, reading MRIs for certain cancers, and any quantitative field—whether it's deciding what loans to approve or detecting credit card fraud.

Such algorithms don't operate in a vacuum. To perform their analyses, they require huge sets of data to train on and vast computational power to process it all. Today's A.I. also functions only in clearly defined single domains. It's not capable of generalized intelligence or common sense—AlphaGo, for example, which beat the world's masters in the ancient game of Go, does not play chess; algorithms trained to determine loan underwriting, likewise, cannot do asset allocation.

With deep learning and the data explosion as catalysts, A.I. has moved from the era of discovery to the era of implementation. For now, at least, the center of gravity has shifted from elite research laboratories to real-world applications. In essence, deep learning and big data have boosted A.I. onto a new plateau. Companies and governments are now exploring that plateau, looking for ways to apply present artificial intelligence capabilities to their activities, to squeeze every last drop of productivity out of this groundbreaking technology (see our next story). This is why China, with its immense market, data, and tenacious entrepreneurs, has suddenly become an A.I. superpower.

What makes the technology more powerful still is that it can be applied to a nearly infinite number of domains. The closest parallel we've seen up until now may well be electricity. The current era of A.I. implementation can be compared with the era in which humans learned to apply electricity to all the tasks in their life: lighting a room, cooking food, powering a train, and so on. Likewise, today we're seeing the application of A.I. in everything from diagnosing cancer to the autonomous robots scurrying about in corporate warehouses.

FROM WEB-LINKED TO AUTONOMOUS

A.I. Applications can be categorized into four waves, which are happening simultaneously, but with different starting points and velocity:

The first stage is "Internet A.I." Powered by the huge amount of data flowing through the web, Internet A.I. leverages the fact that users automatically label data as we browse: buying vs. not buying, clicking vs. not clicking. These cascades of labeled data build a detailed profile of our personalities, habits, demands, and desires: the perfect recipe for more tailored content to keep us on a given platform, or to maximize revenue or profit.

The second wave is "business A.I." Here, algorithms can be trained on proprietary data sets ranging from customer purchases to machine maintenance records to complex business processes—and ultimately lead managers to improved decision-making. An algorithm, for example, might study many thousands of bank loans and repayment rates, and learn if one type of borrower is a hidden risk for default or, alternatively, a surprisingly good, but overlooked, lending prospect. Medical researchers, similarly, can use deep-learning algorithms to digest enormous quantities of data on patient diagnoses, genomic profiles, resultant therapies, and subsequent health outcomes and perhaps discover a worthy personalized treatment protocol that would have otherwise been missed. By scouting out hidden correlations that escape our linear cause-and-effect logic, business A.I. can outperform even the most veteran of experts.

The third wave of artificial intelligence—call it "perception A.I."— gets an upgrade with eyes, ears, and myriad other senses, collecting new data that was never before captured, and using it to create new applications. As sensors and smart devices proliferate through our homes and cities, we are on the verge of entering a trillion-sensor economy. This includes speech interfaces (from Alexa and Siri to future supersmart assistants that remember everything for you) as well as computer-vision applications—from face recognition to manufacturing quality inspection.

The fourth wave is the most monumental but also the most difficult: "autonomous A.I." Integrating all previous waves, autonomous A.I. gives machines the ability to sense and respond to the world around them, to move intuitively, and to manipulate objects as easily as a human can. Included in this wave are autonomous vehicles that can "see" the environment around them: recognizing patterns in the camera's pixels (red octagons, for instance); figuring out what they correlate to (stop signs); and then using that information to make decisions (applying pressure to the brake in order to slowly stop the vehicle). In the area of robotics, such advanced A.I. algorithms will be applied to industrial applications (automated assembly lines and warehouses), commercial tasks (dishwashing and fruit-harvesting robots), and eventually consumer ones too.

THE CHANGES YET TO COME

Because A.I. can be programmed to maximize profitability or replace human labor, it adds immediate value to the economy. A.I. is fast, accurate, works around-the-clock, doesn't complain, and can be applied to many tasks, with substantial economic benefit. How substantial? PwC estimates that the technology will contribute about $16 trillion to worldwide GDP by 2030 (Nelson, 2017).

But that gift doesn't come without challenges to humanity. The first and foremost is job displacement: Since A.I. can perform single tasks with superhuman accuracy—and most human jobs are single-task—it follows that many routine jobs will be replaced by this next-generation tech. That includes both white-collar and blue-collar jobs. A.I. also faces questions with security, privacy, data bias, and monopoly maintenance. All are significant issues with no known solution, so governments and corporations should start working on them now.

But one concern we don't have to face quite yet is the one that may be most common these days, cast in the image of science-fiction movies—that machines will achieve true human-level (or even superhuman-level) intelligence, making them capable presumably of threatening mankind.

We're nowhere near that. Today's A.I. isn't "general artificial intelligence" (the human kind, that is), but rather narrow—limited to a single domain. General A.I.

requires advanced capabilities like reasoning, conceptual learning, common sense, planning, cross-domain thinking, creativity, and even self-awareness and emotions, which remain beyond our reach. There are no known engineering paths to evolve toward the general capabilities above.

How far are we from general A.I.? I don't think we even know enough to estimate. We would need dozens of big breakthroughs to get there, when the field of A.I. has seen only one true breakthrough in 60 years. That said, narrow A.I. will bring about a technology revolution the magnitude of the Industrial Revolution or larger—and one that's happening much faster. It's incumbent upon us to understand its monumental impact, widespread benefits, and serious challenges.

This essay is adapted from Lee's new book, A.I. Superpowers: China, Silicon Valley, and the New World Order (Houghton Mifflin Harcourt). He is the chairman and CEO of Sinovation Ventures and the former president of GoogleChina.

This article originally appeared in the November 1, 2018 issue of Fortune.

HOW ARTIFICIAL INTELLIGENCE CAN HELP PUBLISHERS THRIVE

Just like any other modern industry, news publishing is gradually adopting automation powered by Artificial Intelligence (A.I.)—by its learning and language processing subfields, in particular. Struggling to monetize their content, publishers experiment with ad formats, diversifying revenue streams by introducing paid subscription, while striving to reduce production costs at the same time—and this is where the A.I. can do a trick.

The basic principle of A.I. lies in machine learning that allows computers to process vast amounts of data, and to learn from it without being specifically pre-programmed. First, machines have to rely on a set of rules in order to get sufficient knowledge of how a human would perform a particular task—and then the algorithm is set to go! Below are the most innovative ways of automating content production that are gaining momentum at the biggest news organizations right now:

- Automated reporting
- Reformatting of articles
- Text auto-tagging
- Content translation
- Content moderation
- Chat bots

- Content personalization
- Predictive analytics
- Image recognition and auto-tagging

Automated Reporting

If you're a news publisher, there's no need to hire journalists to cover tons of routine stories — an algorithm can do it for you for free with fewer errors and at better speed. The only requirement is to 'feed' a robot with clear structured data that can be parsed into 'variables'. Some bigger news agencies like Associated Press stepped into generating automated content as early as 2014. The news giant then started producing automated stories on corporate financial results using the Wordsmith platform by Automated Insights. As Philana Patterson, the Assistant Business Editor at A.P. said at that time, the automation of financial quarterly reports freed up to 20% of editors' time, so they could focus on other tasks.

By 2016, according to the report by Tow Center for Digital Journalism, leading publishers such as Forbes, ProPublica, The New York Times and Los Angeles Times also started to use A.I. for content production. However, the technology is still emerging and suited only for the topics where accuracy of data is more important than the quality of writing — i.e. financial reports or breaking news.

Reformatting of Articles

A.P. seem to be amongst the pioneers in this field as well. On average, their reporters used to re-write one article to fit several different channels—all manually. That's why back in 2016, their internal team, in collaboration with a media startup accelerator Matter Ventures, started a new project—development of software that could automate the re-production of a story for all channels, whether for print or broadcast. First, they built a template upon which text for print was transformed into several variations of a copy for digital by shortening the wordage, making sentences more concise and numbers rounded. After a while, a self-learning algorithm, guided by an editor, managed to gain sufficient knowledge to produce multiple versions of the same text autonomously.

Text Auto-Tagging

Creating a digital article, journalists normally have to either rely on the pre-programmed automated tagging available in CMS or add tags manually—the latter may end up as a total clutter. However, there are smarter alternatives such as "Editor," a self-learning interface for text editing implemented by The New York Times that automatically tags text and creates annotation based on information gathered through a set of neural networks.

Content Translation

Most international news outlets strive to win a broader audience across countries and languages—this is where translation and adaptation of the content becomes a challenge. Despite the fact that automated translation software and SaaS like Google Translate have been out there for years, the style of the language and poor localization rarely meets high journalistic standards of the most respected news organizations.

EurActiv.com, a multilingual policy news website, has been experimenting with the automated content translation since its inception, and last year they started using an AI-powered technology by the Latvian company Tilde to streamline their processes. The system analyzes tens of thousands of uploaded stories and their human-made translations to learn the language the site uses and aligns it with the official style guide.

Content Moderation

Evaluation and detection of spam, abusive or inappropriate content in the comment sections has been an issue tackled mostly manually by some bigger news media outlets. Before February 2017, NYT's staff moderators had to examine around 11,000 comments posted to 10% of their open articles daily. However, they have introduced a self-learning algorithm called Perspective that can weed out unreasonable comments on their website automatically. The tool developed by Jigsaw, a technology startup owned by Google's parent company Alphabet, reviews new content and compares it with thousands of comments reviewed and labeled as 'toxic' by human moderators and then scores them accordingly.

With automated AI-powered moderation, NYT is planning to allow 80% of their online content to be commented on by the end of the year. Perspective's API is also currently being used by a number of high-profile news media organizations and can be requested here: https://www.perspectiveapi.com.

Chat Bots

Since early 2016, when Facebook introduced its platform for creating AI-based chatbots for Messenger, news outlets have received another solid alternative for their content distribution — if used wisely. Based on the tool called Wit, publishers can build intelligent bots to automate and personalize interaction with the users. A bot learns a human language and responds to some basic queries like delivering the latest news on a specific topic. However, the adoption of Messenger bots by news outlets is not always smooth. Some have overwhelmed users with too many options or features that do not work correctly; while others dose information wisely so that it can substitute such channels as newsletters or app alerts and bring in even more readers (TechCrunch case).

Content Personalization

Even 5 years ago the possibility to deliver selected content to a specific reader exactly at the right moment—it would not sound realistic. Now an AI-backed personalization via email makes it possible. It works as simple as that: while a user interacts with a website's content, an intelligent algorithm learns one's behavior, defines preferences, and the pages and topics with the highest engagement rate—and compiles a list of the most relevant links to be sent out in a newsletter, exactly when the user is most likely to open and click through to read the content on the website.

According to Boomtrain, a San Francisco-based startup specializing in AI-powered marketing personalization solutions, an average open rate for static emails in the media and publishing industry is around 19.24%, the same metric for personalized emails—increases up to 63.22%; the click rates are 13.16% versus 26.29% accordingly. The data is available in the "The State of AI-powered email marketing report 2017," based on the research of nearly 235 million emails sent out by 65 companies, mainly from the news and publishing industry (Zeta Global, 2020).

Predictive Analytics

This sub-field of A.I. encompasses complex methods of current and historical data analysis required to make predictions on the future of readers' behavior. By automating data forecasts, publishers can shape their monetizing strategy in the most effective way. For example, The New York Times has had a successful experience of employing data science and machine learning to increase subscription-based revenue (Graefe, 2016).

According to their Chief Data Scientist Chris Wiggins, their internal team uses such tools as supervised, unsupervised and reinforcement learning to learn the 'genome' of loyal subscribers and better understand the funnel or reveal risks of cancelling individual subscriptions. Another way the machine learning can help publishers drive the subscriptions is to analyze which content is the most engaging and provide predictive insights to marketers who can promote the content most efficiently and with precise targeting. The API's built by NYT's data science team are open to the public and can be viewed here: https://open.nytimes.com/tagged/data-science.

Image Recognition and Auto-Tagging

Finding an optimal solution for the image storage that would allow faster and better file search is one of the challenges any publishing or a news organization faces inevitably. Another challenge is manual image tagging that involves hours of routine work and probability of a human error. On the other hand, if remain untagged, image archives are hard to navigate so that photo editors may have to re-purchase assets—which means even more waste of time and money for a news outlet. Furthermore, extensive image archives without meta-data lose their monetary value over time, mainly because a publishing company cannot monetize its original proprietary photo content.

Hopefully, this is where AI-powered digital assets management systems can help. Elvis DAM by WoodWing supports integration with APIs of the three biggest providers of the image-recognition algorithms: Google Vision, Amazon Image Rekognition and Clarifai. Each of these is self-taught to recognize physical objects (even such as faces and landmarks), distinguish their characteristics and add them as tags to the file's metadata — which saves time and effort on search and streamlines the process of content creation considerably. A big Swedish magazine publisher Aller Media and their Portuguese colleagues Porto Editora are currently testing the image-recognition functionality within Elvis DAM.

To learn more about how AI-backed DAM can streamline your content creation processes, visit our Elvis DAM page or sign up for our 30-minute free webinar on Sept. 26th: "How Artificial Intelligence brings value to your existing archives".

Summation

A.I. has been with us since the 60's and the possibilities for new applications are increasing at higher rate each year. New applications, new opportunities, new advancements will provide the scholarly publishing, research, academic, tech transfer, etc. with a bundle of new opportunities to advance science. These new opportunities will not happen in a vacuum but will require leadership, tenacity, funding and the guts to advance science. This book Advancing Scholarly Publishing with Blockchain Technologies and A.I. is a thought leader piece to stimulate and challenge the industry to do more and work to be better. Only time will tell how good our crystal ball about the impact of Blockchain and A.I.

REFERENCES

Bush, V. B. (1945, July 1). As We May Think. https://www.theatlantic.com/magazine/archive/1945/07/as-we-may-think/303881/

Diamandis, M. D. P. H. D. (2018, September 7). *The Four Waves of AI: Who will own the future of technology.* https://singularityhub.com/2018/09/07/the-4-waves-of-ai-and-why-china-has-an-edge/

Findlay, R. F. (2020, July 21). *Introducing the Leading Interactive Narrative NLG Platform.* https://www.businesswire.com/news/home/20200721005976/en/

GraefeA. G. (2016, January 7). *Guide to Automated Journalism.* https://www.cjr.org/tow_center_reports/guide_to_automated_journalism.php

IBM. (2020, June 1). *What is artificial intelligence?* https://www.ibm.com/cloud/learn/what-is-artificial-intelligence

Nelson, E. N. (2017, June 27). *AI will boost global GDP by nearly $16 trillion by 2030—with much of the gains in China.* https://qz.com/1015698/pwc-ai-could-increase-global-gdp-by-15-7-trillion-by-2030-with-much-of-the-gains-in-china/#:~:text=AI%20will%20boost%20global%20GDP,of%20the%20gains%20in%20China&text=North%20America%20can%20expect%20a,more%20ready%20to%20incorporate%20AI

Ossawa, E. O. (2018, October 23). *Four Waves of AI and What The Future Holds For It.* https://dzone.com/articles/four-waves-of-ai-and-what-the-future-holds-for-it

Peart, A. P. (2020, October 29). *Homage to John McCarthy, the Father of Artificial Intelligence (AI).* https://www.artificial-solutions.com/blog/homage-to-john-mccarthy-the-father-of-artificial-intelligence

Skinner, M. S. (2021, May 16). *Whatever Hasn't Been Done Yet: AI.* http://www.us-tech.com/RelId/2189332/ISvars/default/Whatever_Hasn_t_Been_Done_Yet_AI.htm

Stezano, W. S. (2018, September 12). *In 1950, Alan Turing Created a Chess Computer Program That Prefigured A.I.* https://www.history.com/news/in-1950-alan-turing-created-a-chess-computer-program-that-prefigured-a-i

Wikipedia. (2021, May 16). *AI Superpowers.* https://en.wikipedia.org/wiki/AI_Superpowers

Zeta Global. (2020, August 6). *The State of AI-Powered Email Marketing.* https://zetaglobal.com/blog/state-of-ai-powered-email-marketing/

KEY TERMS AND DEFINITIONS

A.I. Algorithm: A procedure for solving a mathematical problem (as of finding the greatest common divisor) in a finite number of steps that frequently involves repetition of an operation broadly: a step-by-step procedure for solving a problem or accomplishing some end.

Artificial General Intelligence: Artificial general intelligence is the hypothetical ability of an intelligent agent to understand or learn any intellectual task that a human being can. It is a primary goal of some artificial intelligence research and a common topic in science fiction and futures studies.

Artificial Intelligence: 1) A branch of computer science dealing with the simulation of intelligent behavior in computers; 2) the capability of a machine to imitate intelligent human behavior.

Artificial Narrow Intelligence: Artificial narrow intelligence (ANI or narrow AI) refers to a computer's ability to perform a single task extremely well, such as crawling a webpage or playing chess. Artificial general intelligence (AGI) is when a computer program can perform any intellectual task that a human could.

Artificial Neural Network: Artificial neural networks, usually simply called neural networks, are computing systems vaguely inspired by the biological neural networks that constitute animal brains. An ANN is based on a collection of connected units or nodes called artificial neurons, which loosely model the neurons in a biological brain.

Backpropagation: In machine learning, backpropagation is a widely used algorithm for training feedforward neural networks. Generalizations of backpropagation exist for other artificial neural networks, and for functions generally. These classes of algorithms are all referred to generically as "backpropagation."

Convolutional Neural Network: In deep learning, a convolutional neural network is a class of deep neural network, most commonly applied to analyze visual imagery.

Deep Learning: Deep learning is part of a broader family of machine learning methods based on artificial neural networks with representation learning. Learning can be supervised, semi-supervised or unsupervised.

Expert System: In artificial intelligence, an expert system is a computer system emulating the decision-making ability of a human expert. Expert systems are designed to solve complex problems by reasoning through bodies of knowledge, represented mainly as if–then rules rather than through conventional procedural code.

Forward Chaining: Forward chaining is one of the two main methods of reasoning when using an inference engine and can be described logically as repeated application of modus ponens. Forward chaining is a popular implementation strategy for expert systems, business, and production rule systems.

Generative Adversarial Networks: A generative adversarial network is a class of machine learning frameworks designed by Ian Goodfellow and his colleagues in 2014. Two neural networks contest with each other in a game. Given a training set, this technique learns to generate new data with the same statistics as the training set.

Heuristics: A heuristic technique, or a heuristic, is any approach to problem solving or self-discovery that employs a practical method that is not guaranteed to be optimal, perfect, or rational, but is nevertheless sufficient for reaching an immediate, short-term goal, or approximation.

Inductive Reasoning: Inductive reasoning is a method of reasoning in which the premises are viewed as supplying some evidence, but not full assurance, of the truth of the conclusion.

Machine Learning: Machine learning is the study of computer algorithms that improve automatically through experience and by the use of data. It is seen as a part of artificial intelligence.

Natural Language Processing: Natural language processing is a subfield of linguistics, computer science, and artificial intelligence concerned with the interactions between computers and human language, in particular how to program computers to process and analyze large amounts of natural language data.

Neural Network: Artificial neural networks, usually simply called neural networks, are computing systems vaguely inspired by the biological neural networks that constitute animal brains. An ANN is based on a collection of connected units or nodes called artificial neurons, which loosely model the neurons in a biological brain.

Reinforcement Learning: Reinforcement learning is an area of machine learning concerned with how intelligent agents ought to take actions in an environment in order to maximize the notion of cumulative reward. Reinforcement learning is one of three basic machine learning paradigms, alongside supervised learning, and unsupervised learning.

Strong AI: Strong artificial intelligence (AI) is a theoretical form of machine intelligence that is equal to human intelligence. Key characteristics of Strong AI include the ability to reason, solve puzzles, make judgments, plan, learn, and communicate. It should also have consciousness, objective thoughts, self-awareness, sentience, and sapience.

Turing Test: The Turing test, originally called the imitation game by Alan Turing in 1950, is a test of a machine's ability to exhibit intelligent behaviour equivalent to, or indistinguishable from, that of a human.

ENDNOTE

[1]   https://www.psychologytoday.com/us/basics/artificial-intelligence

Chapter 7
Best Business Practices for Incorporating Change

Peter J. Stockmann
Gamut Strategies, USA & Areopa Group International, USA

ABSTRACT

Organizational changes are made for business decisions that aim to improve performance and achieve short- and long-term strategic goals. The decisions to change are usually based on analysis of the organization, and success is evaluated by improving bottom-line performance. And many changes are unplanned. Despite all the preplanning, external factors can change or even divert the progress of the organization. Change is inevitable, and a good change management process can help ensure the potential for success.

INTRODUCTION

Change presents a challenge. In major transformations companies focus their attention on developing the best strategic and tactical plans. However, it is necessary to consider the human side of change management—the alignment of the company's (Intellectual Capital)—culture, values, people, and behaviors to encourage the desired results. Plans themselves do not capture value; value is realized only through the sustained, collective actions of employees who are responsible for designing, executing, and living with the changed environment.

If we were given a list of possible changes ahead that were positive in nature. Changes that would represent progress and improvement. It's likely that we would embrace all of them. But if the change requires us to change, we may find change harder to do. We don't really resist the change—we resist bring changed (Senge, 2018).

DOI: 10.4018/978-1-7998-5589-7.ch007

Understanding the Human side of change is critical for success. Leaders and employees need a clear understanding of what the change is, why the change is necessary, how it might affect them personally, and how they will benefit, either by better working conditions, higher wages, shares in the company, increasing of knowledge, etc.

Understanding some basic principles and the change process, will lead to success.

CHANGE METHODOLOGY

There are a significant number of change management methodologies (CIOpages. com, n.d.). The leaders in the industry include, Areopa, Lewin's Change Management Model, McKinsey 7-S Model, Kotter's Theory, La Marsh Global, Satir Change Management Model. They all have a set common and unique principles and processes. One of the beliefs in the most successful model states that the easier it is for employees to move along on the change journey, the easier it will be for the organization to move toward success.

No one methodology fits every company, but there is a set of principles, tools, and techniques that can be adapted to most situations. Listed below or some of the most critical guiding principles. Using these as a framework, executives and employees can understand what to expect, how to manage their own personal change, and how to engage the entire organization in the process.

Understanding Human Capital

- Whenever you share your vision and challenge people to achieve something greater, they will tend to fall into three groups. Typically, 25 percent of the people will support you, 50 percent of the people will remain uncommitted or uncertain, and 25 percent of the people will resist. On average 63% of leadership likes change while only 55% of employees like change (Murphy, 2016).
- Any significant transformation creates "people related issues." New leaders will be asked to step up, jobs will be changed, new skills and capabilities must be developed, and employees will be uncertain and resistant.
- Dealing with these issues on a reactive, case-by-case basis puts speed, morale, and results at risk. A formal approach for managing change — beginning with the leadership team and then engaging key stakeholders and leaders — should be developed early and adapted often as change moves through the organization. This demands as much data collection and analysis, planning,

and implementation discipline as does a redesign of strategy, systems, or processes.

- The change-management approach should be fully integrated into program design and decision making, both informing and enabling strategic direction. It should be based on a realistic assessment of the organization's history, readiness, and capacity to change.

- There are 5 phases when presenting a change to people.

  ○ **Phase 1**... The employees may be in a position of shock or denial. They may not be able to digest the fact that they have to undergo change and adapt to something new. They may need time to understand and adjust to the changes.

  ○ **Phase 2**... When the gravity of the situation settles in, and reality becomes clear, employees may begin to feel fear from what lies ahead, and this may turn into anger and resentment. They have been in a comfort zone for so long and knowing that they need to learn, change and adapt may make them uncomfortable.

  ○ **Phase 3**... When employees finally understand the change and realize how they must adapt to new situations and circumstances, they try to understand how they are going to benefit from the change ..... "What's in it for me".

  ○ **Phase 4**... Learning phase may not always be a very happy and comfortable zone for most employees of a workplace. This phase could result in lower productivity.

  ○ **Phase 5**... People begin to embrace the change, accept the situation and start building confidence. They realize and understand the importance of the change and move towards it.

  ○ This insight helps managers in understanding the position at which employees are as far as adapting to change is concerned. This can thus help in creating tailor made methods of communication, guidance and reward system for those on the path of change.

Speak to the Individual

- Change is both an institutional journey and a very personal one. People spend many hours each week at work; many think of their colleagues as a second family. Individuals (or teams of individuals) need to know how their work will change, what is expected of them during and after the change program, how they will be measured, and what success or failure will mean for them and those around them.

- Team leaders should be as honest and explicit as possible. People will react to what they see and hear around them and need to be involved in the change process. Highly visible rewards, such as promotion, recognition, and bonuses, should be provided as dramatic reinforcement for embracing change. Sanction or removal of people standing in the way of change will reinforce the institution's commitment.

- Most leaders contemplating change know that people matter. It is all too tempting, however, to dwell on the plans and processes, which don't talk back and don't respond emotionally, rather than face up to the more difficult and more critical human issues. But mastering the "soft" side of change management needn't be a mystery.

By-In and Support of the Leadership.

- Because change is inherently unsettling for people at all levels of an organization, when it is on the horizon, eyes will turn to the CEO and the leadership team for strength, support, direction and understanding.

- The leaders themselves must embrace the new changes first, both to challenge and to motivate the rest of the company. They must speak with a united voice and model the desired behaviors.

- The executive team also needs to understand that, it is composed of individuals who are going through stressful times and need to be supported.

- Executive teams that work well together are best positioned for success. They are aligned and committed to the direction of change, understand the culture and behaviors the changes intend to introduce, and can model those changes themselves.

Involvement of Everyone

- As transformation programs progress from defining strategy and setting targets to design and implementation, they affect different levels of the organization. Change efforts must include plans for identifying leaders throughout the company and pushing responsibility for design and implementation down, so that change "cascades" through the organization. At each layer of the organization, the leaders who are identified and trained must be aligned to the company's vision, equipped to execute their specific mission, and motivated to make change happen.

Make a Compelling Case

- Individuals are inherently rational and will question to what extent change is needed, whether the company is headed in the right direction, and whether they want to commit personally to making change happen. They will look to the leadership for answers. The articulation of a formal case for change and the creation of a written vision statement are invaluable opportunities to create or compel leadership-team alignment.
- Three steps should be followed in developing the case:
  - Step 1 ... confront reality and articulate a convincing need for change.
  - Step 2 ... demonstrate faith that the company has a viable future and the leadership to get there.
  - Finally, provide a road map to guide behavior and decision making. Leaders must then customize this message for various internal audiences, describing the pending change in terms that matter to the individuals.

Walk the "Talk"

- Leaders of large change programs must overperform during the transformation and be the zealots who create a critical mass among the work force in favor of change. This requires more than mere buy-in or passive agreement that the direction of change is acceptable. It demands ownership by leaders willing to accept responsibility for making change happen in all of the areas they influence or control. Ownership is often best created by involving people in identifying problems and crafting solutions. It is reinforced by incentives and rewards. These can be tangible (for example, financial compensation) or psychological (for example, camaraderie and a sense of shared destiny).

Communicate, Communicate, Communicate

- Too often, change leaders make the mistake of believing that others understand the issues, feel the need to change, and see the new direction as clearly as they do. The best change programs reinforce core messages through regular, timely advice that is both inspirational and practicable. Communications flow in from the bottom and out from the top and are targeted to provide employees the right information at the right time and to solicit their input and feedback. This requires overcommunication through multiple, redundant channels.

Understand the Cultural Landscape

- Successful change programs pick up speed and intensity as they cascade down, making it critically important that leaders understand and account for culture and behaviors at each level of the organization. Companies often make the mistake of assessing culture either too late or not at all. Thorough cultural diagnostics can assess organizational readiness to change, bring major problems to the surface, identify conflicts, and define factors that can recognize and influence sources of leadership and resistance. These diagnostics identify the core values, beliefs, behaviors, and perceptions that must be taken into account for successful change to occur. They serve as the common baseline for designing essential change elements, such as the new corporate vision, and building the infrastructure and programs needed to drive change.

Address Culture Explicitly

- Once the culture is understood, it should be addressed as thoroughly as any other area in a change program. Leaders should be explicit about the culture and underlying behaviors that will best support the new way of doing business and find opportunities to model and reward those behaviors. This requires developing a baseline, defining an explicit future-state or desired culture, and devising detailed plans to make the transition.
- Company culture (Intellectual Capital) is a mixture of shared history, explicit values and beliefs, and common attitudes and behaviors. Change programs involve creating a culture, combining cultures or reinforcing cultures. Understanding that all companies have a cultural knowledge center — the place of thought, activity, influence, or personal identification — is often an effective way to jump-start culture change.

Prepare for the Unexpected

- No change program goes completely according to plan. People react in unexpected ways; areas of anticipated resistance fall away; and the external environment shifts. Effectively managing change requires continual reassessment of its impact and the organization's willingness and ability to adopt the next wave of transformation. Fed by real data from the field and supported by information and solid decision-making processes, change leaders can then make the adjustments necessary to maintain momentum and drive result

THE FIVE STEPS IN THE CHANGE PROCESS (LA MARSH, 1998)

Change occurs as a process, not as an event. Now that we have framework of the change methodology, it time to look at the change process, a logical set of steps to insure successful implementation of change.

Stages the Change

- **The Current State** – The Current State is how things are done today. It is the collection of processes, behaviors, tools, technologies, organizational structures and job roles that constitute how work is done. The Current State defines who we are. It may not be working great, but it is familiar and comfortable because we know what to expect. The Current State is where we have been successful and where we know how we will be measured and evaluated. The Current State is known.
- **The Change State** –The Delta State is messy and disorganized. It is unpredictable and constantly in flux. The Delta State is often emotionally charged—with emotions ranging from despair and anxiety to anger, fear or relief. During this state, productivity predictably declines. The Delta State requires us to accept new perspectives and learn new ways of behaving, while still keeping up our day-to-day efforts. The Delta State is challenging.
- **The Desired State** –The Desired State is where we are trying to get to. It is often not fully defined and can actually shift while we are trudging through the Delta State. The Desired State is supposed to be better than the Current State in terms of performance. The Future State can often be worrisome. The Desired State is unknown.

Prepare for the Change

Key Roles (Must Be Well Defined)

- **Sponsors**—A sponsor is often viewed as the figurehead of a change management initiative. But, is figurehead the correct term? Particularly when a sponsor needs to play a very active role on the project? Project sponsorship means much more than the occasional speech or signature. For a project to truly achieve it's anticipated benefits, real change needs to be embedded within an organization, and this can only be achieved with a pro-active sponsor. Unfortunately, some sponsors make the mistake of not getting involved and remaining distant from the project team and the people affected by the change. Some of the key traits of successful sponsors include:

- ○ Be pro-active ….. "walk to talk"
- ○ Understand the "Human side" of the change
- ○ Develop and communicate the "Value Proposition" – to all employees. Explain the project objective, the timing and the expected outcomes
- ○ Make it clear that resistance will happen and will be addresses
- ○ Commit the resources that are required to understand and reduce or minimize the resistance.
- ○ Do the communicating – often and consistent
- ○ Provide the rewards and reinforcement

- **Change Agents:** A change agent is a person from inside or outside the organization who helps an organization transform itself by focusing on such matters as organizational effectiveness, improvement, and development. A change agent usually focuses his efforts on the effect of changing technologies, structures, and tasks on interpersonal and group relationships in the organization. The focus is on the people in the organization and their interactions. You should have four competencies (Business Jargons, 2016) to become an effective change agent:
  - ○ The focus is on the **Broad knowledge**: You must not only have broad industry knowledge but a broad range of multidisciplinary knowledge, including conceptual knowledge, diagnostic knowledge, evaluative knowledge, an understanding of methodology for change, and ethical knowledge.
  - ○ **Operational and relational knowledge**: You must be able to listen, trust, form relationships, observe, identify, and report. You must be flexible to deal with different types of relationships and behaviors.
  - ○ **Sensitivity and maturity**: You must not only be able to demonstrate sensitivity to others, but you must also be sensitive and mature enough to be aware of your own motivations.
  - ○ **Authenticity**: You must be authentic. You must act in accordance with the values you seek to promote in the organization. For example, if you recommend a form of management that permits subordinate participation, you should not attempt to impose these changes without the participation of the organizational members. In other words, you should practice what you preach.
- **Target:** Understanding who you want to target for change can be relatively simple or more difficult. There factors to consider are Culture, History and potential Resistance.

- Companies have to manage three targets of change and ask three questions to make change happen (Grochowski, 2017)
  - **Individual Change:** change has to capture something inside your soul/habits. Those people who directly experience the problem or are at risk; those people who contribute to the problem through their actions or lack of actions.
  - **Initiative Change:** making change happen on projects.
  - **Institutional Change:** how do we change culture/identity of the firm?
- Key Questions to Address at Each Level of Change:
  - **Why** should we change?
  - **What** should we change to?
  - **How** (e.g., how do you prioritize)?
- Execution occurs at three levels:
  - **Individual:** Do I have the ability to make sustainable change in my personal leadership behavior?
  - **Initiative:** Do we have the ability to accomplish projects or initiatives on time and within budget?
  - **Institution:** Do we have the ability to change our culture so that we have new patterns of how we work

Plan for the Change

Managing the Change

As you move to the planning stage it is important to understanding that this stage one of the keys to success. Doing your homework (information gathering and analysis) and using the various change management process models will keep you on the right path. Companies should establish designate a room(War room) to hold their change meeting. Use the walls to display to do list, timing charts, and other key items.

- **Create**
  - Current State Analysis
  - Desired State Design – What does success look like
  - Delta Dip Assessment – "J curve"
  - Key Role Map Assessment
  - Fishbone of Change Analysis
  - History Audit
  - Culture Audit
- **Populate:** Information Matrix -

- **Generate:**
    - Detailed Road Maps including:
        - To do lists
        - Critical path timeline
        - Meeting Schedule
    - Communication Plan: The content of an effective communications plan parallels or matches where employees are in the process of change. Early communication efforts should focus on explaining why the Current State is not working and must be changed. Communications later on in the change process can begin to focus on details and the eventual results the project or initiative is aiming to deliver. If the first communications to employees focus on the details, milestones and vision of the change, employees are left with unanswered questions that cloud their ability to process the details—namely "why?"
    - Learning & Development Plan: A training plan is a key component of a change management effort. Employees typically need new skills and competencies when adopting a change to their day-to-day work. But the training plan must be effectively sequenced based on where employees are in the change process. A training program that occurs right when employees learn about a change—when they are standing firmly in the Current State—will not be effective (this is an unfortunate reality in many cases, however, where the first response to a change is "send them to training"). Training should be delivered after employees have already started to move out of the Current State and into the Transition State.
    - Process performance measures – Dashboard.
    - Reward system
    - Present the results and plans to management
- **Governance Model**
    - Company
    - Steering Committee
    - Program Management Team
    - Change Management team
    - Communications, Learning and rewards
    - Projects

Implement the Change

- Road Maps
- Assignments
- Accountability

- Key Milestones

Sustaining and Reinforcement the Change

From a change management perspective, reinforcement can be difficult because once a change is finished, we are often moving straight onto the next change. It takes concerted effort and time to make sure a change "sticks," and given the scarce resources and change saturation that many organizations face, reinforcement efforts can often fall short. We see this scenario playing out in the data. A little more than half of organizations are planning for reinforcement and sustainment activities, but fewer than half are dedicating resources to this effort. The data is clear: organizations that are planning and resourcing for reinforcement are more likely to meet or exceed project objectives than organizations that neglect this critical step in the change process (Best Practices in Chain Management, 2014).

- Dashboard – Make it easy to track and monitor the results of change
- Metric – select the data to will indicate that change is successful
- Communication – Communicate, Communicate, Communicate
- Follow up – Establish and implement follow-up processes
- Be flexible and patient

CONCLUSION

The change process is not new. I have collected some of the best information from the leaders in the change methodology. Some of the key lessons learns are:

- Treat the changes you manage as a process, and not as a single event or series of events.
- Individuals experience change as a process. Evaluate and focus your change management activities based on where each individual are in the change process. One size does not fit all.
- No one experiences the change process the same. Understand what your employees what from the change. What is the reward that will motivate them?
- Your organizational change management efforts need to be tied to where you are in the change process.

People are change-weary, yet changes are often in response to a world that is changing even faster. If we want to continue to be ahead of the curve, becoming more effective and accelerating change will continue to offer a competitive advantage.

Following the 10 guiding principles and the 5-step change process will improve our chances of success.

REFERENCES

CIOPages.com. (n.d.). *Top ten change management models: What are change management models?* Retrieved from https://www.ciopages.com/change-management-models/

Grochowski, J. (2017, September 14). *Three targets of change to make organization transformation happen.* The RBL Group. Retrieved from https://www.rbl.net/insights/articles/organization-transformation-three-targets-of-change/

LaMarsh, J. (1998). *Change management.* Ford Motor Company.

Murphy, M. (2016, February 19). Do employees want to change? *Forbes Magazine.*

Chapter 8
Scholarly Publishing's IC in the Age of AI and Blockchain

Brad Meyer
Areopa Group International, UK

Santosh B. M.
Areopa Group International, India

ABSTRACT

In this chapter, the authors explore the potential for actors across the scholarly publishing industry to increase revenues while decreasing costs by using AI and blockchain to capture and leverage many of the intangible assets continually being generated across the industry. Where these assets bring more value than cost, they are referred to as intellectual capital. Areopa's 4-Leaf Model is used to examine how organisations serving the scholarly publishing industry can gain increased future economic benefit from identifying their intellectual capital and then capturing, storing, and making it re-usable.

INTELLECTUAL CAPITAL MATTERS IN SCHOLARLY PUBLISHING

Some departments in traditional organisations in the scholarly publishing industry cycle are downsizing. The downsizing "survivors" are finding their roles being re-examined and, in some case, re-defined. During such a process, it may become increasingly apparent that some knowledge which has been critical to the organisation's smooth running and prosperity has been lost. This lost information, knowledge, know-how, experience and expertise are the organisation's intangible assets.

DOI: 10.4018/978-1-7998-5589-7.ch008

Where those intangible assets added more value than cost, they can be considered Intellectual Capital (IC)(Coakes and Bradbrun, 2005). This IC, that was inherent within the organisation and then lost, was not valued enough when decisions were being made as to who stays and who goes. This is usually because the majority of the IC was mostly tacit, not explicit. In other words, it was residing only in the heads and personal notes of those "in the know", rather than those "on show".

Consider your specific operational niche within the scholarly publishing cycle. Think of someone near you who would leave, or has indeed left, an operational hole behind them, on their departure from the organisation. That hole needs tending to – preferably before the fact, but certainly after the fact. For example, every time you yourself tinker with a process that you are responsible for, every time you improve it so that it takes you or others less time or resources or it produces an improved quality and / or quantity of "output", it probably feels good to you - and the organisation benefits as well. This is obvious.

But what if you have not explicitly captured what you did so that others could learn from, understand and re-use it, to make things run even better? What if no one else could easily continue or re-use your approach because they do not know enough about it and cannot learn much about it in your absence? What if your ideas and actions were not recorded for re-use? What happens if you leave? This too, is obvious.

Two emerging technologies, Artificial Intelligence (AI) and Block Chain (Ruzza et al., 2020), offer new potential ways to identify, capture, secure, validate, make re-usable and monetise your Intellectual Capital and that of all your colleagues (Kamukama et al., 2010). The technologies involved can do this virtually automatically. Imagine everyone earning credit for the work done last year? Imagine still earning that credit after moving on to new things? Think of it as a potential for long-term micro royalties and recognition for work well done – not just for yourself, but for everyone operating in the scholarly publishing cycle.

This chapter introduces you to a few of Areopa's insights on Intellectual Capital matters and how you may be able to tap into and monetise your IC more effectively through the use of the emergent technologies of AI and Block Chain.

Let's take an example now from within the context of academic institutions. More specifically, let us look at the role of a researcher - the source and often a consumer of the content destined to be published....

THE INTELLECTUAL CAPITAL OF RESEARCHERS

Researchers have historically been hired by academic institutions for their continually increasing knowledge, know-how, experience and expertise and are expected to work on innovative and creative projects. With the continual decline in public funding for academic institutions across the globe however, the role of researchers engaged in scholarly activities has become more challenging than ever (American Academy of Arts and Sciences, n.d.).

Most academic institutions (especially, self-financing institutions and institutions that are only partially funded by the state) are struggling to generate enough revenue to remain operational (Yarime et al., 2012). Post globalisation, many institutions across the world have developed sources of revenue generation beyond the royalties earned from publishing. Some have created and tapped into an international student market by establishing campuses in other countries. But despite the intrigue to students that an international academic institution presents, competition in the academic market is heavily influenced by prestige. Researchers play a key role in helping their institutions establish, maintain and enhance this prestige. They achieve this predominantly by publishing scholarly works.

Publishing creates competitive advantage that attracts student enrolments. Publishing also serves as a means of revenue generation for the academic institutions, though it may not be a substantial revenue stream at the moment. Institutions often look to secure additional funding from industry and/or philanthropies. Regardless of the source of funding, to attract these sources, most researchers are compelled to "publish or perish", rather than simply pursue their genuine research goals with passion. And the publishing house protocols naturally narrow down their focus to "success stories" that sell. All of the "ancillary" IC generated along the journey to produce publishable findings is ignored and lost to everybody but the researchers themselves. Since publishable findings represent only a small fraction of that IC that can be tapped for re-use and monetisation, it's worth looking into how this might be accomplished.

Exploring and developing relationships with different funding sources is often considered the responsibility of the researchers themselves, though academic institutions regularly equip them with the required information on various research grants and non-monetary support and assistance. As researchers continually keep an eye out for funding sources, so that they can continue to pursue their innovative and creative projects, in some disciplines such as business management and STEM, they have become research-preneurs. But their focus tends to be on traditional, external sources. They have not yet looked closely enough into the value of their own IC to generate additional funding (Granting Guidelines for F5 Foundation, n.d.).

Whatever the changes in the researcher's role over the last three decades, the role is still considered incomplete without a publication of their scholarly output (e.g. refereed articles, books, book chapters, conference papers, recorded presentations). So, what if there was a way for researchers to publish more verifiable information and insights much more frequently?

At every phase of the research process, Intellectual Capital can be identified. Once identified, the key IC can be captured, stored and made re-usable by others. Once in a re-usable form, it can be capitalised on. Monetised, in fact. But first you have to be able to identify the IC.

Let us briefly look at the basic research phases through the lens of a light-touch Areopa (Figure 1).

Having taken the time to read through the above table, you will now know the first line of questioning to ask, to help you discover the IC that enables, informs and is created by each research phase. Answering these questions thoughtfully will have helped you identify the Intellectual Capital that is at-risk, e.g. when a researcher moves on. It will also help you identify the IC which could be used to generate additional revenue streams if it were captured, stored, made re-usable and then re-purposed with this in-mind.

Let us now look, albeit much more briefly, at the last phase in the research process, that is, producing scholarly publications. At every step in the scholarly publication process, there is an increasing amount of Intellectual Capital being generated. There are some twenty steps within this phase. We will choose just one to mention here; the peer-review step.

The peer-review process is dependent on the reviewers' combined knowledge, know-how, experience and expertise. Each reviewer applies their own IC to the review process. This helps form the foundation upon which the integrity and trust of an article's (indeed, the publisher's) potential for contributing to the growing body of knowledge in the world is established.

In some ways, this historical process foreshadows what Block Chain can contribute to the process going forward. But there is a problem. Block Chain can be costly and for the IC to add more value than cost, certain parameters must be met. Having said this, the current sustenance model of scholarly publishing has been challenged with the advent of the fourth industrial revolution, commonly referred to as Industry 4.0 (I-Scoop, n.d.).

While the traditional scholarly publishing payment model has entailed acquiring or sharing of the authors' Intellectual Property Rights, the future academic and commercial markets may disintermediate the publishers altogether by providing a more direct validation of and potential monetary value for the same material - and much more material as well. Today's Intellectual Property represents only a small proportion of the valuable Intellectual Capital that produced it. There is a customer market for far more of this knowledge than is currently made available by the traditional scholarly publishing cycle.

So, let's jump ahead in the cycle now. Let's step into the space of a customer of the researcher's works.

Figure 1. Intellectual capital assessment

8 RESEARCH PHASES & SOME OF AREOPA'S RELATED IC QUESTIONS TO ASK YOURSELF
01 - Drafting problem statement
What context(s), use(s), practice and experienced-borne efficiencies do the researchers apply to draft a problem statement? In other words, what knowledge, know-how, experience and expertise do they bring to the table to conduct this phase and how much of this will be lost when they move on (because it has not been captured, stored and made available for others to use effectively)? How much of this IC could be re-purposed for creating an additional revenue stream?
02 - Review literature and refine problem statement
What context(s), use(s), practice and experienced-borne efficiencies do the researchers apply when reviewing literature and refining the problem statement? In other words, what knowledge, know-how, experience and expertise do they bring to the table to conduct this phase and how much of this will be lost when they move on (because it has not been captured, stored and made available for others to use effectively)? How much of this IC could be re-purposed for creating an additional revenue stream?
03 - Choose appropriate research design and research method
What context(s), use(s), practice and experienced-borne efficiencies do the researchers apply when choosing an appropriate research design and method based on the literature review and refined problem statement? In other words, what knowledge, know-how, experience and expertise do they bring to the table to conduct this phase and how much of this will be lost when they move on (because it has not been captured, stored and made available for others to use effectively)? How much of this IC could be re-purposed for creating an additional revenue stream?
04 - Gather data
What context(s), use(s), practice and experienced-borne efficiencies do the researchers apply to gathering data using the chosen design and methodology? In other words, what knowledge, know-how, experience and expertise do they bring to the table to conduct this phase and how much of this will be lost when they move on (because it has not been captured, stored and made available for others to use effectively)? How much of this IC could be re-purposed for creating an additional revenue stream?
05 - Analyse data
What context(s), use(s), practice and experienced-borne efficiencies do the researchers apply when analysing the gathered data? In other words, what knowledge, know-how, experience and expertise do they bring to the table to conduct this phase and how much of this will be lost when they move on (because it has not been captured, stored and made available for others to use effectively)? How much of this IC could be re-purposed for creating an additional revenue stream?
06 - Discuss / interpret results
What context(s), use(s), practice and experienced-borne efficiencies do the researchers apply when discussing and interpreting the results of the data analysis? In other words, what knowledge, know-how, experience and expertise do they bring to the table to conduct this phase and how much of this will be lost when they move on (because it has not been captured, stored and made available for others to use effectively)? How much of this IC could be re-purposed for creating an additional revenue stream?
07 - Make conclusions
What context(s), use(s), practice and experienced-borne efficiencies do the researchers apply to arrive at conclusions borne out of the discussions and interpretations of the results? In other words, what knowledge, know-how, experience and expertise do they bring to the table to conduct this phase and how much of this will be lost when they move on (because it has not been captured, stored and made available for others to use effectively)? How much of this IC could be re-purposed for creating an additional revenue stream?
08 - Publish
What context(s), use(s), practice and experienced-borne efficiencies do the researchers apply when documenting and publishing the journey to their conclusion? In other words, what knowledge, know-how, experience and expertise do they bring to the table to conduct this phase and how much of this will be lost when they move on (because it has not been captured, stored and made available for others to use effectively)? How much of this IC could be re-purposed for creating an additional revenue stream?

Trusting What We Read

As frequent desk research consumers (customers) of others' research articles, the authors of this chapter do not always check the veracity of the referenced publications in the bibliography. We note if the article's author has quoted sources or not, but some of us do not always examine the referenced material in-detail. If an article is published by a journal that we are familiar with, we tend to trust that the references have been checked out and the content peer-reviewed. When the source publisher is new to us, then we have a question in the back of our minds as to whether the information presented in the article is true.

But even so, our trust in the article's content is most directly influenced by the formation of the words, sentences and paragraphs on the page. Are they readable? Do they flow, one from the other? Is the hierarchy of ideas being drawn upon presented well enough for us to understand implicitly, if not explicitly? Can we identify the lens through which the writer personally regards the world? Does the article lift us to new lofty heights as well as guide us out across the breadth of life and into the depths of detail? In other words, does our cognitive world expand as we are reading it? If it does, then we are appreciative of having found and read the article. And we will mentally note who the publisher was for future use and deliberately reference it in the future. We might even subscribe online for updates.

But if there appears to be luminous gaps in the writer's thinking and they are appallingly apparent in the article, then we stop reading and move on. And we mentally label the publisher as less worthy of our time as well. We create a stereotypic image by generalizing our experience of the one article into an expectation regarding other articles by the same publisher, without even thinking about it.

Admittedly, these questions represent the authors' personal trust criteria as end consumers / readers of research articles. If there is nothing remarkably "different" or unique highlighted to us early on in what we are reading, if the article follows scholarly protocols but fails to introduce or develop wonder or insight in us, we will probably drop it.

In our desk research on the current state of AI and Blockchain and how these technologies might be incredibly instrumental in the future value chain of publishing scholarly materials, we found some research articles that followed established academic publishing protocol and we found many that did not. We read some fifty articles in all, and came away from this with some impressions in relation to how the scholarly publishing industry might better leverage the value of its Intellectual Capital by using AI and Block Chain.

But first we need to share with you a few things about the lens through which we have read those articles.

Valuing What We Know

Have a look at the following diagram created within Areopa around 2007. It represents the model or lens through which we regard such articles as a whole (Figure 2).

Figure 2.

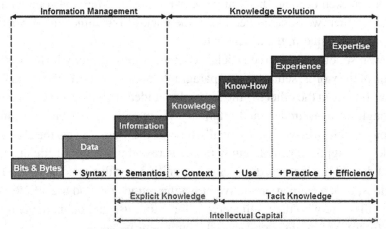

Knowledge Building Process & Intellectual Capital

Scholarly articles reference and form an evidence trail of some of the Intellectual Capital generated from academic research activities. Each article represents an attempt to provide additional explicit knowledge to the world. If the article is read, but not used, it fails to add to the reader's know-how. If it is used, but not repeatedly used in practice, then it may fail to add depth to the reader's experience base. If it is used repeatedly in practice, but no improvements on understanding the value of its content through its efficient re-use occur, then it cannot be regarded as overly instrumental in promoting our evolving expertise in life. In other words, a fuller value for the article and the Intellectual Capital that it represents has not been established or realised.

So, if when reading an article, we detect gaping contextual gaps, we will probably drop it. If we can appreciate the contexts in which it brings value and we read it but we still cannot use it ourselves, we will forget it. If we identify a context in which we can valuably use it one time, but in practice, such contexts are not overly or repeatedly relevant to us, then it will languish on our digital shelf after initial use. If it becomes a continually valuable point of reference for us, then our personal expertise evolves from this re-use. And our re-use of it promotes its value to others that we work with.

So…. how does this relate to the use of AI and / or Block Chain in publishing?

AI interventions already exist that can check each article's content in relation to its semantics, explicit context(s) and even implicit contexts. Consider the potential impact of introducing automatic semantic analysis into the publishing process. Where in your niche of the publishing process, might deploying this approach reduce your re-work costs? Where could it help increase your revenues?

Block Chain interventions already exist that can track each article's reference, indeed the use and re-use of each component within each article. The question is: Where in your niche of the publishing process, might deploying such an approach increase your potential revenue generation opportunities, while reducing your monitoring costs?

Indeed, what if there is there a way to increase the value of every subcomponent in this value chain, i.e. leveraging the value of the Intellectual Capital being generated in each niche within the publishing ecosystem?

Valuing What We Publish and How We Come to Being Able to Publish it

How do you value an intangible asset? If it adds more value than cost, then we can capitalise on it and consider it Intellectual Capital. And if you can identify it, secure it with a right to re-use it for creating future economic benefit, then you can actually put it on your company balance sheet. Check out International Account Standard 38 (IAS 38), if you want to know more. Or contact the authors of this chapter to learn how to take advantage of it.

We can look at the Intellectual Capital of any business or organisation through the lens of Areopa's 4-Leaf Model. Every organisation participating in the scholarly publishing value chain can benefit from looking at themselves through this lens.

The model was created more than a decade ago after a team of thirty people in Areopa conducted the following research;

- Read circa 600 IC-related books
- Studied (virtually) some 2,200 IC-focused projects
- Met with the then six 'gurus' of Intellectual Capital
- Visited (virtually) almost a million websites related to IC

An essential conclusion emerging from this project was that there are just four categories of IC worth considering from a business perspective. These four categories (Structural Capital, Human Capital, Strategic Alliance Capital and Customer Capital) are core to increasing revenues and decreasing costs. To determine the value of your organisation's IC, you need to examine these four categories - on their own and in all of their combinations.

Figure 3 illustrates the combinations.

Figure 3.

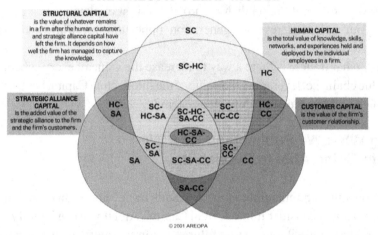

Is your publishing business on auto-pilot? Of course not. If everyone in the company went home and did not return to work, some aspects of your business would continue to exist and "operate", but how soon would it be before the revenue stopped? Your firm's *Structural Capital* is the non-physical or intangible technology, the written procedures and the processes that are "published" and used to streamline the parts of the publishing business value chain niche that you are in. It may be the most tangible of your intangible assets, but using it, realising its full value in profitability terms, is dependent on there being human beings who can and will re-use them in appropriate ways at the appropriate times. And "the times, they are a-changing".

The *Human Capital* required to leverage the inherent value of your Structural Capital is why you count on your colleagues returning to work in the morning. It is their tacit knowledge, know-how, experience and expertise (see the first model) that is needed to minimise costs and generate revenue in efficient ways. And it is their expertise that enables you to adapt your Structural Capital to what is appropriate in these changing times.

But we as human beings do not operate in isolation from each other. We have tacit and explicit networks, populated with other people from other firms in the publishing value chain and beyond. And these networks, these *Strategic Alliances*, help us keep abreast of the marketplace and to look into the future(s) to identify ways that we can influence it that are favourable to our business.

Through our capacity to understand the marketplace and the world in general, we not only identify and interact with our obvious customers but we have the potential to identify new customers as well. Our tacit and explicit *Customer Capital* does more than merely enhance the value of the other three dimensions of our intellectual Capital. It drives them. Or so it should.

SO, HOW ARE YOUR CUSTOMER EXPECTATIONS CHANGING, GIVEN THE ADVENT OF AI AND BLOCK CHAIN?

The current state of AI is in its infancy. But even in infancy, this baby can rock our world. It can change everything: how research is conducted, how the tacit and explicit insights gleaned from this research are captured, how these captured insights are organised and stored and later written about and how once written, they are made re-usable.

Here is a sampling of what others in the scholarly publishing business are already deploying AI to do for them in relation to capturing and leveraging their Intellectual Capital;

- Confirm that a manuscript meets specific requirements with regards to references and structure
- Confirm that its description of the research includes a minimum viable baseline data set, sample size, blind testing approach etc
- Rate the consistency of its reliance on and presentation of statistics
- Examine it for signs of probable plagiarism and other types of fraudulent behaviour
- Identify and automatically summarise the concepts it relies upon and presents
- Discover previously unidentified connections between different disciplines and concepts through automatically examining any number of previously published manuscripts

All of the above examples draw heavily on the tacit and explicit Intellectual Capital of current expertise in the field. This technology does not replace them, but it can significantly increase their work stream efficiencies; reducing the cost of re-work and freeing them up to focus on generating more revenue.

If others are already beginning to use AI technology to do these sorts of things, where else might such technology be used in your particular niche and what impact might this have on your bottom line?

The key is to look at every instance where information is handed over from one person to the next, one process to the next. To reach each hand-over point, there is a need for tacit and explicit knowledge to be expertly applied.

And this leads us nicely into the world of Block Chain.

HOW AI AND BLOCK CHAIN CAN LEVERAGE THE VALUE OF OUR INTELLECTUAL CAPITAL

Block Chains are designed to enable, validate, protect and reference hand-overs by all participants in the Block Chain. As this sentence is being typed, the word processor is automatically saving what is typed in the cloud. What if, in addition to saving and replacing this document, it kept adding new time-stamped versions to the cloud instead? Some word processors already do this. What if instead of merely adding new time-stamped versions, it could also submit each paragraph or section of multiple paragraphs to the scrutiny of an AI program to ensure they meet certain parameters? And then if they did, committed them in a time-stamped form to a closed community of fellow thinkers, writers and readers who could vet the works for authenticity, accuracy and originality? And then what if each well-formed and vetted paragraph were added to an un-mutable historical log of Intellectual Capital hand-over events? Take a moment to imagine what might be possible for you in such a publishing world.

SUMMARY

There is additional, measurable Intellectual Capital value to be gleaned from every step in the scholarly publishing process. This "comes as standard" when deploying an Intellectual Capital Accounting and Management system such as Areopa's ICARuS™ Framework. Deploying AI and Block Chain technologies to identify, extract, refine, validate, secure and monetise more of your IC assets could well make sense.

So why has this technology not been embraced by the scholarly publishing industry more widely than it has been so far? Perhaps it is the belief that the age-old protocols are still and will continue to be profitable and that messing with the food chain is a dangerous thing to do.

The problem with this is that as other industries embrace these technologies, their use of AI and Block Chain may naturally disintermediate the scholarly publishing industry into oblivion.

Here's an experiment you can try:

Imagine that you write down your explanation as to why you are not going to integrate your business processes with AI or Block Chain. And then imagine that you have let the appropriate AI software analyse your explanation and identify any logic faults, explicit and implicit contexts and implied assertions that it finds in your explanation. Does that stimulate your curiosity or slightly un-nerve you? If so, you might want to consider engaging further with the continuous research and development of AI and Block Chain and explore the potential for you to increase your revenues while decreasing your costs through leveraging your Intellectual Capital more effectively than you have ever done before.

This chapter has been produced through the combined efforts of Brad Meyer, Santosh B M and Ludo PYIS from Areopa Group International.

REFERENCES

American Academy of Arts and Sciences. (n.d.). *Section 1: Current Revenue Sources for Public Research Universities*. Retrieved May 3, 2021, from https://www.amacad.org/publication/public-research-universities-understanding-financial-model/section/2

Coakes, E., & Bradburn, A. (2005). What is the value of intellectual capital? *Knowledge Management Research and Practice, 3*(2), 60–68. doi:10.1057/palgrave.kmrp.8500050

Granting Guidelines for F5 Foundation 2020 STEM Education Grants for Non-U.S. Nonprofits. (n.d.). F5. https://www.f5.com/company/global-good/non-us-stem-grant

I-Sccop. (n.d.). *Industry 4.0: the fourth industrial revolution – guide to Industrie 4.0*. Retrieved May 3, 2021, from https://www.i-scoop.eu/industry-4-0/#:~:text=Industry%204.0%20is%20the%20current,called%20a%20%E2%80%9Csmart%20factory%E2%80%9D

Kamukama, N., Ahiauzu, A., & Ntayi, J. M. (2010). Intellectual capital and performance: Testing interaction effects. *Journal of Intellectual Capital, 11*(4), 554–574. doi:10.1108/14691931011085687

Ruzza, D., Dal Mas, F., Massaro, M., & Bagnoli, C. (2020). *18 The role of blockchain for intellectual capital enhancement and business model innovation.* Intellectual Capital in the Digital Economy.

Yarime, M., Trencher, G., Mino, T., Scholz, R. W., Olsson, L., Ness, B., Frantzeskaki, N., & Rotmans, J. (2012). Establishing sustainability science in higher education institutions: Towards an integration of academic development, institutionalization, and stakeholder collaborations. *Sustainability Science, 7*(S1), 101–113. doi:10.100711625-012-0157-5

ADDITIONAL READING

Cokins, G., & Shepherd, N. (2017). The Power of Intangibles. Retrieved from: https://sfmagazine.com/post-entry/may-2017-the-power-of-intangibles/

Global, E. Y. (2019). How blockchain can impact the intellectual property life cycle. Retrieved from: https://www.ey.com/en_uk/consulting/how-blockchain-can-impact-the-intellectual-property-life-cycle

Johnson, R., Watkinson, A., & Mabe, M. (2018). The STM Report. Retrieved from: https://www.stm-assoc.org/2018_10_04_STM_Report_2018.pdf

Lawlor, B. (2019). NFAIS Artificial Intelligence: Finding Its Place in Research, Discovery and Scholarly Publishing. Retrieved from: https://content.iospress.com/articles/information-services-and-use/isu190068

Martin, M. (2018). Reinvent scientific publishing with blockchain technology. Retrieved from: https://www.statnews.com/2018/12/21/reinvent-scientific-publishing-blockchain/

Tennent, D. J. (2017). European Parliament Petition on Elsevier and the Open Science Monitor – The future of scholarly publishing. Green Tea and Velociraptors. Retrieved from: http://fossilsandshit.com/european-parliament-petition-on-elsevier-and-the-open-science-monitor/

Upshall, M. (2019). Using AI to solve business problems in scholarly publishing. Retrieved from: https://insights.uksg.org/articles/10.1629/uksg.460/

Chapter 9

Amazon Blockchain Enabling Commercial and Governmental Applications:
Amazon Leveraging Blockchain for the Advancement of New Technologies

Stephen E. Arnold
ArnoldIT.com, USA

ABSTRACT

The COVID-19 pandemic created significant problems for everyone and every business, but a few enterprises thrived, and Amazon was at the top of the list. Through their AWS (Amazon Web Services), Amazon controls many companies' information flow and data of all sizes. But what the general public does not know is that Amazon has been working on several blockchain and AI initiatives for over a decade. This chapter will provide a detailed narrative about Amazon's activity, patents, databases, and services that will leverage blockchain technology. The many patents filed by Amazon will greatly benefit Amazon both now and in the future.

Much of what we build at AWS is based on listening to customers. It's critical to ask customers what they want, listen carefully to their answers, and figure out a plan to provide it thoughtfully and quickly (Speed matters in business!). No business could thrive without that kind of customer obsession. But it's also not enough. The biggest needle movers will be things that customers don't know to ask for. We must invent on their behalf. We have to tap into our own inner imagination about what's possible.— Amazon CEO Jeff Bezos, 2018

DOI: 10.4018/978-1-7998-5589-7.ch009

INTRODUCTION

Bahrain, Saudi Arabia, and United Arab Emirates are 7,000 miles from Amazon's headquarters in Seattle, Washington. The US eCommerce giant has invested in data centers, hired staff, and pursued commercial and governmental work in these countries. In 2017, Amazon announced it would open data centers for its Middle East Region in Bahrain and Edge Nodes in United Arab Emirates. Amazon's commitment to the Middle East parallels similar efforts from Google and Microsoft.

Amazon wants to provide cloud services to commercial enterprises like Emirates NBD, Dubai's largest lender by assets. The bank is one example of UAE's Smart Dubai project, but the government has an even bolder vision. In the next year or two, UAE wants half of its government's operations to make use of blockchain, a distributed ledger data management system. Saudi Arabia and UAE are exploring a cross-border financial service based on blockchain.

In the spring of 2019, Amazon hosted its AWS Summit Dubai, where one message was stated clearly: Amazon has the technologies to support blockchain and other cloud initiatives. [1] The financial payoff from blockchain is one incentive Amazon and other organizations understand. Estimates of the potential market size for blockchain vary widely. For example, ReportLinker predicts "the global blockchain technology market size is expected to reach USD 57,641.3 million by 2025, registering a compound annual growth rate of 69.4 percent from 2019 to 2025." (ReportLinker, 2019) A more surprising estimate was produced by Fior Markets (Fior Markets, 2019). This consultancy stated, "The global Blockchain market is expected to grow from USD 1.3 Billion in 2017 to USD 169.5 Billion by 2025 at a compound annual growth rate of 83.8% during the forecast period 2018-2025." [2] No one knows, of course, but the figures are indicative of interest even if overstated. For a company seeking new revenue from technology, blockchain emerges a technology to back.

Awareness of Amazon's blockchain capabilities remains low for several reasons. Amazon makes numerous product announcements, making it difficult for observers to determine which of Amazon's more than 80 product announcements in 2019 are likely to have the greatest impact on the company's future cloud business. Second, blockchain is one of many data management systems available. In Dubai at the 2019 Summit, Amazon said it offered fourteen different data management systems. Even Amazon certified professionals can have difficulty differentiating the company's database options. Lastly, Amazon does not provide easily-understood information. Instead the company talks to developers via its sprawling AWS informational Web site. This site is available at https://aws.amazon.com/. Amazon provides a wealth of information, but the specifics are expressed in AWS jargon, code snippets, and abstracts of technical talks like those given at the Dubai summit.

UAE and Dubai are important. For example, UAE and Saudi Arabia have explored a cross border digital currency transaction project (PWC, 2019). This type of project seems ideal for an online service which can provide secure transactions for traditional and digital currency transactions. Just as Dubai's skyline is dominated by Burj Khalifa, a skyscraper half a mile high, Amazon and UAE may be cooperating to make AWS blockchain technology an equally bold and visible landmark for the country. Instead of steel and concrete, UAE's blockchains will be constructed with distributed technology and next-generation inventions. These inventions can automate many activities related to transactions and provide the efficiencies which have made Amazon a leader in online services.

Amazon, Google, Microsoft, and other firms found themselves catching up to the technologies described in the 2008 essay, "Bitcoin: A Peer to Peer Electronic Cash System," allegedly written by a shadow figure using the name Satoshi Nakamoto. Bitcoin and its blockchain foundation became a subject of global interest[3] because the "cash system" created opportunities to bring efficiency to certain financial transactions.

Bezos predicted that "the biggest needle movers will be things that customers don't know to ask for." Blockchain appears to be one of those needle-movers. It's a prime candidate for information technology innovation, not just in the Middle East but in the United States and elsewhere.

Amazon's public announcements about blockchain date from March 2012 when Amazon filed a patent application with the title "Allocating Financial Risk and Reward in a Multi-Tenant Environment." The system and method disclosed the work of two Amazon employees (Gregory Branchek Roth of Seattle, Washington, and Eric Jason Brandwine of Haymarket, Virginia) (Roth, 2013).

Amazon's engineers revealed their research into Nakamoto's technology. Thus between 2008 and sometime before March 2012, Amazon decided blockchain warranted investment, resulting in US 8,719,131, awarded on May 6, 2014.

A comprehensive understanding of a patent requires engineering and legal analysis. For this essay, two points seem important about this invention. First, it directly references Bitcoin and is proof that Amazon directed resources to understand and disclose a novel way to adapt to digital currency used for transactions. Second, Amazon reacted within about 36 months of the Nakamoto white paper (Nakamoto, n.d.), slow by some standards but expeditiously for a $25 billion enterprise like Amazon in 2009. As Amazon revenue more than doubled by 2012, it had the resources to continue its research and development of its blockchain-related technologies. [4]

The table below summarizes selected Amazon blockchain inventions. The criteria used for this subset of Amazon's more than 5,000 patents were simple: These documents reference either Bitcoin or blockchain. Other Amazon patent documents imply blockchain functions, but these are omitted in this essay where the focus is narrowed to specific use cases; for example, law enforcement and intelligence applications, security services, and regulatory services.

Table 1. Selected Amazon blockchain patents

#	Patent Number	Title	Date Filed5	Comment
1	US 8719131 B1	Allocating financial risk and reward in a multi-tenant environment	Mar 29, 2012	Risk assessment in financial or other transactions; for example, digital currency financial systems or traditional securities
2	US 9418213 B1	Delegated permissions in a distributed electronic environment	Feb 6, 2013	Delegated permissions for Bitcoin
3	US 9466051 B1[6]	Funding access in a distributed electronic environment	Feb 6, 2013	Permission system for digital currency supported transactions
4	US 9947033	Streaming data marketplace	Sept 29, 2014	Buy, license, and interact with digital currency and blockchains
5	US 10263994 B2	Authorized delegation of permissions	Aug 3, 2015	Addition of a method to verify that a delegation of permissions is allowed
6	US 10095549 B1	Ownership transfer account service in a virtual computing environment	Sept 29, 2015	Workflow for ownership transfer within a blockchain data structure; for example, a Bitcoin transaction
7	US 2018 0096163 A1 (application)	Immutable cryptographically secured ledger-backed databases	Sept 30, 2016	XML and cryptography provide Amazon-proprietary "immutability" assurance
8	US 10296764 B1	Verifiable cryptographic ally secured ledgers for human resource systems	Nov 18, 2016	Use of blockchain for enterprise applications with workflow, hierarchical structure, logic, amd object tracking
9	US 10237249 B 2	Key revocation	Dec 23, 2016	Revocation data stored in a blockchain
10	US 10291408 B2	Generation of Merkle trees as proof of work	Dec 23, 2016	Use of trees in Amazon's security, access, and validation processes
11	US 10243939 B2	Key distribution in a distributed computing environment	Dec 23, 2016	Method and workflow for delegated key creation and use
12	US 2018 0183592 (application)	Public key rollup for tree signature scheme	Dec 23, 2016	System and method for creating signature authorities and the use of the keys by subordinate authorities.
13	US 10,129,034 B2	Signature delegation	Dec 23, 2016	System and method for the tree method which allows the root of the hash treee to function as the public key for the signature authority
14	US 2019 0026685 A1[7] (application)	Distributed ledger certification	July 19, 2017	Tracking an item but can apply to any entity, event, etc.

Reading the titles of these documents makes evident that Amazon has a system and method for accepting digital currency and managing financial transactions with blockchain services. In fact, the company has had the system and method needed to accept Bitcoin or other digital currencies for more than six years. Just because a patent document exists, Amazon will not automatically introduce a product or service built upon a particular invention. The patents summarized in Table 1: Selected Amazon Blockchain Patents represent significant time, engineering effort, and investment. A dozen or more patent documents reveal that Amazon is not taking a casual approach to blockchain and is intent on preserving a competitive advantage for Amazon Web Services.

Plus, Amazon, like other high-profile technology firms, can reverse direction, often abruptly. For example, Amazon made headlines in the New York Times when it announced that its big budget film "The Aeronauts" would play in IMAX theaters. Eight weeks after that announcement, Amazon reversed direction and killed the IMAX release of the film. The New York Times quoted an industry consultant who said:

On the film side, I still think they are figuring out what they want to be (Sperling, 2019).

Also, Amazon's mobile phone flopped and was terminated. Amazon Spark (a social network-like feature and app), Amazon Restaurants (fresh food delivery), Amazon Storywrite (a service to allow screenwriters to submit scripts to Amazon's video product unit), and Amazon Dash buttons (one click ordering of a single product like laundry detergent), among others fell victim to Amazon's winnowing process.

Amazon, like Facebook and Google, can abandon products and services with minimal financial impact. One must keep in mind that UAE's AWS blockchain work may fail or prove unprofitable. There is no guarantee Amazon's blockchain inventions have the solid support of Amazon's senior managers.

These inventions reveal Amazon's deep understanding of blockchain technology. The problems Amazon may have solved include:

- Access, permissions, verification, and trust in a blockchain-centric system embodying zero trust
- Providing commercial and government customers with tools to build analytic applications; for example, deanonymizing digital currency transactions
- Creating a "low code" system so that new features and solutions can be built, deployed, and managed in less time and for lower cost than developing software in a traditional way

- Delivering cryptographically secure components to help reduce data loss, unauthorized access, inability to track actions, and facilitate interaction among users, systems, and components.

Before looking at these inventions, some terminology must be defined to facilitate understanding of Amazon's blockchain services.

Analytics

Advanced mathematical procedures make it possible to "make sense of data." Among the numerical recipes useful for law enforcement and intelligence work are [a] clustering, that is, grouping of similar people, events, etc.; [b] link analysis, that is, techniques for evaluating relationships (connections) between nodes; and [c] machine learning, that is, identifying patterns and generating inferences, among other methods.[8]

AWS

This acronym for Amazon Web Services refers to the more than 180 functions that Amazon has gathered under the rubric Amazon Web Services. AWS is a cloud computing platform. The platform contains frameworks, systems, applications, databases, tools, and hardware. AWS ranks as one of the leading providers of cloud computing services. Developers and organizations use AWS as a utility; however, AWS offers numerous services and components. The architecture of AWS makes it comparatively easy to "snap in" needed capabilities; for example, virtual machines, analytic functions to generate social graphs, and similar sophisticated capabilities.

Blockchain

The phrase "Amazon blockchain" may be an unfamiliar one even to some AWS customers and users. Blockchain is a distributed ledger system. Both open source and proprietary blockchain software are available. Blockchains can eliminate expensive, time-consuming tasks in many important and widely-used services; for example, financial transactions, land title verification, and product component management. Properly implemented, blockchain technology can increase the efficiency of certain work processes.

Data Marketplace

This phrase means an online store which makes digital information available from a variety of sources. Examples include proprietary sources (content created by employees or contractors), third-party content (information objects created by publishers or by systems, such as public ledgers automatically generated by digital currency systems), and open source information or open source intelligence. An authorized and verified customer selects a data set or a portion of a data set and pays a license fee for access to the data. Online data marketplaces are offered by the Cambridge Information Group, FactSet, and Oracle Corp., among others.

Distributed Ledger

A network of independent computers (nodes) which record, share, and synchronize transactions in each node's electronic ledgers. There is no centralized database of transactions.

Hash Codes

A mathematical function that generates a code to represent an item of data. The storage space required for a hash code is significantly smaller in many cases than the data represented.[9]

Hyperledger Fabric

Hyperledger is a project which provides the framework, standards, guidelines and tools with which to construct open source blockchains and applications. AWS supports the Hyperledger Fabric blockchain framework that runs smart contracts called chaincode, which are written in Go. You can create a private network with Hyperledger Fabric, limiting the peers that can connect to and participate in the network.

Infrastructure

This term refers to AWS's physical and virtual servers, network devices, systems, solutions, functions, and software. The diagram below illustrates one way to conceptualize AWS:

Figure 1. Amazon AWS infrastructure: a multi-purpose computing platform

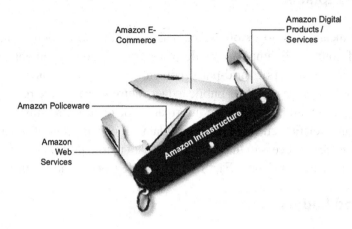

LERIS

An acronym used in this essay to refer to law enforcement, regulatory, intelligence, and security professionals. These individuals typically work for government agencies and enforce rules, regulations, and laws. In addition, some LERIS professionals perform offensive and defensive work designed to prevent cyber crime or other offenses.[10]

Managed Services

AWS Managed Services allow an organization to make use of software and functions; for example, a blockchain to manage person-centric information. These services can automate a range of tasks associated with the software; for example, updates, optimization, and security, among others. AWS Managed Services includes support coverage. The idea is that a managed services can reduces certain costs and change from traditional information technology methods to more modern, efficient approaches.

Multi-Tenant

A cloud or data center architecture set up so that one application serves multiple customers or "tenants."[11] Each tenant's data are separate from other tenant's information. However, the cloud or data center owner has administrative access to the software installations, settings, and other controls required to deliver the service.

Patent Fence

A cluster of patents designed to protect intellectual property or to block claims from other inventors that a particular invention has infringed on another patent.

Policeware

This term refers to Amazon's Public Sector products. Some of these are designed specifically for law enforcement and intelligence professionals. Amazon's activities in the government market have attracted attention from *Technology Review*, but the role of blockchain in the public sector is largely unfamiliar.[12] (Amazon's UAE work is an example of blockchain public sector activity.)

Real-Time

No computing system operates in real time; latency exists. The phrase "real-time" is understood to mean low-latency. Data captured by a surveillance device transfers the data to a network. The network moves the data to their destination. Once received by the destination, data can then be processed. Achieving low-latency data analysis is desirable for some applications. These data are stored and can then be used as historical or reference data.

Serverless Computing

The concept refers to a software design method in which applications are hosted by a cloud computing company like Amazon. The approach eliminates the need for server software and hardware management by the customer.

Smart Contract

The idea is that the terms of the contract are programmed and included in the agreement. The smart contract runs the code without any third-party involvement. The smart contracts are distributed in a distributed, decentralized blockchain.

Streaming

The term "streaming" refers to a flow of real-time data. Examples include real-time video streamed on Amazon's Twitch.tv service, surveillance data from video cameras such as Amazon's DeepLens and Ring products, and intercept data from

Web monitoring systems such as those available from specialist providers like Subsentio, LLC.[13]

Workflow

Tasks require a series of steps to complete. A workflow is a series of tasks orchestrated to achieve a desired outcome. In the context of blockchain, workflow embraces the automation of tasks related to the data in the blockchain as well as to the use of that data in other processes. Workflow in this context is programmatic and may be informed by software programmed to make decisions or by machine learning processes designed to allow workflows to alter some behaviors.

Zero Trust

An approach to security implementing systems and methods for strict identity verification for each user, device, and component requesting data, software, or resources even when coming from within an organization's security perimeter.

AWS BLOCKCHAIN SERVICES

Amazon describes its blockchain services on its Web site. The company, famous for its understatement and lack of transparency, states:

Amazon Managed Blockchain is a fully managed service that makes it easy to create and manage scalable blockchain networks using the popular open source frameworks Hyperledger Fabric and Ethereum*(https://aws.amazon.com/managed-blockchain/).

Note the asterisk. Support for Ethereum, a digital currency comparable to Bitcoin, is not yet available as part of the Amazon Web Services public-facing lineup of functions.

What is available in late 2019? Amazon states that its approach:

is a fully managed service that allows you to set up and manage a scalable blockchain network with just a few clicks. Amazon Managed Blockchain eliminates the overhead required to create the network, and automatically scales to meet the demands of thousands of applications running millions of transactions.

Taking this statement at face value, the AMB (Amazon Managed Blockchain) is just another service. Within AWS, a customer can use Amazon as a utility. The business benefit is that the customer does not have to invest in software, hardware, or specialized engineering to deal with scaling the blockchain service as demand grows.

A customer (established firm or startup) can get started with the Amazon Hyperledger Fabric framework at no cost.[14] If a customer's application requires "an immutable and verifiable ledger database," Amazon provides the Amazon QLDB (Amazon Quantum Ledger Database).[15] Amazon explains:

Amazon QLDB is a fully managed ledger database that provides a transparent, immutable, and cryptographically verifiable transaction log owned by a central trusted authority. Amazon QLDB tracks each and every application data change and maintains a complete and verifiable history of changes over time.

The mechanics for tapping into these functions is consistent with the procedures for the use of other Amazon services. Amazon is set up to allow developers to build a solution using widely supported methods. Amazon has made an effort to provide free training to developers, and the company offers support to educational institutions to "teach the Amazon way" to students. There are YouTube videos, conferences, and presentations in major cities like Washington, DC.

Amazon's explanations of its blockchain services are clear but dispassionate. The company provides no information about how the patented inventions enable the "managed" blockchain service. The trade journal *TechTarget* defined the concept this way:

AWS Managed Services is a set of services and tools that automate infrastructure management tasks for Amazon Web Services (AWS) deployments. The service is aimed at large enterprises that want a simplified way to migrate on-premises workloads to the public cloud and then manage those workloads after migration.[16]

Although simplistic, an AWS customer uses a complex system like blockchain which has been installed and will be maintained by Amazon. Details will vary by customer with service levels defined in the license agreement.

Two of the patents disclose systems and methods which can be understood as mechanisms to reduce risk and enhance the assurances that blockchain data have not been inappropriately modified.

Patent documents speak for themselves. However, the subsequent explorations into Amazon's possible application of these inventions require comments about a selected group of blockchain-related inventions.

The approach is to examine two important patents: One invention discloses Amazon's capability to provide "assurances" for the integrity of data, modifications, additions, and transactions. The second is the invention of a new type of online marketplace, which may be thought of as a variant of Amazon's eCommerce storefront for consumer goods, videos, and other offerings (like data storage for Ring video doorbell customers). The selected inventions provide information about the mechanics of the streaming online market and the assurance workflow system.

The approach is not intended to be exhaustive; rather it provides insight into Amazon's intense engineering for assured blockchain services. Also, Amazon's inventions reveal some information about the components and subsystems required to deploy a streaming data marketplace for what may be business-to-business or government agency-to-agency services. Finally, these enabling inventions provide a competitive advantage to make it more difficult for a competitor to implement similar functions at the risk of either violating or licensing Amazon technology.

Could these and other Amazon inventions be planks in a patent fence? Will Amazon be able to duplicate its success in the eCommerce retail market with the disclosed streaming data marketplace? These are relevant questions but difficult to answer.

AWS Secured Ledgers (US 10,296,764)

The company stated in October 2019:

AWS announced the general availability of Amazon Quantum Ledger Database (QLDB), a fully managed service that provides a high-performance, immutable, and cryptographically verifiable ledger for applications that need a central, trusted authority to provide a permanent and complete record of transactions across industries like retail, finance, manufacturing, insurance, and human resources. [17]

The statement does not mention the use of the system for government applications.

US 10,296,764 Verifiable Cryptographically Secured Ledgers for Human Resource Systems discloses a system and method for the use of blockchain-related operations in an enterprise application; specifically, human resources. Personnel matters are an important organizational concern. However, the patent uses human resource management as a convenient way to illustrate a number of important functions not present in most blockchain implementations.

Amazon's engineers have invented a system and method for a higher-level multi-ledger roll up index. US 10,296,764 Verifiable Cryptographically Secured Ledgers for Human Resource Systems discloses a novel system and method explained as an enterprise application. The reference of "human resource systems" is interesting, but personnel is just one way in which blockchain can be used to develop a dossier about an individual or other entity. Patent diagrams are a unique form of visual communication. Amazon's diagrams present minimal data to the reader. The text of the patent explains how encrypted information with certain data made available in a public or "human readable" form can combine data to answer such questions as:

- What is a person's history; for example, employment, arrest, or similar activity?
- How can access (reads and writes) to blockchains be managed, verified, and tracked? (The patent calls these "assurances.")
- When did a particular transaction take place and what other related actions took place at that time?
- How can a hierarchy of blockchains or other structures be implemented and then used in workflows?

The idea is simple—pull together data from disparate blockchains. But the engineering is complex and computationally intensive. The diagram below shows a simplified version of the AWS meta blockchain.

Figure 2. Amazon's blockchain metadata federation

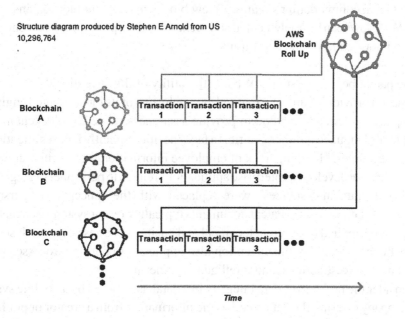

An organization may interact with multiple blockchains. However, obtaining information from blockchains serially using a "one at a time" approach is inefficient and resource intensive. One blockchain might contain digital currency transactions.

Another might track product component supply chain information. Others might create ledgers for business functions like personnel or legal matters. Amazon's meta blockchain provides a single point of access to these data. The invention allows a user or an application to access data from a federated index or ledger of ledgers. Such access can be automated via AWS workflows, infused with adaptive behavior via AWS machine learning, and secured via the AWS blockchain security inventions.

The engineering is complex, and Amazon's inventor (Andriy Batishehev) and Amazon's legal team have gone to great lengths to document the novelty of the invention. There are more than 180 patent documents cited. Other referenced publications range from standards documents to position papers on blockchain technology to Amazon's Snowball data storage appliance to smart shelves for grocery products.

The AWS blockchain meta technology provides three important capabilities to the blockchain infrastructure:

1.   AWS preserves cryptographically secured data while making the data available to authorized users and processes
2.   The system can maintain time-and-state consistency within the meta blockchain while accommodating streams of new blocks in different blockchains
3.   Workflows can be implemented and orchestrated via policy management, alerts and notifications, and audit trails.

The patent begs a question, "What is the utility of this invention?"

Amazon provides scant information about why two of its most talented engineers developed a system and method to provide assurances related to blockchain data. The patent's language is quite specific. In fact, the title explicitly focuses attention on "human resources." Keeping track of employee information is important; however, Amazon has not developed enterprise applications related to personnel management.

What if "human resources" were replaced with the concepts of "person of interest" or "data sources?" Patent documents typically present systems and methods which can be applied to different technical and business use cases. An analyst could reasonably conclude that this invention also applies to important processes in law enforcement, investigations, and intelligence gathering.

Consider the problem of data integrity in a database offered by an online system. The company offering the data receives the information from a creator or publisher. The online vendor does not typically check the data provided for accuracy. Updates are provided by the publisher, and the online information service makes those data available to its customers. For example, LexisNexis receives information from a provider. The data are loaded into the LexisNexis online service, and the customer accesses the data, assuming that it is accurate.

The system and method in US 10,296,764 makes it possible for data to flow into a blockchain. The data can be tracked and made available in a manner similar to the traditional model implemented by, for instance, the Oracle Data Marketplace (Oracle, n.d.).[18] However, when data are added, updated, or removed, a permanent record is created. Those modifications themselves can be tracked. The function is useful, but by itself, is little more than the use of blockchain to manage some type of content.

The invention discloses that a "meta" access point or node is made possible. Therefore, instead of dealing with individual blockchains, the data or the metadata about the blockchain data are federated; that is, there is a single point of access.

The federation complements the invention's disclosure related to assurances. The term appears in the patent document and functions as an umbrella. "Assurance" covers the hierarchies of blockchains, access controls related to blockchains, administrative housekeeping such as verifying purchase authority for data stored in blockchains, and blockchain content modifications.

To sum up, US 10,296,764 adds significant functionality to Amazon's blockchain capabilities. The invention appears, based on the language and diagrams in the patent document, to bring some computational efficiency to blockchain-based data. Furthermore, blockchain technology becomes a ready-to-use service which lowers barriers to the its implementation in enterprise applications or specialized services for law enforcement, regulatory, and intelligence operations. Also, the concept of "assurance" is more robust and subject to programmatic controls. Finally, inclusion in the AWS platform provides "smoothing" features; specifically, automatic scaling to meet usage demands.

The invention is novel, particularly the workflow, automation, and security framework. However, the invention requires an application such as personnel, a supply chain application, or a government agency application to manage tax data. For this essay's focus on law enforcement, intelligence, security, and regulation, an Amazon invention disclosed in another patent provides a specific application—the streaming data marketplace.

STREAMING DATA MARKETPLACE (US 9,947,033)

In November 2019, Amazon announced its AWS Data Exchange.[19] The reason, according to Stephen Orban, General Manager of AWS Data Exchange, was:

Customers have asked us for an easier way to find, subscribe to, and integrate diverse data sets into the applications, analytics, and machine-learning models they're running on AWS. Unfortunately, the way customers exchange data hasn't evolved much in the last 20 years. AWS Data Exchange gives our customers the ability to quickly integrate third-party data in the workloads they're migrating to the cloud, while giving qualified data providers a modern and secure way to package, deliver, and reach the millions of AWS customers worldwide.

The statement that existing online information services have not innovated makes clear that Amazon believes it is introducing a fresh approach to an established product and service.

Data marketplaces are not new, and they have provided an individual or organization with an online store from which data can be licensed. Examples include credit data available from Experian, Equifax, and Fair Isaac. Oracle offers its data marketplace which contains digital information from more than 100 sources. LexisNexis is an online service which provides lawyers and researchers with access to a wide range of data. New vendors like Kustomer and Sift offer advertising-tracking and user-behavior data.

Amazon's novel approach pivots on the word "streaming." Each of the services named typically provide access to information compiled and updated in a traditional way. The data creator updates the files available on the marketplace. There are services which combine historical data with real-time data. Examples include Bloomberg's terminal services and FactSet's data marketplace.

What sets the AWS Data Exchange apart?

Amazon's explanation of its novel approach to its streaming data marketplace includes a handful of Bitcoin, and by definition, blockchain-related references. This example indicates how the data marketplace could be valuable to investigators and government agencies:

Streaming analytics technologies hold the promise of making vast volumes of data available in a low latency fashion. However, while prior technologies may be able to provide data in a low latency fashion, the raw data may have low value (or have less value [sic] than the data could have) until the raw data is enhanced by correlating the raw data with additional data, such as by matching records using common values. In some examples, the useful additional data to correlate with the data stream may not exist in one place but rather may be held by many entities or owners. As the data from each of these entities is correlated and combined with the raw data, the data stream may become more valuable. <u>*One example is a data*</u> <u>*stream that publishes or includes global bitcoin transactions (or any crypto currency*</u> <u>*transaction).*</u> *These transactions are completely visible to each participant in the network. The raw transaction data may have little meaning to a customer unless the customer has a way to correlate various elements of the stream with other useful data.* <u>*For example, a group of electronic or internet retailers who accept bitcoin*</u> <u>*transactions may have a shipping address that may correlate with the bitcoin address.*</u>

The electronic retailers may combine the shipping address with the bitcoin transaction data to create correlated data and republish the combined data as a combined data stream. *A group of telecommunications providers may subscribe downstream to the combined data stream and be able to correlate the IP (Internet Protocol) addresses of the transactions to countries of origin. Government agencies may be able to subscribe downstream and correlate tax transaction data to help identify transaction participants. [Emphasis added]*[20]

Several observations are warranted:

First, this invention describes an online information marketplace which has as its primary focus online, real-time streaming data. The marketplace makes it possible for authorized individuals to locate, obtain, process, and pay for the content. In itself, the invention is not novel. However, Amazon has included capabilities that meet the needs of law enforcement; specifically:

For customers that wish to consume data, the customers may subscribe to the desired data stream and may optionally select desired enhancements that are not already included in the desired data stream. The desired enhancements may be correlative data from one or more additional sources that may be correlated to and combined with the data of the desired data stream. For example, a law enforcement agency may be a customer and may desire to receive global bitcoin transactions, correlated by country, with ISP data to determine source IP addresses and shipping addresses that correlate to bitcoin addresses. *The agency may not want additional available enhancements such as local bank data records. The streaming data marketplace may price this desired data out per GB (gigabyte), for example, and the agency can start running analytics on the desired data using the analysis module. [Emphasis added]*[21]

One use of the Bitcoin data is to facilitate deanonymization of encrypted financial transactions.

Second, the invention operates within AWS. Consequently developers, applications, and third-party software with appropriate authorizations can locate, obtain, and make sense of real-time data within the AWS platform. The streaming data marketplace invention creates a unique solution to deanonymization and possibly other analytic tasks required by law enforcement, regulatory authorities, investigative units of tax authorities, and intelligence agencies.

Third, the streaming data marketplace makes it possible for creators of data as well as users to exploit the "assurances" for security and data validity using blockchain operations. US 9,947,033 discloses:

When data is republished as a combined data stream, the republished data includes the correlated data from previous publishers in the chain. Depending on the configuration, a customer may not necessarily see or be aware of each of the upstream data publishers. Alternatively, a portion or an entirety of publishers or data sellers in the upstream chain may be displayed or available for display to the customer. A data seller may be enabled to choose whether to show the upstream data publishers to the customer. In some examples, customers may find value in visibility of the data sources to ensure validity or accuracy of the data, such as when the data sources are known and trusted by the customer. <u>In one example, each link in the chain may cryptographically sign the chain to make provable to the customer that the data is from the stated source and is not fraudulent.</u> [Emphasis added][22]

The invention also discloses that Amazon has developed additional tools and functions to support the streaming data marketplace. The data subsystem functions include dataset licensing (buying and selling), data federation, analytics, data correlation, link analysis, and reporting. The functions for developers and third parties include coding scripts, performing administrative functions including licensing, data management, generating social graphs (link analyses), and report services. APIs (application programming interfaces) make it possible to incorporate third-party services such as Palantir Technologies' applications, purpose-built applications such as those in use at government agencies, and new capabilities from individual developers, AWS certified partners, and innovative new companies.

One data provider is Thomson Reuters, whose global head of business development and strategy Alphonse Hardel observed:

Reuters curates and distributes over 2.2 million unique news stories per year in multiple languages. Reuters is constantly seeking new ways to broaden the reach of our independent, trusted and unbiased news content and data. We are excited to be among the first providers of such content on AWS Data Exchange, where our multi-language news data will be made available to a diverse range of AWS customers around the globe. With the increasing demand across industries to use news content to train and power their mission critical AI and analytics applications on the cloud, the depth and accuracy of Reuters coverage means AWS customers are now able to seamlessly access the highest quality of data from AWS Data Exchange.[23]

The streaming data marketplace appears to permit a much-needed service for LERIS applications: deanonymizing digital currency transactions. AWS blockchain technology distinguishes the Amazon service from other vendors competing in this market sector.[24]

DEANONYMIZING DIGITAL CURRENCY TRANSACTIONS

News stories like "Bitcoin Accounts for 95% of Cryptocurrency Crime, Says Analyst" indicate that obfuscated and encrypted transactions using digital currency is an issue for government authorities worldwide.[25]

A curious reader could ask "Is Amazon able to provide LERIS professionals a way to perform deanonymization on demand within a streaming data marketplace?" To answer this query, the patents themselves offer some clues; specifically, assurances in US 10,296,764 and a reference in US 9,947,033 to "global bitcoin transactions (or any crypto currency transaction)" analyses. Despite the lack of contextual explanation and specific use cases about analyzing crypto currency transactions, the inventions may support "deanonymization of digital currency transactions." Transactions in Bitcoin and other coins are perceived by some to be anonymous and secure. Deanonymization shines a light on dark transactions and reveals the identities of the parties to illegal transactions such as purchasing child pornography or selling unlicensed weapons. Deanonymization requires using available data, typically from a range of sources, to strip away anonymity.

The methods used by policeware vendors to deanonymize encrypted digital currency transactions are typically trade secrets or classified by government agencies. Nevertheless, a technical paper published by researchers in Qatar provides an explanation of a basic procedure known to deanonymize a high-percentage of digital currency transactions.

The mechanics of deanonymization of Bitcoin and other digital currencies relying on a public database of transactions are iterative; that is, an investigator using the Qatar method must repeat tasks and perform a manual inspection of the output. The approach used by some deanonymization experts was explained

in a 2017 ArXiv paper authored by researchers at Qatar University and the Qatar Computing Research Institute (Al Jawaheri et al., 2017). The main point of the paper is that small leaks can sink great ships; that is, by aggregating single items of data and analyzing these in the context of publicly-available Bitcoin data, it is possible to deanonymize buyers and sellers even in obfuscated environments like the Dark Web network provided by Tor (The Onion Router software bundle) or a similar system.[26]

The general procedure is illustrated in the diagram below, which has been developed from the information provided by the researchers in Qatar:

The Qatar team relied on open source software and publicly-available information; for example, archived tweets from Twitter. The procedure lacks the features of AWS; specifically, automation, machine learning, workflows, and other methods which facilitate real-time data analysis.

Figure 3. The principle steps in deanonymization of a bitcoin transaction

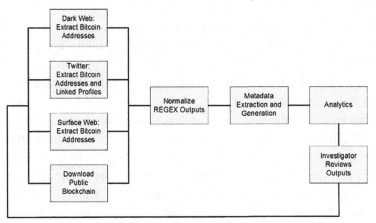

Flow diagram extracted by Stephen E Arnold from Al Jawheri, et al paper.

Based on the data available in the Amazon patents and in Amazon's AWS documentation, the Qatar approach could be implemented within the streaming data marketplace framework. If AWS deanonymization services were available, professionals at the US government Central Intelligence Agency or financial fraud investigators at Germany's Financial Intelligence Unit (FIU) could take advantage of workflow, automation, and machine intelligence as well as apply third-party solutions to deanonymization. Private companies offering deanonymization services could make use of the Streaming Data Marketplace to offer their solution on an industrial scale—unless Amazon decides to compete directly with the specialist firms supporting LERIS tasks. The deanonymization capability could give Amazon a strong grip on providing deanonymization services in the US and in other countries, for instance, Australia, Canada, New Zealand, and the United Kingdom.

Because the streaming data marketplace references law enforcement, the patent makes it possible for Amazon to create an electronic marketplace which can function as a hub for customers like government investigators, data creators or publishers, integrators like AWS certified partners, and established vendors of specialized tools like BAE NetReveal, Lockheed Martin, Northrop Grumman, and others. Should Amazon create a streaming data marketplace with digital currency and blockchain functions, the company could create:

- An efficient way to facilitate cross-agency and multi-vendor data access and federation, a capability not available at the time of this writing

- An online digital currency deanonymization service designed to work on a scale not offered by competitive specialized vendors at the time of this writing
- A platform that can pivot from streaming data to a service offering historical data adapted to meet the needs of other markets; for example, advertising and marketing, financial analysis and investment firms, and health care research, among others
- A potentially significant and new source of revenue for Amazon.

Are the Amazon Blockchain Patents Tactical?

In 2008, Jeff Bezos wrote in his Annual Letter:[27]

In this turbulent global economy, our fundamental approach remains the same. Stay heads down, focused on the long term and obsessed over customers. Long-term thinking levers our existing abilities and lets us do new things we couldn't otherwise contemplate. It supports the failure and iteration required for invention, and it frees us to pioneer in unexplored spaces. Seek instant gratification – or the elusive promise of it – and chances are you'll find a crowd there ahead of you. Long-term orientation interacts well with customer obsession. If we can identify a customer need and if we can further develop conviction that need is meaningful and durable, our approach permits us to work patiently for multiple years to deliver a solution. "Working backwards" from customer needs can be contrasted with a "skills-forward" approach where existing skills and competencies are used to drive business opportunities. The skills-forward approach says ... Working backwards from customer needs often demands that we acquire new competencies and exercise new muscles, never mind how uncomfortable and awkward-feeling those first steps might be. [Emphasis added] (2008 Letter to Shareholders, 2008)

Bezos' comments about innovation stress long-term thinking and iteration. Granted, there is no mention of Bitcoin or blockchain in this letter or subsequent annual letters.

Amazon's interest in blockchain-related technologies dates from the period before September 2012. "Inventing" is difficult to do within a certain amount of time; therefore, prior to September 2012 when Amazon filed Authorized Delegation of Permissions (US 10,263,994), work was required.[28] Amazon does not provide a timeline of its research and development activities. But it is possible to identify these milestones:

- January 2007, a former Central Intelligence Agency professional outlines a vision for analysis of large-scale data flows[29]

- October 2008, Satoshi Nakamoto publishes the Bitcoin paper which describes blockchain (Nakamoto, n.d.)
- September 2012, Amazon files its application for delegation of permissions, an important system and method but not connected to blockchain.

A Patent Fence or a Bold, New Initiative?

What were Amazon's intentions with regard to Bitcoin and blockchain between late 2008 and September 2012? One hypothesis is that Amazon began research and development of systems and methods to address certain enhancements to blockchain. These, if patents were granted, would provide Amazon with a competitive advantage. Due to the complexity of the blockchain patents reviewed in this document, it is reasonable to assume that Amazon invested 24 or more months in this endeavor before filing patent applications.[30]

From minimal public sector activity related to law enforcement and intelligence activities, Amazon moved slowly between 2008 and 2012, the date of the first filing. Between 2012 and 2016, Amazon built upon and extended the disclosure in US 10,263,994 to include blockchain. From the vantage point of 2019, Amazon accelerated its blockchain-related activity, disclosing inventions addressing notable shortcomings in the Nakamoto approach described in his 2008 white paper (Nakamoto, n.d.).

Key features include: [31]

- The linkage of security and permissions
- Delegation of permission use to a third party (either a user or a service)
- Workflow and profile functions
- Permanent record of permission activity
- Metadata generation; for example, user, time, and application, among other items.

However, the system and method disclosed can be viewed in different ways. For instance, these inventions describe systems designed to use blockchain technology. Alternatively, these and the patents discussed in the section which follows, put a "patent fence" in place; that is, these are defensive disclosures. Other viewpoints are possible. Amazon has not discussed these inventions in public, which creates ambiguity about the company's intentions. What Bezos has described as technical "iteration" is evident in these inventions. For example, multiple permission inventions—each of which overlaps to some degree the September 2012 filing and the subsequent AWS permission-centric patents—illustrate an interlocking of the blockchain inventions. Such interdependencies will be observed in the patents discussed in the next section.

ADDITIONAL AMAZON BLOCKCHAIN INVENTIONS

Now, consider this question: "What do the other Amazon blockchain-related patents contribute to AWS capabilities and functions?" A partial answer to this question can be found in the other patent documents listed in Table 1 "Selected Amazon Blockchain Patents." This section will discuss the patent documents not previously considered. [32]

In this way, a chronology of innovation can be documented because Amazon does not publicize its research and development activities. Actual products and services follow patent filings by months or years. Therefore, these public documents provide some, albeit limited, insight into Amazon's approach to innovation.

The Merkle Tree Inventions

Three Amazon inventions pivot on a data structure called Merkle trees. The Merkle tree is a patented procedure refined by Ralph Merkle in the 1970s and subsequently patented.[33] The method is part of Bitcoin and Ethereum blockchains. A Merkle tree is a structure that allows for efficient and secure verification of content in a large body of data. A discussion of the mathematics of the procedure is outside the scope of this essay.

The Amazon Merkle tree inventions are:

- Generation of Merkle trees as Proof of Work (US 10,291,408)
- Signature Delegation (US 10,129,034)
- Public Key Rollup for Tree Signature Scheme (US 20018 0183592).

Generation of Merkle Trees as Proof of Work (US 10,291,408)

Filed in June 2018, Generation of Merkle Trees as Proof of Work (US 10,291,408) discloses a system and method for generating a proof of work. A "proof of work" is a mathematical procedure required to generate an item of data, the computation of which is difficult and costly in terms of time and computing resources. The "proof" makes it more difficult for malicious actors trying to alter the ledger. The phrase gained currency with the emergence of blockchain and the process of "mining" to generate bitcoin.

This invention explains Amazon's use of Merkle trees in demonstrating proof of work. The method is referenced in Amazon's system and method for permission and access processes; when Merkle trees are referenced by Amazon, the application is related to blockchains.

The figure below from US 10,291,408 illustrates Amazon's depiction of a Merkle tree:

Figure 4. Merkle tree US 10,291,408

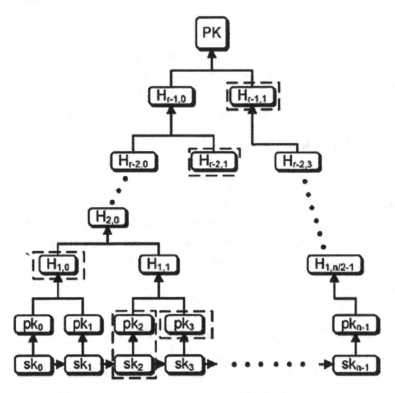

Each transaction is processed with a numerical procedure which, when given a key in the form of a string of letters and numbers, produces an address in a data table. A simple way to visualize how a Merkle tree key works is to visualize retrieving a physical book from a private-library's card catalog. Only some people can enter the library and some may not be permitted to use the cataloging system without an access code provided by the librarian.

A Merkle tree assembles all the transactions in a block, or collection of accession numbers, by producing a digital fingerprint of the complete set of transactions or entries in the data table.[34] A user or other system can verify if a specific transaction is included in a set of transactions by examining a single value. In terms of blockchain, trees are used in Bitcoin and Ethereum blockchains. The purpose of the Merkle tree method is to encode blockchain data efficiently and securely.

Amazon has disclosed a computer-implemented method for tracking and verifying access to a computer system. The system and method makes the Merkle tree one of the foundational elements of Amazon's managed blockchain service. The Merkle tree procedure provides one of the functions upon which AWS provides security, verification, and access for certain services; for example, the streaming data marketplace described in an Amazon patent discussed in a separate section of this essay.

What do these inventions enable? Combining the workflow technology and the streaming data marketplace makes it possible to deanonymize digital currency transactions. These two inventions alone make it possible for Amazon to control access to the streaming data marketplace for buyers, browsers, and sellers.

Signature Delegation (Us 10,129,034)

Filed in December 2016, Signature Delegation is a companion to Key Revocation (US 10,237,249). The problem Amazon inventors address relates to distributed computing; for example, different computing resources require permission (a signature from an authorized person or service) to perform an action.

The invention discloses a hierarchical tree with authorized signatures. The signatures can be verified, distributed, and tracked. These signatures are one-time use encrypted keys. The invention discloses a method to generate keys which can be used on demand.

How many keys are needed for a user or process? The invention references the use of predictive methods. Also, keys and the codes needed for revocation are generated when the hierarchical tree and keys are calculated, thus eliminating the need to calculate keys on demand. When a key is needed, the system verifies that the key is available and issues it to an authorized user or process.

The patent document reveals:

1. A complex procedure to help provide "assurance" that access controls are robust and efficient
2. Use of predictive procedures so that keys can be pre-generated and available when requested
3. A system and method which operates automatically within the AWS platform with functionality extended to other devices such as mobile phones as well as other cloud applications.

This invention and the key revocation disclosure may make it possible for AWS to operate as a virtualized security service. AWS could function on a meta-level; that is, above other security services as a way to obtain the highest possible overview of access permissions. In short, AWS may have the components to provide other systems with secure access keys, a function useful in some federated data tasks.

Public Key Rollup for Tree Signature Scheme (US 2018 0183592)

A patent application for this invention was filed in December 2013. This disclosure explains how an organization's signature authority delegates signing to other signature authorities. These signatures exist in a hierarchical structure so that signature authorities can cascade downwards, thus eliminating cumbersome linear processes needed to process a request, verification, and delegation. The invention references the use of the Merkle tree, and the inventors include references to other methods; for example, Lamport keys or Winternitz keys.[35]

The disclosure casts a wide net for the use of the signature scheme. The inventors identify a range of popular programming languages, representation formats like JSON and XML, content management systems, and support for a range of database systems. One of the more interesting inclusions in the patent is a "kitchen sink" of crytographic methods; namely:

One-way functions (also referred to as "effectively one-way functions") include, but are not limited to, cryptographic hash functions (Hash function, n.d.) such as message authentication codes, (e.g., hash based message authentication code (HMAC)), key derivation functions, such as PBKDF2 and bcrypt (with the password being based at least in part on the plaintext and the cryptographic key, e.g.) and other secure randomization functions which may, but do not necessarily, have a domain (set of possible inputs) that is larger than their range (possible outputs). Other suitable functions (referred to as "f") for various embodiments include, but are not limited to, functions that take at least a plaintext and cryptographic key as input and that have a property of preimage resistance (given a value y, the probability of randomly generating an input x such that f(x)=y is below a specified threshold), second preimage resistance (given an input x1, the probability of randomly generating another input x2, different from x1, such that f(x1)=f(x2) is below a specified threshold) and/or collision resistance (the probability of two different inputs resulting in the same output is less than a specified threshold). The exact threshold for each probability may be context-dependent, with lower probabilities corresponding to higher security contexts. A value can be cryptographically derived using a one-way function. An encryption function can be (or can be a component of) a one-way function from the perspective of an entity that lacks information (e.g., cryptographic key and/or salt) used as input into the encryption function. Hash functions usable as one-way functions in accordance with the techniques of the present disclosure include, but are not limited to, functions described in the National Institute of Standards and Technology (NIST) Special Publication 800-107, Revision 1 "Recommendation for Applications Using Approved Hash Algorithms," which is incorporated herein by reference.

Amazon in this disclosure seems to strive to make its rollup (federation) and hierarchical innovations more comprehensive than some other blockchain implementations.[36]

BLOCKCHAIN MECHANISM INVENTIONS

Amazon's blockchain inventions address certain omissions in the Nakamoto white paper (Nakamoto, n.d.). For the purposes of this essay, selected inventions have been grouped as "mechanisms." These perform a range of functions. The patents in this section of this essay are:

- Funding Access in a Distributed Electronic Environment (US 9,466,051)
- Delegated Permissions in a Distributed Electronic Environment (US 9,418,213)
- Ownership Transfer Account Service in a Virtual Computing Environment (US 10,095,549)
- Immutable Cryptographically Secured Ledger-Backed Databases (US 2018 0096163)
- Key Distribution in a Distributed Computing Environment (US 10,242,939)
- Key Revocation (US 10,237,249)
- Distributed Ledger Certification (US 2019 0026685).

Funding Access in a Distributed Electronic Environment (US 9,466,051)

A version of this invention was filed in March 2012 and as US 8,719,131 in May 2014. This essay summarizes the patent document filed in February 2013, Funding Access in a Distributed Electronic Environment, which implements a variation of the blockchain-based access and permission methods. The invention contains a particularly interesting discussion about buying and selling advertising, including the use of ads as a form of payment[37]. However, in the context of this essay, the disclosures about the mechanism for operating a real-time current account financial system complement the streaming data marketplace.

Key aspects of the invention include:

- Functionality for a real-time, secure accounting process in a multi-tenant, multi-cloud environment
- Use of the access and permission systems explained in other Amazon patent documents
- A novel way to "allow external entities (e.g., users, services, applications, etc.)" to make use of delegation profiles.[38]

The invention discloses the system and method for automating a comprehensive financial services system. Funds, digital or standard electronic, can be processed programmatically. Authorized individuals can use these funds to obtain content in a database offered by a commercial organization such as Dun & Bradstreet, a provider of commercial data about companies. A comprehensive backoffice financial system allows AWS to perform the same functions as a traditional broker dealer. The invention can be applied to more than a streaming data marketplace.

Perhaps the most interesting aspect of this invention is Amazon's inclusion of "profiles." These make it possible for users (humans or systems) to consult the obtained data in order to make real-time decisions about what to show a user, what other functions to initiate, and other actions designed to make the online interaction conform to rules or policies such as access, resources available, funds available to pay for access, and similar managerial and procedural choices. Rule sets can be defined for individuals, classes of individuals, and software processes.

Delegated Permissions in a Distributed Electronic Environment (US 9,418,213)

Filed in February 2013, Delegated Permissions in a Distributed Electronic Environment discloses Amazon's vision for allowing a user or process to have access to certain data; for example, information in a blockchain.

In a sense, this disclosure provides a wide-angle view of a novel access control method. Although blockchain implemented as in a digital currency like Bitcoin offers a measure of security, the approach is narrow; that is, one user, one wallet, one account. Users can set up separate wallets and create new metadata for currency in a wallet, but management can be challenging. Recovering from a catastrophic loss is difficult if not impossible.

Amazon invented a system which provides a management service so that a user or a machine process can delegate permissions. If Bitcoin is a reference model, a Bitcoin user cannot delegate permission to use the account. There are no management controls. Amazon's system addresses this deficiency, not just for a single user but for complex applications or constellations of interrelated processes.

Amazon's summary of the invention is straightforward, although the patent document alludes to other applications of the method:

Permissions can be delegated to enable access to resources associated with one or more different accounts, which might be associated with one or more different entities. Delegation profiles are established that are associated with at least one secured account of at least one customer. Each delegation profile includes information such as a name, a validation policy that specifies principals which may be external to the account and which are permitted to assume the delegation profile, and an authorization policy that indicates the permitted actions within the account for those principals which are acting within the delegation profile. Once a delegation profile is created, the profile can be available for external principals or services that provide a user credential delegated access under the account, where that credential is provided by a trusted identity service. Access can be provided across accounts using the user credential.[39]

One of the key ideas in the invention is that profiles become available to other "principals" or services. Amazon's inventors envision both a delegating system as well as a meta-service capable of interacting with other systems that require a credential to access data or a computer function.

Ownership Transfer Account Service in a Virtual Computing Environment (US 10,095,549)

Filed in September 2015, this invention discloses a system and method for transferring account ownership in a virtual computing environment. The notion of a virtual computing environment makes explicit that Amazon wants to implement serverless methods.

The invention allows policies to perform a number of functions on data; for example, requests, access to computing resources, and transactions related to digital currency.

The invention adds an operational layer to data—what the inventors call account transfers. The idea is that a workflow, based on policies or rules, automates activities performed when a financial or other type of transfer takes place.

Visualize a blockchain system operating for Bitcoin. The "ownership transfer" disclosure permits automation related to a specific activity. In the context of a streaming data marketplace, the invention allows an authorized user to request access, and the AWS system spins up necessary resources, adds metadata for auditing and tracking, and performs authorization processes. Once the request has been fulfilled, or a limit reached, the system and method terminates that access.

The patent document references Bitcoin and blockchain explicitly; however, the scope of the invention extends to other types of financial transactions as well as to novel use cases so that multiple owners of a resource can vote on whether to make a transaction possible.

Several points warrant comment:

1. Additional security operations are implemented to permit control, tracking, and audits of each action
2. The notion of voting can apply to machine resources. Instead of a hard-wired priority in an IBM AS/400-type server, the allocation of resource priority is dynamic.
3. The invention is broad, applying to blockchain as well as other types of transactions, including those in a modern financial trading system, a tax authority's workflow in audits, and policy-based workflows for exploiting resources in a virtualized data center.

Funding Access in a Distributed Electronic Environment (US 9,466,051)

Filed in February 2016, Funding Access in a Distributed Electronic Environment addresses the problem of selling or licensing data only when funds are available to pay the provider. The disclosure's system and method provides backoffice financial mechanisms for transactions.

The system and method makes use of Amazon's blockchain methods. Additional functions of this method include components which perform account activity tracking, debiting, and storing metadata related to the accounts and transactions in digital currency.

The disclosure includes other features of the invention; namely:

- Providing an advertising system
- Workflows to support transactions
- Decision making to determine which user or function will have access to the data on offer.

Immutable Cryptographically Secured Ledger-Backed Databases (US 2018 0096163)

Filed in September 2016, this patent describes a process that extends the AWS security techniques. The system and method disclosed follow the pattern of other assurance and permission inventions; that is, automation implements a workflow.

The actions in the workflow add security functions that are not present in the system described in the Nakamoto white paper (Nakamoto, n.d.).

The invention provides security for the ledger-backed databases deployed by Amazon. The idea is to create an unchangeable, encrypted ledger-based data management system, leveraging the Merkle tree and related methods disclosed in other patents. The system and method provide a major component of the technical infrastructure required to deploy workflow systems designed for large-scale operations. A large-scale operation could be providing infrastructure for a country's immigration and naturalization controls; for example, United Arab Emirates' passports, visas, and related information or the country's intelligence related to security (offensive and defensive actions).

The invention consists of nine functional components plus an interface to AWS. Each component is a "wrapper" or "meta-structure" adding new functionality to a ledger database (blockchain). Amazon's professionals have addressed three shortcomings in blockchain data management:

1. Controls. A mechanism to provide automated control via workflow to an information management system compatible with traditional databases and blockchain.
2. Security. The resulting data management system is cryptographically secured using the mechanisms disclosed in other Amazon blockchain-related patents; for example, access and permissions methods.
3. Automation. The disclosure explains that mechanisms for updating schemas and other components of the cryptographically secured ledger-backed databases can adapt; that is, intelligence is added to the data management system explained in the patent application.

The components disclosed in the patent's block diagram interact with traditional databases in established ways. Thus, reads and writes are possible. One way to conceptualize the invention is as a data management system which combines the blockchain's distributed structure with a non-blockchain database. The result is a hybrid data management system specifically equipped to be extensible. These are capabilities embraced by the "Other Services" block.

The benefit of this invention is that it may provide a developer, user, enterprise application, or some other entity with a best-of-both-worlds solution. Traditional databases are easily manipulated using widely known methods. Blockchain data management systems retain their decentralized structures. Within AWS, the two approaches become a new type of database system with enhanced security.

Figure 5. Function blocks US 2018 0096163

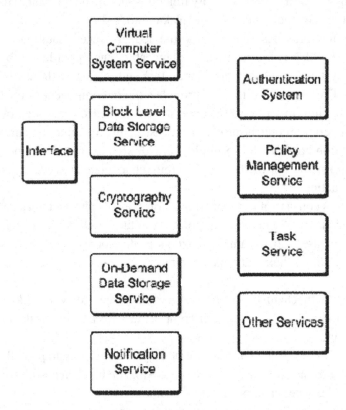

The downside of the application's system and method is that it is yet another system to learn. Developers have mastered traditional data management systems for structured, semi-structured, and unstructured data. Blockchain expertise is less widespread. Therefore, the AWS invention requires an investment in learning, testing, and downstream functions like understanding effective ways to use the invention's methods.

The application includes this statement:

... There is no intention to limit the invention to the specific form or forms disclosed, but on the contrary, the intention is to cover all modifications, alternative constructions, and equivalents falling with the spirit and scope of the invention as defined in the appended claims.

One way to interpret this statement is that Amazon has developed a next-generation information management system. The invention's system and method appears to be a meta-service capable of embracing any other data management system. The resulting system can be used as a multi-purpose data management system for users, developers, and other systems, including those residing on other cloud providers' systems.

Key Distribution in a Distributed Computing Environment (US 10,242,939)

Filed on December 23, 2016, this patent describes another component for the AWS access control service. The system and method disclosed relies upon the hierarchal keys generated by the AWS method explained in other blockchain-related disclosures. The patent references the same procedures disclosed in other Amazon inventions— Ownership Transfer Account Service in a Virtual Computing Environment (US 10,095,549), Key Revocation (US 10,237,249), and Signature Delegation (US 10,129,034), among others.

Points of interest in this patent include:

1. Amazon explicitly identifies other secure key operations as part of an access control system
2. The repetition of the language and the specific components of the system and method make it clear that Amazon is patenting modules of functionality, not rolling each invention into one umbrella patent
3. Amazon wants to make certain that its system and method is protected as a unique approach.

Key Revocation (US 10,237,249)

Filed in December 2016, the key revocation invention discloses a system and method for revoking one-time use keys for generating digital signatures. Such signatures verify instructions regarding transactions requiring approval.

The invention's approach is to implement a hierarchy via a mathematical procedure which allows secure verification of the contents of large data structures. Permissions withdrawals or assignments cascade. Once an authority issues a key, the recipient person or process can perform actions. If the authority attaches additional permissions to the recipient, that person or process can issue keys to other authorized individuals or functions.

The invention can operate within the AWS platform. The approach makes it possible for other implementations as well; for example, a public key component placed on a non-AWS system. The method implements a distribution service and verification service for the keys.

Points to note about this invention:

1. The invention permits creation, management, and revocation of one-time use keys for user or system actions
2. It includes a mechanism to verify or revoke a key in an efficient way via the hash tree method
3. The system allows AWS users and systems to place specific limits on data access for users or systems and adds fine-grained security controls to other AWS blockchain access procedures.

Distributed Ledger Certification (US 2019 0026685)

This recent patent application was filed in July 2017. Distributed Ledger Certification allows AWS to enhance or certify "trust" for a distributed ledger, particularly the initial step in adding data about a product, data file, or other object. The application addresses supply chains and bases trust on a sophisticated workflow system which reaches from the provider and details about the object to the transactions for an object. The document was published in January 2019, and discloses a system and method to authenticate distributed ledgers. Amazon explains the invention this way:

Features are disclosed for an interface for verifiable tracking of an item through a supply chain using a distributed electronic ledger. For example, when an item is added to a catalog system, the item information may be included in the creation element at the start of the ledger for the item. A certification authority may be included to verify that items received correspond to the item included in the catalog based on one or more certification rules. If a certification rule is satisfied, a record may be added to indicate transfer of the item from a provider to the catalog system. The certification information may be dynamically presented with item description information such as in response to searches of the catalog system.

The patent application reveals that AWS can identify ledgers that may not contain valid data. Ledgers which AWS identifies as valid can be used by AWS. The use of the word "catalog" applies to product listings, digital content, or any other object involved in a transaction.

The system and method make it possible for AWS to:

- Certify that a digital ledger is valid; that is, be identified with the equivalent of a "Good Housekeeping Seal of Approval" or a Department of Agriculture identifier for a grade of beef.
- Include "control elements." These can contain information about an object in the distributed ledger or add data to facilitate other operations; for example, policy implementation or pro-active processes.

- Include mechanisms to allow the system to operate in an automated way, making decisions based on "rules" or other "computer implemented method."[40]

The patent document includes more than 20 paragraphs, 0083 to 0105, of language explaining that the "scope" of the invention is not just products and supply chain applications. Indeed, it describes an A to Z approach to tracking tangible and intangible objects entered in a distributed ledger. One can envision a government agency managing its operations with a distributed ledger based on the technology of this invention.

One can argue that Amazon's blockchain inventions, taken as a group of related procedures, mark a turning point in cloud-based data management. The novelty of the Amazon approach, which has been in development almost since Nakamoto's white paper was published, can be summed up by comparing Amazon's data management system with a traditional database system (Nakamoto, n.d.). To make the table's data more concrete, substitute IBM DB2 or Oracle Database for the term "traditional."

Table 2. Traditional data management compared to Amazon's blockchain methods

	Traditional Online Data Vendor	**Amazon Streaming Data Marketplace**
1	Curated databases from commercial database producers, government agencies, and non-governmental organizations	AWS customers can list their data sets for customers in the way sellers of tangible products use Amazon's online store
2	Primarily static data with batch updates	Real-time streams of data
3	Codd architecture (rows and columns)	Codd, unstructured, and blockchain
4	Artificial intelligence not part of the Codd architecture	AWS includes artificial intelligence and workflows to automate standard database transactions in a cryptographically secured system
5	Provides a data utility with options to extend the database functions which can add streaming-related functionality	The Amazon inventions provide a platform and framework for real-time streaming applications and processes
6	Primarily a walled garden; for example, Oracle focuses on Oracle's database and tools	A framework and platform which can operate like a public cloud, a secure private cloud, or a multi-cloud integration system for real-time data management
7	Not engineered to handle streaming real-time data	A real-time streaming system in which binary large objects (blobs) are managed and analyzed by users or other systems
8	Rigid data schemas	Schemas can be updated as required either by an authorized user or service
9	Traditional security via access control lists, record locking, and similar functions	Blockchain-based security methods designed for automated and real-time activity

To sum up the inventions in this mechanisms section, Amazon has systematically addressed specific workflow-related activities. Each of these makes use of the methods disclosed in the tree disclousures. Mapping these inventions to the enterprise application described in Verifiable Crytopgraphically Secured Ledgers for Human Resource Systems and the Streaming Data Marketplace, Amazon has a quite specific vision of technologies required to provide components, procedures, and application support for traditional enterprise solutions as well as novel approaches to the licensing, accessing, and managing real-time streams of data using blockchain as a foundation.

Which of the inventions discussed in this document are the most important? At the time of this writing (November 2019), there are insufficient data to make a credible statement about these inventions. However, it is possible to draw some conclusions about the direction in which Amazon's technology is moving. In the next section of this essay, Amazon's likely journey is explored.

AMAZON'S FLYWHEEL AND MAGNETISM

Amazon's business strategy is described by Amazon as a "flywheel" or momentum (Collins, 2001). The idea is simple: Reinvest and take action. With success, the "flywheel" spins because each step forward accelerates sales, revenue, and customer base. A useful way to track some of Amazon's technologies is to monitor uploads to https://www.slideshare.net/AmazonWebServices

Flywheels can be used to generate magnetism. When electricity passes through a wire, the metal becomes magnetic and creates a magnetic field. Amazon has a similar property. The diagram below illustrates how Amazon's innovation and its services environment "pull" developers, customers, and partners into the AWS platform:

The combination of Amazon's managed blockchain products by itself generates customer interest. The firm's UAE blockchain products illustrate the appeal of AWS capabilities. The combination of the streaming data marketplace produces a stronger magnetic field. The "pull" exerted by AWS creates revenue opportunities for Amazon and at the same time offers benefits to AWS developers, partners, and customers. The effect works like this:

1. Attract developers and organizations who desire to use blockchain technology in a product or as an alternative to another data management system
2. Make it easy for a customer of AWS blockchain to tap into other Amazon offerings; for example, advanced analytics or additional datasets via the Streaming Data Marketplace

3. Build a new application or enterprise solution that provides a comparatively easy-to-use way to efficiently exploit advanced Amazon technology like machine learning and advanced analytics
4. Add next-generation functionality to an existing application or enterprise solution without having to deal with pre-cloud tasks. (This is particularly attractive for LERIS applications because Amazon's GovCloud provides a secure platform for sensitive and classified activity and information.)

Figure 6. AWS service magnetism: organic in-and-up tactic

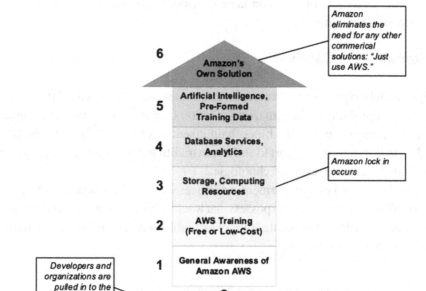

At each level of AWS activity, Amazon invests and makes available higher-level products and services. These include automated data lake functions and pre-built algorithms.

One example of a company "pulled" up and into Amazon is Monkton, a developer specializing in secure mobile applications. The company explored Amazon technology and embraced a number of the firm's services. The company implemented it Web log on AWS, pointing out that the cost was a few dollars per month. The company has continued to develop its expertise with AWS and expand its use of the AWS platform. The firm's mobile application solution is deployed within the Amazon GovCloud (https://monkton.io/).

In each of these representations of AWS services, Amazon tries to implement its "one-click" philosophy; that is, adding services should require a minimal effort.

There are downsides to AWS and its basic, advanced, and next-generation technical offerings. These include becoming dependent on AWS. The Amazon services are flawed in ways that only become evident once a system has been deployed to end users. And AWS next-generation technology may be vaporware or average technology gilded with marketing hyperbole.

The magnetic pull within the flywheel is not well understood by customners. Furthermore, observers of Amazon have overlooked the magnetic forces created by Amazon's momentum.

Blockchain as a Catalyst

A simple thought experiment makes it possible to consider what Amazon's blockchain innovations contribute to the Amazon invention of a streaming data marketplace. Obviously Amazon can use the blockchain inventions to assist the government of United Arab Emirates in its effort to shift from traditional data management systems to distributed and more secure technologies.

The inclusion of law enforcement references in the selected patents begs this question: What data does Amazon possess that would be of use to LERIS professionals?

The diagram below shows data sources available to Amazon for inclusion in the streaming data marketplace:

Figure 7. Selected content flows into AWS streaming data marketplace

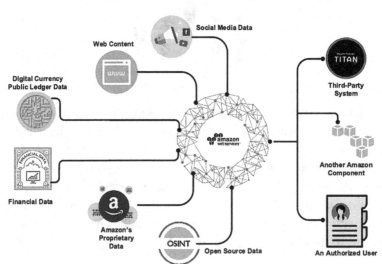

Putting each of these data streams into an Amazon blockchain system creates a solution at scale to several problems:

1. Federating disparate streams of data. The problem for LERIS professionals is obtaining related data at a single go. Pulling data from individual streams is inefficient.
2. Obtaining access to data which may contain information such as reuse of an email handle or a particular Internet Service Provider
3. Indexing or metatagging with date and time stamps, geo-location, category, and similar "tags" or identifiers
4. Proprietary data not available from other vendors.

The Amazon patents reveal that the technology for federating and analyzing data are in the AWS toolset. Indexing of content is also included. Plus, Amazon has proprietary data which are of interest to LERIS professionals. The diagram below shows some of the mechanisms which can feed real-time information into AWS for inclusion in the streaming data marketplace as well as other services offered by the company.

Figure 8. Selected Amazon proprietary data flows

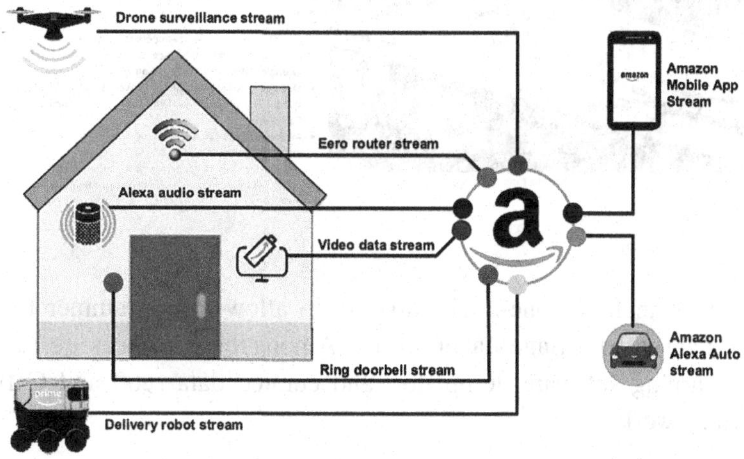

Amazon offers other products and services capable of capturing audio and video data.

One example has received considerable attention. In February 2018, Amazon paid about $1 billion for the company that developed the Ring video doorbell. Five years earlier, Ring had been rejected by the investors on the TV show "Shark Tank." The doorbell makes it possible for a person with the Ring application installed on a mobile phone to see who is at the door and engage in a conversation with that individual.

In mid-2019, information appeared in popular news services about Amazon's providing Ring data to US police departments. One news outlet published a map allegedly showing the more than 400 police departments using Ring data to address criminal activity (Leskin, 2019). The hardware-software system of which Ring is a component performs surveillance. One of the complaints about the Ring device is that its video imagery is poor. Amazon offers a more robust, developer-centric video camera shown below:

Figure 9. Amazon's surveillance device with support for AWS sagemaker

This device includes one-click software to allow a programmer to link the DeepLens' data with the SageMaker service. Among these services are TensorFlow (machine learning software, templates, and curated data sets) and Caffe (deep learning framework).

Amazon and Lego Blocks

Lego blocks are a toy which makes it possible for a young child to create structures by following Lego's directions or by snapping together the blocks and using Lego motors and gears to create using one's imagination. Much like Lego blocks, the Amazon blockchain inventions add additional functions and components to the more than 180 services available to AWS developers, partners, and, of course, the company's own engineering teams.

The diagram below provides a greatly simplified version of how blocks of Amazon functions can be assembled efficiently using Amazon's templates, modules, and features.

Figure 10. Simplified depiction of AWS service structure

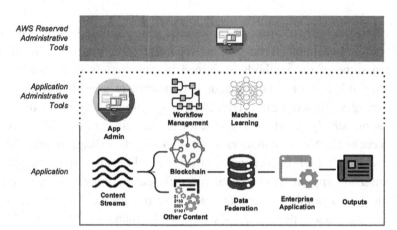

Several observations are warranted:

First, Amazon provides a way for applications for commercial customers and LERIS professionals to take advantage of new technologies like blockchain.

Second, the AWS platform includes machine learning capabilities which can be used to streamline traditional approaches to taking advantage of historical and streaming data.

Third, the workflow features with profiles for users and services, support for rules, and automation features make it possible to apply state-of-the-art systems and methods to tasks either too expensive to deploy or too difficult to implement using traditional software and technology. (The one-click patent, awarded in 1999, illustrates the company's vision for encapsulating multiple processes into software machines.) The one-click patent expired in 2017.

Amazon's momentum—the flywheel metaphor—pulls developers, partners, customers, and users to AWS. Like Amazon's blockchain inventions, this AWS magnetism is a topic that observers of the company have not considered. Therefore, the question "What's the Amazon strategy for its advanced technology?" deserves attention.

The implications of Amazon's streaming data marketplace, the blockchain inventions, and AWS's existing capabilities have the potential to contribute to a re-invention of how LERIS professionals enforce laws. The impact could be comparable to that of Amazon's eCommerce business and how people purchase products for themselves or their businesses.

A LOOK AHEAD

Even a cursory review of Amazon's blockchain inventions reveals systems and methods tailored to financial transactions. To be sure, the transaction mechanisms build upon some of the methods explained in Nakamoto's Bitcoin white paper (Nakamoto, n.d.). The context of Amazon's significant investment in understanding, deconstructing, and inventing novel solutions for distributed ledger data management is the slow but steady growth in demand for blockchain services. IBM Corp. and Microsoft each offer blockchain services. A quick search of Bing, Google, Qwant, or Yandex reveals hundreds of companies offering blockchain services and solutions.

But Amazon's approach to blockchain is different and may be a "unique selling proposition" for a number of markets. Because the patent documents reference deanonymization and other processes directly germane to the work of LERIS professionals, Amazon's AWS is polymorphic; that is, the system looks different depending upon one's point of view and context. Let's look at several examples relevant to LERIS.

A Developer

The devops—development and operations—professional or team decides to use the AWS platform and services. Amazon provides a range of services, many of which can be obtained, configured, and used quickly and easily. Therefore, Amazon is the modern equivalent of a workstation and server room located in the company's data center. The tools the devops team requires are available as open source and without cost. Amazon provides everything else: data management, machine learning, blockchain, high-value data streams, a marketplace, and so on. Amazon is a big, convenient, powerful computer.

A Partner

Amazon offers a partnership program for certified partners. The partner can generate business by advertising that they can advise, implement, maintain, or remediate Amazon applications. The partner sees Amazon as a source of revenue. The partner also assumes that the services provided are valuable to Amazon, filling a gap between the organizational AWS customer and specific needs the customer has. Amazon is not perceived as a competitor; Amazon wants partners to help keep customers satisfied. Partners see Amazon as a business generator.

A Third-Party Software Vendor

A third-party software vendor—for example, Palantir Technologies— uses AWS to deliver some of its services. Amazon is a utility which hosts software developed by a commercial firm. In the case of Palantir Technologies, some of its customers perform Palantir processes on AWS.[41] The expectation is that third-party vendors load code, configure workflows, and provide services to clients of the third-party company. To make this more specific, Palantir Technologies licenses Gotham (an information management and analysis system) to a US government agency. Some of the Gotham functions run on AWS; others may run on secure computers located elsewhere. Palantir Technologies pays Amazon. Palantir bills its customer, the government agency. In this example, third-party software vendors see Amazon as a cloud-based service provider.

An Amazon Customer

Amazon hosts conferences. These conferences explain to the attendees how AWS functions can be used to speed the deployment of services to employees. Furthermore, the AWS approach does not require purchasing additional hardware. AWS scales automatically, additional computing resources are automatically allocated, and advanced services like blockchain are available. Minimal setup and coding are required. The direct Amazon customer sees AWS as an alternative to traditional proprietary software. AWS supports what appears to be mainstream open source technologies; for example, blockchain and Lucene for search and retrieval, among others. Amazon direct customers see AWS as a new paradigm for computing, providing a way to break the shackles of proprietary database systems like Oracle and create needed applications quickly and more economically than the traditional approaches permitted.

These four views are different. The perceptions of Amazon and AWS vary, but they share some common assumptions: Amazon Web Services are:

- Is a neutral utility
- Supports fast, efficient application development
- Is a cloud utility
- Offers next-generation services

- Creates new revenue opportunities for partners.

The information about Amazon's patents presented in this essay provides some insight into AWS technical capabilities. The streaming data marketplace has been a touchstone invention because it is novel. As described in the patent, the streaming data marketplace requires a range of AWS services; for example:

- Managed blockchain services to enable government agencies and third parties to provide data, license it, receive compensation, and have access to reports providing transaction details
- Workflow services to automate information intake, tagging, and other processes such as cross correlation, report output, and security control
- Integration with next-generation AWS services, including machine learning
- Administration of a real-time marketplace in which real-time classified and proprietary data are controlled with regard to permissions
- Financial systems to accept spendable funds, debit funds, and maintain secure records of financial and other transactions
- Reports about transactions, persons of interest, entities of interest, and analyses to permit identification of the parties engaged in a transaction, summaries for auditing purposes, and similar types of information presentation
- AWS administration tools to allow Amazon employees to maintain the infrastructure required to deliver client-built, third-party applications, and other services required by customers, vendors, and developers of marketplace objects.

One answer to the question, "What's the Amazon strategy for its advanced technology?" is that Amazon wants to serve a number of market segments with its blockchain services.

The goal, however, is to generate revenue. On the surface, the business model is straight forward. An engineer assembles or builds applications and pays for AWS services such as storage and compute resources. Partners may pay Amazon for certification. Amazon derives revenues from partner customers who pay the Amazon partner, which in turn buys services from AWS either at list price or a discounted price. The third-party software vendor pays Amazon to use AWS resources to deliver its software's functionality to a customer of the third-party software vendor. The Amazon customer—for example, the US Central Intelligence Agency—pays Amazon for the firm's technical services and other provisions of the Statement of Work for a specified period of time.

No surprises in any of these sources of revenue for Amazon.

Other revenue options exist. One approach is for Amazon to make AWS a separate company which provides services to the Amazon eCommerce unit serving consumers. Amazon can retain an ownership stake in the separate company and then pay the new company to use the AWS infrastructure. Other options exist, but the spin out and options are outside the scope of this essay.[42]

One alternative that is within the scope of this essay is to consider a private brand option.

Amazon Private Brand for LERIS Markets

At the time of this writing, Amazon presents to the public a fragmented series of products and services for LERIS professionals. For the purposes of making Amazon's innovations drive a new business, the Streaming Data Marketplace functions like Amazon's consumer eCommerce business; that is, Amazon's online store has enabled a number of new services. These range from the delivery of digital audio and video to online grocery shopping. The consumer success of Amazon makes the Amazon Prime subscription service attractive for the online shopper and lucrative for the company. Amazon has ventured into private brands. These brands are available along with established brands and third-party merchant products. Vendors of these products find that Amazon's activities have harmed third-party sales (Dzieza, 2018).

A consumer can choose, for instance, a golf shirt offered by Ralph Lauren (an established brand), a third-party merchant (Three Sixty Six), or Amazon Essentials (a house brand). Each is substantially the same. The variable is price. Ralph Lauren golf shirts cost three to four times as much as an Amazon Essentials golf shirt. Third-party merchant golf shirts fall in the middle. The use of house brands is common in the grocery industry.

This is an important question to consider: "What if Amazon offers a house brand for products and services like those available from Monkton (a developer of secure mobile applications), Palantir Technologies (one of the world's leading providers of investigative software), or Webhose.io (an Israel-based company in the business of aggregating Dark Web and other special content for LERIS applications)?

The answer is that Amazon's policeware and intelware offerings become attractive to government agencies under budget pressure with an interest in finding ways to reduce traditional software costs. The arrow figure in the section of this essay labeled "Amazon's Flywheel and Magnetism" illustrates that customers like some government agencies may implement AWS services that are further up the Amazon stack; for example, data sets to train machine learning for an application. The entry point is learning about Amazon and using its free or low-cost services. The next level up is making use of AWS basic services like S3 for storage and EC2 for compute-cycle scaling. AWS advanced services are often little more than one-click away; for example, workflow services and more specialized database systems such as Amazon Aurora, the DynamoDB system, or Amazon ElastiCache, among others. When a customer requires "more," Amazon's engineers provides numerous advanced capabilities; for example, the managed blockchain services, solution templates, and advanced analytics.

It makes good business sense for Amazon to monitor the uptake of its services and what the AWS users are consuming. These data are captured in log files which can be analyzed in real time and compared with historical data. The information can then be processed using AWS' analytical tools.

Does it not seem reasonable that Amazon would introduce its own house brand of products and services tailored to the needs of the LERIS markets?

At this point, in Amazon's consumer facing online store, Amazon has followed this exact path with golf shirts. Amazon's technology and its business tactics make it clear that Amazon can become a provider of house brand services that deliver the same or greater functionality than the products offered by third-parties like Palantir, Monkton, Webhose.io or any of the hundreds of other specialist vendors using AWS to serve the LERIS markets.

The end game is to replicate the success of the consumer facing Amazon online marketplace in the streaming data marketplace.

Why would Amazon push to become a direct competitor with the companies which have been good AWS customers? The facile answer is that investors want to see growth, and taking over a "partner's" marketshare helps provide that.

There is no one answer to the question about why some patents have not been productized, but several possible tactical ideas can be identified by considering the inventions referenced in this essay and Amazon's business trajectory for its consumer facing storefront business.

First, Amazon has developed a system which introduces new and patentable technology which some competitors may find difficult to replicate or fund workarounds for the Amazon patent fence, particularly in managed blockchain services. Competitors may come close, but Amazon's technology is in place and in use. Amazon has first-mover advantages.

Second, government agencies are under budget pressure. Therefore, Amazon is well positioned to offer the equivalent of a comparable or better service at a lower price. Attractive prices coupled with services, extensibility, and technical capabilities can pull some customers to Amazon's own LERIS products and services. If a customer chooses to remain a customer of a third party like Palantir Technologies, Amazon continues to be paid by Palantir for AWS services. At some point, Palantir may shift from the Amazon AWS cloud to another cloud provider, but that may require time and an investment which Palantir may not wish to make as it deals with its financial backers and stakeholders.

Third, Amazon can raise prices to third-party customers. Increasing the cost for AWS services makes the house brand more appealing and may put financial pressure on specialist firms working on narrow margins under government fixed price contracts or budget-conscious LERIS entities. Local police departments seek low-cost investigative solutions. Amazon can raise prices, and third-party vendors have to pass along those costs. Amazon's Ring-centric services can be priced low or offered without charge in order to tempt LERIS professionals into the AWS platform and generate additional revenue from stressed local police agencies. Also, Amazon may gradually raise prices or add services. The pricing pressure will drive some third-party vendors and possibly some Amazon certified partners away from Amazon. From Amazon's point of view, the house brand generates revenue and low prices help retain LERIS customers.

Fourth, Amazon introduces a function-for-function alternative to full-service LERIS products. This means that specialist providers like Verint, a publicly-traded company with a global customer base, face serious competition. Amazon competes directly with Verint and seeks to capture existing Verint customers and win new contracts.

Amazon could be positioning itself to become a dominant player in LERIS markets among the Five Eyes' member countries, US-allied countries, and in some European Union member countries. The revenue potential of the streaming data marketplace warrants an analysis outside the scope of this essay.

Another consequence of the house-brand option can be identified. Should Amazon create house brands and capture customers and some third-party vendors remain on the AWS platform despite Amazon's competitive actions, customers are locked in. The cost of moving off AWS is too great, despite the business threat posed by Amazon's house brands of LERIS products and services. Government agencies lack the resources to shift from AWS to a competitive platform; for instance, Google's or IBM's cloud.

What results is a 21st-century version of IBM lock in. For decades, IBM offered hardware to government agencies. That hardware worked best and often most economically with IBM software. The implementation of the systems, including upgrades, required IBM engineers and service personnel. IBM set up a certified partner network to provide a range of integration, service, and programming support to IBM customers. IBM became the preferred solution for enterprise computing. Unfortunately for IBM, its business model from the 1960s is not working today. IBM has not been able to replicate its lock-in strategy in the distributed computing technology space.

Amazon has an opportunity to achieve lock in by modifying IBM's strategy for today's world; specifically, AWS offers:

- Services and features that combine basic computing functions with next-generation technology
- Software that eliminates many of the costly, time-consuming hurdles traditional development requires; for example, figuring out how to implement blockchain, its workflows, and enhanced security procedures
- Pricing that can be tailored to meet the specific budget requirements of the customer
- Pre-packaged modules, profiles, and data sets designed to allow fast-ramp machine learning for new and existing applications
- Streaming online data, some of which is unobtainable from any other source; for example, AWS drone surveillance videos of persons of interest involved in money laundering. The money laundering was discovered using AWS digital currency deanonymizing services.

At the beginning of this essay, it was mentioned that United Arab Emirates wants to use blockchain for its government's data management. Think of putting half of the data available to a government in blockchain. Those data can then be analyzed, managed, and understood in a way not easily replicated by traditional data management systems. To be sure, one can build a robust system using IBM's, Microsoft's, or Oracle's technology. But Amazon delivers the capabilities in the form of Lego blocks. If the AWS system satisfies UAE, how easy will it be for a competitor to displace AWS? How valuable will an engineer with AWS savvy be? What is the value of AWS to a country like the UAE?

The answer to this question is hundreds of millions of dollars, maybe more, for Amazon.

This essay has introduced one facet of Amazon's technical capabilities. Blockchain inventions have been explained in terms of creating an alternative to traditional ways of managing information. Blockchain enables the buying and selling of streaming data. Blockchain, however, is just one Amazon service.

Figure 11. Amazon's strategy for customer lock in

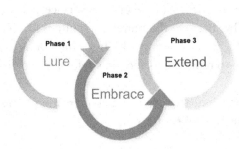

It may be useful to recall that Jeff Bezos spent some of his early career working on Wall Street. He said clearly that Amazon thinks for the long term. The "long term" he mentioned in 1998 is arriving.

Amazon's managed blockchain services will appeal to technology-forward organizations; for example, the government of United Arab Emirates. Those with less technological sophistication will embrace the IBM precept from the 1960s: Proprietary is better, safer, and possibly more familiar. For AWS customers, partners, and users, the cloud platform offers an interesting resource for developers of policeware:

- Innovators can use the AWS platform to create new solutions to problems LERIS professionals face
- Next-generation application builders can build solutions using next-generation technologies to complement existing products or solutions that tap tecnologies simply not affordable under these organizations' conventional methods
- Users—that is, LERIS agencies, whether a local police department or a government's treasury department—can use tools available from a service like the streaming data marketplace.

Amazon can come to dominate LERIS markets in the US and elsewhere. Amazon could emerge as the IBM of policeware and intelware in a few years, but the same model can be applied to the financial sector, health care, transportation, and other business sectors.

Cloud vendors like Amazon generate the bulk of their revenues by renting metered services such as storage, compute cycles, and streaming data. Infrastructure and application workloads have become commodities. Amazon must provide a high-value differentiated service like artificial intelligence, workflow, and next-generation systems like QLDB. These higher-value services amplify the magnetic pull of a company like Amazon and its AWS platform.

The streaming data marketplace, real-time information analysis, and other innovations may well signal a competitive turning point for AWS. For millions of individuals, Amazon is not just a place to buy books online. AWS is one of the principal components of the fabric of one's digital experience.

Thus, a phase change has already taken place, and it will have a significant and positive effect on many business sectors, not just law enforcement and intelligence, security, and regulatory policing. Perhaps those who read this chapter can further their understanding of Amazon's potential business impact on LERIS sectors.

1. AWS inventions create modules of functionality which can be mixed and matched with other AWS components. The overall platform becomes more robust and versatile.
2. Specific inventions like federating blockchains and enabling workflows appeal to both new customers as well as developers and partners. The ecosystem grows as developers find new ways to address the challenges LERIS faces.
3. Blockchain puts Amazon squarely in the business-to-business and business-to-government markets. Blockchain has consumer applications, of course, but AWS now offers next-generation enterprise services.

Examining the inventions summarized in this essay makes it easier to understand the scope of Amazon's blockchain vision. The table below summarizes some of the specific blockchain challenges AWS may resolve:

Table 3. Blockchain issues and Amazon features

	Blockchain Issue	**AWS Solution**
1	Computation	AWS provides automated scaling
2	Database functionality	AWS QLDB invention to complement AWS's SQL and NoSQL systems
3	Set up and optimization	Templates and software-as-a-service make it easy to configure a blcokchain-enabled application
4	Limited assurances / trust	Layered assurance / trust services
5	No hierarchy of blockchains	AWS meta-index of blockchains; that is, federated blockchain data
6	Network latency in distributed architecture	AWS regions and nodes reduce blockchain latency

Plus, Amazon offers software to enable fundamental computing tasks, components which can deliver tactical solutions like serving reports from databases and automatically adding additional compute cycles to handle a surge in usage; operational services to orchestrate different software components and data repositories into a solution; and strategic capabilities such as machine learning, advanced management dashboards, and workflows to automate tasks once handled by technical professionals. Cloud services like Amazon provide a way to avoid some capital costs and sidestep the often time-consuming task of building an application or engineering solution to automate a task or add machine learning to a workflow task.

Amazon faces increased competition. The AWS cloud business is growing at double digits and generates more than $25 billion per year (Griswold, 2019).However, growth going forward requires new products and services to open new markets. The blockchain inventions are not limited to LERIS-centric applications. But these public sector opportunities provide a way to tap into the money governments will spend to deal with criminal activity, regulatory enforcement, and financial regulation.

Will Amazon's blockchain solution become a solution of choice? The answer to the question lies in the future.

REFERENCES

Al Jawheri, Boshmaf, Al Sabah, & Erbad. (2017). *Deanonymizing Tor hidden service users through Bitcoin transactions analysis*. Retrieved from: https://arxiv.org/pdf/1801.07501.pdf

Collins, J. (2001). *Good to great: Why some companies make the leap and others don't* (1st ed.). Harper Business.

Dignan, L. (2019, April 11). *In Amazon shareholder letter, Bezos says AWS targeting 'specialized databases for specialized workloads'*. ZDnet. Retrieved from https://www.zdnet.com/article/in-amazon-shareholder-letter-bezos-says-aws-targeting-specialized-databases-for-specialized-workloads/#:~:text=Bezos%20said%3A%20Much%20of%20what%20we%20build%20at,could%20thrive%20without%20that%20kind%20of%20customer%20obsession

Dzieza, J. (2018, December 19). *Prime and punishment: Dirty dealing in the $175 billion Amazon marketplace*. The Verge. Retrieved from https://www.theverge.com/2018/12/19/18140799/amazon-marketplace-scams-seller-court-appeal-reinstatement

Griswold, A. (2019, February 1). *Amazon Web services brought in more money than McDonald's in 2018*. Quartz. Retrieved from https://bit.ly/2DNBrBs

Hash function. (n.d.). In *Wikipedia*. Retrieved from https://en.wikipedia.org/wiki/Hash_function

Leskin, P. (2019, August 28). Use this map to see if your local police department has access to Amazon Ring's unofficial surveillance network of video doorbells. *Business Insider*. Retrieved from https://bit.ly/31IulXH

Letter to Shareholders. (2008). https://www.sec.gov/Archives/edgar/data/1018724/000119312509081096/dex991.htm

Markets, F. (2019, September 24). *Global blockchain market is expected to reach USD 169.5 billion by 2025*. Intrado GlobeNewswire. Retrieved from https://www. globenewswire.com/news-release/2019/09/24/1919752/0/en/Global-Blockchain-Market-is-Expected-to-Reach-USD-169-5-Billion-by-2025-Fior-Markets.html

Nakamoto, S. (n.d.). *Bitcoin: A peer-to-peer electronic cash system*. Retrieved from https://bitcoin.org/bitcoin.pdf

Oracle. (n.d.). *Oracle Data Cloud Platform Help Center*. https://docs.oracle. com/en/cloud/saas/data-cloud/data-cloud-help-center/AudienceDataMarketplace/AudienceDataMarketplace.html

PwC. (2019). *Establishing blockchain policy. Strategies for the governance of distributed ledger technology ecosystems*. Retrieved from https://www.pwc.com/m1/en/publications/documents/establishing-blockchain-policy-pwc.pdf

ReportLinker. (2019, July). Blockchain technology market size, share, & trends analysis report by type, by component, by application, by enterprise size, by end use, by region and segment forecasts, 2019 – 2025. In *Market report*. Grand View Research. Retrieved from https://www.reportlinker.com/p05807295/Blockchain-Technology-Market-Size-Share-Trends-Analysis-Report-By-Type-By-Component-By-Application-By-Enterprise-Size-By-End-Use-By-Region-And-Segment-Forecasts.html

Roth, G. B., Popick, D. S., & Behm, B. J. (2013). *Delegated permissions in a distributed electronic environment*. Google Patents. Retrieved from https://patents.google.com/patent/US20160352753A1/en

Sperling, N. (2019, October 9). Behind Amazon's change in its film strategy. *New York Times*. Retrieved from https://nyti.ms/2ICg2x0

ENDNOTES

[1]   The AWS Summit Dubai 2019 presentations were available at https://bit.ly/36y5fOY.

[2]   See https://bit.ly/2NZ4E1m.

[3]   https://bitcoin.org/bitcoin.pdf

[4]   It is worth noting that Amazon has not yet implemented company-wide acceptance of digital currencies. An observer of Amazon may wish to consider the question, "Why not?"

5   This is the date displayed on the most recent version of the Amazon patent document.

6   US 8,719,131 B1, "Allocating Financial Risk and Reward in a Multi-Tenant Environment" appears to be the same invention filed in March 2012.

7   This is a patent application. At the time of this writing, no information about the status of the invention is publicly available.

8   Amazon presents some information about its law enforcement and intelligence services at https://aws.amazon.com/federal/us-intelligence-community/.

9   Wikipedia includes a more detailed explanation of hashes, methods, and characteristics. See https://en.wikipedia.org/wiki/Hash_function.

10   Amazon provides some information about its LERIS services at https://aws.amazon.com/federal/us-intelligence-community/.

11   For those interested in multi-tenant methods, Salesforce.com's multi-tenant patents provide a wealth of operational detail; for example, the early 2000 invention disclosed in US 8,533,229.

12   Sharon Weinberger, "Meet America's Newest Military Giant: Amazon," October 8, 2019 at https://www.technologyreview.com/s/614487/meet-americas-newest-military-giant-amazon/

13   Specialist providers like Subsentio typically maintain low profiles due to the nature of their customers and each firm's technical capabilities.

14   https://amzn.to/2MeM8Qs. Note that Amazon urls are modified, usually without warning. Special offers, such as free access to Hyperledger Fabric, can be withdrawn or altered at any time.

15   Information about QLDB is at https://amzn.to/2rdOGo1.

16   "AWS Managed Services," TechTarget, at https://searchaws.techtarget.com/definition/AWS-Managed-Services

17   "Amazon.com Announces Third Quarter Sales Up 24% to $70 Billion," October 24, 2019, at https://yhoo.it/32N8kbJ

18   This Oracle product allows Oracle database licensees to access for a fee the world's largest third-party data marketplace and the standard for open and transparent audience data trading. Oracle Data Marketplace data providers offer more than 30,000 data attributes. (Source: https://bit.ly/2JHKPcr)

19   Amazon, "AWS Announces AWS Data Exchange, November 13, 2019 at https://bit.ly/35bXSLD

20   US 9,947,033 B1, Col. 2, line 52 and following

21   US 9,947,033, B1, Col 4, line 5 and following

22   US 9,947,033 B1, Col. 14, Line 49 and following

23   "AWS Announces AWS Data Exchange," November 13, 2019 at https://bit.ly/35bXSLD

[24]   Data vendors lacking blockchain capability can pay Amazon to use its solution or pursue a different path; for example, internal investment or building the solution using another cloud provider's platform.

[25]   Jen Wieczner, *Fortune Magazine*, April 24, 2019, at https://fortune.com/2019/04/24/bitcoin-cryptocurrency-crime/

[26]   Tor is an acronym for the open source obfuscation software suite called "The Onion Router." More information about Tor is available at https://2019.www.torproject.org/about/overview.html.en.

[27]   Edited to highlight Amazon's approach to innovation. The letter is available at https://www.sec.gov/Archives/edgar/data/1018724/000119312509081096/dex991.htm.

[28]   The September 13, 2012 filing became US 9,098,675. Subsequent Amazon assurance and delegation patents expand and add features to this original invention.

[29]   The video of Robert David Steele's lecture is at https://bit.ly/2NPtzn4. Mr. Steele indicated that Amazon executives showed minimal interest in his ideas and suggestions.

[30]   The public announcement of managed blockchain services' availability took place at the end of April 2019.

[31]   Note that the deficiency in this invention is that blockchain is not referenced explicitly. The iteration of the invention provides Amazon with a novel blockchain capability. There was Application No. 13/614,867 filed in 2012—now US 9,098,675, which is included in "Authorized Delegation of Permissions."

[32]   Some documents are filings; others are patents. Filings appear with a four digit year prefixed to the document number.

[33]   US 4,309,569, "Method of Providing Digital Signatures," published January 5, 1982. The patent had expired before the creation of blockchain.

[34]   In some Amazon Merkle tree implementations, the values are pre-computed so that data can be delivered on demand.

[35]   Lamport keys can be calculated from a cryptographically secure one-way function such as a hash. The Winternitz procedure allows multiple signature functions.

[36]   A list of more than two dozen blockchain technolgy companies appears in "Top Blockchain Technology Companies 2019" at https://www.leewayhertz.com/blockchain-technology-companies-2019.

[37]   US 9,466,051, "Funding Access in a Distributed Electronic Environment," See Col. 1, 24 and following.

[38]   US 9,466,051, "Funding Access in a Distributed Electronic Environment," See Col.4, Line 56 and following.

[39] US 9,418,213 B1, "Delegated Permissions in a Distributed Electronic Environment," cover page, physical page 1 of the published patent. Amazon obtained a patent for Authorized Delegation of Permissions (US 9098675) in August 2015, which was filed in September 2012. Amazon, therefore, was investing in technology related to permissions prior to the reworking of the system and method in US 9,418,213.

[40] US 2019 0026685, "Distributed Ledger Certification", Col 1, 0073

[41] An unsubtantiated item posted by Suburban Prospector on Reddit.com at https://bit.ly/2pHmpsJ on November 2, 2019. The US government allegedly pays AWS $600,000 per month to host the Department of Homeland Security Investigative Case Management service.

[42] Amazon, as a result of an investigation into allegations of monopolistic behavior, may be forced into creating a separate company to deliver AWS services. The reader is invited to consider the likelihood of this outcome and consider the different options available to Amazon's management.

198

Chapter 10
Artificial Intelligence– Led Content Publishing, Metadata Creation, and Knowledge Discovery:
In Quest of Sustainable and Profitable Business Models

Usha B. Biradar
 https://orcid.org/0000-0002-1123-6209
Molecular Connections Pvt Ltd., Bangalore, India

Lokanath Khamari
Molecular Connections Pvt Ltd., India

Jignesh Bhate
Molecular Connections Pvt Ltd., India

ABSTRACT

Digital transitions have had strong headwinds in scholarly publishing for the past decade. It started with digitising content and is resting somewhere between tying up diverse content and catering to diverse end users. The goal is still to keep up with the changing landscape, and a demonstrable way of doing so is to actively participate by quickly adapting to standards. Artificial intelligence (AI) has a proven track record of helping with this and is an integral part of the solution frameworks. The chapter content includes a brief insight into some practices and workflows within

DOI: 10.4018/978-1-7998-5589-7.ch010

Copyright © 2021, IGI Global. Copying or distributing in print or electronic forms without written permission of IGI Global is prohibited.

scholarly publishing that stand to benefit from direct intervention of AI. These include editorial decision systems, metadata enrichments, metadata standardization, and search augmentations. The authors bring to light various developments in scholarly publishing and the status of some of the best implementations of AI techniques in aiding and upkeep of the 'digital transformations'.

INTRODUCTION

Digital transitions have had strong headwinds in Scholarly Publishing for the past decade. It started with digitising content and is resting somewhere between tying up diverse contents and catering to diverse end users. Goal is still to keep up with the changing landscape and a demonstrable way of doing so is to actively participate by quickly adapting to standards. Artificial Intelligence has a proven track record of helping with this and is an integral part of the solution frameworks.

This chapter is aimed at providing an insight into the state-of-the-art Artificial Intelligence applications in scholarly publishing and how these can be leveraged to bring to speed various participants within the ecosystem and as an added benefit, target new engagements and revenue streams. Individual solutions are presented here to demonstrate how Artificial Intelligence can be exploited to automate, gain insights, pave opportunities and streamline existing pipelines across various stages of scholarly publishing

Chapter Content

Authors enumerate some practices and workflows within scholarly publishing that stand to benefit from direct intervention of Artificial Intelligence, namely:

1. Editorial Decision Systems
2. Metadata Enrichments
3. Search Augmentations

EDITORIAL DECISION SYSTEMS

Introduction

Editors play a vital role in the entire process of scholarly publication life cycle. These tasks include but are not limited to literal reviews, directing and distributing incoming content to respective domain experts/peer reviewers, looking out for traffic rates across domains/ subjects of expertise that a particular publication is offering, acceptance and rejection rates across various publications, delays at checkpoints across the workflow and general smooth sailing of the entire process (Oryila & Aghadiuno, 2019).

Responsibilities of certain tasks also include ensuring ethical means are followed along with obvious technical rules and regulations set by the publication and meeting the standards set out by the scholarly community as a whole (Da Silva & Dobránszki 2017). With regards to this any and all help in the form of automating and providing insights is a necessity. Especially so with the volume and expansion in data and content that the world is witnessing currently.

Some of the answers to the questions that editors are in quest for are:

Automations

How can automation be employed to direct incoming traffic to peer reviewers? What prerequisites might one need to employ these automations successfully? How to measure the efficiency and effectiveness of these solutions?

Content Validity and Currentness

What are the densities of published content with respect to topic/subjects that a publication offers. Is there an apparent trend when compared to archives vs recent content? Does this point to any obsolete topics/subjects that are seeing little or no traffic in terms of new publications? How can the adherence of journal scopes to the actual content published be confirmed and validated?

Landscaping

How to identify content overlap amongst publications and remedy/redirect them if necessary? Identify traffic in special issues with respect to topics/subjects vs generic traffic

Inclusivity

How can actionable insights be derived from any feedback forums that are enabled either directly or indirectly in the workflow? Directly in terms of author inputs during submissions and reviews, custom questionnaires and surveys etc., and indirectly via social media.

Opportunity

How can the current and upcoming content needs be recognised and fulfilled? Can the turnaround times be tailored to need of the hour without disrupting the current workflow? How to identify and fulfill content repurposing profitably and efficiently?

Problem Statement

Challenges

To answer or even to make an attempt at answering some of the problem statements listed above, would require considerable personnel and budgetary investment. This is where Artificial Intelligence and any sort of automation using machines, to eliminate efforts from personnel and to ensure efficient solutions plays a pivotal part.

Although a lot of progress has been made in terms of applications of Machine Learning and Artificial Intelligence for knowledge discovery tasks, it remains a very domain dependent, time consuming and costly attempt at a solution (Ware & Mabe, 2015). If the core modules are not flexible enough, with changing variables, cost and time parameters shoot up and scaling becomes increasingly pricey. To ensure return on investments, at the very least, the ML and AI modules must be scalable with a flexibility to remove/add/change a few parameters/inputs at a given point (Biradar, Khamari & Bhate, 2018).

Challenges include; in order of how a solution can be shaped:

1. The volume of data
    How to select a representative set to apply solutions to and how to make sure the representative set is updated with incoming content, in other words; how to keep the selection process flexible in terms of inclusivity but robust and reproducible in terms of the actual solution.
2. Reproducibility
    Designing a solution that is in part reproducible, without constraints on what platforms it is devised to run on is an important consideration. This includes due diligence to ingestible and user end formats that differ from custom platforms that publishers decide to run with or certain widely popular standard publishing platforms.
3. Scalability
    Scalability and cost go hand in hand with any artificial intelligence solution, and there are ways with which cost can be managed efficiently. Flexibility in terms of accommodating growing content if and only if the new content brings a new feature that can be leveraged to improve a solution is definitely a

sound consideration. Data ingestion modules should also be smartly devised to recognise the needs of scalability and not just depend on the volume of the data

Solution and Outcomes

The solutions presented are addressed individually under the buckets they are initially classified into in the introduction section of this excerpt.

Automations

Automations can readily be employed to routine tasks like assigning peer reviewers to author submissions. Prerequisites include; having a sound ontology that connects the expertise of listed reviewers, topics/subjects described in the ontology that also are a part of publication scopes and offerings, that is also readily readable by humans (Users at various stages of publication lifecycle) and a machine on par.

To elaborate on readability; if an AI solution employs a central piece that connects raw content to user end enriched content, it is expected to be both machine readable in terms of applying logic, complex rules, derive what are known as 'features' or unique patterns that a machine associates with particularities of content.

The terms from these ontologies are then treated as labels for training a classification machine learning model. As with all solutions, different models can be tried and tested and even ensemble models have a proven track record of yielding neat results. Decent success is seen with certain multilabel datasets as well.

Another crude approach is to apply topic modelling methods to semi-automate and provide suggestions for traffic routing of incoming content.

Figure 1 is a representation of the said classification model for routing traffic.

Figure 1. Automating traffic downstream using machine learning models; illustrating how classification tags act as decision aids.

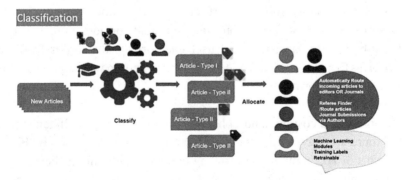

Outcomes

Currently, successful implementations include using a 20-odd topic/top concept ontology to predict and route incoming traffic in physics domain. Binary classification models have also been successfully instituted to determine 'relevant' or not status to content for various downstream processes like metadata enrichment, author disambiguation and general tidying up of sub-standard or old standard scholarly documents.

Content Validity and Currentness, Landscaping, Inclusivity and Opportunity

Problem statements pertaining to Content validity and currentness, Landscaping, Inclusivity and Opportunity all have a single solution that the authors present in the form of intuitive and informative analytics.

Again, a central piece, an ontology that rightly represents the all the content of the publisher is used to connect links between contents and answer all the questions enumerated above. This solution also paves the way for a unique linked data knowledge discovery platform. Authors try and leverage all the metadata available with the content, additionally use an ontology to enrich the metadata and create unique connections that successfully explain observations for a given time period. This model also successfully predicts trends and outliers, which are otherwise known as new opportunities or upcoming possibilities. Figure 2. is a simple pictorial of the solution

Figure 3 helps in identifying trends and out of scope acceptances if any

Figure 2. Data aggregators and analytics to help in editorial decisions

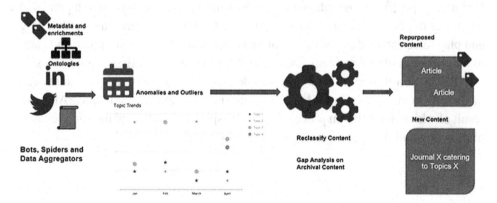

Figure 3. Densities across different topics included in the scope of a particular publication across years.

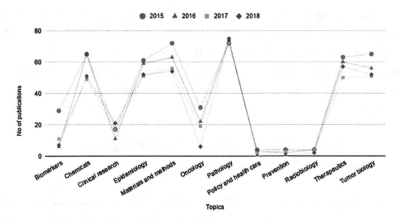

Plagiarism Checks

A special mention on the usage of BERT (**B**idirectional **E**ncoder **R**epresentations from **T**ransformers) (Devlin, Chang, Lee & Toutanova 2018) for plagiarism check is a classic example of a semantic similarity problem and thus can be approached with varied levels of complexity. The same can be extended to other tasks like an automated check point of adhering to publisher rules and guidelines (Read title restrictions, grammar and other content restrictions). At present authors have successfully employed a semantic similarity module for content recommendations (Abdi, Idris, Alguliyev, & Aliguliyev 2015) and semi automated plagiarism check that serve as initial checkpoints/suggestions to reviewers and editors (Franco-Salvador, Rosso & Montes-y-Gómez 2016). Instead of using the entire content of a publication, representative and important sections have been recognized (Title, Abstracts, Section Headings, Specific paragraphs with conclusions etc.,) and this yielded a precision and recall of about 0.85 and 0.87 respectively. Authors recognise that certain plug and play rules can be devised on top of these generic modules to improve and cater to individual publication needs and account for in house submission guidelines

This section thus illustrates how simpler tasks like classification systems can be directly included as editorial decision systems in scholarly publishing. And as a result of which downstream processing can be sped up by eliminating routine tasks of directing and redirecting reviews of incoming content.

METADATA ENRICHMENTS

Under this section, the authors present a unique solution on how metadata enrichment is achieved via fingerprinting of a publication, how this can be automated and how the solution provided can be offered as a service for continued application on incoming content.

Introduction

'Content enrichment' or 'Metadata Enrichment' has emerged as a 'magic bullet' that aims to intelligently imprint tags/identifiers to distinguish types of content: text (journals or books), video, image, audio and also indicate the type of entities (product type, author, publisher, person, organization, named entities of specific domains, chemicals, biological entities) associated with the content, revealing inter/intra connections amongst entities and creating a knowledge pool from which inferences can be derived, paving the way for efficient, time and cost effective, relevant and guided discoverability.

Content enrichment started off as providing relevant data upfront to users enabling them to delve into data without having to rely on any or all background knowledge. With revolutions in IoTs and digitization era, it has now evolved into a more sophisticated solution aimed at creating new discoverability models paving way for innovative products and revenue avenues on existing data. Combined with recent advances in Artificial Intelligence and Machine Learning, content enrichment can also be extended to knowledge acquisition tasks on much larger scales in real time (Brisebois, Abran, Nadembega, & N'techobo, 2017).

To this end, Document Fingerprinting is a unique and high throughput classification system designed at Molecular Connections, which now aids in enhancing the visibility of research articles and publications. Given a scientific article, this system successfully imprints the 'key terms' used in the research along with the probable sub domains of topic that the article deals with. An ontology with 28 odd topics was designed for the purposes of indexing and fingerprinting. These automated systems are intended to provide the critical pointers for a user looking to gather precise and summarized information from digital content. Capabilities of feedback inclusion and a dynamic learning system are one of the prerequisites to improving such systems and keeping the offerings up-to-date.

Challenges

Challenges in ingesting scholarly content include due consideration to content types; articles, editorials, reviews, finding, teaching materials etc., content formats; xmls, word documents, LaTEX, PDFs etc., handling archive data as well as current data, indexing content every time the backbone ontology is updated and APIs to serve fast paced indexing on the go

Solution and Outcomes

Solution architecture is depicted in Figure 4.

Figure 4. Ontology based machine learning module for fingerprinting scholarly articles

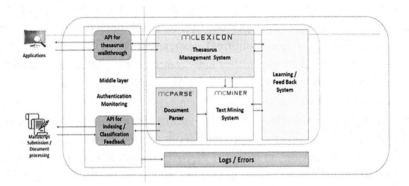

Phases of training and optimizations are described below:

Article Formats

The system successfully ingests both PDFs and xmls with varied content intensity (Full texts, Abstracts, Articles, News and events, Conference proceedings, Lectures etc,)

Training

As a rule of thumb, about 15% of the available publications were selected as representative sets with considerations to period of publication, article type, content format type and file size

Machine Learning

Initial Training

Identifying and weighing candidate terms across the different sub domains, initial training of the machine learning model with a recall of 50% and achieving an average of 50 tags per article

Specificity Training

Weighing contextual terms over other valid terms; precision of 45% and a recall of 58%

Heuristics Training

Leveraging heuristics ranging from sub domain of the article, special focus areas such as articles dedicated to technique/methods/instrumentation as opposed to educational articles. Precision of 51% and a recall of 58%

Lexicon/Ontology Enrichments

Entire archive was leveraged to refine and enrich the lexicon; About 15,00,000 candidate terms screened to arrive at a collective number of 35000. Acronyms, related concepts, synonyms were screened and included.

Ancillary Training

Machine learning models for tagging chemicals and chemical compounds (A precision of 85% and a recall of 89% on its own). Average accuracy at this stage was at 65%.

Model Optimization

Added rule sets to improve on contextual tagging, including complex rules like acronym rules, heuristic weight age of terms, prioritizing chemical tagger and generic tagger etc.,

The accuracy with the optimized model at hand is about 88% on an average. An average of 35 terms per article are tagged with a scoring system.

Author feedback is collected at the very beginning of the lifecycle at submission portals, analysed on a continuous basis and the machine is retrained to reflect some of the suggestions from the feedback.

Proprietary components used in this system are enumerated below.

MC LEXICON™

A proprietary, automated ontology creation, ingestion, maintenance and workflow management system.

MC PARSER™

A proprietary solution to process unstructured contents and XMLs to a standard format

This module acts as a central ingestion module enabling information extraction from spectrum of source data, normalizing the records for downstream processing and packing records in reflections of acceptable standards for delivery in any content enrichment/indexing tasks.

MC MINER™

A proprietary, high accuracy text mining solution. Features include; Complete Machine Learning Modules for classifications and topic modeling, Ensemble named entity taggers – Dictionary (Multiple thesauri/Controlled Vocabularies) + Machine trained models + Rules, Accompanying APIs for each of the modules, Augmentation/Enhancement of existing indexing with versioning information.

Metadata Standardization Discoverability Enhancements

Most standardizations in digital era are centered around semantically linking bits of information. In order to standardize a huge volume of archive/legacy data, it is but natural to look for a cost and time effective solution. Automated standardization using simler AI techniques gives us that opportunity to quickly adapt to changing standards, maintain versioning information, maintain the ability to interoperate in case of callbacks and also to simple be transformation friendly. This is one the in built, customisable components of the fingerprinting system, including automated xml validation, metadata standardizations like institution and author standardization against a well accepted database.

In conclusion, this system is built on a sound ontology that is a perfect fit for automated fingerprinting alongside traditional browse capabilities on platforms. Plug and play modules are integrated automated system with feedback ingestion capabilities. APIs for the Ontology component which are used at the Indexing level as well as the backbone of referee finder and contextual advertising (Ristoski & Mika, 2016) serve multiple purposes. Flexible cores are used in the Ontology and MC MINER™ to accommodate to new requirements/ adjust to new scope horizons keeping the basic functionalities intact. Real-time versioning, update and change management/tracking systems remains the USP of the system.

SEARCH AUGMENTATIONS

Primary goal with any content searching system is to expect minimum possible inputs from a user and evince an efficient answer set to the user query. To that end, 'Augmented browsing', a technique that is focussed towards 'guiding users' by teaching machines to infer and take logical decisions from a query is a readily relatable and need of the hour solution.

This section of the chapter will briefly touch upon state-of-the-art search technologies including augmented browsing in a data model which is centered around semantic entities. All named entities with unique properties and definitions form the central units(along with traditional keywords) also known as 'semantic units'. Also exploited are in this implementation are; multifaceted ontologies that define intra-connections amongst the semantic units. The environment also allows for external communications via inter-connections between semantic units wherever applicable.

The section also touches upon the scope and scalability of augmented browsing. Specific focus will be on the impact of augmented browsing when compound-word searches are used in conjugation with a different combination of words/keywords/entities/phrases. The semantic units include domain entities, geographical locations and heuristic entities. A detailed account of Natural Language Processing as a query parsing component is also explained (Dang, Kalender, Toklu, & Hampel. 2017)

Solution and Outcomes

A traditional approach is depicted in Figure 5. Semantic search pre -requisites and phases of user interaction.

And here is a look at the augmented browsing bit explained using a natural language query:

Suppose users are allowed to enter queries of the sort;

"review articles on nanomaterials in recent times by Massachusetts university"

Traditionally, an end user would have through a string of filters, achieved via 'Advanced search' option on scholarly platforms.

Figure 5. Semantic search pre -requisites and phases of user interaction.

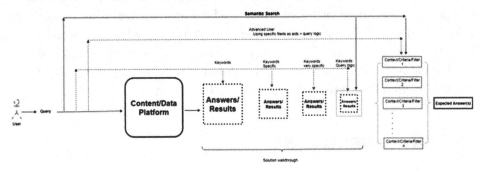

With augmented search and NLP techniques, the query would be processed as follows;

"review articles on <u>nanomaterials</u> in *recent times* by <u>Massachusetts university</u>"

The named entity classes and patterns recognised by NLP engines would be,

Review articles as Content type

Nanomaterials as a Concept/Term from an Ontology

Recent times as an indication of a sort/filter application

Massachusetts university as a Named Entity ofthe type Institution/Organization

The said query is then translated and extended to include all the following traditional keywords.

"Review articles (in Content Type)" AND

"(Nanoparticle OR Nanofibre OR Fullerene OR Fullerenes OR ....)" AND

"(Massachusetts university OR University of Massachusetts) (in Organization from author/author affiliation metadata)"

We see that the query engine has made full use of the semantic units and expanded the query to include lexical variants and synonyms. The result sets are then ranked based on a model trained to recognise frequencies, weighted averages of scores on each semantic unit based on where and how they occur within the content (Di Iorio, Lange, Dimou, & Vahdati, 2015).

Some of the Natural Language helper modules that can be exploited include (McEntire et al., 2016):

Phrase Search

Search using a string of keywords instead which are not recognised as any named entities or semantic units for very specific result retrievals

For instance;

A query of "generally recognized as safe" will retrieve all records containing the phrase "generally recognized as safe"

Query Completion

Refers to the classic auto suggest capabilities embedded into the search bar. So, a user is prompted to enter known variations of the keywords.

Query Flexibility

An extension of Query completion, where an end user has the option of toggling between controlled vocabularies and free text to form his/her queries.

Aided Query Parsing

Refers to specific instructions passed through queries. Pre set prefixes are used to search in specific metadata of the content. This of course includes a help and training section to sensitise users to the system.

Query fall backs and spelling suggestions also form a very important part of these augmented browsing experiences.

To touch upon multifaceted linked data, the named entities can be expanded to retrieve allowed search results from the internet in different languages and other open source platforms if required and create a unique set of results for the user to evaluate and aid in extended knowledge discovery

Authors have implemented this solution in one of their other offerings, a food regulation and compliance platform that is used by common people, industry experts, regulators, product companies and academic community. Different versions of it is currently under various phases of user acceptance testing. All in all, this technology and its scalable results record a unique proof of concept implementation of user centric search and browsing modules on platforms, directly on data lakes and on structured indexed content.

CONCLUSION

With this chapter, the authors intend to bring to light various developments in scholarly publishing and the status of some of the best implementations of Artificial Intelligence techniques in aiding and upkeep of the 'digital transformations'. Authors also aim to open up discussions on the need to adapt to standards and address the questions surrounding standard operating procedures if any or lack thereof. There is ample evidence supporting content repurposing with minimal efforts by including artificial intelligence and machine learning based solutions at specific stages of a new product development. Some of the solutions presented here also have a component that exploits open data revolution to keep the product as up to date as possible. Additional information and demonstrations of the methods discussed and solutions stated can be arranged by contacting the authors with a short communication on intended usage and specifications of problem statements.

REFERENCES

Abdi, A., Idris, N., Alguliyev, R. M., & Aliguliyev, R. M. (2015). PDLK: Plagiarism detection using linguistic knowledge. *Expert Systems with Applications*, *42*(22), 8936–8946. doi:10.1016/j.eswa.2015.07.048

Biradar, U. B., Khamari, L., & Bhate, S. (2018). Transforming 50 years of data: A machine learning approach to create new revenue streams for traditional publishers. *Information Services & Use*, (Preprint), 1-5.

Brisebois, R., Abran, A., Nadembega, A., & N'techobo, P. (2017). A semantic metadata enrichment software ecosystem based on sentiment and emotion metadata enrichments. *International Journal of Scientific Research in Science, Engineering and Technology*, *3*(02), 625–641.

Da Silva, J. A. T., & Dobránszki, J. (2017). Excessively long editorial decisions and excessively long publication times by journals: Causes, risks, consequences, and proposed solutions. *Publishing Research Quarterly*, *33*(1), 101–108. doi:10.100712109-016-9489-9

Dang, J., Kalender, M., Toklu, C., & Hampel, K. (2017). *U.S. Patent No. 9,684,683*. Washington, DC: U.S. Patent and Trademark Office.

Devlin, J., Chang, M. W., Lee, K., & Toutanova, K. (2018). *Bert: Pre-training of deep bidirectional transformers for language understanding*. arXiv preprint arXiv:1810.04805.

Di Iorio, A., Lange, C., Dimou, A., & Vahdati, S. (2015, May). Semantic publishing challenge–assessing the quality of scientific output by information extraction and interlinking. In *Semantic Web Evaluation Challenges* (pp. 65–80). Springer. doi:10.1007/978-3-319-25518-7_6

Franco-Salvador, M., Rosso, P., & Montes-y-Gómez, M. (2016). A systematic study of knowledge graph analysis for cross-language plagiarism detection. *Information Processing & Management*, *52*(4), 550–570. doi:10.1016/j.ipm.2015.12.004

McEntire, R., Szalkowski, D., Butler, J., Kuo, M. S., Chang, M., Chang, M., ... Cornell, W. D. (2016). Application of an automated natural language processing (NLP) workflow to enable federated search of external biomedical content in drug discovery and development. *Drug Discovery Today*, *21*(5), 826–835. doi:10.1016/j.drudis.2016.03.006 PMID:26979546

Oryila, S. S., & Aghadiuno, P. C. (2019). Editing Scholarly Communication in the Age of Information and Communication Technology. *Library Philosophy and Practice*, 1-18.

Ristoski, P., & Mika, P. (2016, May). Enriching product ads with metadata from html annotations. In *European Semantic Web Conference* (pp. 151-167). Springer. 10.1007/978-3-319-34129-3_10

Chapter 11
Internet of Things and Its Impact on Financial Services

Deepika Dhingra
https://orcid.org/0000-0001-5967-8834
Bennett University, India

Shruti Ashok
Bennett University, India

ABSTRACT

The internet of things (IoT) is proving to be a seminal development amongst this century's most productive and pervasive high-tech revolutions. Increased reliance on the internet of things (IoT) is one of the foremost trends, and the financial services industry is a major contributor to that trend. IoT's influence on our daily lives is noteworthy, and it has become imperative for financial services organizations to evolve to adapt to these changes. Digital devices have started to interconnect with each other and possibly with other peripheral entities. Owing to the explosion of these devices and digitization in the banking and financial services industry, businesses are discovering the possibility of IoT in finance to control data and to minimize the risk. This chapter focuses on the impact of internet of things on financial services. It discusses the various applications, trends, challenges, and risks associated with adoption of IoT by financial services institutions. This chapter also discusses Indian and global cases of application of internet of things by financial services institutions.

DOI: 10.4018/978-1-7998-5589-7.ch011

INTRODUCTION

Over the past few years, financial services have gravitated towards the intangible – from counterparty risks and bill payments to other traditionally tangible things like share certificates and even money. Engaging with the Internet of Things (IoT) and the data generated by it, offers a gripping opportunity for financial institutions (FIs) to transform their products and services. On the flip side, the inability to do so in time may jeopardize their future prosperity, making them susceptible to competitors and new players.

The mechanisms of this evolving ecosystem are complicated and unique to the conservative world of financial services. Billions of linked devices, apparently infinite possibilities, and a giant wave of data are uniting to bring convolutions. Now is the time for FIs to reflect upon the diverse positions they can take in the IoT ecosphere, the roles they can adopt, and the preliminary use-cases which will give them a marketable position. Study by Perera et.al (2021) concluded that Internet of things (IoT) is a game plan of interrelated registering gadgets, both mechanical and advanced machines gave novel identifiers (UIDs), that are bound with the capacity to move information over an organization without the requirement for human-to-human or human-to-PC cooperation.

There is a dire need for leaders working in the finance sector to understand the opportunities as well as challenges that IoT poses in the finance sector and the other industries that work in proximity to the Finance Sector. Several industries have managed to look past the hype that surrounds IoT applications and have seen it for its true merit - with analysts and technology providers forecasting a rise in the economic value between $300 billion to $15 trillion by the end of this decade (Accenture, 2021).

As per a study by Bestarion, analysts across the globe expect IoT to have a metamorphic effect on almost every aspect of the economy by 2020. IoT based on the theory of physical objects exploiting the internet to interconnect data about their condition, position, or other attributes is expected to grow significantly and will matter a great deal to enable Financial Service Institutions (FSIs) to be active participants in this transformation.

It should, therefore, be easy for FSI leaders to foresee the probable benefits ensuing from having more comprehensive, real-time data about their own or their client's financial assets. The applications of IoT can be seen in industries such as "smart" commercial real estate, building-management systems, auto insurance, and telematics. This paper explores IoT's potential impacts on the financial services industry.

BACKGROUND

Internet of Things (IoT) is taking up all the industries by a storm and is shaping up to the century's most ubiquitous and prolific technological revolution. Nearly everything we do on digital devices will be interconnected to other digital devices in less than three years, giving rise to one of the quickest IOT developments accompanied by market adoption. IOT will have a significant impact on our lives and hence, financial services companies should start preparing for those changes the sooner the better.

The IoT technology in monetary offerings is to help a consumer save time, work smarter, and live a greater energetic lifestyle. IoT within the banking and finance sector is still in the planning stage but there is an incredible scope of innovation in it. IoT facilitates a financial institution in each aspect, ranging from an increase in sales to higher consumer offerings.

Digital gadgets like computing devices, smartwatches, or even a car will communicate not only with each other but also with other outside entities. IoT is anticipated to have a massive impact on every component of our monetary lives from banking and coverage to fitness, financial planning, and health. Interconnected intelligent gadgets will become ubiquitous and healthy seamlessly into everyday activities. Adopting IoT brings opportunities and challenges across all industries, with clear impacts on manufacturing, logistics, and life sciences. But how will IoT impact financial services organizations, and how can banks and insurance companies make the best of this emerging opportunity?

Sundmaeker et.al (2010) elaborated on the enormous impact of Internet of Things on every aspect of our financial lives—from banking and insurance to financial planning, health, and fitness. Interconnected intelligent devices will become pervasive and fit seamlessly into day-to-day activities. Adopting IoT brings opportunities and challenges across all industries, with clear impacts on manufacturing, logistics, and life sciences. But how will IoT impact financial services organizations, and how can banks and insurance companies make the best of this opportunity, are that need to be answered.

Experts believe insurance, healthcare, and banking will provide the new prospects for using the Internet of things with room for innovative financial products and services popping up. Looking forwards, we will have a fair number of unknowns on the exact impact of IoT on banks and insurance companies. There is substantial groundwork required to manage and embrace these upcoming changes.

Figure 1 shows the potential growth of IoT in the financial services sector worldwide.

Figure 1. Potential growth in worldwide sensor deployment by FSI sector use (2013-2020)
Source: Chart created by Deloitte Centre for financial services center based on Gartner research:"
Forecast: Internet of Things, endpoints and associated services, Worldwide, 2014", Gartner Inc,
October 20, 2014

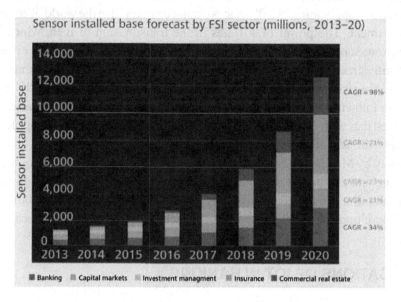

RESEARCH METHODOLOGY

The qualitative approach applied in this study analyses the impact of the Internet of things on financial services and the strategies adopted by existing as well as new players to challenge or support this.

Research Objectives

- To understand the growing importance of IoT in the financial services sector.
- To identify the need for the adoption of IoT in banking.
- To study the various applications of IoT in the banking industry across the world.
- To study the future role of IoT in the financial services sector.
- To recognize the challenges in the adoption of IoT faced by the financial sector.

ADOPTION OF IOT IN BANKING

Banking as an industry has always traded on the impalpable, therefore something tangible like the Internet of things may not seem directly associated with it. However, the impact and application of IoT devices cannot be ignored in the world of commerce and investment. The power of IoT lies in the transmission of data, which is the primary source of information for FSI. The most notable example of investment in the IoT infrastructure has been by retail banks. Khanboubi and Boulmakoul (2018) discussed the rising investments made by on of banks in connective technologies-otherwise known as "fintech"- to make payments and transactions seamless. It is anticipated that with further integration of Finance and Technology, tangible forms of money will become completely extinct.

A study by Mckinsey (2018) examines how IoT, can make banks become digital to the core and can propel the financial industry to another level. Though most of the IoT adoption situations in banking appear far-fetched and overly ambitious, the pace of development of IoT proves that connected banking is within reach.

APPLICATIONS OF IOT IN BANKING

Internet of Things has manifold applications in the banking and financial services sector. An article by Cyber Security Observatory on 'bank of things' has discussed the application of IoT in the Financial sector in detail. Banks have been constantly improvising to facilitate a faster payments system, better operability, and more responsive mobile services. All these objectives are achievable by adopting and exploring the various facets of IoT. To offer a more personal, contextual, and unique experience, IoT has found the following applications in the banking space. Some of the most promising applications of IoT in banking as discussed below:

- **Biometrics and IoT Aid in Compliance and Reporting** –The use of biometrics to sign in into devices has surged significantly owing to its safety feature in comparison to the traditional passwords or PINs where the fear of being lost or stolen was always there. The latest innovations are facial recognition and thumbprint features. Most apps now allow users to sign in using face recognition or thumbprint which is one of the safest ways to log in. Caixa Bank in Spain recently implemented the option to sign into ATMs using facial recognition technology.
- **24/7 Access to Financial Services**: IoT has provided a platform to banks wherein they can give secure access to customers to financial services during off-hours. Citibank has been using 'beacon' technology that allows customers

to cardless entry to ATM lobbies after banking hours through a Bluetooth connection on their phones. This technology transforms an individual's Apple watch/ I-phone into virtual keys for unlocking the lobby's door thereby allowing 24-hour ATM access to customers. This service provides a more convenient and welcoming banking experience for clients. On the other hand, the bank gets a marketing advantage by allowing it to present customers with offers while they're at the bank. It also allows Citibank to track traffic and the number of customers visiting the ATM lobbies.

- **Voice-Enabled Identification:** Voice-enabled biometric solution has also made customer identification easier and more convenient for telebanking customers. Such a technology automatically verifies the user's identity within seconds of a phone call. Citibank has been using this voice recognition solution for some time now.

- **Banking on Wearables**: Many banks are strongly focusing on wearable devices to improve the overall banking experience. In collaboration with big brands, bank accounts are being facilitated to be linked with wearable devices. This has been the easiest 'win' for banks so far, due to the increasing ecosystem of devices and the relatively low cost, the penetration of wearable devices has been significant. Many banks have developed applications suitable for popular wearables like Apple Watch and Fit Pay. Some banks have developed their own devices like Barclay's which launched bPay wearable contactless payment solutions. Australia's Westpac, Caixa Bank, and Hellenic Bank have also developed wearable bands.

- **Pumping up Payments**: IOT can facilitate payments to order food, drinks, avoiding long waits for the customer. In a trial conducted at a bar in London, Barclay's pay @ pump allowed the users to order, pay and get their drink in flat 60 seconds.

- **Branching out to Connected Cars**: IOT can enable banking facilities to reach the customer rather than vice versa. It provides a unique opportunity for car manufacturers to offer services in connected cars that can boost revenues and improve customer relationships. Idea Bank operates cars that are customized with an ATM and an integrated security deposit box. The deposits at this car-based mobile ATM are 3 times higher than at the bank branches. Banks are increasingly exploring the possibility of wealth management apps, that can be displayed on car windscreens enabling the passengers to review their portfolios while on the way to their destinations.

- **Block Chain-Based Smart Contracts:** Many banks across the globe are effectively using blockchain technology to complete global trade transactions. The potential of Blockchain's potential to keep a secure record of genuine transactions is being put to effective use through this. Wells Fargo, Brighann

Cotton, a trading firm, and Commonwealth Bank of Australia have recently concluded a transaction involving the shipment of cotton from Texas to China using Blockchain.

- **Smarter Branches:** IoT empowers bank branches to operate as smart branches by using facial detection technology and offering web access through interactive touchscreens. This results in a better customer experience. Clydesdale and Yorkshire Banking Group's (CYBG) customer innovation lab in London, tested several smart devices to improve the customer experience.

- **Banking at Home:** Applications of IoT have enabled banking at home using Amazon's Alexa to pay customer bills. Starling Bank in the UK has been experimenting using its integrated API with smart speakers that allow users to carry out balance queries and payments through voice commands.

- **Chatbot Services:** Chatbot is a computer program that communicates on the internet, using auditory or textual methods. Its adoption in retail banking is an easy and affordable way to automate customer service inquiries. Many start-ups and banks are recognizing and are utilizing this opportunity. Some examples like Royal Bank of Scotland's 'RBS Assist' Chatbot for banking FAQs, DBS's 'Kasisto Kai' AI platform allows customers to transfer and pay bills.

- **Product Planning and Management:** By studying past data trends on customer reactions and preferences for banking products, banks can gain better perspectives on the preferred product services, product launches, timing of product introduction, and the key customers to target.

- **Tailored Marketing:** With the availability of data of the present economic condition, buying behavior & individual needs of a client, IoT has made tailored marketing a reality. Banks can now keep a track of all consumer activities and present personalized solutions tailored to meet the needs and desires of the client.

- **Proactive Service Delivery:** Due to real-time information availability, banks can service the customers better in case of service faults or product changes. This reduces the resolution turnaround time for banks, improves customer service, and ensures customer retention.

- **Wealth Management Personalization:** Wealth Management outfits across the globe have been using data processing algorithms to produce meaningful insights to aid financial advice. The application of the Internet of Things in financial services is expected to increase the precision and speed of the collection of information. IoT-enabled wealth management solutions will also alarm the users in case their financial stability is under threat. With access to real-time financial data, business managers will be able to improve the quality of the decision-making process.

- **Optimized Capacity Management: The** Internet of Things can be used in optimizing capacity management at bank branches. It can aid bank managers in keeping real-time track of the number of customers visiting a bank branch per day. This information can help in deploying the requisite staff to achieve peak efficiency warranting effective time and cost management. IoT can also help bank managers to predict the amount of cash needed at dispensing machines at each location.
- **Voice Assistants:** IoT helps banks embrace voice-driven communications. In 2016, Capital One introduced a unique skill for Amazon's Alexa which allows bank customers to use the voice command feature to process sensitive financial data. This allows the bank clients to check current loans outstanding, credit card balance accesses their financial accounts in real-time, etc. Some examples of voice communications that a user can ask a voice assistant using IoT are mentioned below:
  - How much did I spend in a selected period?
  - What is my current bank balance?
  - When are my bills due next?
  - How much is my next payment?
- **Robust Mobile Banking:** In the internet era, mobile banking is fast becoming the new way to the bank. Mobile banking apps are devising new features to augment customer experience. Through graphical representation, these mobile banking apps categorize the monthly spending pattern enabling better tracking and budgeting for the account holders. Many others offer all banking solutions under the banking app, chatbot service, integrations with mobile wallets, and more.

Figure 2 summarises the potential uses of IoT in the financial services sector.

INDIAN AND GLOBAL CASES ON THE USE OF THE INTERNET OF THINGS IN FINANCIAL SERVICES

Fintech has always been a resurrecting factor in widening the scope of the business of banking. Khanboubi, et.al (2019) analyzed the impact of digital trends and IoT on the of a traditional bank. Just like ATMs, online banking, and mobile banking, IoT will now help the banking sector to enhance its potential. This section gives an insight into the various IoT technologies and their applications that have been adopted by customers the world over. This article aims to provide case studies documenting the journey of financial service institutions in incorporating IoT-based applications to enhance the overall customer experience. A paradigm of banks, Indian Overseas

Bank (IOB) and Barclays, are mentioned to illustrate how they are using IoT to fulfil their respective objectives.

Indian Overseas Bank (IOB)

Indian Overseas Bank (IOB), one of the leading public sector banks, launched an IoT-based customer service application to fulfill its "Customer First" initiative. To initially test the application, it was launched at the Cathedral branch in Chennai, India. Mr. R K Shetty, general manager at IOB, introduced 3 initiatives to ensure customer satisfaction.

Figure 2. Potential use of IoT in the Financial Services sector
Source: Deloitte Centre for Financial Services Analysis

Sector	Scenarios	
Banking	• Improved commercial loan risk management • Using IoT data to assess creditworthiness • Monitoring students and their debt • Banks as platforms for micropayments • Logical banking • Retail banks finance replacement of failing appliances • Potential for employer services/payroll • Intelligent homes revolutionize mobile payments	• Thing-based consumer finance • Sensors will revolutionize recordkeeping • IoT-sensitive lease pricing • International trade financing instruments • IoT-facilitated account security • IoT-driven energy project finance • "Googlization" of retail banks
Investment and wealth management	• Change in the investment management business model • Data acquisition in the age of perfect information • Predicting the harvest • Portfolios informed by real-time IoT data • IoT unearths new investment opportunities • IoT undermines derivatives in corporate bond market	• Entrepreneurs' telematics as a metric for startup valuation • Increased returns and reduced risks from POL analysis • Linking health monitors to wealth management • Riskology—the new investment science • Using data to profile customers and conduct intelligent upsell • Using IoT ecosystem data to tailor investment recommendations
Insurance	• Insuring individuals in high-risk areas • Using sensor data to provide smart cargo insurance • Unbiased vehicle insurance management • Health insurance premiums adjusted for lifestyle choices	• Insuring assets in risk-prone areas • More accurate pricing of product liability insurance • Cyber-insurance companies use IoT to determine premiums • Natural hazard detection to spread risk and reduce claims
Capital markets	• Leveraging IoT for crowd-investing • Development of crowd-sourced capital pools	• Making virtual currencies physical • New commodity datastreams
Commercial real estate (CRE)	• A new "smart construction" era begins • Real-time bidding markets for CRE	• Real-time information allows occupancy optimization • Improved risk management in CRE construction and lending

First Initiative- Sound Pressure Level Meter

At the branch's service counter, a sound pressure level meter is placed. This meter ensures that the bank's branch manager and the designated official are alerted about any sort of discord or fuss.

Second initiative- Tablet for Recoding Feedback

A tablet will be provided to the customers visiting the branch, in the tablet the customers may fill their response. A customer service team will then take suitable action depending on the 'Happy' or 'Unhappy' emotions displayed on the customer service application.

Third Initiative- Missed Call Feedback

To gain sincere customer feedback, the branch has implemented a missed call-based feedback system for its customers.

Idea Bank- Mobile ATM Fleet

Idea Bank is Poland's most innovative bank. Its mobile- ATM car initiative was recognized as the greatest Innovation in Payments in the BAI- Infosys Finacle Global Banking Innovation Awards. Under this initiative, unlike the traditional ATM system where an individual has to find an ATM and reach its location, The ATM-laden cars can be summoned by the individual to deposit cash through a smartphone application at any location and at any point of time.

As per the bank's data, on average, the deposit at one of its mobile, car-based ATMs is three times higher than at the branch. Hence, it can be inferred that this initiative has been successful.

Commonwealth Bank of Australia and Wells Fargo (USA)

Using Blockchain-based smart contracts and IoT, the Commonwealth Bank of Australia, Wells Fargo of the USA and Brighann Cotton have executed the world's first global trade transaction between two independent banks. In this transaction, Cotton was shipped from Texas in the USA to Qingdao in China.

The blockchain-based smart contract technology is like the one used for mining Bitcoins. This technology mimics letter of credit (LOC) through a privately distributed ledger between the parties and their respective banks based in the USA and Australia. When compared to the traditional process and trade instruments, IoT ensures:

- More transparency between the buyers and sellers,
- Higher level of security,
- Higher cost efficiency,
- Real-time shipment tracking,
- Reduction in errors,
- Removal of inefficiency which is usually faced in international transactions.

Barclays

Using IoT to extract customer-related data through analytics and then shaping this information into consumables, can create a lot of potential for the banking and financial sector.

Barclays is already using IoT to extract customer-related data through analytics using apps like BPay. BPay is a wearable contactless mobile payment product that allows the bill payer to transfer payment electronically from their linked debit or credit cards. Mainly there are two BPay wearable devices available in the market in the form of a fob and a wristband, which facilitate such transactions.

THE FUTURE ROLE OF IOT IN THE FINANCIAL SERVICES INDUSTRY

As digital transformation becomes a necessity, the financial IoT can only be expected to grow. An article by Financial Brand (2018) explored the rising eminence of Digital transformation in banking and discusses how it is about more than just providing online and mobile functionality. Wünderlich et.al (2013) discussed the need for *t*raditional banking providers need to combine digital speed and convenience with human interactions that are both thoughtful and caring at crucial IoT is expected to play a larger role in increasing value for a financial institution in diverse ways. Some of them are listed below:

- **Improved Transparency:** IoT holds enormous promise for the banking sector in the future. Loan providers will have access to detailed data on customers: their credit history, asset details, and value. Loan terms and conditions can be customized based on the customer's credit history, behavior, and objectives. This will ensure financial institutions have better processes for credit grants. The data provided by IoT would induce transparency in banks and equip them to devise effective risk management strategies to deal with unreliable debtors in the future.

- **Telematics:** Usage of telematics (measuring item usage with sensors) has the potential to completely alter the way insurance claims are currently processed. From car insurance to homeowner's insurance, data on real-time detection of injuries can help predict and measure losses when a customer files an insurance claim.

- **Data Gathering:** With IoT devices permeating everyday activities, through mobile devices, wearable technology, and other forms, the financial services industry is being presented with unlimited opportunities to gather actionable, business-relevant data. This information can be best used by financial organizations to improve the underwriting process and provide customized offers.

- **Simplifying Account Access:** IoT-powered technology will help banks use biometrics – voice or touch – to simplify account access through digital channels. Processes that require physical signatures to sign in would have the option to use "Wet Ink" technology, which allows users to sign in through any of the touch screen devices giving the option to clone that signature on physical paper with "Wet Ink". This will allow clients to conduct business even when they are not physically available and eliminate barriers related to paper-based transactions.

- **Leasing Finance Automation:** IoT-enabled digital leased assets can be monitored in real-time for wear and tear. Information on idle time and asset usage can provide crucial input data facilitating the pricing of leased assets. This could help banks widen product offering of leased assets - turning traditional products into services by digitally enabling them. With greater control over leased assets, the leased asset could be locked or disabled remotely by the bank. A study by Wang on Edgeverve.com identified IoT as an efficient enabler in simplifying leasing terms due to better control and automation, terms and conditions.

- **Smart Collaterals:** IoT technology can empower banks to get better control over a customer's mortgaged assets like cars, expensive home appliances, etc. This could enable a retail or SME customer to raise finance by offering machinery, cars, or expensive home appliances as collateral. Financing requests and transfer of ownership could be completely digitalized and automated. Application of IoT-enabled digital identity for individuals can transfer ownership of an asset in seconds. This would ensure immediate issuance of loans and monitoring of collateral status in real-time, without physical custody of the asset. The bank would be authorized to remotely disable or enable the machine anytime based on defined business rules. For instance, in case of non-payment of EMIs, the engine could be disabled.

- **Automated Payment through Things:** The number of payment endpoints will be increased as a result of the Integration of payment functionality and IoT. The power of IoT has enabled machines to perform transactions with other machines in real-time on a marginal cost basis and has rendered the traditional methods of payments obsolete. As the financial transactions integrate with other services and become automated – almost all transfer/payment could be automated. If digital identities and personal biometrics are done right it could enhance security in payments. This not only presents greater convenience to the end-users but also leads to smarter retailers, payments companies, transactions, manufacturers, banks, and more.

- **Wallet of Things**: As the devices are "smart" and digital, wallets might be associated with each device. Consumer equipment, the home appliance could eventually host a pre-funded, embedded wallet capable of making payments on its own. For instance, a car, using its embedded wallet could pay for its parking, gas, rental, or even maintenance service.

- **Contextualized PFM:** Early PFM focused more on generic insights and expenditure categorization for users – like benchmarking finance management with "People like Me". PFM tools in the future will offer advice and more contextualized alerts by accessing IoT data from client's leased or owned devices. For instance, alerts on air conditioner electricity consumption or parking fees will be contextualized based on real-time data. These alerts would be based upon the owner's estimated parking fees or on the personal budget for electricity consumption. This paradigm will facilitate better management of operating expenses and service consumption and enable services and devices to be capped to a pre-defined amount.

- **Frictionless Customer Onboarding and KYC:** Banks cross-sell relevant products and correctly profile a customer by having insights into customers' financial behavior during onboarding. However, at this stage not only is the information available with banks scarce but it also fails to provide a comprehensive view of the customer's financial behavior. With IoT, client's devices are linked with their digital identity, which makes access to the client's digital footprint possible. A blockchain-based unique digital signature can be used for most transactions as people extensively use their Gmail/Facebook ids to log in to different websites. This might also be used for KYC processes in the future.

- **Tailor-Made Auto Insurance:** IoT can also provide tailor-made insurance to customers based on the wear and tear of their vehicles, driving habits, and the health of the engine. Many companies are already offering devices that provide driving behavior data to their clients by plugging the device into the diagnostic port of their cars. The owners can also be eligible for discounts based on their recorded driving habits. Even insurance companies can calculate the probability of accidents, by studying the GPS data, enabling them to price insurance premiums appropriately.

- **Real-time Life Insurance:** IoT can transform the way life insurance policies are currently issued. IoT makes it possible for life insurance companies to automatically issue insurance. People now can get life insurance instantly anytime, anywhere with the help of health metrics generated from wearables coupled with biometric digital identity and medical history. This would also drastically reduce the time required for underwriting to near real-time.

- **P2P Finance on Tangible Assets:** A futuristic application of IoT can help extend the P2P (peer to peer) model to newer areas and impact the way traditional financial services are provided. Leasing is one service that can be made completely online through IoT. As the owner of the assets is transferred from lessor to lessee, leasing can be completed in real-time within seconds after the payment confirmation, using a digital identity. Exploring this paradigm has the potential to unleash a completely new business model, facilitating any digital peer-to-peer financial dealings, changing the way banks carry on leasing and mortgage activities.

CHALLENGES IN IOT ADOPTION IN THE FINANCIAL SECTOR

The power of IoT devices to bring in change is boundless, so is their vulnerability. An article by Petracek (2018) discusses that owing to the nature of financial transactions coupled with the accuracy and security concerns, the promises and risks of IoT application in the financial services sector increase manifold. All the benefits shown above will bring some problems related to the confidentiality and security of customers' data. The financial platforms using IoT connections should ensure the safety of customer's data.

As suggested by Technosip, an IoT development company, below are some of the weaknesses of IoT applications in FinTech.

- **Data Accessibility:** With the exponential jump in data generation made possible through connected devices, the possibility of highly sensitive and valuable consumer information being hacked increases significantly. As more data continues to be generated, becoming increasingly accessible through a large number of connected devices, the risk of being hacked goes up too. Organizations must, therefore, figure out a way to store, track and protect it, and quickly.

- **Privacy and Security:** The potential danger to privacy and security of financial transactions using IoT cannot be ignored. As per a report by GSMA (2019), privacy and security are of utmost importance in the financial industry, and they need to accord the highest priority to certify customer data protection. Whenever financial and personal information is transmitted using IoT networks, the possibility of breaching and hacking is huge, so the privacy and security concern means a lot, and attention should be paid to it.

- **No Common Standards:** The lack of common standards in IoT maintenance is one of the reasons for the failure in the functionality of IoT devices. As IoT involves linking multiple devices and software, it also remains a fact that different devices require different maintenance approaches. Due to the lack of common standards for maintaining IoT equipment, it seems impossible to resolve this issue. All the hardware used in IoT is manufactured by different suppliers without any common maintenance standard. This issue can be resolved only if there is one monopolistic manufacturer of all equipment, but this seems completely impossible.

- **Complex System:** Being a complex system of devices linked with each other, the bounds for IoT expansion are limitless. This chain of IoT devices can function properly only if all the devices in the link function efficiently. Break down in any one link can halt the entire system, this applies both to hardware and software devices. Therefore, it becomes important that high-quality hardware manufacturers and experienced software companies are chosen.

- **Higher Unemployment Rate:** With the advent of IoT in banking, the need to automate work processes becomes important. This might result in some bank processes being replaced by machines, especially if these work positions were held by unskilled employees. This trend might grow with the use of IoT in banks and financial institutions.

- **The Invisibility of IoT Devices:** An additional risk arises because IoT devices are often "invisible"; it becomes easy to forget about them and hence the security of the devices poses a threat to the organization. In case of any update required in the software, due to invisibility, organizations might skip the updates exposing the company to multiple external and internal risks.

- **Risk due to Design:** IoT devices are not protected by design. In the absence of any compliance standards during manufacturing, these devices are often shipped and distributed as hackable devices. Thus, the financial products, that use these devices to transfer money and personal data, become convenient targets for cybercriminals. Once an insecure device is breached, the data within the entire network can be trickled. This compromises the utility of IoT's application in FSI and thus puts the data of every customer at risk.

- **Risk due to Greater Exposure:** Due to inadequate security, IoT devices are often exposed through their cloud or web application services. The wireless networks surrounding IoT devices are also susceptible and penetrable, where multiple devices from many users are concerned. Thus, these can be accessed from the organization's network or any Wireless fixed connection.

CONCLUSION

The pertinence and the necessity of IoT in banking and FSI cannot be disregarded. Taking into consideration the multiple risks involved, it becomes imperative for organizations to acknowledge and detect the risks IoT brings forth with its diverse benefits. Technology is an essential factor for gaining a competitive advantage in any sector of the economy. There are many examples, like Reliance Jio Infocomm Limited that highlight the implication of technology in producing disruptive ideas.

Organizations need to recognize that the threat landscape has altered and that there are billions of devices and each device is unique. The traditional way of perceiving threats through signature scanning is no more relevant. Smarter and next-generation ingenious methods based on sophisticated machine learning and behavioral analysis need to be designed to meet the challenges posed by IoT.

Steps that organizations can follow to make IoT application more secure and beneficial are:

- Be able to track where each IoT-connected device is.
- Have proactive, effective risk management policies in place much before the damage.
- Warrant continuous visibility (24×7), update, or patch.
- Fully understand the risk level of each device in the network.

Various banks and financial institutions must innovate to increase customer satisfaction. The government should invest in the Fintech sector for using its potential for improving the country's financial condition. Lack of financial literacy is another problem that FSIs need to consider bridging the gap between people and facilities.

REFERENCES

Accelerating digital transformation in banking. (2021). Available at: https://www2. deloitte.com/us/en/insights/industry/financial-services/digital-transformation-in-banking-global-customer-survey.html.html

Accenture. (2021). *Let there be change*. Available at: https://www.accenture.com/us-en

Bestarion. (n.d.). *The Internet of Things (IoT)*. https://bestarion.com/portfolio/internet-of-things/

Cyberstartup Observatory. (n.d.). *The Bank of Things - The Application of IoT in the Financial Sector*. https://cyberstartupobservatory.com/the-bank-of-things-the-application-of-iot-in-the-financial-sector/

EdgeVerve. (2017). *IOT Banking Enabling Banks Digital Future*. https://www.edgeverve.com/finacle/finacleconnect/trulydigital-2017/perspective/iot-banking-enabling-banks-digital-future/

Forecast: Internet of Things, Endpoints and Associated Services, Worldwide. (2014). Available at: https://www.gartner.com/en/documents/2880717/forecast-internet-of-things-endpoints-and-associated-ser

Gsma.com. (2019). Available at: https://www.gsma.com/mobilefordevelopment/wp-content/uploads/2019/02/ProofOfID_R_WebSpreads.pdf

Khanboubi, Boulmakoul, & Tabaa. (2019). Impact of digital trends using IoT on banking processes. *Procedia Computer Science*, *151*, 77–84.

Khanboubi, F., & Boulmakoul, A. (2018). A roadmap to lead risk management in the digital era. *ASD 2018: Big data & Applications 12th edition of the Conference on Advances of Decisional Systems*.

McKinsey. (2018). *Transforming a bank by becoming digital to the core*. https://www.mckinsey.com/industries/financial-services/our-insights/transforming-a-bank-by-becoming-digital-to-the-core

Perera, C., Liu, C. H., Jayawardena, S., & Chen, M. (2021). A Survey on Internet of Things From Industrial Market Perspective. *IEEE Access: Practical Innovations, Open Solutions*, *2*, 1660–1679. https://www.academia.edu/28144983/A_Survey_on_Internet_of_Things_From_Industrial_Market_Perspective

Petracek, N. (2021). Council Post: Is Blockchain The Way To Save IoT? *Forbes*. Available at: https://www.forbes.com/sites/forbestechcouncil/2018/07/18/is-blockchain-the-way-to-save-iot/?sh=3356dda35a74#65d086d25a74

Sundmaeker, Friess, & Woelfflé. (2010). *Vision and challenges for realizing the Internet of Things. European Commission Information Society and Media*. Available at: http://www.internet-of-things-research.eu/pdf/IoT_Clusterbook_March_2010.pdf

Technosip. (n.d.). *IoT Development Services and Solutions*. https://www.technosip. com/internet-of-things-iot/#:~:text=The%20Internet%20of%20Things%20 (IoT,human%2Dto%2Dcomputer%20interaction

The Four Pillars of Digital Transformation in Banking. (2018). Available at: https:// thefinancialbrand.com/71733/four-pillars-of-digital-transformation-banking-strategy/

Wünderlich, N. V., Wangenheim, F. V., & Bitner, M. J. (2013). High Tech and High Touch: A Framework for Understanding User Attitudes and Behaviors Related to Smart Interactive Services. *Journal of Service Research*, *16*(1), 3–20. doi:10.1177/1094670512448413

Chapter 12
Blockchain and the Research Libraries:
Expanding Interlibrary Loan and Protecting Privacy

Anthony L. Paganelli
Western Kentucky University, USA

Andrea L. Paganelli
Western Kentucky University, USA

ABSTRACT

This chapter will examine the theoretical uses of blockchain technologies in research libraries. Technology has enhanced the services and operations of research libraries since the early implementation of computerized cataloging systems. Blockchain technology provides research libraries with the opportunity to decentralize services, while also maintaining and strengthening digital rights management. Research libraries will be able locate services that can be decentralized to provide patrons with a more effective and efficient service. The blockchain technology has the potential to expand library collections through distributed verifiable sovereign identity, which would allow patrons to securely access information from multiple libraries while maintaining their privacy. Libraries will be able to evaluate services and programs to determine best uses for blockchain technology.

DOI: 10.4018/978-1-7998-5589-7.ch012

INTRODUCTION

When people mention technology, most would relate the term technology with computers or some form of electronic device. However, libraries have embraced technology as a broader term that is inclusive of pre-digital tools implementing various forms of technology well before computers. Libraries have utilized technology for centuries that includes the Gutenberg printing press that increased library collections. Due to the increase of collections, print book catalogs were created for librarians and patrons to access books. Eventually, the catalog books were changed to cards that would provide accurate record of the collection without having to reprint the catalog book as books were acquired or withdrawn. The card catalogs were enhanced with the invention of the typewriter, which the Library of Congress created in 1902.

A major technological advance for libraries was the implementation of the Machine Readable Cataloging (MARC) format in the mid-1960s that automated the cataloging process and eventually led to the creation of catalog cards. Because of the Machine Readable Cataloging format, libraries were able to use that format to create the Online Public Access Catalog, which is what most people are familiar with as the library's online catalog of the library's collection. From this technological format, libraries later created the database management systems that allows users to go directly to the data entry or record for the information, whether it be a book in the collection or an electronic source. The computer technology has provided libraries to process, manage, and access information effectively and efficiently.

While this internal technological transformation for libraries was beneficial for libraries to maintain the needs of patrons, computer technology also altered workflows and traditional services. Many of these traditional services, such as reference services, processing print books and materials, and cataloging were drastically changed. In some instances, these jobs were eliminated or greatly reduced Again, technology is on the verge of changing how research libraries operate with the introduction of Blockchain technology. The technology has the potential to alter the ways research libraries will acquire academic materials, collaborate with publishers and vendors, and conduct scientific research.

Since the introduction of computer technology in the library, academic library leaders have continued to predict the technological trends and innovations that will prepare the library to meet the needs of their patrons and the institution. With the advent of new technology implementations, libraries have embraced technology that will have an impact on many facets of library organizations' operations. Currently, Blockchain has been considered as disruptive technology that will have an impact on many facets of organizations' operations Therefore, library administrators are carefully considering how to better understand Blockchain prior to attempting implementation.

Blockchain technology is another innovation that library administrators are viewing as a possible important technological tool. The importance of library administrators' perspective of technology will provide a foundation in the future of how the technology will be used and create best practices to be more effective for the organization and patrons. Some library administrators view technology as transformational, which is often the case as technology can be disruptive to an organization's operations (Cox, Pinfield, & Rutter, 2019). As a librarian you can't help but wonder, is Blockchain the next revolution in library practice or just a passing trend?

Why Blockchain and the Research Libraries?

According to Cox, Pinfield, & Rutter (2019), technology drives social change, which pressures libraries to stay abreast of new technology to meet the needs of patrons. Major industries are implementing the technology for various reasons, such as to aid in fraud prevention, which can cost companies millions of dollars. Lindenmoyer and Fischer (2019) noted that "the following industries are implementing some type of Blockchain: the diamond industry, medical industry, retail law offices, energy management, accounting, and education to a small extent" (p. 77). This includes the health sector that has increased usage of Blockchain in regards to supply-chain management (Bhargava, 2019; Hirsh & Alman, 2019).

If this many fields that manage large amounts of data are having success using Blockchain technology how could it aid or impact library function and technology programming? As libraries are continually striving to remain relevant in our increasingly technology savvy society by utilizing the latest technology that includes the implementation of Virtual and Augmented Reality devices, Makerspaces, 3D printers, and eBooks. The need and drive to increase technology availability for patron in librarian use can be a costly endeavor. In a political climate that sees a continual reduction in funding from federal and state agencies maximizing available resources is a must. As such, libraries are seeking more efficient ways to provide services and programming.

The urgency to keep libraries relevant due to the decrease funding has also changed library operations towards an entrepreneurship approach. Basically, libraries are being pushed more toward an operating model that resembles a business like organization. Creating opportunities and challenges for libraries to become more cost effective. This drive to utilize technology and operate more as a business model begins with the use of technology. Libraries and librarians can use technology to support functional operations in an efficient and effective manner. Blockchain has the promise to deliver as both efficient and effective tool.

Blockchain technology has reached significant attention due to the use of Blockchain to create cryptocurrency. The draw of interest has further increased around Blockchain technology because organizations are identifying uses outside of cryptocurrency. These uses such as smart contracts and supply chain management have potential to be revolutionary. The technology has received attention from government agencies, which are implementing legislation and regulation regarding Blockchain technology. The impact for libraries and Blockchain technology is heavily influenced by the government's implementation, perspective, and regulation of the budding technology. In other words, as governments continue to recognize and implement the technology, the potential for research and public libraries to utilize Blockchain technology may become a reality.

A recent survey by the Deloitte accounting firm released data from 1,386 international senior executives that noted over 50 percent viewed Blockchain as a new technology that would be needed in their organizations (Hirsh & Alman, 2019). The same expectations are also noted in government organizations that are beginning to realize the potential of Blockchain technology. Based on the increase usage of the technology in the financial sector and the business community, eventually libraries will have to consider whether the technology will be a feasible and practical technological tool.

In other words, libraries will have to remain diligent about how and when to use Blockchain technology. For instance, library administrators will have to think about what type of data needs to be stored on a Blockchain, the type of information that maybe significant in changing the organization's operations, the impact of the technology in regards to users, and the expenditures (Hirsh & Alman, 2019). Research libraries will also have to consider security by maintaining confidentiality, integrity, and user availability of data, because of the Family Educational Rights and Privacy Act (FERPA).

The utilization of Blockchain Technology has the possibility to positively impact research libraries' services and operations. Primarily, libraries have to consider the fundamental elements of Blockchain in regards to implementing the technology. Most importantly, Blockchain is an option for library administrators to change operational workflows by removing a centralized system, preserving and archiving metadata, and research publications, as well as other opportunities to reduce expenditures and enhance services and operations. Overall, Blockchain could be a useful tool for research libraries.

HIEARCHY OF IMPLEMENTING BLOCKCHAIN INTO RESEARCH LIBRARIES

To implement Blockchain technology in the research library, there are a few factors that library administrators will have to note, such as costs, privacy, security, and trust.

However, the technology may be implemented based on the hierarchy of government institutions. For libraries to fully utilize Blockchain technology, libraries will examine and review how technology is used in other government agencies, which begins with legislation that provides regulations, universities implementation and assessment of the technology, and a universal standard that is agreed upon by the library community. Therefore, the hierarchy begins and moves from government officials, to government agencies, to higher educational institutions, and then research libraries. By examining and reviewing the outcomes of these other organizations, research libraries will have a better understanding of how the technology works, determine best standards and practices, and best uses for Blockchain in research libraries.

Legislation

Because most research libraries are funded through federal and state government agencies, libraries will have to abide governmental regulations, such as FERPA or information technological restrictions. Therefore, the implementation of Blockchain technology will be regulated by governmental legislation, which numerous state governments are researching and approving legislation regarding Blockchain technology. The government's interest in Blockchain began with the trend of cryptocurrency and regulating the financial aspects of the currency. Afterwards, the introduction of smart contracts associated with Blockchain caused state governments to determine how to best regulate and eventually utilize the technology in their own organizations.

Government agencies "have recognized the technology's potential for the delivery of public services, and are at various stages of implementation" (Ray, p. 10). The Delaware Blockchain Initiative introduced by former Governor of Delaware Jack Markell, "Smart Contracts offer powerful innovative way to streamline cumbersome back office procedures, lower transactional costs for consumers and businesses, and manage and reduce risk" (Ray, p. 10). Delaware's Blockchain Initiative allows corporate registration and other Uniform Commercial Code (UCC) filings. Illinois and Arizona are also implementing some form of Blockchain technology. Illinois has a series of pilot programs that want to "transform the delivery of public and private services, redefine the relationship between government and the citizen in terms of data sharing, transparency and trust, and make a leading contribution to the State's digital transformation" (Ray, p. 10). Arizona has made legislation and regulations regarding contract signatures, transactions, and contracts that will allow their residents to pay their income tax in cryptocurrencies (Ray, 2019).

On February 14, 2018, the U.S. House of Representatives Committee on Science, Space, and Technology held a joint hearing stated, "This hearing is an opportunity to learn more about the standards, guidelines and best practices that may be necessary to ensure effective appropriate implementation of Blockchain technology" (Ray, p. 11). The hearing also resulted in the discussion of "ways to improve government efficiency and private sector success with this technology" (Ray, p. 11). A form of efficiency is the use of Blockchain in voting, because the technology would provide full transparency and accurately count each vote (Bhargava, 2019).

Smart Contract is the actual code on the Blockchain that determines the agreement between two or more parties (Beraducci, 2019). Beraducci (2019) provided an example of a Smart Contract by describing a person who creates a Smart Contract that states "if the Cleveland Browns win a game next year, I will buy everyone a lunch" (p. 25). According to Beraducci (2019), the contract "would be open, available, inspectable, and I could not tamper with the rules set in the code" (p. 25). Once the code has been completed, it cannot be changed.

While the smart contract appears to be a legal contract, Rohr (2019) notes that smart contracts are "not necessarily legal contracts" (p. 68). He stated that once the code was completed it cannot be altered or ended, which is a challenge when the parties involved have a dispute about the contract that would make the agreement an expensive breach of contract. In these instances, the courts will have to review and interpret Smart Contracts.

Despite the concept that Smart Contracts are not actually a contract, state legislatures are recognizing smart contracts as legal entities. The State of Tennessee approved legislation in 2018 that stated, "smart contracts may exist in commerce. No contract relating to a transaction shall be denied legal effect, validity, or enforceability solely because that contract is executed through a smart contract" (Beraducci, 2019, p. 70). California, New York, Arizona, and Nevada have also passed legislation since 2017 regarding the language and usage of Blockchain technology and smart contracts.

In Beraducci's article (2019) he uses Nick Szabo's analogy that a vending machine represents the Blockchain concept, which describes any person can place money in a vending machine that is coded to only accept the payment terms. Once the money has been entered into the vending machine the transaction cannot be breached by the purchaser. Plus, if there is a breach it would be extremely expensive to undo the transaction.

The vending machine analogy also brings into account that smart contracts at this particular stage of implementation struggles with open-ended phrases, because the code of the vending machine relies on closed-ended terms that is easily understood by both parties. In other words, the owner of the vending machine and the purchaser agree on the exchange of goods for a set price. More complicated contracts that would require open-ended terms and phrases could be subject to debate, which would be difficult to add to a Blockchain. Basically, more research is needed to implement traditional contracts into the new smart contract concept.

Higher Education

As government agencies continue to recognize this technology as a tool and resource, they will begin to utilize Blockchain more frequently, which may include the transactions between government agencies, universities, libraries, and other sources in the future. This type of involvement with Blockchain could be more noted in library administrative and leadership roles. However, Lindenmoyer and Fischer (2019) stated, "Higher education is an industry where Blockchain has not been implemented on a major scale" (p. 78). Yet, higher education has the potential for numerous areas to utilize Blockchain technology, because Blockchain's basic structure of a ledger system will greatly enhance the various record keeping systems of a higher educational institution.

Of course, FERPA is the major issue that universities would have the most challenge implementing the Blockchain technology. Therefore, higher education would have to rely mostly on a consortium Blockchain. The consortium closed Blockchain that allows restrictions on those who read the data and create data on the Blockchain (Lindenmoyer and Fisher, 2019). Due to the Blockchain's ability to prevent external sources from altering the data and the technology is immutable, Blockchain is a tool that could be a keeper of data that could not be altered or corrupted.

According to Tapscott & Tapscott (2018), four aspects of higher education will be affected by Blockchain technology that include "Identity and student records, new pedagogy, costs (student debt), and the meta-university (new models of universities). There will be several uses for higher education to utilize Blockchain that will include the ability for students to verify and control their academic progress and achievements. According to Hoy & Brigham (2017), "Early in 2016, Sony announced plans to build a Blockchain for the 'open and secure sharing of academic proficiency and progress records'" (p. 276).

In other words, students will be able to access all of their academic information that would include all assignments, tests, courses completed, and submitted works. The technology would also prevent academic dishonesty. For instance, tests and assignments on a student's Blockchain could be activated to prevent students from printing or sending to other students. The Blockchain could also send an alert if a student attempted to access an old test or assignment (Lindenmoyer & Fischer, 2019).

Most importantly, Blockchain uses the Self-Sovereign Model that gives the user complete control over their data. Due to this control, students have the opportunity to control their information as they progress through their college tenure. Basically, students will be able to review their academic progress, financial records, and other school related materials.

The current concept of Blockchain in higher education is verifying certificates and degrees. Massachusetts Institute of Technology (MIT) offers students that are graduating in finance and obtaining a masters in media arts the option to receive a digital diploma following graduation, which would allow potential employers to verify degree completion utilizing Blockcerts. Similar opportunities exist with verifying certificates or completion of training programs for government and businesses. By providing this type of information on a Blockchain, universities could reduce costs, remove the centralized workflow (transcript offices or departments), and provide a secure platform for the student's diploma and data (Hirsh and Alman, 2019; Bhargava, 2019).

According to Alammary, et al. (2019), listed numerous other opportunities for higher education to utilize Blockchain that includes fees and credit transfers, obtaining digital guardianship consent, the evaluation of student's professional skills in regards to workforce demands, and Digital Rights Management. The final item, Digital Rights Management is a service that will impact research libraries should Blockchain technology be utilized, along with other library services.

Research Libraries

Libraries will need to assess the need for Blockchain technology before spending time and expenditures on technological equipment and personnel. The purpose for the assessing the needs is to determine whether the technology would be best option to serve the institution, the library, and the patrons. They will have to look for areas in the library that can be decentralized and become transparent. The use of blockchain technology in the library must be understood that this a closed-term system. In other words, if the library would like to implement the blockchain technology then the system must be setup so that any agreement with another party is clearly understood between both parties, such as the vending machine concept noted earlier (Berraducci, 2019).

Library leaders and experts have discussed other factors to consider when planning for Blockchain technology, such as the creation of universal standards, implementation of the technology internally, understanding that data entered on the Blockchain is immutable, and public and private keys are irreplaceable (Smith, 2019; Hirsh & Alman, 2019).

In regards to transparency, the supply-chain management is a concept that provides transparency and would be useful for research libraries in regards to acquisitions or metadata. Sissman & Sharma (2018) noted that "Supply chains are made up of network of individuals, organizations, technology, resources and activities that spread from the initial creation of a product to delivery. Therefore, Blockchain would useful for research libraries creating a Blockchain for archiving and preservation of materials.

Hirsh and Alman (2019) noted several options where Blockchain technology can be implemented into libraries that include interlibrary loan services, universal library cards, archiving records. Other experts in the library profession seeking other uses for Blockchain. For instance, the utilization of Blockchain for scholarly communications, Digital Rights Management, securing contracts with publishers, maintain patrons' records, and creating metadata (Hirsh & Alman, 2019; Alammary, et al., 2019).

BLOCKCHAIN TECHNOLOGY IN THE RESEARCH LIBRARY

Preparing for Blockchain

Despite the numerous potential opportunities, research libraries must prepare for Blockchain technology. Most importantly, research libraries will need to keep in mind that Blockchain technology will rely on trust between more than one organization, if a library is entering a consortium or some type of collaboration with other organizations. In addition, this decentralization system must rely on an agreement by all parties. Therefore, research libraries collaborating with other research libraries will have to create a set of standards for sharing the data entered into the Blockchain.

The creation of standards must consider the fundamentals of Blockchain technology, which is a distributed ledger that is transparent, but maintains security and integrity. Based on the fundamental properties of a Blockchain, research libraries collaborating with other libraries or even internally will have to agree to how the data is entered, shared, and interpreted. The agreement or standards that are created must include any legal implications, because the information entered on the Blockchain is immutable. Due to the inability to change data on a Blockchain, legal experts and legislators are determining ways to interpret these issues.

Once research libraries create a plan that includes an agreement or set of standards and guidelines, library administrators can begin planning for implementation. Due to the recent introduction of this technology in governmental agencies and libraries, library administrators or other personnel may begin a small internal project to fully understand the Blockchain process. By starting on a small scale, stakeholders will have a better understanding of the technology needed and the personnel required to enter information and maintain the technology.

Other factors to include in this pre-planning stage is how Blockchain technology will either benefit or hinder the libraries' mission to provide services to patrons and meet the goals of the institution. First factor to consider is whether the technology is necessary to complete the mission of the library and will the technology efficiently enhance library services. Organizations that are implementing this technology have realized the potential Blockchain and have invested in the personnel and the equipment. Financial costs is a factor some experts have noted about utilizing Blockchain, due to the equipment needed to mine the text and data. Therefore, library administrators will have to determine if the expenditures to implement Blockchain is beneficial to providing services to patrons and the operations of the library.

Metadata

The premise of Blockchain is to remove an authoritative centralized unit, which libraries have a centralized unit in creating metadata. Therefore, the potential disruptive technological service that Blockchain would have an impact on for research libraries is creating and preserving metadata. Librarians have been creating metadata for decades, therefore libraries are familiar with the concept of metadata, which is the basis of Blockchain technology. Yet, research libraries rely mostly on a third party to assist with creating metadata primarily due to the continuous budget cuts to libraries. For instance, most research libraries utilize the Online Computer Library Center (OCLC) to provide metadata on materials purchased.

OCLC is the largest Online Public Access Catalog that provides bibliographic metadata for libraries that are members of the OCLC. The standards that research libraries utilize is the Library of Congress Classification system, which is a system that has the metadata standards for archiving preserving, and retrieval of information. The Library of Congress is another source that librarians receive metadata information due to the classification system. In 2012, the Library of Congress began to change the source for bibliographic metadata from MARC to the 2016 version BIBFRAME (Bibliographic Framework). The newest version to create metadata was based on new technology being introduced into libraries.

Research libraries have the opportunity to collaborate with other libraries to create a standards based on the Library of Congress Classification system utilizing Blockchain. The collaboration and creation of bibliographic metadata would decentralize the need of a third party, such as OCLC and the Library of Congress. Libraries could create and distribute the metadata that could be updated and tracked. This would mean that libraries did not have to pay a membership fee to OCLC to have their metadata included through acquisitions or through an external source. Through this system libraries could share their MARC or bibliographic metadata with other libraries.

OCLC is a large corporation that has been a producer and owner of metadata since 1971, therefore libraries may have a difficult decision whether to discontinue a reliable service and use Blockchain to create and share bibliographic metadata. However, Blockchain does provide the option for research libraries to create a metadata system. Blockchain could provide the opportunity to create an international metadata system (Hirsh & Alman, 2019). This system could offer libraries the position of the selling and purchasing of metadata, which could generate revenue or even reduce costs of utilizing a third party. In addition, using Blockchain to create metadata could alter the workflow of an organization's operation.

Another purpose that research libraries would utilize Blockchain for metadata is the preservation and archiving items (Hirsh & Alman, 2019). Special collection libraries are responsible numerous items that include historical artifacts and documents. By utilizing Blockchain technology, archivist will be able to create metadata that could be shared with other institutions for research and other preservation needs.

Digital Rights Management

Digital Rights Management is an element of libraries that can be better maintained through Blockchain. Since research libraries act as providers of scientific digital content for patrons, libraries are held accountable of copyrighted digital works and bound by the works' legal permission to use (Abu Sirhan, et al., 2019). Current Digital Rights Management tools includes the encrypted conversion of text and decoding encrypted text in digital media, identification and authenticity systems, digital signatures, digital watermarks that are created in the work, digital fingerprints that allow access through identification, copy detection systems, and payment methods (Abu Sirhan, et al., 2019).

Through Blockchain, publishers and authors will have more control of their works. First of all, Blockchain can create the verifiable transaction, which authors and publishers can establish specific licensing fees for the works. Secondly, owners of the works can control how the work is utilized or even reproduced. According to Hoy & Brigham (2017), Blockchain can assist in the reproduction of digital materials. Hoy & Brigham (2017) stated, "Because the Blockchain creates a unique, verifiable record that can be accessed by anyone, it could be tied to digital materials and used as a method to show 'provable scarcity' of that resource. This would allow digital materials to be uniquely identified, controlled, and transferred" (pp. 276-277).

The Music Modernization Act was signed into law on October 11, 2018 that created the Mechanical licensing Collective to create and maintain an open database by January 1, 2021 of copyrighted works. The database will provide copyright owners' works that will make it easier for licensing agreements to be established between owners and consumers. The purpose of the act was to increase more control to the copyright owners, primarily due to the large streaming platforms, such as Amazon, Apple, Google, Pandora, YouTube, and Spotify.

The open database is also aligned with new technology such as AI and Blockchain. According to Panay, Pentland, & Hardjono (2019),

Layered on top of open, shared standards, new technologies like Blockchain and AI have the potential to allow all participants in the digital music supply chain

– songwriters, performers, producers, labels, publishers, music services, rights societies, licensors and critically, consumers - to safely and securely transact and collaborate with each other, offering unprecedented access to information and data and giving rise to rich new consumer experiences that are currently out of reach due to an antiquated, centuries-old infrastructure.

This is another way in which Blockchain can impact research libraries, because libraries will be able to assist patrons with identifying digital works and establish licensing agreements with the copyright owner, which could be a best practice. Of course, Blockchain also creates other opportunities for copyright owners that includes authors and owners of copyrighted works being able to sell or license their works directly to the consumer. Through Blockchain technology, authors or creators of works are not bound to a third party, such as a publisher or other organization to sell their works to consumers, because Blockchain will allow a secure transaction of the work.

Scholarly Communication and Publishing

Blockchain can provide researchers the opportunity to collaborate with other researchers on specific topics. Researchers could be given a problem that multi researchers can contribute through Blockchain by tracking and providing data pertinent to the research, while maintaining a peer-reviewed system. In addition, researchers will not have to rely on publishers to publish the research, because the work would exist on the Blockchain, which is easily available for those seeking information on the topic instead of searching multiple databases. This form of collaboration would also reduce redundancies in research topics being conducted and published by different researchers in multiple locations (Hirsh & Alman, 2019; Smith, 2019).

In regards to scholarly communication, van Rossum (2018) mentions two platforms that have the potential to disrupt scholarly communication. Scienceroot and Plato are platforms for researchers to collaborate on research topics and to publish their findings. According to van Rossum (2018), "Scienceroot is an open access Blockchain-based scientific ecosystem that combines all of the functionalities required during the scientific discovery process – from funding through research to publishing" (p. 98). The Plato platform is an etherium Blockchain that does not rely on the traditional centralized workflow process to conduct and publish research.

Authors and researchers also have the opportunity to sell their works directly to the buyer, thus again avoiding publishers and providing freedom to openly share information. Digital first sale can be important for libraries if it is an open platform that allows authors to have more control of their works. In other words, libraries could purchase works directly from the authors. The platform DECENT is a Blockchain application that would allow libraries to purchase works directly from the author, which would avoid costs set by publishers or subscription fees from digital subscribers. Through this platform it would provide the consumer with the transparency to know the source of the work, which address issues of credibility.

Open Educational Resources, Supply-Chain Management, and Smart Contracts

Supply-Chain Management would be utilized in the acquisition of Open Educational Resources (OER), which are textbooks or educational materials that are free or at a reduced costs to students. Based on the supply-chain management system, Blockchain could assist with the demand to reduce college student debt by offering OER. Based on the supply-chain's transparency, textbook materials could be produced through Blockchain where faculty could follow the OER chain to determine if the resource is a credible source to support the course curriculum. Basically, the supply-chain management concept offered by the Blockchain technology will allow faculty to trace the origins of information entered in the chain to better evaluate the source for the educational purposes.

In addition, the supply-chain management that Blockchain offers will enhance the record keeping of research libraries in regards to operational expenditures. Due to the budget regulations by government agencies, libraries can be more transparent of their purchases to their stakeholders through the use of Blockchain technology. According to Sissman & Sharma (2018), "Blockchain provides an increased level of transparency across the production of goods in supply chain management" (p. 46). Currently, the U.S. Department of Commerce and the U.S. Department of Defense are utilizing Blockchain to be more transparent and increasing knowledge to track supplies (Sissman & Sharma, 2018). Libraries could also purchase materials with cryptocurrency, as well as purchase international goods or services, such as Interlibrary Loans using cryptocurrency that would be more efficient than using international exchange rates.

In addition, the smart contract concept allows libraries to utilize Blockchain in the place of an Integrated Library System. The Integrated Library System is the primary system that interacts with patrons' services, such as checking out a book or using the Interlibrary Loan service. Through Blockchain, library administrators can maintain patron data and library services. The concept of smart contracts that Blockchain technology offers can be created to place holds on patron's account and accept payments. The technology will also allow libraries the opportunity to set fines, restrictions on borrowing materials, and create a patron history database. The smart contract concept will also allow libraries to analyze patron data effectively by the transparency of the patrons' usage of library services, that includes reference, computer, printer and Interlibrary Loan usages.

Interlibrary Loan and Distance Education

Interlibrary Loan is a library service that libraries provide when patrons request materials that are not in their main library collection, which libraries will then borrow books from other libraries on behalf of the patron. This service is a centralized system, wherein the patron has to request the service from an Interlibrary Loan department or specialist. Through Blockchain, libraries can remove the centralized system by authenticating patron's credentials to borrow books from any library within the consortium Blockchain.

The concept could also apply to Distance Education Library Services where some institutions require a centralized entity, typically a distance education library department or distance education librarian provides the materials to students at satellite campuses or other locations. These entities are third parties that interact as an agent for the library and provides services to distance education students. Basically, if libraries created a consortium Blockchain with other libraries then a student would be issued a library card that would work at any of those libraries through the Distributed Verifiable Sovereign Identity.

Annie Norman, State Librarian of Delaware and Director, Division of Libraries stated that Blockchain could expand stronger securities for patron identity and open several opportunities for public libraries to increase the value of libraries. She noted, "New technological solutions such as a distributed ledger could provide the necessary authentication and privacy capabilities for public libraries to support a universal library card, a union catalog with provenance and ownership verification, data sharing, and more" (Hirsh & Alman, 2019, p. 52).

If libraries could create the standards and a consortium to provide patrons with a universal library card with Blockchain, then this would decentralize Interlibrary Loan and Distance Education services. Of course, the standards for a universal library card would have to ensure patron's data was secure and complied with FERPA regulations. Strengthening personal data is being implemented in the health care field, as health care organizations are attempting to use Blockchain to exchange patient's health information within other health care organizations.

Universal library cards that allow patrons to access multiple library collections through a secure authentication system will increase available collections for patrons and eliminate the need for an Interlibrary Loan department or librarian, as well as Distance Library Education services. By removing the centralized Interlibrary Loan and Distance Education services, research libraries will be able to reduce costs associated with personnel and other operational expenditures.

Educate Students and the Community

If research library administrators determine that Blockchain is not needed for their libraries or cannot justify implementing Blockchain technology into their organization, the library can provide educational workshops or provide information about Blockchain technology to students, faculty, or even the community (Hirsh & Alman, 2019; Smith, 2019). As Blockchain continues to increase usage in businesses and governmental agencies, the demand to gain knowledge of the new technology will increase.

Libraries have an opportunity to provide patrons and the community the best information regarding Blockchain technology. The information can be presented to patrons in workshops or through reference services, as well as the library's collection. Overall, libraries will need to have information about Blockchain as the technology continues to be utilized in other organizations. For research libraries, educating students on the technology is significant in giving students the necessary education about Blockchain to be knowledgeable of Blockchain's potential use in the workforce.

PROBLEMS

While there are numerous possibilities to implement Blockchain technology into a research library, the risk factors do need to be stated. The first and most noted issue with Blockchain technology is the cost. In order to implement and maintain a Blockchain system is to have costly equipment, which requires a server or many servers depending on the size of Blockchain. The servers are expensive and they also require a facility that can store and maintain the correct temperature of the room. Opponents of Blockchain have concerns that the amount of energy used to utilize Blockchain technology is not sustainable and hazardous to the environment. Also, bandwidth is an issue noted by library professionals, due to the amount of bandwidth required to store data.

Secondly, data entry error and immutable is an issue when interacting with Blockchain technology. If information is entered and accepted into the chain, the information could no longer be changed. While the technology is significant in providing data that cannot be altered, the issue of needing to change the data can cause several issues. Due to this problem with Blockchain, attorneys and legislatures are addressing these concerns.

Thirdly, Blockchain is a decentralized concept, yet if a majority is recognized on a Blockchain then an authoritative unit that emerges can control the Blockchain. This creation is also called the 51% Rule, where a person or organization that gains

51 percent of the Blockchain then they are the majority and would have the ability to control the data in the chain. Choo, Yong Park, & Lee, (2017) state that the integrity of the Blockchain can be held if the 51% are good nodes and have no intention of breaking the integrity of the chain. The 51% can also allow for hackers to take control.

Additionally, accessing the Blockchain requires a private or public key, which is the main authentication of the user. If a user loses the key or the information to access the Blockchain, the user cannot access the information on the chain. There have been instances where people invested in cryptocurrency and lost their key along with the money invested in the cryptocurrency. Unlike a third party or centralized system where users that lost their password can request access. Therefore, this would be an issue if a user or an organization loses access to the Blockchain, which could affect library patrons.

Finally, privacy issues for research libraries is concern for library administrators as they comply with FERPA regulations. Despite the secure infrastructure that Blockchain provides, the concept of shared student personal data with external organization is a problem that research libraries and higher educational institutions will have to address.

CONCLUSION

Library administrators have many facets of technology to consider as new technology is being introduced at a rapid rate. For example, Artificial Intelligence (AI) is already being assessed for usages in the library. Cox, Pinfield, & Rutter (2019) noted that AI has the potential to be a disruptive technology for reference services. As AI improves, the opportunities to implement AI in reference services will become more frequent, because AI has the ability to search and retrieve information. This implementation in regards to reference services could change the workforce, as AI could be used to answer reference questions 24 hours a day, seven days a week.

While Blockchain technology is being implemented in various businesses, government organizations, and education, research libraries will have the opportunity to evaluate the role Blockchain will have in their institutions. Furthermore, libraries will be able to create standards and guidelines that will dictate how Blockchain will be utilized in the future. Due to the early inception of Blockchain technology being implemented in organization, research libraries have the opportunity to participant in the design and provide valuable insight as to the usage Blockchain technology will have in research libraries and other libraries. Libraries have been noted as late adopters, therefore library administrators will need to determine when or if they want to implement Blockchain.

As for Digital Rights Management, libraries have the opportunity to be involved in the creation of industry standards as publishers and copyright owners begin to negotiate best practices for using Blockchain technology. Without input from libraries, publishers, copyright owners, and vendors of scientific information could increase costs or even establish restrictions regarding the use of copyrighted works. Therefore, library administrators have the opportunity to be involved in the technology or at least be aware of trade practices.

REFERENCES

Abu Sirhan, A., Abdrabbo, K., Ahmed Ali Al Tawalbeh, S., Hamdi Ahmed, M., & Ali Helalat, M. (2019). Digital rights management (DRM) in libraries of public universities in Jordan. *Library Management, 40*(8/9), 496–502. doi:10.1108/LM-05-2018-0044

American Library Association. (2017). Blockchain. *Library of the Future*. Retrieved from http://www.ala.org/tools/future/trends/blockchain

Berarducci, P. (2019). Collaborative approaches to blockchain regulation: The Brooklyn Project example. *Cleveland State Law Review, 67*(1), 22–30.

Bhargava, R. (2019). Blockchain technology and its application: A review. *IUP Journal of Information Technology, 15*(1), 7–15.

Choo, S., Yong Park, S., & Lee, S. R. (2017). Blockchain consensus rule based dynamic blind voting for non-dependency transaction. *International Journal of Grid and Distributed Computing, 10*(12), 93–106. doi:10.14257/ijgdc.2017.10.12.09

Coghill, J. G. (2018). Blockchain and its implications for libraries. *Journal of Electronic Resources in Medical Libraries, 15*(2), 66–70. doi:10.1080/15424065. 2018.1483218

Cox, A. M., Pinfield, S., & Rutter, S. (2018). The intelligent library: Thought leaders' view on the likely impact of artificial intelligence on academic libraries. *Library Hi Tech, 37*(3), 418–435. doi:10.1108/LHT-08-2018-0105

Cox, A. M., Pinfield, S., & Rutter, S. (2019). Academic libraries' stance toward the future. *Portal (Baltimore, Md.), 19*(3), 485–509.

Griffey, G. (2018). Blockchain & libraries from Carnigie Mellon – Qatar. *Pattern Recognition*. Retrieved from http://jasongriffey.net/wp/2018/03/22/blockchain-libraries-from-carnegie-mellon-qatar/

Hirsh, S., & Alman, S. (Eds.). (2019). *Blockchain*. Neal-Schuman.

Hoy, M. B., & Brigham, T. J. (2017). An introduction to the Blockchain and its implications for libraries and medicine. *Medical Reference Services Quarterly, 36*(3), 273–279. doi:10.1080/02763869.2017.1332261 PMID:28714815

Lindenmoyer, J., & Fischer, M. (2019). Blockchain: Application and utilization in higher education. *Journal of Higher Education Theory & Practice, 19*(6), 71–80.

Ojala, M. (2018). Blockchain for Libraries. *Online Searcher, 42*(1), 15.

Panay, P. A., Pentland, A., & Hardjono, T. (2019). Why success of the Music Modernization Act depends on open standards. *Open Music Initiative*. White Paper. Retrieved from https://static1.squarespace.com/static/56d5e44060b5e9e20a94b16c/t/5bd7199e8165f5a5e9241ae9/1540823454789/Open+Music-Music+Modernization-Open+Standards+White+Paper.pdf

Ray, B. (2019). Blockchain symposium introduction: Overview and historical introduction. *Cleveland State Law Review, 67*(1), 1–21.

Rohr, J. G. (2019). Smart contracts and traditional contract law, or: The law of vending machine. *Cleveland State Law Review, 67*(1), 67–88.

Sissman, M., & Sharma, K. (2018). Building supply management with blockchain: New technology mitigates some logistical risks while adding for a few others. *Industrial and Systems Engineering at Work, 50*(7), 43–46.

SJSU iSchool. (2019). Ways to use blockchain in libraries. *Blockchains for the Information Profession*. Retrieved from https://ischoolblogs.sjsu.edu/blockchains/blockchains-applied/applications/

Smith, C. (2019). Blockchain reaction: How library professionals are approaching Blockchain technology and its potential impact. *American Libraries, 50*(3/4), 26–33.

Tapscott, D., & Tapscott, A. (2017). The blockchain revolution & higher education. *EDUCAUSE Review, 52*(2), 10–24.

Van Rossum, J., & Lawlor, B. (2018). The Blockchain and its potential for science and academic publishing. *Information Services & Use, 38*(1/2), 95–98.

Zalatimo, S. (2018). Blockchain in publishing: Innovation or disruption? *Forbes. Com*. Retrieved from https://www.forbes.com/sites/forbesproductgroup/2018/05/03/blockchain-in-publishing-innovation-or-disruption/#2b632a2a5456

ADDITIONAL READING

Agnew, G. (2008). Digital rights management: A librarian's guide to technology and practice (Chandos information professional series). Oxford, UK: Chandos Publishers.

Assessing Blockchain applications for the public sector: Blockchain basic for governments. (2019). Deloitte. Retrieved from https://www2.deloitte.com/us/en/insights/industry/public-sector/blockchain-public-sector-applications.html

Bashir, I. (2018). *Mastering blockchain: Distributed ledger technology, decentralization, and smart contracts explained* (2nd ed.). Packt Publishing.

Blanchard, D. (2010). *Supply chain management best practices*. John Wiley & Sons.

De Filippi, P., & Wright, A. (2018). *Blockchain and the law: The rule of code*. Harvard University Press. doi:10.2307/j.ctv2867sp

Suber, P. (2012). *Open access*. MIT Press Essential Knowledge Series. MIT Press. doi:10.7551/mitpress/9286.001.0001

KEY TERMS AND DEFINITIONS

Decentralization: The removal of an authoritative central system.

Digital Rights Management: A systematic approach for authors and publishers to protect digital media copyrights.

Immutable: Information stored on a Blockchain cannot be changed.

Integrated Library System: A system that maintains library data for the library's collection and patron information.

Interlibrary Loan: A service provided to library patrons, where the patron's library borrows materials from other libraries.

Metadata: A format that provides data regarding data, such as a bibliographic record that includes data about the author, title, date, information about the work, etc.

Open Educational Resources: A textbook or other educational resources that is accessible for students for free or at a reduced cost.

Scholarly Communication: The research process where research is conducted, evaluated, and preserved for the scholarly community.

Chapter 13
Automating Quality Checks in the Publishing Process

Leslie McIntosh
Ripeta, USA

ABSTRACT

While technology advances, the applications of those technologies within the scientific publishing ecosystem have lagged. There has never been a greater time to increase the speed and accuracy of scientific reporting. Researchers are under immense pressure to conduct rigorous science, and the publishing industry continues to act as a facilitator. Yet, inefficiencies stall the speed and prohibit the consistency of communicating research. This chapter proposes automating quality checks as a means to scale science. The author also explores the publishing process and potential places to use machine learning and natural language processing to enhance the quality—and thus rigor—of reporting scientific research.

OVERVIEW

Ensuring reliable, verifiable, and reproducible research is increasing in complexity yet crucial when translating research to practice (Millman & Pérez, 2014). Various funding agencies have developed standards enforcing rigor, reproducibility, and reporting practices (National Science Foundation, 2014; Collins & Tabak, 2014; Pilat & Fukasaku, 2007). Many of these policies are generalized to diverse methods and materials across clinical, life, and social sciences qualified for federal funding. Yet, it is still difficult to robustly assess the scientific rigor used in research based on the available information in scientific publications. The crisis that science and

DOI: 10.4018/978-1-7998-5589-7.ch013

scholarship have been facing has been well documented by *The Economist, Science,* and *Nature,* among others ("Challenges in Irreproducible Research," 2018; "The Scientific Method: Let's just try that again," 2016; McNutt, 2014). Retractions and failures to replicate studies have resulted in a severe trust and verifiability issue for the public and the broader scientific community. This has a reverberating impact, beyond the individual researcher - it also negatively affects the publisher, funding agency, and affiliated institutions or companies. Research of poor quality, or not applying a rigorous scientific method, has been shown to impact these organizations on a financial level (Munafó, et. al., 2017). Thus, tools and technology are needed to screen and assess manuscripts, proposals, and documentation for proper scientific method components.

Standards for enforcing rigor, reproducibility, and reporting practices are rapidly expanding, yet it is still difficult to robustly assess the scientific rigor used in research based on the available information in scientific publications. One must know the criteria to use (e.g., an appropriate checklist, what 'reproducible' elements should exist) across a broad spectrum of fields (e.g., statistical, study design, domain) then manually assess a publication for its merit.

At *Ripeta,* the team will use a transformative approach to automate the detection and extraction of reproducible elements within scientific publications using machine learning and natural language processing and offer examples throughout the chapter.

Automation is not the antithesis of current practices, but instead a tool to assist in achieving larger goals. There will always be a need for manual intervention in scientific processes. Though *what* tasks take manual momentum today may change in the future. Currently, the human component to publishing is critical in curating knowledge dissemination to broader audiences. In this chapter, the author explores ways in which machine learning can be implemented to break the current stagnation in publishing progress.

CURRENT LANDSCAPE

The scientific community contains many stakeholders: researchers, funders, institutions, publishers, and the public. Each stakeholder plays a key role in this ecosystem, yet no one has full control. Publishers are not responsible for the science but hold the crucial role of reporting the research. Funders are responsible for paying for but typically not conducting the science. Researchers conduct the science and are experts who may still lack expertise in all areas of fully reporting science. Improvement in research quality will come when multiple actors in this network make changes.

To radically change the scientific publishing review, the scientific community must move from manual processes based on peer-review and editor knowledge to automated pipelines programmatically assessing the reported research. Technically this entails items such as i) Obtaining machine-readable information from publications across disciplines and publishers; ii) Transforming the data into a normalized and meaningful structure for future use; then, iii) Using machine learning and natural language processing to accurately identify and extract text. As with any technological solution, there also needs to be the ability to have this solution adopted in practice. Let us first delve into the stakeholders and current practices taking place to ensure scientific rigor in preventing the dissemination and consumption of non-rigorous, non-reproducible science.

Researchers

Maintaining relevance and keeping up with current expectations within *and* outside their discipline challenges every researcher. In addition, they must secure funds for projects and demonstrate the impact of their work. Researchers are recognized as experts in their field and are expected to produce apposite work that is consistent, accurate, and nuanced. Yet, they must have seemingly heroic powers to also incorporate best practices of data sharing and management - among many others - into their work and communication. The 'other' duties required results in researchers expending precious time and energy to support their research but not conduct it.

Research support may exist with good mentorship, supportive institutions, and ample resources, but none of these are guaranteed and the combination of multiple support mechanisms for researchers is fragmented at best. Thus, developing and incorporating automation solutions could have a positive impact on researchers. For this to be successful in supporting researchers, the solutions offered should be for known problems and incorporated into the research workflow.

Academic Institutions

Academic institutions act as the facilitators and conservators of scientific work, modulating their reputations through rigorous and prestigious research. The institution represents the individuals that constitute them and showcase their moral standings through collective action (Kerasidou 2017). Consequently, institutions have the challenge of aligning their researchers' goals with their own while supporting each individual's pursuits. This relationship functions like a distributed system; essentially a collection of independent researchers working in different disciplines, but communicating through the institution to achieve a common goal. So, it is the institution's job to appear as a cohesive unit while utilizing the aggregated knowledge of its researchers to maximize its academic reach. Ideally, this means that the cumulative works of its researchers will reinforce their academic foundation, and compensate for any weaknesses within the system. Yet, even within a single institution, understanding and making decisions upon the distributive landscape of academic research proves opaque. Again, there is another argument to be made to automate the understanding of the academic research landscape.

Funders

As a group, funders include non-governmental/nonprofit entities, governmental sources, and private donors who serve a unique purpose as the arbiters of the research because of access to funds. Each funder has an institutional mission to uphold and ostensibly would like to improve research in the designated field. This may include financially supporting a scientific domain but could also encompass broader activities such as the development of research reporting guidelines (e.g., ARRIVE, CONSORT) (Percie du Sert et. al., 2020; Schultz et. al., 2010). Yet, research grants are becoming increasingly more competitive, and funders are limited in the amount of grant money they can provide to applicants. Therefore, detailed records of the outputs from their funded projects or adherence to guidelines are required to ensure their investments are sound, but the process is difficult. Hence, for similar reasons to academic institutions, an automated solution that provides a landscape view of funders' portfolios could be useful.

Publishers

From entities offering preprint services to formal review and publications, publishers provide exposure and possible validation of scientific research available for consumption and discussion. A spectrum of publishing practices permeates the scientific ecosystem - from reviewing manuscripts to curating information, to hosting papers. Yet, increasing competition, pressure, and expectations have all created a myriad of challenges for publishers to contend with. A successful journal generally will improve scientific discovery and discussion while also being profitable as a company. Preprint services provide an opportunity to increase the speed of scientific discovery and discussion but at the price of quality checks. However, adhering to ideals and scaling to the needs of quality research communication has proven challenging. In addition to the challenges described for researchers, which could result in lower quality publications, publishers must contend with intentional threats to undermine publications. Supporting quality publications at scale can be augmented through a balancing of automatic checks with human curation.

Dividing responsibility among various stakeholders, while natural, impedes the overall improvement of science and scientific rigor. In the current environment, while each stakeholder has a specific responsibility, much of that burden of good science ultimately falls to the researchers. To realize a quality publication process, an understanding should occur of each stakeholder group and the challenges that they must grapple with concerning their responsibilities and incentives (Table 1).

Table 1. Integrating Automation Into Publishing

Researchers	Institutions	Publishers	Funders
Responsibilities Ensure research rigor and methodological transparency. First do no harm.	**Responsibilities** Ensure research aligns with institutional mission and vision.	**Responsibilities** Publish the full scientific workflow. Ensure the dissemination of good science	**Responsibilities and Incentives** Support well-conducted research and ensure funded research is in line with the organizational missions or improving human health.
Incentives Add to scientific discovery, improve personal reputation, increase citations.	**Incentives** Improve, maintain, and/or promote institutional or departmental reputations.	**Incentives** Facilitate scientific discovery, gain citations, increase value.	**Incentives** Facilitate scientific discovery.

While the author has discussed the stakeholders of research, let us look at the process for communicating scientific work and where automation can be embedded. Moving back to the original point, there is a necessity to simultaneously improve science while making science faster. One solution is to incorporate automated quality checks into the publication pipeline. It may be the job of publishers to curate the circulation of knowledge with integrity; it can be the job of the machines to catch what humans do not and do so faster.

Broadly speaking, at some point during the research process, a manuscript is drafted, submitted, reviewed by the editor, peer-reviewed, reviewed by the editor, and possibly published. The process can stop at any point, of course, and there are other mechanisms for publications such as through conference proceedings or preprint services (Figure 1). It is easy to see that to improve the speed and accuracy of scientific research, publishing is one area to incorporate automated processes. As depicted in the figure, areas for quality checks of research can facilitate manuscript screening, peer-review, editor review, and decision making. Moreover, automated checks of published papers can provide metrics and metadata to understand the quality of research from an individual paper to a portfolio of research.

Figure 1.

Current review process and where to introduce automation denoted by ☼ .

As with most human activities, the review process offers many opportunities for improvement. Some limitations to the current process include: Rules are not clear and transparent; Favors the wealthy and well-supported researchers; Lack of consistency in reviews. There is not only a potential for error at every step, but also a potential for misplaced effort leading to poor revisions on authors' manuscripts.

To quickly judge if a researcher supports reproducibility and responsible research, a human can look for a few key items in an article or grant: use of unique author identifiers (e.g., ORCIDs), a well-stated hypothesis, data availability, data citations, code sharing, ethical approval, funding citations, and limited self-citations. Each of these examples has a level of trust; If there is a data availability statement but all it states is to contact the author, the consumer may have less trust in their work than if they have given specific instructions for obtaining the data or a link to the data. But will a person perform these checks consistently? The objective of automation is to program these human judgements into algorithms as accurately as possible.

Ethics and Biases

While out of scope for this chapter, it must be noted that machine algorithms will have biases just like humans, which need to be identified and mitigated. The thought that humans will be better or worse than machines - or vice versa - is false. Yet, machines will move more quickly than people will ever be able to, thereby amplifying both quality and the potential for biases.

As of this writing, the author suggests starting with automating checks in the structure of scientific presentation and keeping the scientific review to humans to support ethical research practices while understanding the mitigating risks of algorithmic biases. This is because before one automates checks in science, there must be a handle on understanding the biases in scientific reviews - algorithms produce results with a probability of being correct, not an absolute assurance of accuracy.

Automating Quality Checks

So options exist to optimize the publishing process and have given some examples of what could be optimized - quality checks of manuscripts. Now the question is *how* is this done? Each quality check must be identified and defined allowing the development of one algorithm that will require different customizing and context. Only after knowing what to look for by clearly defining items should the annotation and algorithm development commence. While many nuances make natural language processing complex, the overarching order of operations is rather straightforward.

For the purposes of this chapter, the author will focus on quality checks that inform the structural quality of manuscripts. This responds to the question: Does the manuscript have the necessary parts? These structural checks include the rigor and transparency of reporting research and have been described elsewhere (McIntosh & Juehne, 2019; McIntosh et. al., 2017). There are other checks both in the quality of the reporting (e.g., statistical checks) as well as the quality of the computations (e.g., data and code checks) (Goulier & Konkol, 2020). Ripeta, Penelope, Gigantum and Code Ocean are all examples of services facilitating these checks. Other chapters in this book will highlight the importance of and uses for other technological applications to publishing such as blockchain. This is an exciting potential for sharing otherwise sensitive data, so let us keep that in the back of our minds for now.

Specifically, let us start with two checks that should be in most research manuscripts and help improve the quality of the paper: a study objective and data availability statement (DAS). The first check sets the stage for the publication while the latter speaks more to the substance of the science. From an AI perspective, searching for the study purpose has a different challenge as compared to checking for a DAS, however they both start in the same manner to develop two algorithms.

Though the results seem instantaneous, automation takes many manual steps. To begin, experts define, differentiate, and further describe (Table 2 and Table 3) each item. This is important, as it creates the data dictionary for which algorithms can be developed and allows for various experts (e.g., information science, domain experts, and algorithm developers) to align understanding and outputs. This is vital to develop an algorithm to produce the expected results expect and reduce the biases baked into the algorithms. This data dictionary provides the foundation for the algorithm development.

An algorithm model is then developed to extract text snippets for each of the target quality checks such as the study objective and DAS. A baseline system is built using straightforward unigram/bigram/trigram bag-of-words (BOW) in a model trained using Naïve Bayes. The data scientists next compare the baseline system to more sophisticated models, including word embeddings generated by deep learning recurrent neural networks; distributional semantic models; and part-of-speech (POS) models, all providing input to several algorithms, including at a minimum, Support Vector Machines (SVM), Random Forests, and Conditional Random Fields. The model is evaluated using the standard metrics for precision, recall, and F-measure. The best-performing model is then embedded in a Python-based NLP pipeline.

Table 2.

Study Objective	
Definition	The main aim of a study (not necessarily the hypothesis though it may overlap) A concise statement in the introduction of the article, often in the last paragraph, that establishes the reason that the research was conducted.
Differentiation	• This is not what makes a good statement, it is the statement itself. • Location matters. This cannot be found in the abstract, methods, results, or discussion. That is a different quality indicator where appropriate.
Typical Location	Introduction, Objective(s)
Also Known As	Study, purpose, hypothesis
Examples	• *The objective of this study is to measure the effective coverage of hypertension screening services at the provincial level in Thailand, using an applied effective coverage framework.* • *We hypothesized that we could identify patients with high psychosocial complexity at risk for increased health care utilization by using only data available in a patient's EHR.* • *In this study, the primary aim was to validate the LACE index in an older Singapore population and the secondary aim was to improve the predictive performance of the LACE index.*
Notes	Usually, the study purpose is in the last paragraph of the Introduction. It is important to note that we are looking for a study purpose stated in the body of the text; we do not include study purposes stated in the abstract in this instance.

Some checks will have binary responses and can easily be extracted with regular expressions (e.g. data objector identifiers (DOI)). The majority of checks are more challenging to identify by a machine because of the nuances of human expression and scientific publications. Developing algorithms using ML/NLP requires first detecting if the text is present for the variable, then understanding the semantic meaning within the text. For example, in assessing if the data is shared, the data scientists can extract data availability statements, yet there are many ways of saying the data is *not* readily available (e.g., "The data is available upon request"). The complexity of the checks dictates the amount of work to develop an algorithm, fewer annotated manuscripts are needed to detect and extract the variables with high precision and recall on the structurally easier text. However, the more complex variables need at least hundreds or thousands of annotated manuscripts for the same level of precision and recall.

For our examples, the data scientists take a set of texts that should contain what is needed - in this case, research manuscripts that should include both a study objective and DAS. From these texts, they attempt different methods for text extraction and iterate over our results to optimize the algorithm. Because Data Availability Statements are separate statements within a paper, they are easier to develop into an algorithm. While study objectives tend to be located at the end of the introduction section of a research paper, their complexities in expression, word use, and topics require more nuanced machine learning training. Hence, the DAS takes less time to develop into an algorithm as compared to the study objective.

As the algorithms are applied to expanding domains of knowledge, the machine learning process requires additional resources to address the differences in semantics and domain-specific vocabulary. Expanding functionality to other domains requires: 1) Defining of quality, reproducibility, and transparency best practices within domain-specific methods; 2) Developing of new algorithms to extract these domain-specific practices, 3) Curating sufficient sample of domain-representative publications to test the recall and precision of the newly developed domain variables. All of these processes will require devoted time and resources, though much of the previous development and lessons learned make this future development in new domains more efficient.

Table 3.

Data Availability Statement (DAS)	
Definition	A statement (in a separate section offset from the main body of text) explaining how/if one can access a study's data.
Differentiation	If there is data availability information within a "Supplementary Materials" or "Supplementary/supporting information" section, it is not a DAS though such information may be included as part of "Data Location."
Typical Location	In an individual section before References or near Acknowledgments at the end of the paper. May also be stated at the very beginning of the paper. Placement of the data availability statement often depends on the journal.
Also Known As	Data and Code Availability Statement; Data and Materials
Examples	• *All raw sequencing data and ancillary analyses are deposited in the GEO database under the accession number GSE94518.* • *All data generated or analyzed during this study are included in this published article (and its Supplementary Information files).* • *Public use datasets are available at https://www.icpsr.umich.edu/icpsrweb/ICPSR/series/253.* • *The datasets generated and/or analyzed during the current study are not publicly available due to embedded protected health information in conversations, but are available from the corresponding author upon reasonable request.* • *Data sharing is not applicable to this article as no datasets were generated or analyzed during the current study.*
Notes	This is different from data location. Rather than looking for the information itself, this variable is looking for the statement as a whole. The examples above are only two of the many variations for the title of the DAS section.

RIPETA AS A CASE STUDY IN AUTOMATION IN PUBLISHING INNOVATION

While publisher and funder guidelines for quality, transparency, and reproducibility exist, they are not comprehensive, often ambiguous, and resource-intense to implement. Ripeta streamlines the publication review process by automating quality checks using machine learning and natural language processing. The unique approach generates usable findings in an audience-agnostic and easily intelligible format, providing an intuitive and evidence-supported method for multiple stakeholders to evaluate the quality of published literature. As depicted in Figure 2, understanding the quality indicators of research augments the complete research lifecycle from creation and planning to discovery and reuse.

Figure 2.

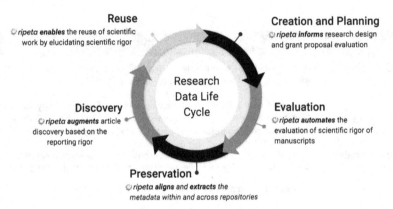

Reuse
ripeta **enables** the reuse of scientific work by elucidating scientific rigor

Creation and Planning
ripeta **informs** research design and grant proposal evaluation

Discovery
ripeta **augments** article discovery based on the reporting rigor

Research Data Life Cycle

Evaluation
ripeta **automates** the evaluation of scientific rigor of manuscripts

Preservation
ripeta **aligns** and **extracts** the metadata within and across repositories

To illustrate the implementation of quality checks into the publishing process, the author will use a recent case. The Coronavirus 2019 (Covid-19) pandemic revealed a vital need to increase the speed of verified, scientific scholarship. Using data from COVID-19 preprints in March 2020, Ripeta conducted an analysis of 535 preprints based on the inclusion of six key quality checks: study objective, authorship, funding statement, DAS, data location, and code availability. Through automation, data scientists rapidly checked the manuscripts for each of these measures and scored the papers according to their completeness. The overall results are described elsewhere, but four results highlight the differences among text and potential use cases (Sumner, et. al., 2020).

As shown in Table 4, the four preprints contained varying degrees of quality checks - from one that did not report funding, DAS, data sharing location, or code availability to one that reported all of those (Ahmed, Quadeer, & McKay, 2020; Gautret, et. al., 2020; Pradhan et. al., 2020; Zhao, et. al., 2020). Thus, their quality rankings vary from low to high.

Table 4.

Covid Preprint Analyses	Study Objective	Funding Statement	DAS	Data Location	Code Availability	ripetaRank
Similarity nCoV spike protein DOI: 10.1101/2020.01.30.927871	Yes	No	No	None	No	Low
Hydroxychloroquine DOI: 10.1101/2020.03.16.20037135	Yes	Yes	Yes	On request	No	Medium
ABO Blood Group DOI: 10.1101/2020.03.11.20031096	Yes	Yes	Yes	In paper	No	Medium
Potential vaccine targets DOI: 10.1101/2020.02.03.933226	Yes	Yes	Yes	External repo	Yes	**High**

There are a couple of interesting takeaways from this research. First, it is possible to automate quality checks on papers that can inform further publication decisions. There are clear differences in the quality of each paper that could inform editorial decisions. Depending on the decision, a ranking could inform how to quickly move the paper back to the author for immediate revisions or to the editors for consideration for peer review. Second, if these checks were implemented at the pre-print stage, the information could also assist readers in weighing the strength of the paper quality.

Table 5.

Covid Preprint Analyses	ripetaRank	Outcome	Citations
Similarity nCoV spike protein DOI: 10.1101/2020.01.30.927871	Low	Withdrawn	50
Hydroxychloroquine DOI: 10.1101/2020.03.16.20037135	Medium	Questioned, Published	**3000**
ABO Blood Group DOI: 10.1101/2020.03.11.20031096	Medium	Overhyped, Not Published	150
Potential vaccine targets DOI: 10.1101/2020.02.03.933226	**High**	**Published**	450

Currently, as shown in Table 5, the quality of the paper does not correlate with its outcome or citations. While the Hydroxychloroquine study garnered much public attention and scientific scrutiny, some structural improvements - or at least salient structural questions - could have been asked before given the attention it garnered (Gautret, et. al., 2020). For example, Where are the data?

On the other hand, the ABO Blood Group also fared decently in the preprint's structure but did not gain as much attention. It did gain international attention when it posited that there was a lower risk of Covid-19 infection associated with blood group O compared to non-O blood groups (Zhao et. al. 2020). For them, the hype overpowered the science and led to an otherwise decent paper not being published.

CONCLUSION

Right now, the world is watching science. The distrust of science has been gaining momentum for decades even though science and scientists are still greatly trusted. Every overhyped non-finding has the potential of spreading inaccurate information just as relevant, rigorous research could be overlooked. These factors coupled with the sheer volume of research papers put further pressure on the publishers to produce studies that are accurate, reproducible, and ultimately instill *trust* in science as opposed to suspicion. As illustrated in the above examples, automating the reviewing process would have caught potentially misleading results, and in turn, allowed the publishers to focus their attention on the quality of the work. With a greater influx of scientific research, there needs to be further checks and at a faster speed. By the end of 2020, the number of preprints in bioRxiv and medRxiv grew to nearly 12,000 (COVID-19 SARS-CoV-2 preprints from medRxiv and bioRxiv, 2021). Humans alone can not keep up with the needed checks, but augmenting audits through computer automation can improve the pace and rigor of science.

ACKNOWLEDGMENT

This work is made possible through a collaborative effort of fantastic individuals working to improve the quality of science including: Cynthia Hudson Vitale, Leah Haynes, Paola Ortega Saborío, Josh Sumner, August Devore Welles, Chris Westling, Ruth Whittam. Thanks to August Devore Welles for editing the chapter.

REFERENCES

Ahmed, S. F., Quadeer, A. A., & McKay, M. R. (2020). Preliminary identification of potential vaccine targets for the COVID-19 coronavirus (SARS-CoV-2) based on SARS-CoV immunological studies. *Viruses*, *12*(3), 254. doi:10.3390/v12030254 PMID:32106567

Challenges in Irreproducible Research Nature. (2018). https://www.nature.com/news/reproducibility-1.17552

Collins, F. S., & Tabak, L. A. (2014). Policy: NIH plans to enhance reproducibility. *NATNews*. PMID:24482835

COVID-19 SARS-CoV-2 preprints from medRxiv and bioRxiv. (n.d.). https://connect.medrxiv.org/relate/content/181

Gautret, P., Lagier, J. C., Parola, P., Meddeb, L., Mailhe, M., Doudier, B., . . . Honoré, S. (2020). Hydroxychloroquine and azithromycin as a treatment of COVID-19: results of an open-label non-randomized clinical trial. *International Journal of Antimicrobial Agents*, 105949. doi:10.1101/2020.03.16.20037135

Goulier, L., Nüst, D., & Konkol, M. (2020). *Publishing computational research-a review of infrastructures for reproducible and transparent scholarly communication*. doi:10.118641073-020-00095-y

Kerasidou, A. (2017). Trust me, I'm a researcher! The role of trust in biomedical research. *Medicine, Health Care, and Philosophy*, *20*(1), 43–50.

McIntosh, L. D., & Juehne, A. (2019). Automating the pre-review of research. *Information Services & Use*, 1-6. doi:10.3233/isu-190048

McIntosh, L. D., Juehne, A., Vitale, C. R., Liu, X., Alcoser, R., Lukas, J. C., & Evanoff, B. (2017). Repeat: A framework to assess empirical reproducibility in biomedical research. *BMC Medical Research Methodology*, *17*(1), 143.

McNutt, M. (2014). Reproducibility. *Science*, *343*(6168).

Millman, K. J., & Perez, F. (2014). Developing Open-Source Scientific Practice. In *Implementing Reproducible Research. R series*. CRC Press Taylor & Francis Group, LLC. doi:10.1201/b16868

Munafò, Nosek, Bishop, Button, Chambers, du Sert, Simonsohn, Wagenmakers, Ware, & Ioannidis. (2017). A Manifesto For Reproducible Science. *Nature Human Behaviour*, *1*(1). doi:10.103841562-016-0021

National Science Foundation. (2014). *A Framework for Ongoing and Future National Science Foundation Activities to Improve Reproducibility, Replicability, and Robustness in Funded Research*. Off Management Budget.

Percie du Sert, N., Hurst, V., Ahluwalia, A., Alam, S., Avey, M. T., & Baker, M. (2020). The ARRIVE guidelines 2.0: Updated guidelines for reporting animal research. *Journal of Cerebral Blood Flow and Metabolism, 40*(9), 1769–1777.

Pilat, D., & Fukasaku, Y. (2007). OECD principles and guidelines for access to research data from public funding. *Data Science Journal, 6*, OD4–OD11.

Pradhan, P., Pandey, A. K., Mishra, A., Gupta, P., Tripathi, P. K., Menon, M. B., . . . Kundu, B. (2020). *Uncanny similarity of unique inserts in the 2019-nCoV spike protein to HIV-1 gp120 and Gag*. doi:10.1101/2020.01.30.927871

Schulz, K. F., Altman, D. G., & Moher, D.Consort Group. (2010). CONSORT 2010 statement: Updated guidelines for reporting parallel group randomised trials. *Trials, 11*(1), 32.

Sumner, J., Haynes, L., Nathan, S., Hudson-Vitale, C., & McIntosh, L. D. (2020). *Reproducibility and reporting practices in COVID-19 preprint manuscripts* [preprint]. doi:10.1101/2020.03.24.20042796

The Scientific Method. Let's just try that again. (2016). Retrieved January 04, 2021, from https://www.economist.com/science-and-technology/2016/02/06/lets-just-try-that-again

Zhao, J., Yang, Y., Huang, H. P., Li, D., Gu, D. F., Lu, X. F., . . . He, Y. J. (2020). *Relationship between the ABO Blood Group and the COVID-19 Susceptibility* [preprint]. doi:10.1101/2020.03.11.20031096

Chapter 14
DJournal:
A Blockchain-Based Scientific-Paper-Reviewing System With a Self-Adaptive Reviewer Selection Sub-System

Shantanu Kumar Rahut

iD https://orcid.org/0000-0001-9507-7630
Saarland University, Saarland, Germany

Razwan Ahmed Tanvir
East West University, Bangladesh

Sharfi Rahman
East West University, Bangladesh

Shamim Akhter
*International University of Business Agriculture and Technology (IUBAT),
Bangladesh*

ABSTRACT

The paper reviewing process evaluates the potentiality, quality, novelty, and reliability of an article prior to any scholarly publication. However, a number of recent publications are pointing towards the occurrence of the biasness and mistreatments during the progression of the reviewing process. Therefore, the scientific community is involved to standardize the reviewing protocols by introducing blind and electronic submission, selecting eligible reviewers, and supporting an appropriate checklist to the reviewers. The amplification of reviewing with decentralization and automation can solve the mentioned problems by limiting the possibility of human interaction. This chapter proposes and implements a decentralized and anonymous paper reviewing

DOI: 10.4018/978-1-7998-5589-7.ch014

system (DJournal) using blockchain technology. DJournal eliminates all the trust issues related to the reviewing process but improves reliability, transparency, and streamlining capabilities with up-gradation of the machine learning-based reviewer selection approach.

INTRODUCTION

Scientific paper reviewing is a process of critically appraise, examine and evaluate research quality and secure essential features, substantive appearance, related evidence current findings on theoretical and methodological innovations and their proofs by the domain experts (Mulligan, Hall & Raphael, 2012, p. 132-161). Therefore, reviewing can be considered as the backbone and the final metric of analysis for publishing a research work, for approving a grant application, or for offering a reward, and etc. Considering the above involvement of reviewing in scientific communities, it is necessary to keep reviewing more transparent, trustier and freer from human relate prejudices including author's reputation, gender, and institution rather than their submission quality. Reviewing should provide a valuable judgment and constructive feedback, and thus helps to contribute to the scientific discoveries (Kelly, Sadeghieh & Adeli, 2014, p. 227–243). In this regard, publishers or relevant organizations follow devise strategies including blind reviewing, double-blind reviewing, and etc. to improve their reviewing and ensure fewer biases but more trustful and more transparent system. However, still many peer-reviewing frauds are detected and removed from various journals for biased reviewing (Stoye, 2019) (Mahoney, 1977) including Sage publications removed 60 research papers for exploiting peer reviews (Fanelli, 2009). In the traditional reviewing process, the biasness can occur at the very beginning (assignment phase) of a systematic reviewing process. Here, a submitted paper can be influenced by the editor and can contribute biasness. Reviewers can also be biased or offer biased reviews. The whole reviewing process is questionable if anyone from the editor or reviewers forgets his/her ethical norms and drowns into dishonesty. Thus, a new peer-reviewing system is needed to solve the drawbacks of existing traditional reviewing system and assigns reviewers a submitted research paper automatically without any human interaction (Clarke, 2013). In this paper, we present a reviewing system without any explicit influencing factors, biasness, or un-trust issues, but with more trustful and more transparent. The proposed system improves the reviewing process and resolves all un-trustful issues with the following contributions:

1. The article implements a blockchain-based decentralized and automated reviewing system named "DJournal", with the help of a smart-contract and IPFS.
2. DJournal integrates a machine learning-based self-adaptive process for choosing appropriate reviewers for a submitted paper.
3. DJournal supports a ranking algorithm for ranking the eligible reviewers.
4. DJournal provides an easier interface to help authors for submitting papers, and reviewers for receiving papers.
5. In addition, a novel hybrid decentralized system or HDS for diminishing the possibility of fake or fraudulent users (reviewer/author) from registration in "DJournal" is also discussed.

The remainder of the paper is organized as follows: "Related Work" features the state-of-the-art automated reviewing system. "Background" features some background information related to blockchain, smart-contract, and IPFS. "System model and implementation of DJournal" overviews the proposed system with a summary of the workflows is provided with the system design and description of different parts of our proposed decentralized reviewing system (DJournal). This section also includes the work methods of DJournal, Research field prediction mechanism using machine learning approach and demo application. A series of experiments with detailed result analysis is provided in "Result analysis". "Discussion" section features the discussion over the implemented system, its limitations, and future modifications. "Conclusion" concludes the paper with concluding remarks.

RELATED WORK

Currently reviewing is the "most standard" process for any scholarly publication. Almost 90% scientist recommends reviewing is effective for the development and improvement in technological areas (Mulligan et. el., 2012, p. 132-161). Researchers and Scholars are getting their works reviewed by peers, which helps them to work further and gives room for improvement. Even with so much popularity, the process has many drawbacks including poor evaluation, personal conflicts, gender biases, stealing thoughts, etc. Thus, in recent years, people have attempted for a better and automated reviewing system. Besides the single-blind reviewing (Cho, Kwangsu & Schunn, 2007) and peer reviewing, modern computerized reviewing system can be categorized broadly into two (2) different categories including centralized and distributed.

Paper in (Cho et. el., 2007) introduces a centralized reviewing system. Here, the authors presented a web-based client-server application named SWoRD (Scaffolded Writing and Rewriting in the Discipline) and its working strategies. Authors in (Gehringer, 2001) introduced another web-based reviewing system for grading assignments of students. There were six phases from signing up to web publishing of the assignment. In (Kahani, Mohsen & Borchardt, 2017), authors discussed a way for exploiting a flaw in SMTP protocol to include email spoofing, and that can lead to manipulate the overall centralized reviewing system. They also suggested a solution for this kind of reviewing problem by introducing unique random ID to the authentic reviewers with their authentic email address.

Centralized web-based review systems in (Cho et. al., 2007), (Gehringer, 2001) and (Kahani et. al., 2017) are prone to cyber-attacks thus compromising the security of the submitted papers. Cyber attackers could easily delete, modify, and update any kind of information or reviewing decision from the centralized system. They could also steal the research items and publish it elsewhere with their own identity. In addition, if a centralized server is destroyed, all information regarding submitted, reviewed and published researches may loss forever. Distributed review systems bear the same problems of being prone to cyber-attacks. However, it diminishes the possibility of losing information regarding reviewed or submitted or published research works.

Decentralized blockchain-based reviewing systems are a new addition to the automated reviewing system. In our previous book chapter (Rahut, Tanvir, Rahman & Akhter, 2019) we proposed a methodological framework for decentralized reviewing system using blockchain, smart-contract, and IPFS. The paper introduces three (3) sections – submission, selection, and review. The paper also introduces reputation-point as modified crypto-currency, which would be used as modified gas money ("What is Gas? | MyEtherWallet Knowledge Base," n.d.) to find the eligible reviewer and to fuel the decentralized review process. Paper (Tenorio-Fornés, Jacynycz, Llop-Vila, Sánchez-Ruiz & Hassan, 2019) also directs toward a similar approach and proposes a decentralized reviewing system using blockchain, smart contract, and IPFS. Paper in (Jan, 2018) focuses on recognition and rewarding system for reviewers. In this system, authors can submit a punishment or a reward to reviewers according to their reviewing decision using blockchain.

However, the explained systems are in the theoretical domain and waiting for implementation. In paper (Avital, 2018), the authors presented a token-based payment system for reviewers using blockchain. Although, the papers in (Tenorio-Fornés et. al. 2019), (Jan, 2018) and (Avital, 2018) are discussed monetary value as a payment and similar things using crypto-currency but do not focus on the arise problems due to the monetary value including the attempt of bribing, or asking/offering money in exchange for getting favors in reviewing. Dishonest reviewers could find the public key of the author and ask for crypto-currency or authors could find out the public key of the reviewers and send some crypto-currency in exchange for favors. Having multiple user wallets or accounts for a person wouldn't create any problem during the uses of blockchain system in currency transaction purpose problems. However, in the case of blockchain based paper reviewing system multiple user wallets or accounts for a single person poses severe threats. While registering as a reviewer for a decentralized paper reviewing system, a person (dishonest) can claim himself or herself as a higher rank expert and demands to have a large number of publications on a particular subject.

In all current blockchain systems, there is no perfect way of making sure that the information given during registration in the blockchain is true or not. This happens because of the interior structure of blockchain where multiple accounts of a person are possible but impossible to trace the multi-accounts holders. In our proposed system, this will create a major or dominating threat. One author-reviewer may have multiple review accounts with high-rank expertise and large publication numbers will influence our system to choose him/her as multiple reviewers and the situation becomes even more complex when he is the author of the submitted article. Author becomes the only (multiple) reviewers of his submitted paper. This will cause loss of credibility of the system, rise biasness and bring forth trust issues regarding the blockchain based peer-review systems.

The Papers by (Tenorio-Fornés et. al., 2019), (Jan, 2018), (Avital, 2018) and also our previous proposed model in (Rahut et. al., 2019) do not state or even discuss the above-mentioned problem or its feasible solution(s). Thus, in this paper we are going to extend our previous proposed research (Rahut et. al., 2019), using machine learning approaches for Tag prediction for finding eligible reviewers. Besides, we are proposing a novel approach for a hybrid decentralized system to diminish the possibility of fake or fraudulent users from registration (reviewer, editor, and authors) in this system.

BACKGROUND

Blockchain

Blockchain is a special type of distributed ledger (shared database) with a set of distinct features including transactions that are verified by all network computers and stored information into a block. Blockchain guarantees the immutability of the ledger, as any form of modification in the block needs to manipulate every copy of the blockchain on the network. Any transaction that happens on blockchain is irreversible. There is no single point of failure in the blockchain. In a blockchain network, adding data into a block is considered as a transaction in the network. Every transaction in the blockchain network has a lifecycle and it is summarized below:

- A transaction is initiated by a node in the network. Thereafter the transaction is sent to the other participants of that network for the verification of that transaction.
- There are some rules to decide a transaction is valid or not. These rules are validated by the computers of the network.
- After the verification, the transaction is included in a block and a cryptographic hash is generated to sign that block. This hash generation process is also called mining. Cryptographic hash ensures the security of the block so that no one can tamper the inside data and thus keeps the immutability. After signing the block, it is broadcast to the other nodes in the network to verify if the block is valid against some preset validation rules. Upon validation, the node is added to the existing chain of blocks of the network. This process is done through the consensus mechanism. This mechanism is generally applied to multi-agent systems in a distributed process to make the system fault-tolerant. Unlike traditional databases, blockchain has no single authority to maintain the state of the ledger, so a public blockchain network must use a mechanism that can ensure the integrity of the ledger. There are multiple consensus mechanisms currently being used in different systems with different methods. The consensus algorithm that is used by the Ethereum network is called Proof of Stake (PoS) (Saleh, 2018). Due to consuming less energy to process transactions, it minimizes the cost of verifying network transactions. It states that higher value of the stake has higher right to add new blocks to the system.
- A transaction is processed, validated and added to the block with the participation of all the nodes in the network. It makes the system resilient and trusted as there is no involvement of any third party to tamper with data.

Smart Contract

Figure 1 gives a brief idea about smart-contracts. A smart-contract is a feature provided by Ethereum blockchain. A smart contract can be considered a sophisticated node and an autonomous account of a blockchain network. This node can store data and execute pre-written commands autonomously based on certain conditions. This autonomous feature of the smart contract makes them a potential substitute for intermediaries. Therefore, intermediaries can be eliminated if smart contracts are used to execute a contract. We use Solidity language to develop our smart contract because it is the most used and effective language for developing smart contracts at present. The developed smart contract is deployed on the Rinkeby test network to verify its components, and for debugging purposes. This test network is also free to use. So, it is sufficient and appropriate to deploy the test run of the smart contract on Rinkeby. After the final development, this contract is deployed to the main network.

Figure 1. Life cycle of blockchain with smart-contract governing the transactions

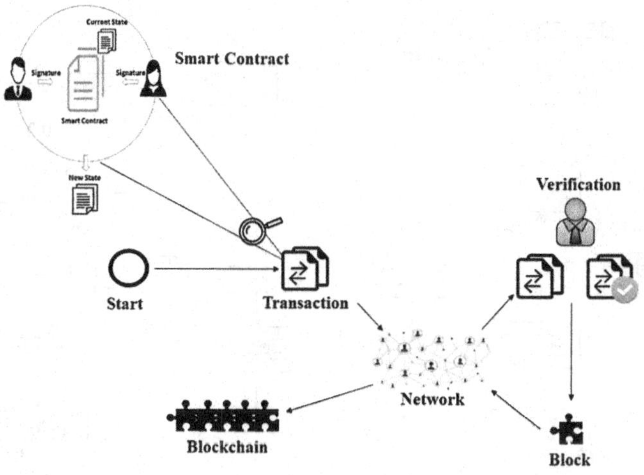

IPFS Technology

Storage in the blockchain network is very costly as the information replicates in the whole network. So, it is inefficient to store large files into blockchain. Inter Planetary File System (IPFS) (GitHub, 2019) is a technology where files are uploaded and generated corresponding hash codes. A file can be accessed by the network participants using its unique hash code. Thus, this technology is integrated with blockchain and brings effectiveness in the file storage.

Keccak-256

Ethereum integrates Keccak-256 method (Keccak, 2019) to generate hash values. The input space for Keccak-256 is infinite and the output string is of 32 Bytes or 256 bits. All the blocks are connected and secured by these hash values. This Keccak-256 method takes a large text or even files and encrypts them. Every file has a unique hash value and it uses to validate that no change is made to the source file. This hash function is used to sign the transactions in the Ethereum blockchain. Moreover, this function helps to make the chain secure so that no one can compromise the integrity of the platform.

Figure 2. Dataflow diagram of DJournal

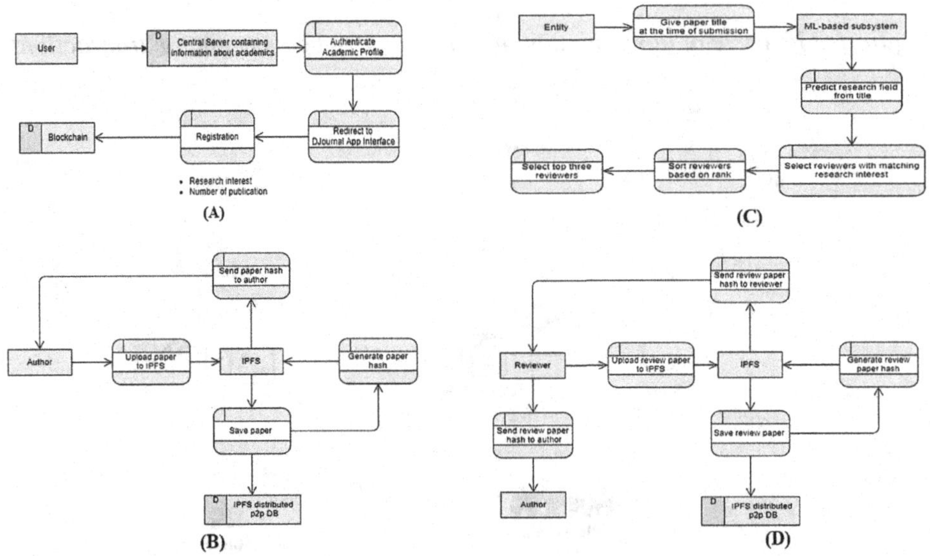

SYSTEM MODEL AND IMPLEMENTATION OF DJOURNAL

The full system model of the proposed DJournal with its implementation threats and technical challenges are presented here. The system consists of two (2) kinds of actors including Author and Reviewer. A registered user can act as Author, or Reviewer, or both. The role of the authors is to submit papers for reviewing process. The role of the reviewers is to review a submitted paper. In our proposed system, there is no role for editor because it is played by the system itself. The system in fact works as an automated editor. The system finds an eligible reviewer based on a new algorithm proposed in (Rahut et. al., 2019). Thus, the complete paper reviewing system is divided into four different sub-sections including Registration, Submission, Selection and Review. Figure 3. presents the sequence diagram of DJournal.

A brief overview of the whole reviewing process is given below:

Figure 3. Sequence diagram of paper reviewing process

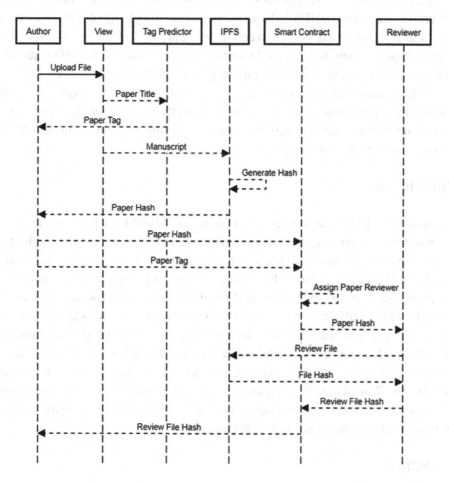

Registration

The whole system is implemented with a smart contract using solidity for backend and ReactJs for frontend or user interface. Backend of the application (DJournal) contains a smart-contract and it is written in solidity language. The frontend program is written using ReactJs. Anyone who wishes to use the system has to register first. The data flow for the registration process is shown in Figure 2(A).

The registration process needs to ensure that one person shouldn't have multiple accounts. Having multiple accounts can severely threaten the credibility of the reviewing system. In a situation, where someone uploads a paper from one account, and review the same paper using different account can direct towards a big security loophole. There is also another possibility of creating accounts with false information.

Our proposed DJournal registration system adds a novel approach towards Hybrid Decentralized System or HDS, to bypass these two security loopholes of conventional decentralized systems. It includes a centralized gateway website that is responsible to open a user account with their educational institute's mail id and all the required fields including research interest, publication number, Google scholar link, and etc. After getting confirmation from the gateway, the user is redirected to the decentralized application's webpage, in this case, the interface of the paper review/ paper submission system described. Thus, HDS implementation in registration improves the security of the system.

Submission

The workflow of the system begins with the act of submitting a paper to the system for reviewing purpose. Large file transmission in blockchain is very costly, thus a new associative framework IPFS (Inter Planetary File System) is integrated to handle the large files. A user, who wishes to submit a paper, can submit papers via the client-side application. The application grabs the selected file and uploads it to IPFS. Thereafter, IPFS then returns a hash string which is a downloadable link for the uploaded paper. The link is then sent to the smart contract through the user-interface. The client-side application then takes that link and sends it to the reviewers inside the system with the help of blockchain and smart contract. A dataflow diagram explains the flow of data throughout the paper submission process in Figure 2(B). The paper also introduces a new sub-system based on machine learning for selecting and sending the paper to an eligible reviewer.

Selection

A Reviewer is deemed fit for doing a review if he or she has -

1. Same research area as the submitted paper.
2. Number of published papers on that particular research-area.

The system selects the best possible reviewers to review a submitted paper automatically based on the algorithm proposed in our previous work in (Rahut et. al., 2019). The system tries to match the research domain of the submitted paper and the research domain of the users of the system. To do that, the system collects the research domain and publication numbers from a user (Reviewer) at the time of his or her registration process. The system with the help of the sub-system collects the research domain of the submitted paper automatically from the paper title. The sub-system predicts text-based tags from the paper title given by the author at the submission time. Later, these tags are used to find an eligible match from the reviewer's information. If there is a match, the system then sorts the matched users (Reviewers) based on their number of publications on the specific research domain.

The first three eligible reviewers are ranked using the ranking algorithm based on Eq. (1). The reviewer is selected based on same research domain as the submitted paper, and larger number publications on the field.

$$R\gamma = \sum_{\varphi=1}\left(NP\varphi + RP\varphi\right) * RS\gamma$$

where

$R\gamma$ = Rank of the γ th reviewer
$NP\varphi$ = No. of publication at φ th instance
$RP\varphi$ = Reputation point at the φ th instance
$RS\gamma$ = Review status of the γ th reviewer

A user of DJournal, who is willing to review a paper, may choose "active" or "busy" status. If someone chooses "busy" status, his or her total no. of publication and reputation points will be multiplied by 0 (zero). Thus, busy reviewers will get the lowest rank and thus won't be selected as reviewers. If someone chooses "active" status, his or her total no. of publication and reputation points will be multiplied by 1 (one). Thus, he or she will be ranked according to his or her capability. If the system sends a review request to an unwilling user and he or she does not respond by either accepting or rejecting, the review request will hang there for an indefinite time. This modified algorithm ranks only those users who are willing to review as reviewers. This whole process is done automatically by the system with the help of a developed smart contract. As, in this system, the smart contract selects the reviewer, and thus it acts as smart editor! Figure 2(C) illustrates the reviewer selection process using a dataflow diagram. Figure 4 illustrates the research domain prediction subsystem model. The dataset includes 20000 research paper titles with keywords. They are labeled based on their keywords. The model uses 80% data for training and 20% data for testing. Data are first pre-processed using Tokenization, Lemmatization, and Stop word removal techniques. Punctuation marks are also removed. Then using the Tfidfvectorizer, features were extracted from the processed data. Tfidfvectorizer follows the bag-of-words model, and it is a very common method of feature extraction. The extracted features are fed into the ML algorithms for classification purposes. After training, the model is able to predict the class of a newly given paper title. After completing the research field prediction process from submitted paper title, the predicted research field is used for ranking potential reviewers according to an algorithm represented by Eq. (1).

Figure 4. Proposed model of research field prediction from submitted paper title using machine learning

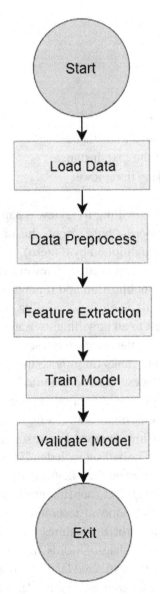

Review

The last part of the workflow is the review process. After the Reviewers are selected by the smart contract (sub-system), they receive the download link from the IPFS. The reviewers then download the paper. Then they review it. After successful reviewing, they submit their review report(s) using the similar technique of file submission with the help of IPFS and smart contract. Figure 2(D) explains the data flow inside the system throughout the review process. The smart-contact mentioned earlier is responsible for sending the reviews to the authors automatically right after the reviews have been submitted.

Demo Application of DJournal

An application is created with Solidity and ReactJs for experimenting with the accuracy of the proposed framework. The sections provided in Figure 5 will try to give a view of the developed application based on the proposed framework. The whole application has five (5) different sections. The upper left section presents the user registration form. Interested researchers can become a user of the system by giving the research interest in the "Tag" marked box and total number of publications in "Number of publication" marked box.

The upper right section of the application is used for submitting a paper for the review process. First, the title of the paper needs to place in the "Paper Title" box. The research domain is selected using the research domain prediction mechanism using machine learning of that uploaded paper and inserted into the "Paper Tag" box. After that, he or she presses the "Submit" button. Then the user taps on the "Choose File" button, he or she can then select a paper to upload. After everything is taken care of, he or she presses the "Send it" button places a transaction. The developed smart contract for this system selects Reviewers based on the matching of the research domain with the submitted paper and the number of publications. Selected reviewers will then receive the download link of the submitted paper.

The lower right section is the part where Reviewers can choose to accept or deny the reviewing request of a submitted paper. A user can press the "Check Review Request" button to check if the system is asking him or her to review a paper. He or she can accept the request for reviewing the paper by pressing "Accept Review Request" or reject/deny the request by pressing "Reject Review Request". Reviewers can also choose active or busy status by clicking "Become Active" or "I am Busy" button. If the Reviewer accepts the review request for a submitted paper, he or she then can collect the downloadable link of that paper produced by IPFS, by clicking "Check Assigned Paper Hash". After the review, the Reviewer can submit his or her review comments as a file. He or she can select the file by clicking "Choose

File" then press 'Send it" to send the review directly to the author of the submitted paper through a transaction.

The transaction is governed by the developed smart contract for the system. The Author who has submitted a paper for reviewing can check the review of his or her work. The lower-left section of the application is dedicated for that purpose. If the review is sent by the reviewers, by clicking the "Get Review on Submitted Paper" button, the user can see the download links of the files containing review comments.

The middle left section of the application is used for viewing necessary and associated information of the submission. After submitting a paper for reviewing, the user can see his or her own Ethereum address, research field of the paper (paper tag), IPFS generated hash code of the submitted paper, his or her total number of paper, address of the smart contract (address of the genesis block where the contract is stored), transaction hash, current number of blocks in the blockchain and the price of the transaction (gas price) in ether by clicking "Get Transaction Receipt".

Figure 5. DJournal application interface

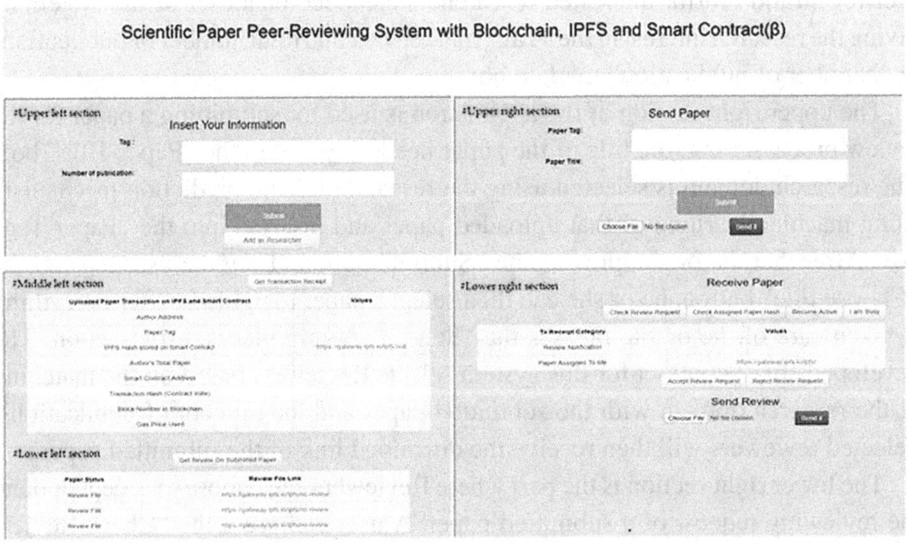

RESULT ANALYSIS

Testing Submission Process (Paper Submission and Review Submission)

The system uses IPFS as a distributed database. Uploading and downloading papers from IPFS are two major tasks of the system, thus performance of IPFS is very crucial. We tested the load on the IPFS network and it showed promising results. Different sizes of files were uploaded to IPFS and their uploading time was measured in seconds. It is usual to submit research papers in Latex, pdf, doc, docx, etc. format, for reviewing. DJournal also supports these conventional file

formats. Research paper files of these formats usually from 5MB to 20MB size. Figure 6 presents that it takes 0.16-0.7 seconds for uploading files of such size. So, the proposed system gives a good performance in its main task of submitting a paper for review by the author and submitting a review by the reviewer. The experiment was done using a machine with Intel 7th gen core i7-7500U processor, and 8GB ddr4 RAM.

Figure 6. Upload time on IPFS

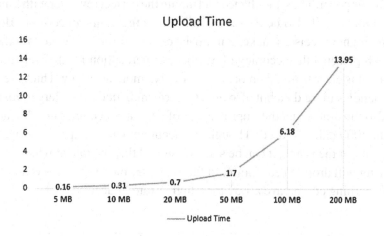

Testing Machine-Learning Based Automatic Reviewer Selection-

The newly proposed ML-based subsystem for research field prediction is very important for making automation in the process of reviewer selection. Figure 7 shows the comparisons between Gradient boosting, Multi-layer perceptron, Naïve Bayes, Support Vector machine, and Logistic regression algorithms in terms of precision, recall, f1-score, and accuracy. This experiment was done using a machine with an Intel core i7-8700K processor and 16GB ddr4 RAM. It is clear from Figure 8 that Multi-layer perceptron gives better results in the case of research domain prediction.

A Multi-layer perceptron gives a score of 77% in precision. Precision directs to the ratio of correctly predicted observed class and total predicted observed class. Higher precision leads to a lower number of false positives. Recall is the ratio of correctly predicted positive observed class and total positive observed class. Higher recall leads to a lower number of false negatives. F1-score is the weighted average of precision and recall. Accuracy is the ratio of correctly predicted between observed class and total observed class. In this case, Multi-layer perception shows the highest precision. It means that the model based on this algorithm will perform well in case of correctly guessing the research domain from a paper title.

A little mistake in title increases the chance of predicting the wrong research domain for the paper. Thus, the chance for finding the perfect reviewer with a matched research domain will also be decreased and this is the main concern of DJournal. So, having higher precision makes a multi-layer perceptron best suited for the task.

Figure 8 presents the accuracy of Multi-layer perception for different amounts of data and it is clear from that more data will give more accuracy. Thus, the model not only handles more data but also able to perform better with a larger volume of data. It also illustrates that the improvement of accuracy becomes non-linear when more than 4000 data are used. Though the accuracy keeps improving, due to the non- linearity of the graph, it can be safely assumed that the rate at which accuracy is improving will drop in near future. In future, better models with new approaches like deep learning could pave a way for a higher rate of accuracy.

CONCLUSION

Creating an unbiased, anonymous and autonomous paper review system can affect scientific society greatly. Biased review, idea heist, and etc. can gravely injure the scientific community and withheld progress of civilization. This article successfully proposes and implements a decentralized paper reviewing system DJournal with autonomous Reviewer selection based on a ranking algorithm and machine learning-based research field prediction. This article also finds out two (2) security loopholes on decentralized systems and proposes a novel HDS (Hybrid Decentralized System) approach to solve the security issues. The article also suggests the modernization of DJournal by addressing the recommender system. Thus, the article investigates, experiments and instigates decentralization and automation with the help of blockchain and machine learning based paper reviewing. In future the system can be improved as a recommender system for recommending Reviewers to choose an article for reviewing. Authors can also provide rating (on 10) of a submitted article according to their research domains and reviewers can also provide his/her choice rating during his registration. The system can also auto-track each Reviewer engagement (likes/comments/preferences) with various articles, and thus the system will have Reviewer choice profile vectors and the article vectors, and these vectors can be used to predict which articles will be similar to the reviewer's taste. Therefore, along with new articles in a week, a separate recommendation can be made to a particular Reviewer based on the articles which he hasn't read already.

Figure 7. Comparison of different ML algorithms for research field prediction

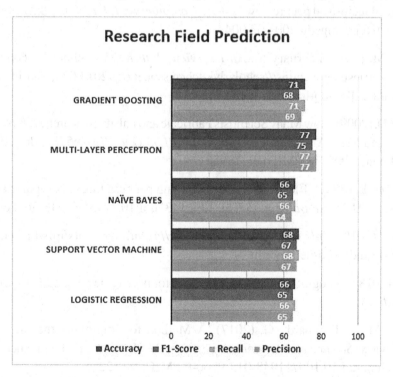

Figure 8. Multi-layer perceptron accuracy vs data-size

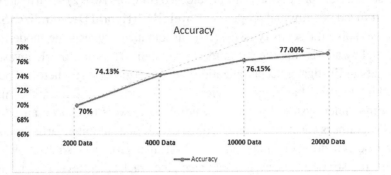

REFERENCES

Avital, M. (2018). Peer Review: Toward a Blockchain-enabled Market-based Ecosystem. *Communications of the Association for Information Systems*, *42*, 646–653. doi:10.17705/1CAIS.04228

Cho, K., & Schunn, C. (2007). Scaffolded writing and rewriting in the discipline: A web-based reciprocal peer review system. *Computers & Education*, *48*(3), 409–426. doi:10.1016/j.compedu.2005.02.004

Clarke, M. (2013, February 5). *An Interview With Keith Collier, Co-Founder of Rubriq*. Retrieved from https://scholarlykitchen.sspnet.org/2013/02/05/an-interview-with-keith-collier-co-founder-of-rubriq/

Fanelli, D. (2009). How Many Scientists Fabricate and Falsify Research? A Systematic Review and Meta-Analysis of Survey Data. *PLoS One*, *4*(5), e5738. doi:10.1371/journal.pone.0005738 PMID:19478950

Gehringer, E. (2001). Electronic peer review and peer grading in computer-science courses. *ACM Sigcse Bulletin.*, *33*(1), 139–143. doi:10.1145/366413.364564

GitHub. (2019). *ipfs/ipfs*. Available: https://github.com/ipfs/ipfs/blob/master/README.md#who-designed-it

Jan, Z. (2018). Recognition and reward system for peer-reviewers. *CEUR Workshop Proceedings*.

Kahani, M., & Borchardt, G. (2017). A Method for Improving the Integrity of Peer Review. *Science and Engineering Ethics*, *24*(5), 1603–1610. Advance online publication. doi:10.100711948-017-9960-9 PMID:28812275

Keccak Team. (2019). Available: https://keccak.team/index.html

Kelly, J., Sadeghieh, T., & Adeli, K. (2014). Peer Review in Scientific Publications: Benefits, Critiques, & A Survival Guide. *EJIFCC*, *25*(3), 227–243. PMID:27683470

Mahoney, M. J. (1977). Publication prejudices: An experimental study of confirmatory bias in the peer review system. *Cognitive Therapy and Research*, *1*(2), 161–175. doi:10.1007/BF01173636

Mulligan, A., Hall, L., & Raphael, E. (2012). Peer review in a changing world: An international study measuring the attitudes of researchers. *Journal of the American Society for Information Science and Technology*, *64*(1), 132–161. doi:10.1002/asi.22798

Rahut, S. K., Tanvir, R. A., Rahman, S., & Akhter, S. (2019). Scientific Paper Peer-Reviewing System With Blockchain, IPFS, and Smart Contract. *Advances in Systems Analysis, Software Engineering, and High Performance Computing*, 189–221. doi:10.4018/978-1-5225-9257-0.ch010

Saleh, F. (2018). Blockchain Without Waste: Proof-of-Stake. SSRN *Electronic Journal*. doi:10.2139srn.3183935

Stoye, E. (2019). *Studies flag signs of gender bias in peer review*. Chemistry World.

Tenorio-Fornés, A., Jacynycz, V., Llop-Vila, D., Sánchez-Ruiz, A., & Hassan, S. (2019). Towards a Decentralized Process for Scientific Publication and Peer Review using Blockchain and IPFS. *Proceedings of the 52nd Hawaii International Conference on System Sciences*. 10.24251/HICSS.2019.560

What is Gas? (n.d.). *MyEtherWallet Knowledge Base*. Retrieved February 14, 2020, from https://kb.myetherwallet.com/en/transactions/what-is-gas/

Chapter 15

Blockchain and Scholarly Publishing Industry:
Current Use Cases – New Efficiencies in Scholarly Publishing

Darrell W. Gunter
(iD) https://orcid.org/0000-0001-5717-8342
Gunter Media Group, Inc., USA

ABSTRACT

This chapter will explore how blockchain and AI technology will address the current problems in the current publishing workflow including the author manuscript submission systems, peer review process, editing, production process, and dissemination process. Further, after the article has published, blockchain and AI technologies will allow all of the stakeholders in the value chain to benefit from a more efficient and effective upstream and downstream publishing process. This chapter will explore rights and royalties, anti-piracy and ebooks, and how blockchain and AI will create new research and business opportunities.

INTRODUCTION

This chapter aims to discuss the current challenges and opportunities that Blockchain and AI can provide the scholarly publishing community to improve the efficiencies and transparencies of the manuscript submission, peer review, dissemination of published manuscripts, the recording of the reading, and use of this content. In this chapter, I will present several hypotheses and ideas to address the current

DOI: 10.4018/978-1-7998-5589-7.ch015

challenges and opportunities. Throughout the last few years, there have been quite a few Blockchain project developments, but it appears that the outcomes of these projects remain uncertain.

If the industry is serious about leveraging Blockchain and AI, it will require a keen sense of leadership, drive for excellence, and investment.

There is so much information about Blockchain, its origin, its applications, capabilities, etc., but here is a pretty good definition of Blockchain. *Blockchain is a shared, distributed ledger on which transactions are digitally recorded and linked together to provide the entire history or provenance of an asset. A transaction is added to the Blockchain only after it has been validated using a consensus protocol, ensuring it is the only version of the truth. Each record is also encrypted to provide an extra layer of security. Blockchain is said to be "immutable" because it cannot be changed and transparent because all participants to trade have access to the same version of the truth.*

Scholarly publishing has many challenges and opportunities in the manuscript submission, peer-review process, publication process, dissemination, and ultimately the articles' use and reporting. Authors are challenged by the various manuscript systems utilized by the estimated 5,000 – 10,000 publishers (Ware and Mabe, 2015). The authors have no choice but to acquiesce to the manuscript systems of the publishers. Each of these manuscript systems has common threads of features and has their unique workflow that each author must follow to submit their manuscript.

In addition to the publisher's manuscript system, the current peer review system does not provide the author protection against a peer reviewer sampling the idea, hypothesis, data, etc., from a paper under their review, and there is no way to discern if a peer reviewer has utilized any information from an article under consideration. However, if the peer review platform uses Blockchain, this information will be readily available. We will provide a potential solution later on in this chapter.

MANUSCRIPT SUBMISSION

The author's manuscript's submission is the first step in what some authors have characterized as a long and demanding process. A critical fundamental question is why does the peer review process takes so long. One study stated that the average review process of 74 days. Secondly, that that manuscripts were returned 1.73 times per manuscript. One of the critical areas of discrepancy was grammar. In addition to the papers having to be sent back to the author once the article was deemed acceptable for review, the average review time was 22 days (Cornelius, 2012).

Blockchain and AI can significantly enhance this first step of the article submitted by the author. Regarding AI, at least two companies have implemented tools for the researcher that would help them submit a manuscript with new grammar and the other company to check their manuscript to determine if it meets the Open Science, Integrity, and Reproducibility requirements.

The first company Writefull uses Artificial Intelligence, corrects grammar, punctuation, word use, and more - tailored to research writing. Writefull's suggestions appear to the right of your text. You can accept or reject them with a single click. Writefull recently completed a program with Hindawi. The pilot, which began on December 9, allowed authors to use Writefull before submission to Hindawi journals. Uptake, particularly from Chinese and US authors, has been impressive. To date, over 1,600 manuscripts have been submitted for revision to the service. I

Hindawi's objective is to improve the service to their authors, editors, and peer reviewers. Writefull has excellent potential as a tool that could help to level the playing field for researchers from non-English speaking countries by ensuring good research doesn't fall at the language hurdle (Kelesidou, 2020) This service is an excellent example of how AI can help improve the scholarly research process.

Ripeta's AI tools help the researcher, institution, publisher, and funders evaluate a manuscript for its compliance to Open Science standards, Trust in Authorship, and Reproducibility (https://ripeta.com/about/). The ripetaReview is a review of a single manuscript for each of the areas mentioned above. The ripetaReport is an aggregate report of several manuscripts, and the executive summary provides details of the key quality indicators that are and are not present.

Ripeta started 2020 with STM to analyze 300,000 manuscripts for the STM Research Data Year project (STM Research Data, 2021). The 21 participating publishers that contributed to the 300,000 manuscripts were able to view their publications Data Availability Statements. Throughout 12-months, the program tracked that the average number of journals with data policies across participating publishers went up 80% (from 29 pct to 52 pct) while the number of articles that contained data availability statements (DASs) more than doubled, from 7% to 15%.

Their other client The Welcome Trust a non-profit funder of APCs (Article Processing Fees) want to see to what effect their funding policies are being followed. They wanted to compare all of their funded manuscripts from 2016 vs. 2019. The Ripeta AI tool would provide them unprecedented data about their manuscripts in a very efficient and effective manner. The ripetaReport by Ripeta was able to provide them the data comparison in minutes versus a very laborious method of having humans to do the comparison. Ripeta's AI based ripetaReport provided them the strategic information at a fraction of the human labor cost.

It is great to see the scholarly publishing industry embrace these new AI technologies, and more opportunities will help advance academic research if the industry opens to them.

Ripeta also had an engagement with Research Square that focused on the evaluation of the submitted pre-prints for publication. The authors were offered the opportunity to have their preprint reviewed by Ripeta. Thirty-three percent of the authors updated their preprint with the ripetaReview's recommendation. This is an important point as the Ripeta tool provides significant data and information in seconds versus the number of hours for a human to do the same exercise.

PEER REVIEW

The peer-review process, as previously stated, is painfully slow and can be enhanced to improve the overall strategy that will benefit the advancement of scholarly research. There are many areas where Blockchain and AI can improve peer review.

Imagine a Blockchain peer review that will ingest potential manuscripts into the open or closed trusted distributed network containing potential verified reviewers who are authorities in the subject matter. The reviewers are provided two full weeks to review the manuscript and provide their comments, suggestions, and recommendations. This Peer Review Blockchain Platform (PRBP) would offer everyone the following benefits in the value chain in Peer Review.

The first benefit is transparency and timing. The clarity will be on many different levels. The author will know precisely when the manuscript was received and viewed by the editor. The following notification will be when the manuscript is distributed to the peer review panel. If the peer-review process is a blind process, then the reviewer's name would not be revealed. Once the Peer Reviewers have completed their respective reviews, the PRBP will detail the evaluation dates and time stamps. If the manuscript is returned to the author for further editing, all of these actions are provided a day and time stamp that preserves each activity's critical path.

This type of transparency is unprecedented and eliminates all grey areas concerning dates and times of the peer review's critical path. Further, it will provide a digital record of who reviewed the manuscript. If the peer reviewer published an article of similar content in the future and if they did not cite the original author in their manuscript, it could potentially expose a bad actor. Since the PRBP has a record of everyone who viewed the article and if the PRBP utilizes semantic search that would allow the searcher to find articles in context, this could be another opportunity for the industry to build more trust and integrity in scholarly publishing.

Over the last few years, there have been several experiments from significant publishers to start-ups. Back in September 2018, it was announced that Karger Publisher and The Wellcome Trust would join the Blockchain for Peer Review Project (BPRP) (Blockchain, n.d.). The BPRP would comprise three phases. The participants in Phase 1 would also include the original members, Cambridge University Press, Digital Science, Katalysis, ORCID, Springer Nature, and Taylor & Francis.

Phase 1: Pilot Phase

(participation almost closed).

1. Develop the first version of review information data store for selection of publishers/titles (exact data stored TBD)
   a. Review process can be independently verified
   b. Review info is fed to ORCID researcher profiles
   c. Short-term collaboration and confidentiality agreement among initial organizations
2. Investigate the long-term structure of the initiative
   a. Financial model (e.g., similar to Crossref, ORCID)
   b. Type of organization (e.g., non-profit membership)
3. Set up steering committee
   a. Governance
   b. Reporting
4. Investigate legal aspects (e.g. GDPR)

Phase 2: Minimal Viable Product

Together with members of phase 1 we will describe the framework for phase 2.
High-level goals are as follows (subject to change based on phase 1 discussions):

1. Add additional publisher partners
2. Implement long-term financial & organizational model
3. Extend functionality

Phase 3: Advanced Development

To be decided but the approach is likely to involve:

1. Onboard more publishers
2. Investigate applications outside of peer review

At the time of the writing of this chapter, the status of the BPRP is not known.
A November 15, 2019 Frontiers in Blockchain publication, titled, *A Framework Proposal for Blockchain-Based Scientific Publishing Using Shared Governance,* the

authors provide a complete overview of the Peer Review Blockchain developments. The companies cited companies included ARTiFACTS, Pluto, Orvium, and ScienceMatters-EUREKA, who actively pursued Peer Review Blockchain initiatives.

At the center of this framework is a model that adopts shared governance and validates inclusion via a Democratic Autonomous Organization (DAO). A DAO (Blockchain, 2019) is an entity wherein the organizational rules are implemented and executed via smart contracts. The DAO will comprise participants of validated individuals and organizations who are publishers, editors, peer-reviewers, and citizen scientists to manage and oversee the framework (Mackey et al., 2019).

This article discusses 7 phases of their proposed project with complete detail about the proposed project's principles features.

The 7 phases are as follows:

Phase 1: Author Submission
Phase 2: Manuscript Handling
Phase 3: External Peer-review
Phase 4: Editorial Assessment
Phase 5: Revision Stage
Phase 6: Production and Post Peer-Review
Phase 7: Post Publication Phase

CITATIONS, JOURNAL IMPACT FACTORS, AND OTHER FACTORS

Reporting on the various statistics of scholarly research is quite complex. There are many measurements that the industry relies on to report on the use and citation of a journal article.

The Bernard Becker Medical Library provides a guide that defines the various types of metrics to measure a manuscript's reading.

Article Metrics and Altmetrics

Article metrics are metrics based on usage of a scholarly work or components of work such as figures, or a non-article work such as software or slides, and its subsequent application or use. A peer-reviewed journal article is one example of a scholarly work.

An example of a traditional article metric is a citation to a work noted in the scholarly literature, which allows for an in-context understanding of the nature, purpose, and motivation of the citing author/s. See the Citations tab for more information (Quantifying the Impact of My Publications: Article Metrics., 2021).

With the advent of sophisticated digital applications, publishers and vendors developed other types of article metrics based on usage of the work in its digital format, such as the number of times a work is read, viewed, or downloaded. These are also referred to as altmetrics or alternative metrics.

Other examples of altmetrics or alternative metrics represent an immediate set of metrics that can be captured to determine how work is shared among others, disseminated further, or commented upon using various social media-based platforms. Results can be in other formats besides the traditional journal article, such as figures, slides, datasets, software, and unpublished works. These metrics are generated by various audiences, including non-academic audiences, and are considered to be representative of the level of "public or social engagement" activity based on work.

Examples:

- **Bookmarks** or **Saves** to online reference managers such as Mendeley
- **Mentions** in social network sites such as Twitter or Facebook
- **Discussions** in blogs and mainstream media
- **Favorites or Likes** in sites such as Slideshare, YouTube, or Facebook
- **Recommendations** in sites such as Figshare
- **Comments/annotations** from readers in platforms such as PubMed Commons
- **Reviews** in post-peer review resources such as F1000Prime

Why are Altmetrics or Alternative Metrics Useful?

Non-citation metrics can be useful as they provide additional metrics that authors can use to quantify the influence or impact of their works and go beyond the traditional peer-reviewed journal article to include other scholarly works such as datasets, software, slides, figures, unpublished works such as a policy brief, etc. Some metrics such as online views or comments or recommendations represent early-stage engagement indicators of how and by whom work is being shared, used, commented on, and disseminated further. Who is reading the new work? Who is tweeting about the new work? Where are they tweeting from? Is the work being commented on in a blog posting? By whom? A scientist or a policy-maker, or a layperson? Are users bookmarking the work in Mendeley? Is the result the topic of an article in the press? Is a user viewing the slides in Slideshare? Is a user viewing the figure in Figshare?

The idea behind non-citation metrics is to monitor the initial influence or attention work on various online platforms. It is evidence of the outreach of work and serves as a complementary means to traditional citations, and allows authors to highlight multiple scholarly output examples (Quantifying the Impact of My Publications: Article Metrics., 2021).

Digital Science's Altmetric has established itself as one of the premier altmetric tools to provide a daily overview of what the scholarly community is saying across all social media outlets, wikis, newsletters, blogs, etc. Altmetrics provides the market a broader view of a manuscript's impact.

Suppose the scholarly publishing manuscripts are in a Blockchain distributed network environment. In that case, it will capture not only all view and usage metrics but also the people who have viewed the manuscript and where it was posted. The transparency will not only capture the view, posting activity, and its impact, but it will also a timeline of its use and the context of its use. This type of data reporting provides the market insight into what research is being conducted and potentially where research is headed.

DATA AVAILABILITY STATEMENTS AND OTHER INFORMATION

The current Open Science, Integrity, and Reproducibility movement requires authors to provide a host of data in their manuscript. While this movement is gathering steam, Funders and Publishers formulate their policies to ensure that the three areas of Open Science, Integrity, and Reproducibility standards are being met. There are no agreed to measures to determine if these policies are being met consistently. Ripeta has launched their ripetaReview product to allow a researcher, institution, publisher, and funder to determine if their manuscripts are genuinely open. Another significant issue is determining if the reader of these publications are reading, copying, citing these data points. If they are reading and using these data points in their manuscript, how will the original author get proper credit?

In a blockchain distributed ledger environment, all of the previous questions would be answered as details of what data was viewed, who viewed the data, and when the data was considered would be immediately available. The benefits to the author, publisher, researcher, and scholarly publishing community would be pretty extensive.

COPYRIGHT AND ROYALTIES

The current copyright and royalty process is quite complex, and it takes the publisher significant time to receive their payment. In a Blockchain distributed ledger environment, the ability to discern all of the particulars around the reading and using an article is high-speed and transparent. The publishers' benefit is that they will have precise information about who read their writing when the paper was read, if they purchased the complete text, and where the article was used. The article fee would be electronically transferred within 24 hours. The Blockchain royalty network will create a new paradigm of article usage and payment.

CONCLUSION

Blockchain and AI can provide the scholarly publishing community with a host of new tools, applications, and t to improve academic research and flow. These new potential tools will require the industry to demonstrate leadership like it has not demonstrated before. In addition to the administration, it will require significant investment to develop the MVP (Minimum Viable Product) and the proper testing and communication to the marketplace to ensure that the market leaders are aware of the blockchain applications are being developed.

This current situation around Blockchain reminds me of the 2021 PSP Annual Conference, where there was a session titled, "The E-book: Crouching Dragon or Hidden Tiger?" which debated whether or not all books would be eventually digitized. I was so disappointed and annoyed by the session that I advised the then Director that I would not return if PSP continued to pursue topics that discouraged innovation. In my 2014, *Against The Grain* article, titled, "As Worlds Collide – New Trends and Disruptive Technologies" (Hinds, 2014), I chronicled this event as it is my opinion that the scholarly publishing industry is slow to adopt new technologies. It is quite understandable for the industry to vet new technologies to ensure that any investment in new technology would result in a unique benefit to the researcher, which ultimately supports the industry's mission.

The book segment of the scholarly publishing industry suffered a significant blow for the next several years. Many of the publishers delayed the digital conversion of their book programs which meant that ultimately the researcher was denied the ability to conduct their research most productively.

The proliferation of research around COVID-19 in 2020 created a new paradigm of sharing research information to address the Global Pandemic. This cooperation led to the development of a vaccine in record time. Imagine a scholarly publishing world with several Blockchain and AI applications to advance academic research; in my humble opinion, the industry will experience significant positive growth. Blockchain and I will usher in a new era of quality, fairness, and scholarly research advancement.

REFERENCES

BlockChain. (2019, July). *Tokenized networks: What is DAO?* Blockchainhub Berlin. Retrieved from https://blockchainhub.net/dao-decentralized-autonomous-organization/

BlockChain. (n.d.). *About the project.* BlockChain for Peer Review. Retrieved from https://www.blockchainpeerreview.org/about-the-project/

Cornelius, J. L. (2012). Reviewing the review process: Identifying sources of delay. *The Australasian Medical Journal, 5*(1), 26–29. doi:10.4066/AMJ.2012.1165 PMID:22905052

Hinds, L. (2014, July 18). *V26 #3 As worlds collide – New trends and disruptive technologies (by Darrell W. Gunter).* Charleston Hub. Retrieved from https://www.against-the-grain.com/2014/07/v26-3-as-worlds-collide-new-trends-and-disruptive-technologies/

Kelesidou, F. (2020, March 16). *We piloted Writefull, an AI-based academic language platform* [blog post]. Hindawi. Retrieved from https://www.hindawi.com/post/we-piloted-writefull-ai-based-academic-language-platform/

Mackey, T. K., Shah, N., Miyachi, K., Short, J., & Clauson, K. (2019, November 15). *A framework proposal for blockchain-based scientific publishing using shared governance.* Frontiers. Retrieved from https://www.frontiersin.org/articles/10.3389/fbloc.2019.00019/full

Quantifying the Impact of My Publications: Article Metrics. (2021, February 15). *BeckerGuides.* https://beckerguides.wustl.edu/impactofpublications/ALM

STM Research Data. (2021, March 22). *Share – Link – Cite.* Retrieved from https://www.stm-researchdata.org/#:~:text=STM%20has%20declared%202020%20the,with%20Data%20Availability%20Statements%20(DAS)

Ware, M., & Mabe, M. (2015, March). *The STM Report: An overview of scientific and scholarly journal publishing* (4th ed.). University of Nebraska – Lincoln.

Chapter 16
Blockchain and Scholarly Publishing Industry:
Potential Uses Cases – Applications of Blockchain in Academic Publishing

Edward Reiner
New York University, USA

Darrell W. Gunter
(iD) https://orcid.org/0000-0001-5717-8342
Seton Hall University, USA

ABSTRACT

Blockchain has broad application in academic publishing and addresses necessary benefits in cost containment, improved workflow, and business management. In particular, blockchain facilitates greater control over copyrighted content and royalty administration, citations, and billing and collection. Blockchain is a user-friendly technology that can improve profitability and cash flow while reducing administrative errors. Blockchain technology has become ubiquitous within various market segments but slow to be adopted within academic publishing environments, but with the pressure on revenue growth and cost containment, blockchain represents a new tool in the arsenal of workflow products to create more accurate reporting. In particular, royalty accounting has been an area of varying reliability and uncertainly, relying on many data sources and data aggregation generally confusing to authors, researchers, and writers. Blockchain takes the guesswork out of this process by documenting digital content access and usage through artificial intelligence engines and machine learning tools.

DOI: 10.4018/978-1-7998-5589-7.ch016

BLOCKCHAIN POTENTIAL USE CASES

The advancement of digital technology has enabled greater management and business administration within the academic publishing ecosphere, including many aspects of the relationship between author and publisher, publisher and its vendors, as well as the author and publisher with the marketplace. One key advancement are the improvements in Blockchain technology, moving this application to "the masses" which enables better documentation, authentication and facilitation of transactions within the publishing supply chain. Blockchain has also dramatically improved various "back office" functions such as Finance, Accounting, Contracts, Compliance and Royalties by automating many manual processes. Traditionally, published content and the eventual sale or license of content to readers has resulted in ad hoc reporting of content publication of copyrighted or protected material based on third party reporting. This reporting is managed for use in accounting for revenue, royalties and copyright protection as well as contract administration and general accounting.

Blockchain opens up new opportunities for efficiency, accuracy and improved operating performance for academic publishing, both commercial and non-profit. Even small society publishers will derive greater operating efficiencies with Blockchain. Improvements from Blockchain may include faster collections, more accurate disbursements, more "automated" financial reporting and better compliance with vendors and suppliers. Blockchain is no longer the purview of technology companies; as such, academic publishers are looking for efficiencies to capture protection of copyright, royalty accounting and reporting, rights and permissions, as well as efforts to document contractual payments. Blockchain for academic, non-profit and society publishers is easily accessible and can be implemented cost effectively (Brody, 2019)

THE LIBRARY ECONOMY

Pricing pressures placed on academic publishers in the current "academic publishing economy" for library supported content has placed greater demand on cost containment and operating efficiencies. It is quite obvious that the need to control expenses, accelerate collections, reduce costly errors and improve back office efficiency are necessary to remain competitive in today's academic publishing marketplace. Blockchain facilitates this with a high degree of efficiency and accuracy.

Applying technology-supported applications to reduce cost, improve efficiency and generating user confidence will promulgate greater industry acceptance. It is expected that the uptake of Blockchain applications in academic publishing will accelerate as more publishers embrace the platforms and applications as has been realized in other aspects of the content industry.

Definition: A blockchain is a decentralized, distributed, and oftentimes public, digital ledger that is used to record transactions across many computers so that any involved record cannot be altered retroactively, without the alteration of all subsequent blocks. This allows the participants to verify and audit transactions independently and relatively inexpensively. A blockchain database is managed autonomously using a peer-to-peer network and a distributed timestamping server. They are authenticated by mass collaboration mass collaboration powered by collective self-interest. Such a design facilitates robust workflow where participants' uncertainty regarding data security is marginal. The use of a blockchain removes the characteristic of infinite reproducibility from a digital asset. It confirms that each unit of value was transferred only once, solving the long-standing problem of double spending (Wikipedia, 2021). A blockchain has been described as a value-exchange protocol. A blockchain can maintain title rights because, when properly set up to detail the exchange agreement, it provides a record that compels offer and acceptance.(Euromoney, What is Blockchain, 2021).

ROYALTIES

In academic publishing, sales and royalty reporting have largely been "running on faith" in which the publisher reports publication, sales or licensing of content to libraries, bookstores, web services, syndicators and subsidiary rights holders. Print content is typically reported twice per year via sales reports which are aggregated to generate royalty statements upon which royalties are paid. For digital content, the expansion of the Internet allowed for the tracking of electronic terms, phrases and subject matter through digital object identifiers (DOI) which enables content creators to maintain a permanent "handle" or nomenclature to refer to content. Unfortunately, the complexities of DOI is that there is no simple mechanism to track, analyze and report on content usage. This includes academic materials, STEM or educational or other copyright protected material managed under the stewardship of the publisher. While DOI usage has grown, it remains the domain of technologists who actively track usage through complex search engines to find DOIs relevant to authors. (American Psychological Association, What is a digital object identifier, 2020).

Artificial intelligence systems have improved dramatically to leverage Natural Language Processing (NLP) and machine learning systems to recognize specific terms, nomenclature, and even textual content to maintain accurate tracking of authored content. Ai systems rely on algorithms to recognize text, images, music, photos that are the property of authors and writers. These Ai engines can locate, confirm and report on content usage based on the authentication of the original content (Wikipedia, 2021).

The new enablement of Blockchain now permits authors and publishers to accurately track, manage, confirm and record usage of content attributable to an author or writer. Based on algorithms using the author's content, images, music, composition, terminology, textual expression, etc., Ai engines can isolate, confirm and report on digital content that belongs to an author (and licensed to a publisher). The confirmation is determined through a machine learning platform which compares the original content to the identified content and can confirm that these are indeed from the same source. The use of Ai with Blockchain can now enable authors to confirm digital usage of content that would otherwise be invisible or unreported to the original author or even the publisher. This application of Blockchain now facilitates reporting such that authors can confirm royalty payments provided by publishers as well as review sales and licensing of content to third parties and prevent and protect against pirating or content misuse.

Based on this application, academic publishers will be encouraged to use Blockchain to provide more accurate royalty and licensing reporting and to improve accuracy of subsidiary rights reporting and monitor copyright usage. Utilizing Blockchain smart contracts will provide the necessary transparency and fulfillment (IBM, What are smart contracts on Blockchain?, 2021).

INFORMED SEARCH

Another application of Ai and Blockchain is the management of informed search engines using Blockchain. Since transactions are secured and reportable, academic search engines that respond to student/faculty queries can improve search results and improve the identification of content related to the query. When search results are reported, Blockchain can protect the integrity of the results of the search by identifying royalty-eligible content that records the query and the resulting access of that copyrighted material to confirm royalty or licensing payments to authors. Improved accuracy with reduced manual effort will increase the confidence of accurate royalty reporting and disbursements and create a level of competence for the Blockchain "member". (Pankaj, Difference between Informed and Uninformed Search in AI, 2021).

ACCOUNTING AND COLLECTIONS

Academic publishers, faculty/authors and non-profit entities can apply Blockchain technology for all contracts, transactions, searches and results in a fully documentable, auditable trail that maintains the integrity of the operational data flow. Staff requirements to adapt to Blockchain among academic publishers is minimal and can be applied across roles in Finance, Legal and Accounting with automated tracking and reporting. Cloud-based, menu-driven, secure and auditable transactions will improve daily workflow and reduce manual effort.

Additionally, Blockchain applications in academic publishing includes "chains" of pending collections from agents and consortia who represent libraries and buying groups bound by subscriptions contract or agreements. Billing and collection efforts are dramatically reduced by automating the process of renewals, invoicing and cash receipts under the domain of Blockchain, thereby improving cash flow and minimizing error. This may reduce the overhead burden and permit price discounting for agents, consortia or buying groups who "join the chain" and automate the renewal effort. This is largely due to the number of intermediaries who can facilitate a transaction. No longer will libraries claim that they did not receive the invoice, or that it was sent to an unmonitored mailbox. Documentation and confirmation are certain in the Blockchain link which will avoid awkward collection efforts or contractual confusion.

CITATION AND REFERENCES

One of the mainstays of academic research is the application of citations and references to existing bodies of work. These references are key to driving the Citation Index ranking as well as the impact factor. Blockchain technology can confirm these references and links and document the accuracy of these links, thereby improving the reliability of relevance and "proximity" to the underlying work. Blockchain technology will therefore establish levels of accuracy for work in which the citations, references and footnotes of academic work is related to the current research. Blockchain is precisely the technology that links related works to each other through these citations and references such that these will augment the current linking conducted through currently available abstracting and indexing services. Books and journal articles will have improved confirmation of the links via Blockchain that reduce the workload to confirm references manually.

let's take a look at a few of the Blockchain projects that are underway in the scholarly publishing industry.

- Taylor and Francis & Cambridge Univ Press Join Springer Nature - Blockchain for Peer Review
- IEEE
- Orvium
- Open Science Organization

Taylor and Francis & Cambridge University Press Join Springer Nature – Blockchain for Peer Review

Taylor & Francis and Cambridge University Press join Springer Nature as publisher partners, all three organisations will share key information around publisher and peer review workflows, and make a number of journals available to the pilot for development purposes. Katalysis will provide technical expertise to the creation of the test platform and ORCID will share insights on personal identifiers and authentication. Digital Science will continue to manage this non-commercial industry initiative (Digital Science, *Taylor & Francis and Cambridge University Press Join Blockchain for Peer Review Project, 2019*).

IEEE

MATRIX will be joining the IEEE P2418.1 blockchain standards working group for blockchain applications in IoT, organized by Dr. Ramadoss. Owen and Bill introduced Dr. Ramadoss to our development team, and gave an overview of our capabilities in blockchain and AI. Dr. Ramadoss is one of the leads for the IEEE Blockchain Global Initiative, launching four new regional blockchain groups in China this year, with a dozen groups to be launched all over the world by the end of the 2018 (Matrix AI Networks, MATRIX Supporting IEEE's Global Efforts to Advance Blockchain Applications in IoT, 2018).

Orvium

Executive Summary Problem Overview The scientific publishing industry is one of the most profitable in the world. The top five publishers account for 50% to 70% of all publications, and their profit margins have been reported to exceed those of companies such as Google, Amazon and Apple. In 2015, the global market for scientific, technical, and medical (STM) publications was an estimated $25 billion. In contrast to any other publishing industry, private scientific publishers have pushed the publication efforts and costs to the research community. Scientific publishers have created an awkward triple-pay system: (1) governments fund most of the research, (2) volunteer scientists—usually paid by the government or research institutes—review the work, and (3) publishers sell the product back to governmental institutions and universities. Scientists and research institutions regularly criticize this outrageous economic model, which compromises the dissemination and growth of scientific knowledge, a process responsible for some of the most revolutionary changes in human history. Moreover, the current publication model has several problems affecting the research community, including high publication costs; copyrights held by publishers rather than authors; long, opaque and biased process; lack of rewards and recognition for researchers; and a proliferation of low-quality journals. Solution Orvium works to eliminate market inefficiencies and improve the quality and effectiveness of scientific publishing. The ultimate objective is for Orvium to be the leading publication platform for the research community while returning the benefits of science to the society.

The Orvium platform features:

- Proof of ownership for manuscripts
- Copyright and licenses are owned and transferable by authors
- Optimal publication and access costs
- Create decentralized journals with low maintenance and operational costs
- Integration between research data and results
- Public recognition and economic reward for peer reviewers
- Journal subscription freedom. No journal subscription model is enforced
- Accommodates gray literature and its validation
- Calculation of quality metrics such as impact factor and peer review quality
- Eliminates current "predatory" practices and conflicts regarding plagiarism, idea ownership and registration
- Social platform

Open Science Organization

The current system has been proven to be ill-suited for the modern scientific research. The current problems in research such as irreproducibility, high publication and subscription fees, publish or perish mentality, funding-crisis, etc. stem from the current inefficient system. So, the research ecosystem needs a complete overhaul and with the right use and adoption of technology it is not impossible. The Open Science Organization (OSO) is developing a community-managed system to make research open, unbiased, and efficient. The OSO platform which is a *decentralized Idea platform* and can be a research ecosystem in itself; a single place for all the activities in a research cycle i.e. funding to publishing. The platform will contain all the components required to manage (own, create, publish, review, revise, fund) an idea. The proposed platform will significantly reduce the cost of scientific research and inherently incentivizes openness and cross-pollination of ideas. In their platform, idea creators (e.g. researchers) will be able to receive funding from anyone and anywhere in the world and the general public and investors can fund any ideas.

OSO Idea Platform is:

- **A decentralized ideaplatform.**
  - Just like Ethereum is a smart contract platform i.e. a set of protocols to deploy self- executing code in a decentralized fashion, OSO platform is a set of protocols to deploy (own, host, revise, share, etc.) your ideas. OSO network is a global network of ideas just like Internet is a global network of computers.
- **A global decentralized research lab.**
  - Just like Github is a popular site to develop and share open-source softwares. OSO platform is a place to develop and share ideas. It strives to be a single place that will host the evolution of global human knowledge.

The fundamental characteristics of the OSO platform are:

- **Open:** The platform is open-source in nature; everything related to the platform (e.g. protocols, software, etc.) are made public. It is designed to incentivize rapid and open sharing of ideas while ensuring that the value created by an idea is appropriately shared to its creator(s).
- **Decentralized:** The platform is made up of modular web3 components to avoid central point of ownership and failure.
- **Community-based:** The platform is collectively owned and managed by a community of users and interested stakeholders.
- **Collaborative:** The platform incentivizes collaboration by design. It incentivizes the cross-pollination among the ideas, thereby encouraging collaboration among the Idea creators (e.g. researchers). The end goal of OSO platform is to transform research from the current "publish or perish" mentality into harmonious collective endeavor.
- **Flexible:** The platform will be flexible in design to allow different needs of the users. It will contain the core protocols to manage ideas in a decentralized way and others can build applications on top of the platform to provide services to the users.

The **flexible design of OSO platform** will be able to serve the different needs of the users. The core OSO platform will have technical components required to own, create, iterate, review, store, publish, and fund ideas. Within the OSO network, users can customize the use of protocols to form *sub-networks* within the OSO-network and the sub-networks can overlap with each other. See Figure 1. Just like a group of users with similar interests can create a sub-Reddit in the Reddit platform to suit their topic of interest and make their customized rules to govern the sub-reddit, users (e.g. researchers) can create sub-networks inside the OSO network to suit their custom needs. For example, a group of researchers can create a sub-network for their research domain. There can be multiple sub-networks for a subject domain. Users will have the complete freedom to create sub- networks and switch in-between them. We expect this design will create a healthy competition and collaboration among sub-networks.

Within a sub-network created for a research domain, researchers can create idea-sharing or publishing *channels*. Channels are themed publication tracks with custom focus and rules (similar to traditional journals). There can be multiple channels in a sub-network and channels can span multiple sub-networks. Channels will have their own custom rules (e.g. specialization track, selectivity, review policy, etc.) Sub-networks can have their own rules about the creation and management of the channels.

OTHER CONSIDERATIONS

The application of Blockchain technology within academic publishing allows publishers to enjoy operating efficiencies that apply to industrial or manufacturing companies with complex supply chain needs. Academic publishers need to consider the benefits of Blockchain applications with subscription agents, academic libraries, consortia and buying groups. Blockchain applications can extend to pricing changes, adding/subtracting partners or members to the chain, and ultimately to manage cash flow. Manuscript submissions and content protection can also be included in the Blockchain platform, reducing legal risk and improving copyright protection.

SUMMARY

As you can see, there are many great Blockchain initiatives and developments in the scholarly publishing industry. Blockchain is being adopted in other industries as well. JP Morgan Chase Bank announced their establishment of a digital coin for payments and State Farm and USAA joined forces to test Blockchain for auto claims (Reuters, JP Morgan Chase to create digital coins using Blockchain for payments) (Adriano, State Farm USAA join forces to test Blockchain solution for auto insurance claims, 2019). Our lives are driven by contracts to purchase homes, cars, equipment, to rent apartments and the list goes on. Smart Contracts utilizing

Blockchain will be quite prevalent as the Blockchain technology emerges over time. This article from Medium demonstrates the many areas (50) that Blockchain will improve the efficiency, effectiveness and productivity of many industries. These applications will be developed overtime. While the internet came about in the early 90's, we were happy to just connect to URL's and we never imagined how the web and applications would develop over time. The same will be true of Blockchain. (Medium, 50+ Examples of How Blockchains are Taking Over the World, 2018)I am placing a proverbial stake in the ground that Blockchain will begin to show an early stage dominance in 2020 and beyond.

- The intention of this blog post is to keenly raise the scholarly publishing industry's awareness of Blockchain and inspire the many players to give thought to the many opportunities to develop Blockchain applications and improve the workflows and capabilities of the publishing value chain.
- We, the leaders in the scholarly publishing industry must accept the responsibility, charge and challenge of defining ***not*** if we should adopt a new technology, but ask the question(s) as to how the technology could be of benefit to the publishing industry. Let us be the leaders who are seeking technology to solve the many problems facing our industry.

Blockchain is a reliable, advanced and secure platform for data and transaction management with academic publishing companies. Blockchain automates many manual processes and improves the accuracy and precision of transaction documentation by maintaining an unbreakable link or chain between transactional parties. Blockchain will automate an auditable accounting of transactional relationships that must be maintained through the term of the contract.

REFERENCES

Adriano, L. (2019, June 3). *State Farm, USAA join forces to test blockchain solution for auto insurance claims.* https://www.insurancebusinessmag.com/us/news/technology/state-farm-usaa-join-forces-to-test-blockchain-solution-for-auto-insurance-claims-168858.aspx

American Psychological Association. (2020, August 1). *What is a digital object identifier, or DOI?* Https://Apastyle.Apa.Org/Learn/Faqs/What-Is-Doi#:~:Text=A%20digital%20object%20identifier%20(DOI,Published%20and%20made%20available%20electronically

Brody, P. B. (2019, December 6). *Plastic darts wall art gallery How public blockchains are making private blockchains obsolete*. Https://Www.Ey.Com/En_us/Innovation/ How-Public-Blockchains-Are-Making-Private-Blockchains-Obsolete

Digital Science. (2019, April 26). *Taylor & Francis and Cambridge University Press Join Blockchain for Peer Review Project*. https://www.digital-science.com/ press-releases/taylor-francis-and-cambridge-university-press-join-blockchain-for-peer-review-project/

Euromoney. (n.d.). *What is blockchain?* Https://Www.Euromoney.Com/Learning/ Blockchain-Explained/What-Is-Blockchain#:~:Text=Blockchain%20is%20a%20 system%20of,Computer%20systems%20on%20the%20blockchain

IBM. (n.d.). *What are smart contracts on Blockchain?* https://www.ibm.com/topics/ smart-contracts

MATRIX AI Network. (2018, September 11). *MATRIX Supporting IEEE's Global Efforts to Advance Blockchain Applications in IoT*. https://matrixainetwork.medium. com/matrix-supporting-ieees-global-efforts-to-advance-blockchain-applications-in-iot-829e1f7e36cc

Medium. (2018, May 30). *50+ Examples of How Blockchains are Taking Over the World*. Https://Medium.Com/@essentia1/50-Examples-of-How-Blockchains-Are-Taking-over-the-World-4276bf488a4b

pp_pankaj, P. P. P. (2021, February 26). *Difference between Informed and Uninformed Search in AI*. Https://Www.Geeksforgeeks.Org/Difference-between-Informed-and-Uninformed-Search-in-Ai/#:~:Text=Informed%20Search%3A%20Informed%20 Search%20algorithms,Greedy%20Search%20and%20Graph%20Search

Reuters. (2019, February 14). *JPMorgan Chase to create digital coins using blockchain for payments*. https://www.reuters.com/article/us-jp-morgan-blockchain/jpmorgan-chase-to-create-digital-coins-using-blockchain-for-payments-idUSKCN1Q321P

Wikipedia. (2021, May 16). *Authentication*. https://en.wikipedia.org/wiki/ Authentication

Wikipedia. (n.d.). *Double Spending*. https://en.wikipedia.org/wiki/Double_spending

ADDITIONAL READING

Open Science Organization. (n.d.). www.oso.com

Orvium. (n.d.). https://orvium.io/

Peer-to-peer. (n.d.). https://en.wikipedia.org/wiki/Peer-to-peer

Record. (n.d.). https://en.wikipedia.org/wiki/Storage_record

Reproduction. (n.d.). https://en.wikipedia.org/wiki/Reproduction_(economics)

Robust. (n.d.). https://en.wikipedia.org/wiki/Robustness_(computer_science)

Self-Interests. (n.d.). https://en.wikipedia.org/wiki/Self-interest

Title Rights. (n.d.). https://en.wikipedia.org/wiki/Title_(property)

Workflow. (n.d.). https://en.wikipedia.org/wiki/Workflow

Compilation of References

Letter to Shareholders. (2008). https://www.sec.gov/Archives/edgar/data/1018724/000119312509081096/dex991.htm

Abdi, A., Idris, N., Alguliyev, R. M., & Aliguliyev, R. M. (2015). PDLK: Plagiarism detection using linguistic knowledge. *Expert Systems with Applications*, *42*(22), 8936–8946. doi:10.1016/j.eswa.2015.07.048

About Bitcoin.org. (n.d.). Retrieved from Bitcoin.org: https://bitcoin.org/en/

Abu Sirhan, A., Abdrabbo, K., Ahmed Ali Al Tawalbeh, S., Hamdi Ahmed, M., & Ali Helalat, M. (2019). Digital rights management (DRM) in libraries of public universities in Jordan. *Library Management*, *40*(8/9), 496–502. doi:10.1108/LM-05-2018-0044

Accelerating digital transformation in banking. (2021). Available at: https://www2.deloitte.com/us/en/insights/industry/financial-services/digital-transformation-in-banking-global-customer-survey.html.html

Accenture. (2021). *Let there be change*. Available at: https://www.accenture.com/us-en

Adriano, L. (2019, June 3). *State Farm, USAA join forces to test blockchain solution for auto insurance claims*. https://www.insurancebusinessmag.com/us/news/technology/state-farm-usaa-join-forces-to-test-blockchain-solution-for-auto-insurance-claims-168858.aspx

Ahmed, S. F., Quadeer, A. A., & McKay, M. R. (2020). Preliminary identification of potential vaccine targets for the COVID-19 coronavirus (SARS-CoV-2) based on SARS-CoV immunological studies. *Viruses*, *12*(3), 254. doi:10.3390/v12030254 PMID:32106567

Al Jawheri, Boshmaf, Al Sabah, & Erbad. (2017). *Deanonymizing Tor hidden service users through Bitcoin transactions analysis*. Retrieved from: https://arxiv.org/pdf/1801.07501.pdf

American Academy of Arts and Sciences. (n.d.). *Section 1: Current Revenue Sources for Public Research Universities*. Retrieved May 3, 2021, from https://www.amacad.org/publication/public-research-universities-understanding-financial-model/section/2

American Library Association. (2017). Blockchain. *Library of the Future*. Retrieved from http://www.ala.org/tools/future/trends/blockchain

American Psychological Association. (2020, August 1). *What is a digital object identifier, or DOI?* Https://Apastyle.Apa.Org/Learn/Faqs/What-Is-Doi#:~:Text=A%20digital%20object%20 identifier%20(DOI,Published%20and%20made%20available%20electronically

Anderson, K. (2013, January 8). *Have Journal Prices Really Increased Much in the Digital Age?* The Scholarly Kitchen. Retrieved from: https://scholarlykitchen.sspnet.org/2013/01/08/ have-journal-prices-really-increased-in-the-digital-age/

ANSI/NISO Z39. 43-1993 (R2017) standard address Number (SAN) for the publishing industry. (n.d.). Retrieved May 07, 2021, from http://www.niso.org/publications/z3943-1993-r2017#:~:text=The%20Standard%20Address%20Number%20(SAN,%2C%20publishers%2C%20 etc.)

Anwar, H. (2018, July 19). *101 Blockchains - Home»Guides»Smart Contracts: The Ultimate Guide for the Beginners.* Retrieved from 101Blockchains.com: https://101blockchains.com/ smart-contracts/#15

Aschermann, T. (2018, August 30). *Was weiss das Auto über mich?* [What does my car have on me/know about me?"]. CHIP. Retrieved from https://praxistipps.chip.de/was-weiss-mein-auto-ueber-mich-diese-daten-speichert-ihr-kfz-ueber-sie_100613

Avital, M. (2018). Peer Review: Toward a Blockchain-enabled Market-based Ecosystem. *Communications of the Association for Information Systems, 42,* 646–653. doi:10.17705/1CAIS.04228

Bartoletti, M. (2020). *Smart Contracts Contracts. Frontiers in Blockchain, 5.*

Beall, J. (2016). *List of Publishers.* Scholarly Open Access.

Berarducci, P. (2019). Collaborative approaches to blockchain regulation: The Brooklyn Project example. *Cleveland State Law Review, 67*(1), 22–30.

Bergstrom, T. C., Courant, P. N., McAfee, R. P., & Williams, M. A. (2014). Evaluating big deal journal bundles. *Proceedings of the National Academy of Sciences of the United States of America, 111*(26), 9425–9430. doi:10.1073/pnas.1403006111 PMID:24979785

Bestarion. (n.d.). *The Internet of Things (IoT).* https://bestarion.com/portfolio/internet-of-things/

Bhargava, R. (2019). Blockchain technology and its application: A review. *IUP Journal of Information Technology, 15*(1), 7–15.

Biradar, U. B., Khamari, L., & Bhate, S. (2018). Transforming 50 years of data: A machine learning approach to create new revenue streams for traditional publishers. *Information Services & Use,* (Preprint), 1-5.

BlockChain. (2019, July). *Tokenized networks: What is DAO?* Blockchainhub Berlin. Retrieved from https://blockchainhub.net/dao-decentralized-autonomous-organization/

BlockChain. (n.d.). *About the project.* BlockChain for Peer Review. Retrieved from https://www. blockchainpeerreview.org/about-the-project/

Brenig, C., Accorsi, R., & Muller, G. (2015). Economic Analysis of Cryptocurrency Backed Money Laundering. In C. Brenig, R. Accorsi, & G. Muller (Eds.), *ECIS 2015 Completed Research Papers* (p. 19). Association for Information Systems.

Brisebois, R., Abran, A., Nadembega, A., & N'techobo, P. (2017). A semantic metadata enrichment software ecosystem based on sentiment and emotion metadata enrichments. *International Journal of Scientific Research in Science, Engineering and Technology, 3*(02), 625–641.

Brito, J., & Castillo, A. (2013). *Bitcoin: A Primer for Policymakers.* Mercatus Center: George Mason University.

Brody, P. B. (2019, December 6). *Plastic darts wall art gallery How public blockchains are making private blockchains obsolete.* Https://Www.Ey.Com/En_us/Innovation/How-Public-Blockchains-Are-Making-Private-Blockchains-Obsolete

Bush, V. B. (1945, July 1). As We May Think. https://www.theatlantic.com/magazine/archive/1945/07/as-we-may-think/303881/

Challenges in Irreproducible Research Nature. (2018). https://www.nature.com/news/reproducibility-1.17552

Cho, K., & Schunn, C. (2007). Scaffolded writing and rewriting in the discipline: A web-based reciprocal peer review system. *Computers & Education, 48*(3), 409–426. doi:10.1016/j.compedu.2005.02.004

Choo, S., Yong Park, S., & Lee, S. R. (2017). Blockchain consensus rule based dynamic blind voting for non-dependency transaction. *International Journal of Grid and Distributed Computing, 10*(12), 93–106. doi:10.14257/ijgdc.2017.10.12.09

CIOPages.com. (n.d.). *Top ten change management models: What are change management models?* Retrieved from https://www.ciopages.com/change-management-models/

Clarke, M. (2013, February 5). *An Interview With Keith Collier, Co-Founder of Rubriq.* Retrieved from https://scholarlykitchen.sspnet.org/2013/02/05/an-interview-with-keith-collier-co-founder-of-rubriq/

Coakes, E., & Bradburn, A. (2005). What is the value of intellectual capital? *Knowledge Management Research and Practice, 3*(2), 60–68. doi:10.1057/palgrave.kmrp.8500050

Coghill, J. G. (2018). Blockchain and its implications for libraries. *Journal of Electronic Resources in Medical Libraries, 15*(2), 66–70. doi:10.1080/15424065.2018.1483218

Coindesk. (2020). *Coindesk-Mt. Gox-Tokyo.* Retrieved from Coindesk: https://www.coindesk.com/company/mt-gox

CollegeBoard. (2020a, October). *Trends In Higher Education Series Trends in College Pricing and Student Aid 2020.* Retrieved from: https://research.collegeboard.org/pdf/trends-college-pricing-student-aid-2020.pdf

CollegeBoard. (2020b, October). *Trends In Higher Education Series Trends in College Pricing and Student Aid 2020*. Retrieved from: https://research.collegeboard.org/pdf/trends-college-pricing-student-aid-2020.pdf

CollegeBoard. (2020c, October). *Trends In Higher Education Series Trends in College Pricing and Student Aid 2020*. Retrieved from: https://research.collegeboard.org/pdf/trends-college-pricing-student-aid-2020.pdf

CollegeBoard. (2020d, October). *Trends In Higher Education Series Trends in College Pricing and Student Aid 2020*. Retrieved from: https://research.collegeboard.org/pdf/trends-college-pricing-student-aid-2020.pdf

Collins, F. S., & Tabak, L. A. (2014). Policy: NIH plans to enhance reproducibility. *NATNews*. PMID:24482835

Collins, J. (2001). *Good to great: Why some companies make the leap and others don't* (1st ed.). Harper Business.

Contributors, W. (2020a, August 2). *Byzantine Fault*. Retrieved from Wikipedia, The Free Encyclopedia: https://en.wikipedia.org/w/index.php?title=Byzantine_fault&oldid=970825345

Contributors, W. (2020b, August 2). *Decentralization*. Retrieved from Wikipedia, The Free Encyclopedia: https://en.wikipedia.org/w/index.php?title=Decentralization&oldid=970789219

Contributors, W. (2020c, July 5). *Distributed Ledger*. Retrieved from Wikipedia, The Free Enclyopedia: https://en.wikipedia.org/w/index.php?title=Distributed_ledger&oldid=966156176

Contributors, W. (2020d, july 5). *Distributed Ledger*. Retrieved from Wikipedia, The Free Encyclopedia: https://en.wikipedia.org/w/index.php?title=Distributed_ledger&oldid=966156176

Contributors, W. (2020e, July 27). *Peer-to-peer*. Retrieved from Wikipedia, The Free Encyclopedia: https://en.wikipedia.org/w/index.php?title=Peer-to-peer&oldid=969866372

Contributors, W. (2020f, May 11). *Secure by Design*. Retrieved from Wikipedia, The Free Encyclopedia: https://en.wikipedia.org/w/index.php?title=Secure_by_design&oldid=956142127

Cornelius, J. L. (2012). Reviewing the review process: Identifying sources of delay. *The Australasian Medical Journal*, *5*(1), 26–29. doi:10.4066/AMJ.2012.1165 PMID:22905052

COVID-19 SARS-CoV-2 preprints from medRxiv and bioRxiv. (n.d.). https://connect.medrxiv.org/relate/content/181

Cox, A. M., Pinfield, S., & Rutter, S. (2018). The intelligent library: Thought leaders' view on the likely impact of artificial intelligence on academic libraries. *Library Hi Tech*, *37*(3), 418–435. doi:10.1108/LHT-08-2018-0105

Cox, A. M., Pinfield, S., & Rutter, S. (2019). Academic libraries' stance toward the future. *Portal (Baltimore, Md.)*, *19*(3), 485–509.

CryptoNinjas-Home-What Are Smart Contracts. (2020). Retrieved from CryptoNinjas.com: https://www.cryptoninjas.net/what-are-smart-contracts/

Cuen, L. (2019, November 11). *Coindesk - Business.* Retrieved from Coindesk.com: https://www.coindesk.com/how-to-turn-a-17-million-ico-into-104-million-the-cosmos-story

Cyberstartup Observatory. (n.d.). *The Bank of Things - The Application of IoT in the Financial Sector.* https://cyberstartupobservatory.com/the-bank-of-things-the-application-of-iot-in-the-financial-sector/

Da Silva, J. A. T., & Dobránszki, J. (2017). Excessively long editorial decisions and excessively long publication times by journals: Causes, risks, consequences, and proposed solutions. *Publishing Research Quarterly, 33*(1), 101–108. doi:10.100712109-016-9489-9

Dang, J., Kalender, M., Toklu, C., & Hampel, K. (2017). *U.S. Patent No. 9,684,683.* Washington, DC: U.S. Patent and Trademark Office.

Devlin, J., Chang, M. W., Lee, K., & Toutanova, K. (2018). *Bert: Pre-training of deep bidirectional transformers for language understanding.* arXiv preprint arXiv:1810.04805.

Di Iorio, A., Lange, C., Dimou, A., & Vahdati, S. (2015, May). Semantic publishing challenge–assessing the quality of scientific output by information extraction and interlinking. In *Semantic Web Evaluation Challenges* (pp. 65–80). Springer. doi:10.1007/978-3-319-25518-7_6

Diamandis, M. D. P. H. D. (2018, September 7). *The Four Waves of AI: Who will own the future of technology.* https://singularityhub.com/2018/09/07/the-4-waves-of-ai-and-why-china-has-an-edge/

Digital Science. (2019, April 26). *Taylor & Francis and Cambridge University Press Join Blockchain for Peer Review Project.* https://www.digital-science.com/press-releases/taylor-francis-and-cambridge-university-press-join-blockchain-for-peer-review-project/

Dignan, L. (2019, April 11). *In Amazon shareholder letter, Bezos says AWS targeting 'specialized databases for specialized workloads'.* ZDnet. Retrieved from https://www.zdnet.com/article/in-amazon-shareholder-letter-bezos-says-aws-targeting-specialized-databases-for-specialized-workloads/#:~:text=Bezos%20said%3A%20Much%20of%20what%20we%20build%20at,could%20thrive%20without%20that%20kind%20of%20customer%20obsession

DOAJ. (n.d.). *Transparency & best practice.* Retrieved from https://doaj.org/apply/transparency/

Dua, A., Law, J., Rounsaville, T., & Viswanath, N. (2020, December 4). *Reimagining higher education in the United States.* McKinsey & Company. Retrieved from: https://mck.co/3u0vM2S

Dzieza, J. (2018, December 19). *Prime and punishment: Dirty dealing in the $175 billion Amazon marketplace.* The Verge. Retrieved from https://www.theverge.com/2018/12/19/18140799/amazon-marketplace-scams-seller-court-appeal-reinstatement

EdgeVerve. (2017). *IOT Banking Enabling Banks Digital Future.* https://www.edgeverve.com/finacle/finacleconnect/trulydigital-2017/perspective/iot-banking-enabling-banks-digital-future/

Elev8. (2019, August 23). *Elev8 Blog.* Retrieved from Elev8.com: https://www.elev8con.com/what-is-blockchain-3-0-a-guide-to-the-next-phase-of-dlt/

Enago Adacemy. (2020). *Will Crowd-based Peer Review Replace Traditional Peer Review?* Enago Adacemy.

Euromoney. (n.d.). *What is blockchain?* Https://Www.Euromoney.Com/Learning/Blockchain-Explained/What-Is-Blockchain#:~:Text=Blockchain%20is%20a%20system%20of,Computer%20systems%20on%20the%20blockchain

Fanelli, D. (2009). How Many Scientists Fabricate and Falsify Research? A Systematic Review and Meta-Analysis of Survey Data. *PLoS One, 4*(5), e5738. doi:10.1371/journal.pone.0005738 PMID:19478950

Ferry, G. (2015). Medical periodicals: Mining the past. *Lancet, 385*(9987), 2569–2570. doi:10.1016/S0140-6736(15)61151-5 PMID:26122152

Findlay, R. F. (2020, July 21). *Introducing the Leading Interactive Narrative NLG Platform.* https://www.businesswire.com/news/home/20200721005976/en/

Forecast: Internet of Things, Endpoints and Associated Services, Worldwide. (2014). Available at: https://www.gartner.com/en/documents/2880717/forecast-internet-of-things-endpoints-and-associated-ser

Franco-Salvador, M., Rosso, P., & Montes-y-Gómez, M. (2016). A systematic study of knowledge graph analysis for cross-language plagiarism detection. *Information Processing & Management, 52*(4), 550–570. doi:10.1016/j.ipm.2015.12.004

Frankenfield, J. (2019a, November 8). *Block Time.* Retrieved from Investopedia: https://www.investopedia.com/terms/b/block-time-cryptocurrency.asp

Frankenfield, J. (2019b, October 8). *Investopedia-Cryptocurrency-Blockchain.* Retrieved from Investopedia.com: https://www.investopedia.com/terms/s/smart-contracts.asp#:~:text=Smart%20contracts%20were%20first%20proposed,bitcoin%2C%20which%20he%20has%20denied

Frankenfield, J. (2020, February 2). *Investopedia-Cryptocurrency-Cryptocurrency Strategy & Education.* Retrieved from Investopedia: https://www.investopedia.com/terms/m/mt-gox.asp

Gasiorowski-Denis, E. (2020, July 7). Towards a trustworthy AI. Retrieved May 07, 2021, from https://www.iso.org/news/ref2530.html

Gautret, P., Lagier, J. C., Parola, P., Meddeb, L., Mailhe, M., Doudier, B., . . . Honoré, S. (2020). Hydroxychloroquine and azithromycin as a treatment of COVID-19: results of an open-label non-randomized clinical trial. *International Journal of Antimicrobial Agents*, 105949. doi:10.1101/2020.03.16.20037135

Gehringer, E. (2001). Electronic peer review and peer grading in computer-science courses. *ACM Sigcse Bulletin., 33*(1), 139–143. doi:10.1145/366413.364564

Ghosh, P. (. (2019, October 31). *Dataversity - Data Topics - Data Education>Smart Data News, Articles, & Education>The Future of Blockchain.* Retrieved from Dataversity.net: https://www.dataversity.net/the-future-of-blockchain/

GitHub. (2019). *ipfs/ipfs.* Available: https://github.com/ipfs/ipfs/blob/master/README.md#who-designed-it

Goulier, L., Nüst, D., & Konkol, M. (2020). *Publishing computational research-a review of infrastructures for reproducible and transparent scholarly communication.* doi:10.118641073-020-00095-y

Goyal, S. (2018, November 3). *101blockchains.com-Reviews.* Retrieved from 101 Blockchains: https://101blockchains.com/history-of-blockchain-timeline/

Graefe A. G. (2016, January 7). *Guide to Automated Journalism.* https://www.cjr.org/tow_center_reports/guide_to_automated_journalism.php

Grant, C. (2018). We are the change we want to see. *Information Services & Use, 38*(1-2), 45–59. doi:10.3233/isu-180011

Granting Guidelines for F5 Foundation 2020 STEM Education Grants for Non-U.S. Nonprofits. (n.d.). F5. https://www.f5.com/company/global-good/non-us-stem-grant

Greenberg, A. (2017, January 25). *Wired.com - Security.* Retrieved from Wired.com: https://www.wired.com/2017/01/monero-drug-dealers-cryptocurrency-choice-fire/

Griffey, G. (2018). Blockchain & libraries from Carnigie Mellon – Qatar. *Pattern Recognition.* Retrieved from http://jasongriffey.net/wp/2018/03/22/blockchain-libraries-from-carnegie-mellon-qatar/

Griswold, A. (2019, February 1). *Amazon Web services brought in more money than McDonald's in 2018.* Quartz. Retrieved from https://bit.ly/2DNBrBs

Grochowski, J. (2017, September 14). *Three targets of change to make organization transformation happen.* The RBL Group. Retrieved from https://www.rbl.net/insights/articles/organization-transformation-three-targets-of-change/

Gsma.com. (2019). Available at: https://www.gsma.com/mobilefordevelopment/wp-content/uploads/2019/02/ProofOfID_R_WebSpreads.pdf

Güçlütürk, O. G. (2018, August 1). *Medium.com - Cryptocurrency.* Retrieved from Medium.com: https://medium.com/@ogucluturk/the-dao-hack-explained-unfortunate-take-off-of-smart-contracts-2bd8c8db3562

Hash function. (n.d.). In *Wikipedia.* Retrieved from https://en.wikipedia.org/wiki/Hash_function

Hileman, D. G., & Rauchs, M. (2017). *Global Cryptocurrency Benchmarking Study.* Centre for Alternative Finance - University of Cambridge.

Hinds, L. (2014, July 18). *V26 #3 As worlds collide – New trends and disruptive technologies (by Darrell W. Gunter)*. Charleston Hub. Retrieved from https://www.against-the-grain.com/2014/07/v26-3-as-worlds-collide-new-trends-and-disruptive-technologies/

Hirsh, S., & Alman, S. (Eds.). (2019). *Blockchain*. Neal-Schuman.

Hoy, M. B., & Brigham, T. J. (2017). An introduction to the Blockchain and its implications for libraries and medicine. *Medical Reference Services Quarterly, 36*(3), 273–279. doi:10.1080/02763869.2017.1332261 PMID:28714815

Hyperledger.org. (2020). *Hyperledger - How Walmart*. Retrieved from Hyperledger.org/Learn: https://www.hyperledger.org/learn/publications/walmart-case-study

IBM. (2020, June 1). *What is artificial intelligence?* https://www.ibm.com/cloud/learn/what-is-artificial-intelligence

IBM. (n.d.). *What are smart contracts on Blockchain?* https://www.ibm.com/topics/smart-contracts

ICS. (2019, May 23). Retrieved May 07, 2021, from https://www.iso.org/standards-catalogue/browse-by-ics.html

I-Sccop. (n.d.). *Industry 4.0: the fourth industrial revolution – guide to Industrie 4.0*. Retrieved May 3, 2021, from https://www.i-scoop.eu/industry-4-0/#:~:text=Industry%204.0%20is%20the%20current,called%20a%20%E2%80%9Csmart%20factory%E2%80%9D

Janicke Hinchliffe, L. (2020, April 8). *Seeking Sustainability: Publishing Models for an Open Access Age*. The Scholarly Kitchen. Retrieved from: https://scholarlykitchen.sspnet.org/2020/04/07/seeking-sustainability-publishing-models-for-an-open-access-age/

Janicke Hinchliffe, L. (2019). *Transformative Agreements: A Primer*. The Scholarly Kitchen.

Jan, Z. (2018). Recognition and reward system for peer-reviewers. *CEUR Workshop Proceedings*.

Jinha, A. (2010, July 1). *Article 50 million: An estimate of the number of scholarly articles in existence*. Retrieved May 07, 2021, from https://onlinelibrary.wiley.com/doi/abs/10.1087/20100308

Jinha, A. E. (2010). *Article 50 million: An estimate of the number of scholarly articles in existence*. Academic Press.

Kahani, M., & Borchardt, G. (2017). A Method for Improving the Integrity of Peer Review. *Science and Engineering Ethics, 24*(5), 1603–1610. Advance online publication. doi:10.100711948-017-9960-9 PMID:28812275

Kamukama, N., Ahiauzu, A., & Ntayi, J. M. (2010). Intellectual capital and performance: Testing interaction effects. *Journal of Intellectual Capital, 11*(4), 554–574. doi:10.1108/14691931011085687

Keccak Team. (2019). Available: https://keccak.team/index.html

Kelesidou, F. (2020, March 16). *We piloted Writefull, an AI-based academic language platform* [blog post]. Hindawi. Retrieved from https://www.hindawi.com/post/we-piloted-writefull-ai-based-academic-language-platform/

Kelly, J., Sadeghieh, T., & Adeli, K. (2014). Peer Review in Scientific Publications: Benefits, Critiques, & A Survival Guide. *EJIFCC, 25*(3), 227–243. PMID:27683470

Kerasidou, A. (2017). Trust me, I'm a researcher! The role of trust in biomedical research. *Medicine, Health Care, and Philosophy, 20*(1), 43–50.

Khanboubi, F., & Boulmakoul, A. (2018). A roadmap to lead risk management in the digital era. *ASD 2018: Big data & Applications 12th edition of the Conference on Advances of Decisional Systems.*

Khanboubi, Boulmakoul, & Tabaa. (2019). Impact of digital trends using IoT on banking processes. *Procedia Computer Science, 151*, 77–84.

Kirkland, R. (2020, March 31). *Execs to Watch - Execs to Know.* Retrieved from WashingtonExec. com: https://washingtonexec.com/2020/03/how-jose-arrieta-became-a-blockchain-champion/#. XynYeihJF3g

Kopfstein, J. (2013, December 12). *New Yorker.com-Tech.* Retrieved from New Yorker: https://www.newyorker.com/tech/elements/the-mission-to-decentralize-the-internet

Kronick, D. A. (1976). *History of Scientific and Technical Periodicals* (2nd ed.). Scarecrow.

LaMarsh, J. (1998). *Change management.* Ford Motor Company.

Larivière, V., Haustein, S., & Mongeon, P. (2015). The Oligopoly of Academic Publishers in the Digital Era. *PLoS One, 10*(6), e0127502. doi:10.1371/journal.pone.0127502 PMID:26061978

Leskin, P. (2019, August 28). Use this map to see if your local police department has access to Amazon Ring's unofficial surveillance network of video doorbells. *Business Insider.* Retrieved from https://bit.ly/31IulXH

Levine, B. (2018, June 11). *Martech: Marketing.* Retrieved from Martech Today: https://martechtoday.com/a-new-report-bursts-the-blockchain-bubble-216959

Library Journal. (2019). *Deal or No Deal: Periodicals Price Survey 2019.* Author.

Lindenmoyer, J., & Fischer, M. (2019). Blockchain: Application and utilization in higher education. *Journal of Higher Education Theory & Practice, 19*(6), 71–80.

Mackey, T. K., Shah, N., Miyachi, K., Short, J., & Clauson, K. (2019, November 15). *A framework proposal for blockchain-based scientific publishing using shared governance.* Frontiers. Retrieved from https://www.frontiersin.org/articles/10.3389/fbloc.2019.00019/full

Mahoney, M. J. (1977). Publication prejudices: An experimental study of confirmatory bias in the peer review system. *Cognitive Therapy and Research, 1*(2), 161–175. doi:10.1007/BF01173636

Markets, F. (2019, September 24). *Global blockchain market is expected to reach USD 169.5 billion by 2025*. Intrado GlobeNewswire. Retrieved from https://www.globenewswire.com/news-release/2019/09/24/1919752/0/en/Global-Blockchain-Market-is-Expected-to-Reach-USD-169-5-Billion-by-2025-Fior-Markets.html

Marques, M. (2016, October 24). *Offsetting models: Update on the Springer Compact deal*. JISC. Retrieved from https://scholarlycommunications.jiscinvolve.org/wp/2016/10/24/offsetting-models-update-on-the-springer-compact-deal/

Marsh, A., & Brush, S. (2019, March 3). *Bloomberg Technology*. Retrieved from Bloomberg.com: https://www.bloomberg.com/news/articles/2019-03-03/why-crypto-companies-still-can-t-open-checking-accounts

Marvin, R. (2017, August 30). *PCMag Australia - Features*. Retrieved from Au PCMag: https://au.pcmag.com/features/46389/blockchain-the-invisible-technology-thats-changing-the-world

MATRIX AI Network. (2018, September 11). *MATRIX Supporting IEEE's Global Efforts to Advance Blockchain Applications in IoT*. https://matrixainetwork.medium.com/matrix-supporting-ieees-global-efforts-to-advance-blockchain-applications-in-iot-829e1f7e36cc

Mayer, K. (2006). *Journal subscription costs continue to climb*. UW News.

McEntire, R., Szalkowski, D., Butler, J., Kuo, M. S., Chang, M., Chang, M., ... Cornell, W. D. (2016). Application of an automated natural language processing (NLP) workflow to enable federated search of external biomedical content in drug discovery and development. *Drug Discovery Today*, *21*(5), 826–835. doi:10.1016/j.drudis.2016.03.006 PMID:26979546

McIntosh, L. D., & Juehne, A. (2019). Automating the pre-review of research. *Information Services & Use*, 1-6. doi:10.3233/isu-190048

McIntosh, L. D., Juehne, A., Vitale, C. R., Liu, X., Alcoser, R., Lukas, J. C., & Evanoff, B. (2017). Repeat: A framework to assess empirical reproducibility in biomedical research. *BMC Medical Research Methodology*, *17*(1), 143.

McKinsey. (2018). *Transforming a bank by becoming digital to the core*. https://www.mckinsey.com/industries/financial-services/our-insights/transforming-a-bank-by-becoming-digital-to-the-core

McNutt, M. (2014). Reproducibility. *Science*, *343*(6168).

Medium. (2018, May 30). *50+ Examples of How Blockchains are Taking Over the World*. Https://Medium.Com/@essential/50-Examples-of-How-Blockchains-Are-Taking-over-the-World-4276bf488a4b

Merton, R. K. (1963). Resistance to the Systematic Study of Multiple Discoveries in Science, *European Journal of Sociology*, *4*(2), 237–282. doi:10.1017/S0003975600000801

Miller, R. (2018, September 24). *Walmart is betting on the blockchain to improve food safety*. Retrieved from TechCrunch.com: https://techcrunch.com/2018/09/24/walmart-is-betting-on-the-blockchain-to-improve-food-safety/

Millman, K. J., & Perez, F. (2014). Developing Open-Source Scientific Practice. In *Implementing Reproducible Research. R series*. CRC Press Taylor & Francis Group, LLC. doi:10.1201/b16868

Mingers, J., & Leydesdorff, L. (2015). A Review of Theory and Practice in Scientometrics. *European Journal of Operational Research*, *246*(1), 1–19. doi:10.1016/j.ejor.2015.04.002

Mitchell, J. (2020, October 19). How Apprenticeship, Reimagined, Vaults Graduates Into Middle Class. *Wall Street Journal*.

Mittermaier, B. (2015). Double Dipping in Hybrid Open Access – Chimera or Reality? Forschungszentrum Jülich.

Modern Language Association. (2002). *Report from the Ad Hoc Committee on the Future of Scholarly Publishing*. Author.

Mow, S. (2017, August 7). *Fortune-Commentary-Bitcoin*. Retrieved from Fortune.com: https://fortune.com/2017/08/07/bitcoin-cash-bch-hard-fork-blockchain-usd-coinbase/

Mulligan, A., Hall, L., & Raphael, E. (2012). Peer review in a changing world: An international study measuring the attitudes of researchers. *Journal of the American Society for Information Science and Technology*, *64*(1), 132–161. doi:10.1002/asi.22798

Munafò, Nosek, Bishop, Button, Chambers, du Sert, Simonsohn, Wagenmakers, Ware, & Ioannidis. (2017). A Manifesto For Reproducible Science. *Nature Human Behaviour, 1*(1). doi:10.103841562-016-0021

Murphy, M. (2016, February 19). Do employees want to change? *Forbes Magazine*.

Nakamoto, S. (n.d.). *Bitcoin: A peer-to-peer electronic cash system*. Retrieved from https://bitcoin.org/bitcoin.pdf

National Science Foundation. (2014). *A Framework for Ongoing and Future National Science Foundation Activities to Improve Reproducibility, Replicability, and Robustness in Funded Research*. Off Management Budget.

Nelson, E. N. (2017, June 27). *AI will boost global GDP by nearly $16 trillion by 2030—with much of the gains in China*. https://qz.com/1015698/pwc-ai-could-increase-global-gdp-by-15-7-trillion-by-2030-with-much-of-the-gains-in-china/#:~:text=AI%20will%20boost%20global%20GDP,of%20the%20gains%20in%20China&text=North%20America%20can%20expect%20a,more%20ready%20to%20incorporate%20AI

Ojala, M. (2018). Blockchain for Libraries. *Online Searcher*, *42*(1), 15.

OpenAccess. (2019, January 15). *"Publish and Read" contract with Wiley concluded* [Notes]. Retrieved from https://openaccess.mpg.de/2336450/deal-contract-with-wiley-signed

Oracle. (n.d.). *Oracle Data Cloud Platform Help Center*. https://docs.oracle.com/en/cloud/saas/data-cloud/data-cloud-help-center/AudienceDataMarketplace/AudienceDataMarketplace.html

Orcutt, M. (2017, September 11). *MIT Technology Review/Blockchain/Cryptocurrency.* Retrieved from MIT Technology Review: https://www.technologyreview.com/s/608763/criminals-thought-bitcoin-was-the-perfect-hiding-place-they-thought-wrong/

Oryila, S. S., & Aghadiuno, P. C. (2019). Editing Scholarly Communication in the Age of Information and Communication Technology. *Library Philosophy and Practice*, 1-18.

Ossawa, E. O. (2018, October 23). *Four Waves of AI and What The Future Holds For It.* https://dzone.com/articles/four-waves-of-ai-and-what-the-future-holds-for-it

Panay, P. A., Pentland, A., & Hardjono, T. (2019). Why success of the Music Modernization Act depends on open standards. *Open Music Initiative.* White Paper. Retrieved from https://static1.squarespace.com/static/56d5e44060b5e9e20a94b16c/t/5bd7199e8165f5a5e9241ae9/1540823454789/Open+Music-Music+Modernization-Open+Standards+White+Paper.pdf

Parity.io. (2017, November 15). *Parity.io - Security- A Postmortem on the Parity Multi-Sig Library Self-Destruct.* Retrieved from Parity.io: https://www.parity.io/a-postmortem-on-the-parity-`multi-sig-library-self-destruct/

Peart, A. P. (2020, October 29). *Homage to John McCarthy, the Father of Artificial Intelligence (AI).* https://www.artificial-solutions.com/blog/homage-to-john-mccarthy-the-father-of-artificial-intelligence

Percie du Sert, N., Hurst, V., Ahluwalia, A., Alam, S., Avey, M. T., & Baker, M. (2020). The ARRIVE guidelines 2.0: Updated guidelines for reporting animal research. *Journal of Cerebral Blood Flow and Metabolism, 40*(9), 1769–1777.

Perera, C., Liu, C. H., Jayawardena, S., & Chen, M. (2021). A Survey on Internet of Things From Industrial Market Perspective. *IEEE Access: Practical Innovations, Open Solutions, 2,* 1660–1679. https://www.academia.edu/28144983/A_Survey_on_Internet_of_Things_From_Industrial_Market_Perspective

Perryman, E. (2020, January 26). *Yahoo! Finance.* Retrieved from Finance.yahoo.com: https://finance.yahoo.com/news/blockchain-interoperability-key-successful-projects-140034557.html

Petracek, N. (2021). Council Post: Is Blockchain The Way To Save IoT? *Forbes.* Available at: https://www.forbes.com/sites/forbestechcouncil/2018/07/18/is-blockchain-the-way-to-save-iot/?sh=3356dda35a74#65d086d25a74

Pilat, D., & Fukasaku, Y. (2007). OECD principles and guidelines for access to research data from public funding. *Data Science Journal, 6,* OD4–OD11.

Piwowar, H., Priem, J., Larivière, V., Alperin, J. P., Matthias, L., Norlander, B., Farley, A., West, J., & Haustein, S. (2018). The state of OA: A large-scale analysis of the prevalence and impact of Open Access articles. *PeerJ, 6,* e4375. doi:10.7717/peerj.4375 PMID:29456894

Polkadot. (2020, May 25). *W3F Initiates Launch: Polkadot is Live*. Retrieved from Polkadot.network: https://polkadot.network/web3-foundation-initiates-launch-polkadot-is-live/#:~:text=26%20 May%202020%2C%20Zug%2C%20Switzerland,together%2C%20seamlessly%20and%20at%20 scale.

Posnak, E. (2019, May 27). *Medium.com - On the Origin of Polkadot*. Retrieved from Medium.com: https://medium.com/on-the-origin-of-smart-contract-platforms/on-the-origin-of-polkadot-c7750e2fc5ff#:~:text=History,figure%20in%20Ethereum's%20early%20 history.&text=While%20still%20at%20Ethereum%2C%20Wood,hereafter%20referred%20 to%20as%20Parity)

Poynder, R. (2020, December 2). *Open access: Information wants to be free*. Retrieved from https://richardpoynder.co.uk/Information_Wants_to_be_Free.pdf

pp_pankaj, P. P. P. (2021, February 26). *Difference between Informed and Uninformed Search in AI*. Https://Www.Geeksforgeeks.Org/Difference-between-Informed-and-Uninformed-Search-in-Ai/#:~:Text=Informed%20Search%3A%20Informed%20Search%20algorithms,Greedy%20 Search%20and%20Graph%20Search

Pradhan, P., Pandey, A. K., Mishra, A., Gupta, P., Tripathi, P. K., Menon, M. B., . . . Kundu, B. (2020). *Uncanny similarity of unique inserts in the 2019-nCoV spike protein to HIV-1 gp120 and Gag*. doi:10.1101/2020.01.30.927871

Publons. (n.d.). Retrieved May 07, 2021, from https://publons.com/account/login/?next=%2Fd ashboard%2Ftools%2Fcreate-rid%2F

PwC. (2019). *Establishing blockchain policy. Strategies for the governance of distributed ledger technology ecosystems*. Retrieved from https://www.pwc.com/m1/en/publications/documents/ establishing-blockchain-policy-pwc.pdf

Quaderi, N. (2021, April 22). *The JCR reload and a look ahead to the introduction of early access content in 2021*. Retrieved May 07, 2021, from https://clarivate.com/webofsciencegroup/article/ the-jcr-reload-and-a-look-ahead-to-the-introduction-of-early-access-content-in-2021/

Quantifying the Impact of My Publications: Article Metrics. (2021, February 15). *BeckerGuides*. https://beckerguides.wustl.edu/impactofpublications/ALM

Rahut, S. K., Tanvir, R. A., Rahman, S., & Akhter, S. (2019). Scientific Paper Peer-Reviewing System With Blockchain, IPFS, and Smart Contract. *Advances in Systems Analysis, Software Engineering, and High Performance Computing*, 189–221. doi:10.4018/978-1-5225-9257-0.ch010

Ray, B. (2019). Blockchain symposium introduction: Overview and historical introduction. *Cleveland State Law Review*, *67*(1), 1–21.

Raymaekers, W. (2015). Cryptocurrency Bitcoin: Disruption, challenges, and opportunities. *Journal of Payments Strategy & Systems*, 30-46.

Raymond, E. S. (1996). *The New Hacker's Dictionary, 3e*. MIT Press.

Compilation of References

Rebouillat, S., Steffenino, B., Lapray, M., & Rebouillat, A. (2020). New AI-IP-EI trilogy opens innovation to new dimensions: Another chip in the innovation wall, what about emotional intelligence (EI)? *Intelligent Information Management, 12*(04), 131–182. doi:10.4236/iim.2020.124010

Registration Agencies, D. O. I. (n.d.). Retrieved May 07, 2021, from https://www.doi.org/registration_agencies.html

Reiff, N. (2020, February 1). *Investopedia - Blockchain Explained.* Retrieved from Investopedia: https://www.investopedia.com/terms/b/blockchain.asp

ReportLinker. (2019, July). Blockchain technology market size, share, & trends analysis report by type, by component, by application, by enterprise size, by end use, by region and segment forecasts, 2019 – 2025. In *Market report.* Grand View Research. Retrieved from https://www.reportlinker.com/p05807295/Blockchain-Technology-Market-Size-Share-Trends-Analysis-Report-By-Type-By-Component-By-Application-By-Enterprise-Size-By-End-Use-By-Region-And-Segment-Forecasts.html

Researcher, I. D. (n.d.). Retrieved May 07, 2021, from https://www.researcherid.com/#rid-for-researchers

Reuters. (2019, February 14). *JPMorgan Chase to create digital coins using blockchain for payments.* https://www.reuters.com/article/us-jp-morgan-blockchain/jpmorgan-chase-to-create-digital-coins-using-blockchain-for-payments-idUSKCN1Q321P

Ristoski, P., & Mika, P. (2016, May). Enriching product ads with metadata from html annotations. In *European Semantic Web Conference* (pp. 151-167). Springer. 10.1007/978-3-319-34129-3_10

Robbins, C., Khan, B., & Okrent, A. (2020, January 15). *Science & Engineering Indicators.* National Science Foundation. Retrieved from: https://ncses.nsf.gov/pubs/nsb20201/global-r-d

Rohr, J. G. (2019). Smart contracts and traditional contract law, or: The law of vending machine. *Cleveland State Law Review, 67*(1), 67–88.

Roth, G. B., Popick, D. S., & Behm, B. J. (2013). *Delegated permissions in a distributed electronic environment.* Google Patents. Retrieved from https://patents.google.com/patent/US20160352753A1/en

Ruzza, D., Dal Mas, F., Massaro, M., & Bagnoli, C. (2020). *18 The role of blockchain for intellectual capital enhancement and business model innovation.* Intellectual Capital in the Digital Economy.

Saleh, F. (2018). Blockchain Without Waste: Proof-of-Stake. SSRN *Electronic Journal.* doi:10.2139srn.3183935

Save on Course Materials – Cengage Unlimited. (n.d.). Cengage. https://www.cengage.com/unlimited/

Schiffrin, A. (2001). *The Business of Books: How International Conglomerates Took Over Publishing and Changed the Way We Read.* Academic Press.

Schiffrin, A. (1996). The Corporatization of Publishing. *Nation (New York, N.Y.)*, 29–32.

Schulz, K. F., Altman, D. G., & Moher, D.Consort Group. (2010). CONSORT 2010 statement: Updated guidelines for reporting parallel group randomised trials. *Trials*, *11*(1), 32.

Sedgwick, K. (2020, Jan 22). *News - Blockchain - Polkadot Will Finally Launch*. Retrieved from News.Bitcoin.com

Shaywitz, D. (2019, January 16). Novartis CEO who wanted to bring tech into pharma now explains why it's so hard. *Forbes*. Retrieved from https://www.forbes.com/sites/davidshaywitz/2019/01/16/novartis-ceo-who-wanted-to-bring-tech-into-pharma-now-explains-why-its-so-hard/?sh=370f17cd7fc4

Shortdoi Service. (n.d.). Retrieved May 07, 2021, from http://www.shortdoi.org/

Siegel, D. (2015, June 25). *Coindesk.com - Markets*. Retrieved from Coindesk.com: https://www.coindesk.com/understanding-dao-hack-journalists

Sissman, M., & Sharma, K. (2018). Building supply management with blockchain: New technology mitigates some logistical risks while adding for a few others. *Industrial and Systems Engineering at Work*, *50*(7), 43–46.

SJSU iSchool. (2019). Ways to use blockchain in libraries. *Blockchains for the Information Profession*. Retrieved from https://ischoolblogs.sjsu.edu/blockchains/blockchains-applied/applications/

Skinner, M. S. (2021, May 16). *Whatever Hasn't Been Done Yet: AI*. http://www.us-tech.com/RelId/2189332/ISvars/default/Whatever_Hasn_t_Been_Done_Yet_AI.htm

Smith, C. (2019). Blockchain reaction: How library professionals are approaching Blockchain technology and its potential impact. *American Libraries*, *50*(3/4), 26–33.

SPARC. (2020). *Big Deal Cancellation Tracking*. SPARC.

Sperling, N. (2019, October 9). Behind Amazon's change in its film strategy. *New York Times*. Retrieved from https://nyti.ms/2ICg2x0

Standards by ISO/TC 307. (2021, May 5). Retrieved May 07, 2021, from https://www.iso.org/committee/6266604/x/catalogue/

Stezano, W. S. (2018, September 12). *In 1950, Alan Turing Created a Chess Computer Program That Prefigured A.I.* https://www.history.com/news/in-1950-alan-turing-created-a-chess-computer-program-that-prefigured-a-i

STM Research Data. (2021, March 22). *Share – Link – Cite*. Retrieved from https://www.stm-researchdata.org/#:~:text=STM%20has%20declared%202020%20the,with%20Data%20Availability%20Statements%20(DAS)

Stoll, J. D. (2020, November 9). This College Degree Is Brough to You by Amazon. *Wall Street Journal*.

Store, I. S. O. (2020, April 17). Retrieved May 07, 2021, from https://www.iso.org/store.html

Stornetta, M. F. (2019). Retrieved from Google Docs: docs.google.com/document/d/1xYmwJQK-pi9fr6yOq5RzQBaRzoQuEpSUQyvjOzkAjQc/edit?usp=sharing

Stornetta, W. S. (2018, September 6). *The Missing Link between Satoshi & Bitcoin: Cypherpunk Scott Stornetta* (N. Brockwell, Interviewer). Academic Press.

Stoye, E. (2019). *Studies flag signs of gender bias in peer review*. Chemistry World.

Sumner, J., Haynes, L., Nathan, S., Hudson-Vitale, C., & McIntosh, L. D. (2020). *Reproducibility and reporting practices in COVID-19 preprint manuscripts* [preprint]. doi:10.1101/2020.03.24.20042796

Sundmaeker, Friess, & Woelfflé. (2010). *Vision and challenges for realizing the Internet of Things. European Commission Information Society and Media*. Available at: http://www.internet-of-things-research.eu/pdf/IoT_Clusterbook_March_2010.pdf

Systematic reviews: The process: Grey literature. (n.d.). Retrieved May 07, 2021, from https://guides.mclibrary.duke.edu/sysreview/greylit

Talks, T. (2019, February 20). *Blockchain: Decentralization is Central*. TEDxBeaconStreet.

Tapscott, D., & Tapscott, A. (2016). *The Blockchain Revolution: How the Technology Behind Bitcoin is Changing Money, Business and the World*. Penguin Group.

Tapscott, D., & Tapscott, A. (2017). The blockchain revolution & higher education. *EDUCAUSE Review*, *52*(2), 10–24.

Technosip. (n.d.). *IoT Development Services and Solutions*. https://www.technosip.com/internet-of-things-iot/#:~:text=The%20Internet%20of%20Things%20(IoT,human%2Dto%2Dcomputer%20interaction

Tenopir, C., & King, D. W. (1997). Trends in Scientific Scholarly Journal Publishing in the U.S. *Journal of Scholarly Publishing*, *28*(3), 135–170. doi:10.3138/JSP-028-03-135

Tenorio-Fornés, A., Jacynycz, V., Llop-Vila, D., Sánchez-Ruiz, A., & Hassan, S. (2019). Towards a Decentralized Process for Scientific Publication and Peer Review using Blockchain and IPFS. *Proceedings of the 52nd Hawaii International Conference on System Sciences*. 10.24251/HICSS.2019.560

The Anatomy of an OPM and a $7.7B Market in 2025. (2020, August 18). HolonIQ. Retrieved from: https://www.holoniq.com/news/anatomy-of-an-opm/

The Economist. (2015, October 31). *The Great Chain of Being Sure About Things*. Author.

The Economist. (2018). European countries demand that publicly funded research should be free to all. *The Economist*.

The Four Pillars of Digital Transformation in Banking. (2018). Available at: https://thefinancialbrand.com/71733/four-pillars-of-digital-transformation-banking-strategy/

The Royal Society. (2015). *Philosophical Transactions: 350 years of publishing at the Royal Society (1665–2015).* Author.

The Royal Society-Publishing. (2010). *Philosophical Transactions of the Royal Society of London – History.* Author.

The Scientific Method. Let's just try that again. (2016). Retrieved January 04, 2021, from https://www.economist.com/science-and-technology/2016/02/06/lets-just-try-that-again

United Nations. (2020, August). *Policy Brief: Education during COVID-19 and Beyond.* United Nations. Retrieved from: https://www.un.org/development/desa/dspd/wp-content/uploads/sites/22/2020/08/sg_policy_brief_covid-19_and_education_august_2020.pdf

Van Rossum, J., & Lawlor, B. (2018). The Blockchain and its potential for science and academic publishing. *Information Services & Use, 38*(1/2), 95–98.

Vilner, Y. (2019, April 25). *Forbes - Crypto & Blockchain.* Retrieved from Forbes.com: https://www.forbes.com/sites/yoavvilner/2019/04/25/down-the-next-rabbit-hole-exploring-biockchains-second-layer/#2f57c4af278f

Vincent, J. (2019, April 10). *The first AI-generated textbook shows what robot writers are actually good at.* The Verge. Retrieved from https://www.theverge.com/2019/4/10/18304558/ai-writing-academic-research-book-springer-nature-artificial-intelligence

Ware, M., & Mabe, M. (2015, March). *The STM Report: An overview of scientific and scholarly journal publishing* (4th ed.). University of Nebraska – Lincoln.

What is Cosmos? (2020). Retrieved from Cosmos.Network: https://cosmos.network/intro

What is Gas? (n.d.). *MyEtherWallet Knowledge Base.* Retrieved February 14, 2020, from https://kb.myetherwallet.com/en/transactions/what-is-gas/

What is iso 9001:2015 and why is it important? (2019, February 1). Retrieved May 07, 2021, from https://www.qualitymag.com/articles/95235-what-is-iso-90012015-and-why-is-it-important#:~:text=ISO%20consists%20of%20161%20standards,776%20technical%20committees%20and%20subcommittees

White, K. (n.d.). *Science & engineering indicators.* Retrieved May 07, 2021, from https://ncses.nsf.gov/pubs/nsb20206/#:~:text=This%20report%20utilizes%20data%20from,million%20to%202.6%20million%20articles

Wikipedia. (2021, May 16). *AI Superpowers.* https://en.wikipedia.org/wiki/AI_Superpowers

Wikipedia. (2021, May 16). *Authentication.* https://en.wikipedia.org/wiki/Authentication

Wikipedia. (n.d.). *Double Spending.* https://en.wikipedia.org/wiki/Double_spending

Wolfe, D. (2020). *SUNY Negotiates New, Modified Agreement with Elsevier*. Libraries News Center University at Buffalo Libraries.

Wünderlich, N. V., Wangenheim, F. V., & Bitner, M. J. (2013). High Tech and High Touch: A Framework for Understanding User Attitudes and Behaviors Related to Smart Interactive Services. *Journal of Service Research*, *16*(1), 3–20. doi:10.1177/1094670512448413

Yarime, M., Trencher, G., Mino, T., Scholz, R. W., Olsson, L., Ness, B., Frantzeskaki, N., & Rotmans, J. (2012). Establishing sustainability science in higher education institutions: Towards an integration of academic development, institutionalization, and stakeholder collaborations. *Sustainability Science*, *7*(S1), 101–113. doi:10.100711625-012-0157-5

You are Crossref. (n.d.). Retrieved May 07, 2021, from https://www.crossref.org/ ANSI/NISO

Zalatimo, S. (2018). Blockchain in publishing: Innovation or disruption? *Forbes.Com*. Retrieved from https://www.forbes.com/sites/forbesproductgroup/2018/05/03/blockchain-in-publishing-innovation-or-disruption/#2b632a2a5456

Zeta Global. (2020, August 6). *The State of AI-Powered Email Marketing*. https://zetaglobal.com/blog/state-of-ai-powered-email-marketing/

Zhao, J., Yang, Y., Huang, H. P., Li, D., Gu, D. F., Lu, X. F., . . . He, Y. J. (2020). *Relationship between the ABO Blood Group and the COVID-19 Susceptibility* [preprint]. doi:10.1101/2020.03.11.20031096

About the Contributors

Darrell Wayne Gunter is very active in the information industry with memberships in AAP/PSP, ISTME and SSP and serving as an SIIA CODiE judge since 2007. He Co-Chaired, PSP's Committee for Digital Innovation from 2011-2018 and is a former Associate Editor of the Learned Journal published by the ALPSP. A graduate of Seton Hall University's W. Paul Stillman School of Business, he obtained his BS Business Administration (Marketing) and earned his MBA from the Lake Forest Graduate School of Management. He also graduated from Rutgers CUEED's Entrepreneur Pioneer's Initiative program and completed the MIT Sloan Exec Edu – Blockchain Technologies: Blockchain Innovation & Application online certificate program and other certificates. He serves as an advisor to startups (Aptology, Breezio and MyScienceWork) and non-profit boards (USA Boxing and Women's Venture Fund) and is an adjunct professor at Seton Hall University where he teaches Professional Sales. His radio program "Leadership with Darrell W Gunter" in its 11th season airs 8:00 am EST Saturday on WSOU HD 89.5 FM / WSOU.net. His previous shows are available on his iTunes Podcast.

* * *

Shamim Akhter is working as Professor, Department of Computer Science and Engineering (CSE), IUBAT—International University of Business Agriculture and Technology, Bangladesh. He received his Ph.D. in Information Processing from Tokyo Institute of Technology (TokyoTech), M.Sc. in Computer Science and Information Management from Asian Institute of Technology (AIT) and B.Sc. in Computer Science from American International University Bangladesh (AIUB) in 2009, 2005, and 2002 respectively. He was also a JSPS Post Doctoral Research Fellow in National Institute of Informatics (NII) from FY 2009-2011, Visiting Researcher in Tokyo Institute of Technology, Japan from FY 2009-2011, Research Associate at the RS and GIS FoS, Asian Institute of Technology, Thailand in 2005, Global COE Research Assistant from Sep 2007~ Aug 2009 in Tokyo Institute of Technology, Japan and full-time contact faculty at Thompson Rivers University, CANADA in 2013. He was awarded "The Excellent Student of The Year, FY2008", Global COE Program, Photonics Integration-Core Electronics (PICE), Tokyo Institute of Technology, Japan and Magna-Cum Laude for academic excellence from American International University Bangladesh in 2002. Dr. Akhter has around 50 research publications in renowned journals and conferences. His research interests are Artificial Intelligent, Evolutionary Algorithms, and Models for their Paralleliza331 Remote Sensing (RS) and GIS applications, High-Performance Computing (HPC), Algorithm and Complexity Analysis. He is a senior member of IEEE, a member of JARC-Net, and a member of IEEE CS technical committee for intelligence informatics and parallel processing. He serves as a reviewer of various renowned journals and numerous international conferences.

Stephen E. Arnold is a technology and financial analyst with more than 30 years of experience. Stephen has extensive operational and entrepreneurial experience, able to bridge the gap between new ideas and the financial implications of a technology. His most recent search project is writing the open source search profiles for IDC, one of the world's leading consulting companies. Profiles will appear every 10 through the end of 2012. (Information about one of the profiles appears at https://www.idc. com/getdoc.jsp?containerId=236086.) His professional career has spanned 40 years. In 2000, he worked on the cost analysis, security, and technical infrastructure for the US government's FirstGov.gov Web site. After 9/11, he worked on the US government's Threat Open Source Intelligence service. In addition to performing technical and business analyses about search and content processing companies, Stephen wrote three monographs about Google's technology: The Google Legacy, Google Version 2.0, and Google: The Digital Gutenberg. He writes a monthly column about Google for IMI Publishing's Enterprise Technology Management and columns for Information Today (search), KMWorld (content analytics), and Online (open source search technology). He was the author of Enterprise Search Report, a 600 page encyclopedia of search published between 2004 and 2007. With co-author Martin White, he wrote Successful Enterprise Search Management in 2009. In 2011, he wrote The New Landscape of Enterprise Search. Mr. Arnold worked at Halliburton Nuclear after college. He then joined Booz, Allen & Hamilton in 1976. He was vice president, online, at the Courier Journal & Louisville Times in the firm's database unit. He worked at Ziff Communications until starting his ArnoldIT.com strategic information Services business in 1991. Since 1991, Stephen has worked as an advisor to organizations worldwide. In 1993, He and Chris Kitze founded a search system, Point (Top 5%) of the Internet, selling that property to Lycos, Inc. in 1996. He was a member of the planning team for USWest's electronic yellow pages. He has worked for a number intelligence and enforcement organizations, including the US Senate Police, the General Services Administration, among others. He is the recipient of the following awards: ASIS Eagleton Lectureship, 1986; Online Best Paper Award, 1989, the Malcolm Hill Award, 2003, the OSS Golden Candle Award in 2007. He is the author of more than 70 journal articles. A partial list is available on LinkedIn at http://www.linkedin.com/profile/view?id=155724&trk=tab_pro. Mr. Arnold's Web log "Beyond Search" is a widely read collection of critical commentary and opinion about information systems and methods available at http://arnoldit.com/wordpress. He also publishes online information services about analytics and content intelligence. See www.inteltrax.com and www.textradar.com. Picture: http://www.arnoldit.com/bio/art/seatif02.zip.

Shruti Ashok is an academician, researcher & a Finance professional with Ph.D. from Faculty of Management Studies, Delhi University and B. Com (Hons) From SRCC, Delhi University. Currently working as an Assistant Professor in Finance with Bennett University, she has over 14 years of experience across academia and corporate. Her Industry engagements spanning 3 years, include HSBC Bank Dubai, Citibank, HDFC Bank and State Bank of India. She is skilled in equity valuation, corporate finance, corporate restructurings and Portfolio management. She has presented her research work at conferences organised by IITs, IIMs and FMS and her scholarly work has been published in reputed international journals.

Jignesh Bhate is the Founder and CEO of Molecular Connections Pvt. Ltd(MC). A chartered accountant, Cost Accountant, lawyer by profession - Mr. Bhate has played a major role in taking MC from a startup company to a globally respected informatics major. He envisioned very early the need for service platforms like text mining, literature curation and annotation, development of informatics tools, knowledgebase for the drug discovery industry and brought a top team of scientists together to start Molecular Connections. Founded in the year 2001, MC, is a pioneering In Silico discovery services company. MC's vision is to be the most admired informatics company with best-in-class products & services delivered with a sharp customer focus, through best-in-class talent. The company has acquired institutions that are older than Molecular Connections and hence today, for over 30years the company has a formidable track record of serving the big pharmas like Altana, Aventis, Becton & Dickenson, GlaxoSmithKline, Harvard, Imperial College, Merck, Max Planck, Sanger etc., Publishers and universities across the globe. His personal mission is to make Molecular Connections the leader of the Informatics industry which can sustain and thrive through the changing generations of scientific requirements of the Life Sciences industry.

Usha B. Biradar received her Master of Technology in Bioinformatics from the R V College of Engineering, Visveswaraya Technological University in 2014. She is the recipient of multiple gold medals in undergraduate and graduate courses. She is currently the Lead – Decision Sciences and Text at Molecular Connections Pvt. Ltd. She is keen on exploiting flexible, end to end AI and blockchain solutions and cross platform integration of these solutions. Open, interoperable standards is another area she is exploring and eager to contribute to and often participates in conferences and industry gatherings to share ideas. ORCiD: https://orcid.org/0000-0002-1123-6209. LinkedIn: https://www.linkedin.com/in/usha-b-biradar-37b04988.

Deepika Dhingra is an academician, Finance professional, Trainer & Consultant with over 13 years of rich experience in Academia and industry. Strong education professional with a Ph.D. in Finance from Faculty of Management Studies, Delhi University and M.B.A in Finance from Guru Gobind Singh Indraprastha University. She teaches finance courses to postgraduate as well as undergraduate students & is also guiding Ph.D. students at Bennett University. Dr. Deepika has moderated panel discussions, chaired sessions, and delivered invited talks at Seminars. She has undertaken training for several PSU's such as Engineers India Limited, NBCC, GAIL & is also empanelled as a Faculty/Trainer with the Institute of Company Secretaries in India. Dr. Deepika has published & presented her research at various conferences held at IIM Bangalore, IIM Raipur, IIM Calcutta, IIM Indore, IIT Roorkee, etc.

Roland D. J. Dietz is Chairman of Focused Growth Partners, Inc., a global boutique advisory and investment firm with offices in the USA, Europe and Latin America. At CABI Roland served as board director and chair of the remuneration committee, member of the audit committee, and contributed strongly regarding strategy involving innovation, commercialization, publishing and technology areas. CABI is a UK based multinational organization, focused on agricultural, biological and environmental research and development with 10 centers around the world. Previous board roles include: Chairman Adonis B.V., Chairman ScienceServer LLC, Director Ticer BV and CCO/ Executive board director Elsevier. At Elsevier (NYSE: RELX), the world's largest science publisher, he was brought in to lead the transformation from print to digital, cloud based, media. He built a $734m information licensing business, growing the combined print and digital business with a CAGR of 7% (double market growth). He negotiated ground-breaking deals with national governments (Japan, China, Mexico. Brasil, NL, UK) and built an industry leading customer centric sales and marketing organization. He was asked to turn around Endeavor Information Systems, Inc. Roland addressed the undelivered client commitments ($4M) and brought back profitability. He pioneered a new digital archiving solution by forging a public-private partnership with the National Library of New

Zealand. This product delivered a 25% growth on revenues in the first year and became the standard for preservation of digital information worldwide. He sold the company to private equity above expected value. Roland built his career on the core values of: Leadership, Customer Centricity and Strategic Creativity which enable an approach towards growth and value creation initiatives that is soundly Evidence-based. He takes particular pride in the good group of executives that he has coached and mentored, and who have become successful senior leaders of their own. He is an accomplished martial artist and certified trainer/coach in various body-mind fitness disciplines. Roland is a dual citizen of the USA and the Netherlands, speaks 5 languages and lives in Scottsdale, AZ. He is married and has two adult children. His holds a M.Sc. from Delft University of technology (A.I.) and a Candidate's (equiv. Bachelors) in biomedical engineering. He has attended executive education courses delivered by Harvard, Stanford and Oxford Universities.

Lokanath Khamari is the Chief data officer at Molecular connections Pvt Ltd. He has led the Data mining solution provider team at Molecular Connections for more than a decade. His passion for giving practical, implementable solutions adds efficiency to the content development workflows. A techno enthusiast and an avid birder, Lokanath takes immense interest in proving UI/UX solutions for the complex problem in life sciences. Find more about him at https://www.linkedin. com/in/lokanath/.

Joost Kollöffel is a publishing professional with over 25 years of international business experience. He excels in setting up and leading innovative and game-changing projects and is experienced in the online scientific, technical medical & education information industry. Creating and managing a new business with good margin through creative approaches is what drives his passion. As an innovative and quick sales and marketing professional with experience working in and with the academic and corporate markets of the publishing industries, he can help you drive growth. He offers a deep understanding of the varied audiences: academic and corporate librarians, information professionals and researchers. Combined with using digital and traditional sales and marketing techniques, he can translate your business goals into resonating campaigns and effective activities. He is Level 5 Pragmatic Marketing certified. He believes in an integrated marketing approach; from the top of the marketing funnel, for example by creating online and offline strategic content, placed in smart outlets that will raise brand recognition and brand awareness, to lead generation activities, such as webinars and life meetings, to setting up customer retention programs (for example advisory boards for strengthening relationships with key clients to receive strategic input). These assets need to be in place in a way that creates synergy. In his view, marketing is a precursor to sales; the two go hand in hand. His prior responsibilities were mainly in Sales and Marketing, so he is able to combine the two functions. In fact, they should not be seen separated… Joost Kollöffel holds a Masters degree in Biology, specialised in Molecular Genetics from the Free University of Amsterdam, the Netherlands. He speaks and writes fluently in Dutch, English and German.

John H. Larrier is a lifelong learner who is a versatile marketing and sales professional with varied career experiences. With a love of history and trained in film and video production, John produced television commercials early in his career working primarily for Steve Steigman, the photographer famous for the Maxell audio tape "Blown Away Guy" photo. John subsequently moved into the entertainment field, producing music videos for some of the most successful R&B artist of the time, including Boyz II Men, Tony Braxton, and Patti Labelle. His business experience from the television commercial world made him a trusted partner to young directors, unfamiliar with managing the financial resources entrusted to them. He then transitioned to successfully take on the role of Festival Manager, for what was then known as the Acapulco Black Film Festival. John was an integral part of the team that ran the festival during its growth years, attracting award winning actors such as Denzel Washington, Halle Berry and Morgan Freeman. It has become the leading film festival showcasing films by an ethnically diverse group of film makers. John joined Elsevier shortly after Reed Elsevier purchased Harcourt General. He managed Library and Tradeshow Marketing for the N. American Sales Team and successfully integrated the Harcourt and Elsevier tradeshow programs in the US, setting an example that was used by the global tradeshow program. He also led the expansion of the Science Direct High School Program providing database access to the leading science and technology high schools in the US, preparing students for the growing use of online based research in their college years. John eventually took on the role of Science & Technology Global Exhibitions at Elsevier managing teams in Amsterdam and New York. He worked tirelessly with colleagues to improve Elsevier's standing within the scholarly and librarian community, including collaborating with industry pioneer Karen Hunter on planning the Digital Library Symposium at several ALA Midwinter conferences. He served on conference planning committees representing Elsevier or the scholarly publishing community with the American, Special and Medical Library Associations, as well as the Society for Neuroscience. John is currently Director of Digital Marketing Business Development for Small Business Like A Pro, an advisory and coaching business for entrepreneurs and small business owners. He is also working closely with its founder to launch the learning platform, Small Business Pro University. John is a graduate of the University of Michigan, Rackham Graduate School and Northwestern University's School of Communication. He also has a certification in Digital Marketing from the University of Vermont.

Carlo Scollo Lavizzari specializes in copyright law, licensing and litigation. He is an attorney admitted to practice in Switzerland, South Africa, England and Wales. Carlo's law firm is based in Basel, Switzerland. Carlo advises STM and other publishers world-wide on copyright law, policy and legal affairs, as well as some film, record and software producers. Carlo writes articles and speaks frequently about copyright and related matters.

Santosh M. is a transnational professional consultant specialised in facilitating organisational change in the higher education institutions. He has over two decades of experience in assisting leaders, managers and their teams at all levels of management in achieving performance excellence through applied business ethics and integrated innovation strategies. His consulting, research, change leadership and academic engagements, and learning while travelling pursuits (incl. long drives) have taken him to unfamiliar locations and situations in the developed, developing and least developed regions of the world. These destinations include Australia, Singapore, India (southern, northern, eastern and western states), Malaysia and Bhutan. His collaborative research-consulting entails working across multiple time zone differences with a globally distributed, culturally diverse and a multi-lingual clientele. He holds a PhD in Business Studies (Organisational Downsizing) from Australian Catholic University (a publicly funded university), Brisbane.

Leslie McIntosh, PhD, is the founder and CEO of Ripeta, a company formed to improve scientific research quality and reproducibility. Now part of Digital Science, the company leads efforts in rapidly assessing scientific research to make better science easier. She served as the inaugural executive director for the US region of the Research Data Alliance and is still very active with the RDA. She has experience leading diverse teams to develop and deliver meaningful data to improve scientific decisions. Dr. McIntosh is an accomplished biomedical informatician and data scientist as well as an internationally known consultant, speaker, and trainer who is passionate about mentoring the next generation of data scientists. She holds a Masters and PhD in Public Health with concentrations in Biostatistics and Epidemiology from Saint Louis University and a Certificate in Women's Leadership Forum from Washington University Olin's School of Business.

Brad Meyer has been helping people find reasons (first) and then ways (second) to collaborate more effectively. His underlying ethos is that "there is no such thing as 'strictly business', everything is personal." His knowledge management work over two decades within the contexts of the oil and gas, finance, sustainable development, social inclusion, justice and legal domains affords him a breadth and depth of insights which surface and refine themselves during his professional and personal engagements. Author of two books and referenced in others, Brad sometimes sets his organizational change work aside to help with red squirrel conservation in the Lake District, England where he lives.

Andrea Paganelli is an Associate Professor in the School of Teacher Education, Libraries, Informatics and Technology in Education Program at Western Kentucky University. Her research is focused on innovative practice in libraries, educational technology, school libraries and makerspaces.

Anthony Paganelli is a library instructor for Western Kentucky University as the law collection specialist. Research includes Blockchain technology, makerspaces, library trends, and music history.

Neil Posner is a senior executive, entrepreneur, and consultant with over 35 years of experience. He is currently Managing Partner of Digital Publishing Partners LLC which he co-founded in 2010. Focusing on the formulation and implementation of winning pricing strategies, tactics, and processes, his mission is to drive profitable growth and value capture for his clients in various industries including software, information, and electronic publishing. Neil was a co-founder, COO and CFO of DotHealth LLC which obtained venture capital funding and successfully acquired the rights from ICANN to operate the .Health gTLD (generic top level domain registry). Neil was previously VP Pricing Strategy for several multi-billion dollar international companies including Avaya (2004-2008) and Elsevier (1997-2004). He holds an MBA in Finance from Fordham University in New York, and a BS in Business Administration from the State University of New York at Albany. Neil currently serves on the Board of Directors of the New Jersey Metro and Rockland County Chapter of the Juvenile Diabetes Research Foundation (JDRF) whose primary mission is finding a cure for Type 1 diabetes.

Sharfi Rahman is a research enthusiast in the Computer Science and Engineering. Currently Working in the role of Research and Development Engineer in eGeneration. Graduated in Computer Science and Engineering from East West University, Bangladesh. Research Interests are: Blockchain, Data Science, Artificial Intelligence, Machine Learning. Interested in exploring more areas of computer science for research purpose.

Shantanu Kumar Rahut is a researcher by passion. He has been doing research on computer science from a young age. He has several published papers on Machine Learning and Blockchain. He completed his BSc in Computer Science and Engineering from East-West University in December 2018. He has also served as a Teaching

Assistant in his Department. Currently, Mr. Shantanu Kumar Rahut is pursuing his Master's in Data Science and Artificial Intelligence at Saarland University, Germany.

Edward Reiner is a corporate executive with IQVIA (a publicly traded clinical research organization) with extensive experience in academic publishing. He has worked for Simon and Schuster, Prentice-Hill, McGraw-Hill and for over 10 years with Elsevier Science. He has worked at General Electric and also supports sales and marketing for Humanities E- Book, formerly a division of ACLS. Ed is an adjunct professor at the Graduate School at New York University's School of Professional Studies (MS in Digital Media and Publishing) where he has taught in the Center for Publishing for 20 years. He is also a frequent speaker in matters of financial operations to Society for Scholarly Publishing and Association of American Publishers and continues to remain active in scholarly publishing.

Virginie Simon trained as an engineer in biotechnology at the Technological University of Compiègne (UTC), Paris. She then received her doctorate in nanotechnology for cancer therapy from the University Pierre and Marie Curie (UPMC), Paris. She has over 3 years' professional experience in a nanomedicine start-up, which confirmed her desire to become an entrepreneur. Virginie Simon is the CEO & Co-Founder of MyScienceWork since 2010. MyScienceWork is an innovative, professional technological platform, offering a Web 3.0 environment aimed at researchers. MyScienceWork offers the first global scientific platform. Virginie Simon currently leads a team of 15 people.

Peter Stockmann's professional business career spans over 50 years as an entrepreneur, corporate leader, a training and development provider, and hospitality consultant. Peter has a vast knowledge and dedication in establishing, promoting, marketing, and operating a variety of businesses. His customer service expertise, leadership capacities, team-building skills, and business professionalism have enabled him to successfully launch and manage several unrelated businesses Peter's extensive work experiences (Ford Motor Company – finance and strategic planning, product development, manufacturing operations and corporate training – designed, managed the building and operated the state-of-the-art, 300,000 square foot, Learning and Conference Center) have provide him with the foundation required for being successful in the ever-changing business environment. Peter also possesses, demonstrated expertise, in the areas of conference design and operations and has completed consulting work for University of Michigan, Ford Motor Company, General Motors, Kmart, Best Buy, FedEx, Microsoft, Engineering Society of Detroit, Harley Ellis, and Spectrum Strategies.

Razwan Ahmed Tanvir is a programmer by profession. He completed his BSc in Computer Science and Engineering from East West University in December 2018. He also served as a Graduate Teaching Assistant in his Department before joining to the current workplace. HIs current research interest includes various applications of Blockchain, Machine Learning and Data Science.

Index

IGI Global Author Services

Providing a high-quality, affordable, and expeditious service, IGI Global's Author Services enable authors to streamline their publishing process, increase chance of acceptance, and adhere to IGI Global's publication standards.

Benefits of Author Services:

- **Professional Service:** All our editors, designers, and translators are experts in their field with years of experience and professional certifications.
- **Quality Guarantee & Certificate:** Each order is returned with a quality guarantee and certificate of professional completion.
- **Timeliness:** All editorial orders have a guaranteed return timeframe of 3-5 business days and translation orders are guaranteed in 7-10 business days.
- **Affordable Pricing:** IGI Global Author Services are competitively priced compared to other industry service providers.
- **APC Reimbursement:** IGI Global authors publishing Open Access (OA) will be able to deduct the cost of editing and other IGI Global author services from their OA APC publishing fee.

Author Services Offered:

English Language Copy Editing
Professional, native English language copy editors improve your manuscript's grammar, spelling, punctuation, terminology, semantics, consistency, flow, formatting, and more.

Scientific & Scholarly Editing
A Ph.D. level review for qualities such as originality and significance, interest to researchers, level of methodology and analysis, coverage of literature, organization, quality of writing, and strengths and weaknesses.

Figure, Table, Chart & Equation Conversions
Work with IGI Global's graphic designers before submission to enhance and design all figures and charts to IGI Global's specific standards for clarity.

Translation
Providing 70 language options, including Simplified and Traditional Chinese, Spanish, Arabic, German, French, and more.

Hear What the Experts Are Saying About IGI Global's Author Services

"Publishing with IGI Global has been **an amazing experience** for me for sharing my research. The **strong academic production** support ensures quality and timely completion." – **Prof. Margaret Niess, Oregon State University, USA**

"The service was **very fast, very thorough, and very helpful** in ensuring our chapter meets the criteria and requirements of the book's editors. I was **quite impressed and happy** with your service." – **Prof. Tom Brinthaupt, Middle Tennessee State University, USA**

Learn More or Get Started Here: For Questions, Contact IGI Global's Customer Service Team at cust@igi-global.com or 717-533-8845

IGI Global
PUBLISHER of TIMELY KNOWLEDGE
www.igi-global.com